An Introduction to

FILM

Thomas Sobchack
The University of Utah

Vivian C. Sobchack

An Introduction to
FILM

LITTLE, BROWN AND COMPANY
Boston
Toronto

Library of Congress Catalog Card No. 79–90617

ISBN 0–316–802506

10 9 8 7 6 5 4 3 2

HAL

Published simultaneously in Canada by Little, Brown & Company (Canada) Limited

Printed in the United States of America

ACKNOWLEDGMENTS

Portions of *Glossary of Film Terms*, John Mercer, compiler (Journal of the University Film Association, Monograph no. 2), are reprinted by permission of John Mercer and the editor of the Journal of the University Film Association. Copyright © 1978.

"The Use of Music in Michael Ritchie's *Smile*" is printed by permission of the author, Jean Tarascio. Copyright © 1980 by Jean Tarascio.

"Politics in Movies" is printed by permission of the author, Ellen Jacob. Copyright © 1980 by Ellen Jacob.

"The Caper Film" is printed by permission of the author, Stephen Kendorski. Copyright © 1980 by Stephen Kendorski.

Text and cover photographs are from The Lester R. Glassner Collection and are reprinted by permission.

PREFACE

> The movies are part of my culture, and it seems to me that their special
> power has something to do with their being a kind of "pure" culture, a lit-
> tle like fishing or drinking or playing baseball — a cultural fact, that is,
> which has not yet fallen altogether under the discipline of art.
> Robert Warshow, *The Immediate Experience*

There is a popular assumption that movies are mindless escapism. On
entering a movie theater, we assume that the movie will divert us from
our ordinary experiences by entertaining us. Many movies, however,
do more than provide us with entertainment; as well as diverting us,
they enlighten us. Chaplin's *City Lights* and Coppola's *The Godfather*,
for example, are highly entertaining and widely popular movies. Yet
both are also films which make us recognize human relationships, social
inequities, and their own artistry. A knowledgeable filmgoer, then, enters the theater receptive, open to the possibilities of both entertainment and enlightenment, realizing that a film can be experienced from
a variety of perspectives — cultural, ideological, and aesthetic.

An Introduction to Film assumes that familiarity with these perspectives and others will increase the viewer's understanding and will also
add to the pleasures of the commonplace moviegoing experience. A
grasp of the basics of filmmaking will develop a respect for the complicated choices made by the artists and artisans responsible for a completed work. An awareness of the variety of cultural and theoretical
approaches to the film will help a person appreciate a range of films
wider than those usually shown at local movie theaters and on television. And a sense of film history will connect each individual film, not
only with other films, but also with the growth, development and evolution of technology and culture in the twentieth century. A basic un-

derstanding of these aspects of film and filmmaking cannot help but create a more conscious and visually literate viewer, a viewer who is able to respond fully to the array of images which present themselves on theater and television screens throughout a lifetime. *An Introduction to Film*, in short, seeks to help the general student of the humanities, the fine arts, and the sciences to become an active rather than a passive film viewer.

To achieve this end, *An Introduction to Film* is comprehensive yet decidedly nontechnical. While technical matters are covered when they are crucial to a thorough understanding of a point, as a rule technical material is not given for its own sake. For example, we discuss many of the technical processes of animation because they are necessary to a full, intelligent understanding of animated films, but we do not discuss, in our comments on the function of lighting, the many terms used to designate the various sizes, kinds, and characteristics of lighting equipment, because these terms are not crucial to an understanding of how light functions aesthetically in film. Our aim has been to make the text readable and straightforward, to emphasize not the variety and complexity of equipment, but the variety and complexity of aesthetic choice and its result in finished works. In a like manner, while the text is far-reaching in its concerns, certain topics of little relevance to the general student have been omitted. Except for passing references, consideration of the economics and business practice of the motion picture industry, and of certain types of film such as the industrial and scientific film, are omitted. As well, for reasons of length and complexity, we have chosen to outline only briefly the basics of film theory. Conversely, we have chosen to stress some topics which, though given little space in most introductory texts, occupy a great deal of the reader's viewing time outside the classroom. Both genre films and documentary films, for example, are treated extensively.

An Introduction to Film is divided into four parts. Part I (Cinematic Form), by considering space, time, and sound, discusses basic film aesthetics. Part II (Cinematic Content: The Fiction Film) and Part III (Cinematic Content: The Nonfiction Film) discuss a variety of film types, film movements, and filmmakers, with an emphasis on the cognitive rather than sensuous experience of film viewing. Finally, Part IV (A Guide to Film Analysis and Criticism), beginning with the development of the varied critical and theoretical approaches to film, goes on to consider the problems faced by the student writer (illustrated with examples of student writing). Each of the four parts of the text includes Historical Overviews, which supply the reader with a connected, chronological account of relevant technological and cultural events so that discussions of film form and content will not occur in a historical vacuum. Finally, the text concludes with a bibliography designed to help the student find published source materials and a glossary of terms boldfaced in the text. Although the text can be read straight through as presented, chapters can also be assigned selectively without a loss of coherence. Each chapter is self-contained, and the numerous headings within chapters will even enable instructors to assign only portions of chapters if they wish. Because each part of *An Introduction to Film* is independent, there is necessarily some repetition of key material. Certain films, filmmakers, and historic events are referred to more often than others. Such repetition or emphasis is justified, we believe, by the acknowledged aesthetic or historic importance of the film, filmmaker, or event. Almost all the films referred to in the text are taken from the American Film Institute's recent survey of the feature titles most used in film study classes around the country. Not only are these films commonly agreed to have intrinsic artistic merit and importance within the context of film history, but they are also the most readily available for rental and purchase and so tend to appear regularly as the "core" films in introductory and advanced courses. The text also refers to certain short films such as *An Occurrence at Owl Creek Bridge*, which, although absent from the AFI survey, are often used in the college classroom. It has been our consistent intent to refer to films which students will most likely have the opportunity to see, and to balance citations of classic films with contemporary films, foreign-language films with English-language films, and esoteric films with popular films.

Still photographs are another form of cinematic citation used in the text. Although stills cannot duplicate or even approximate the temporal and changing nature of the film experience, they can provide an image which jogs the memory of that experience or whets the appetite for it. Certainly, it is impossible to demonstrate what a tracking shot is or does with a group of selected stills; even if every frame of the shot were represented, the illusion of continuous time and space and motion would be shattered into separate photographs on the page. Nevertheless, it is true that the discussion of tracking shots is made clearer for the reader when some photographs are included. And stills can effectively illustrate cinematic elements such as lighting and composition. Some of the photographs in *An Introduction to Film* are studio stills (that is, publicity photographs taken on the set during filming, many of them posed or shot under ideal lighting conditions and which therefore have only a tangential relationship to comparable images in the released film). Others are frame enlargements from the films themselves. Frame enlargements are preferred of course, since what one sees in the photograph is what one sees (for a split second) in the film, yet frame enlargements often do not reproduce very well and, in some instances, are simply not available. Although the text uses both studio stills and frame enlargements, the captions indicate (either directly or indirectly) whether a particular shot actually appeared as shown in a given film. Unless credited otherwise, all the pictures are from The Lester R. Glassner Collection.

To illustrate the text further, various filmmakers and craftsmen are quoted in appropriate sections. These quotations clarify our discussion and provide provocative statements which may occasion thought and spark discussion. They have been chosen as much for their liveliness as for their appropriateness in prefacing a specific section of the text.

A brief mention must be made regarding the use of pronouns. Plural forms ("viewers," "they") were often used to avoid sexist emphasis, but sometimes common usage of the pronoun "he" seemed less unwieldy or distracting than the plural "they," the awkward "one," the coinage "s/he," and the unfortunately still startling "she." The aim was first and foremost clarity, the primary emphasis film as the subject. The authors take responsibility for this decision and wish there was some way of resolving a real dilemma which we are conscious of perpetuating.

Many people must be thanked for their help and guidance in the writing of this book. Sylvan Barnet's incisive editing made this a more concise, readable text. Lester Glassner's sensitive and indefatigable efforts in locating stills cannot be adequately measured. Duane Powell added his expertise in still production. The chapter on sound owes much of its substance to one marathon conversation with Win Sharples, Jr. and the clear technical explanation provided by Dale Christensen of Trolley Theatres of Salt Lake. The early enthusiasm and support of Little, Brown editors Charles Christensen, Katie Carlone, and Sheryl Gipstein kept the project going, and in the final months of revision and production Jan Young and Karen Lavroff saw the book through to completion. Throughout the many revisions, Karen Anastasopoulos, Sharon Bennett, Karen Donahue, Lisa Hancock, and Pat Tiemens typed and retyped the manuscript; their efforts are most appreciated. Special mention must also be given our son, Christopher, whose patience and understanding belie his nine and a half years. And finally, we must thank our students. While we extend particular gratitude to Ellen Jacob, Steve Kendorski, and Jean Tarascio, who kindly consented to let us use their class papers, we are also indebted to our students at the University of Utah, UCLA, and University of Vermont, who helped create this text from their insights, questions, problems, and interest. Without them, this book would have neither substance nor relevance.

Thomas Sobchack
Vivian C. Sobchack

CONTENTS

PART II
CINEMATIC CONTENT: THE FICTION FILM

PART III
CINEMATIC CONTENT: THE NONFICTION FILM

★★★ **Historical Overview:**
The Development of the Documentary Film   342

7   The Documentary Film   352

★★★ **Historical Overview:**
The Development of Experimental, Independent, and
Animated Filmmaking   377

PART I
CINEMATIC
FORM

★★★   **Seeing and Hearing Film**

Imagine two film images of a dog barking. One of them is a close-up of
the dog's head and clearly shows his open mouth and sharp teeth; it
suggests the dog's savagery and power. The other image is taken from
high above the dog and looks down on its entire body within the context
of a large space; it may suggest the dog's helplessness and fright. The
content (a dog barking) gets its meaning partly from the *form* in which
it is presented. Because form and content are interdependent — *what*
something means depends partly on *how* it is said or shown — it might
seem pointless to attempt to separate form and content for the purpose
of critical study.

And yet sometimes while one is looking at a film, and certainly after,
it is possible — and even pleasurable — to contemplate such a division,
for example to separate the actor from the character portrayed, *what*
the film was about from *how* it was created. True, this separation is
arbitrary, but it can prove fruitful, giving us a deep and informed
appreciation of the complexity and capacity of the medium.

Part I of this book is about how the filmmaker shapes what we see and
hear in a motion picture, or to put it a bit differently, how a filmmaker
uses technique to shape meaning. Seeing and hearing a film is in many
ways similar to seeing and hearing the rest of our daily life. We see people on the street, we see them on television, we see them on the stage,
we see them on the screen. There are specific ways, however, in which
seeing people on film is controlled by the filmmaker. To take the most
obvious: on the street we can usually look at a person from top to toe,
and we can focus on what we want to, but in a film we can see only that
part of a person that the filmmaker presents on the screen. The sounds
we hear are similarly controlled by the filmmaker, who can provide —
or not provide — soaring music to accompany the lovers we see running
toward each other across a meadow.

Most people enjoy seeing films, but to understand and more fully
appreciate the power and art of the film, one must first understand the
ways in which various cinematic components — the mechanical, the
technological, and the creative aspects — work together to create the
film which we finally experience as a unified and entire work. Thus
Part I examines the means to the end, *how* film communicates the "what"
of its content by manipulating space, time, and sound to become the
film we see and hear.

Historical Overview: The Development of the Image

EARLY MECHANISMS

The invention of photography in the early part of the nineteenth century by Joseph Niepce and Louis Daguerre in France was the first step towards capturing the moving image of reality, a dream held by artists and philosophers for thousands of years. Once still photography had been achieved, attempts to invent *moving* photographic pictures began. There already were mechanical devices to give motion to *drawn* figures: the Stroboscope, a slotted disc (1832); the Zoetrope, a slotted revolving drum (1834); and the Praxinoscope, a more complicated form of the Zoetrope, which eventually was combined with the Magic Lantern (1877) to project its little figures of clowns, horses, and acrobats upon a wall (Figure 1). These devices were the ancestors of our animated films, a series of drawings — each showing the figure in a slightly different pose — viewed in rapid succession so that the figure seemed to move. There were also experiments which attempted to use the photographic process to give motion to images of real figures; a series of still photographs taken by Eadweard Muybridge in the 1870s with a battery of twenty-four cameras so as to capture increments of motion in a racehorse was projected on a screen in rapid succession to give the illusion of movement. But the final stages of the development of a practical motion picture camera and projection system had to wait until the perfection of a flexible film which could replace glass photographic plates. Soon after a celluloid film base was discovered by an amateur inventor, the first roll film was marketed by George Eastman in 1888.

It was the team of William Dickson and Thomas Edison, however, who used the flexible film for cinematography rather than still photographs. By

★ **1**   Throughout the nineteenth century, inventors tried to solve the problem
of creating the illusion of motion. Based on Roget's theories about the
"persistence of vision," these parlor toys were the first steps towards the
motion picture. The movements drawn in individual pictures blend together
to give the impression of continuous motion when the machines are revolved.
The key to the illusion is that each of the little pictures must be seen
separately and distinctly. The Zoëtrope (top left) uses slits to isolate each
increment of motion; the motion picture process uses a shutter.

1889, problems with moving the celluloid strips through the camera (dubbed the Kinetograph in 1891) had been solved, and in the laboratory Dickson not only demonstrated to Edison a motion picture of Dickson walking forward and lifting his hat off his head, but he also linked his voice to the picture — recorded on the recently developed phonograph. Edison, however, had no plans for full-scale exploitation of the sound part of the invention. He did, on the other hand, decide to market a device into which one could peer and see the unprojected images in motion. Although only one viewer could see the film at a time, the Kinetoscope, as it was called, was a great success. By 1894 there were peep-show parlors all across the country and around the world as well.

Within a year inventors from every industrial nation came out with their own versions of cameras that could take moving pictures, and it was only a short step to adapt the mechanism for projection on a large screen. For example, Auguste and Louis Lumière devised their Cinématographe, which took, printed, and projected the films they made; their contribution to the development of an effective projection system was their invention of a clawlike device which moved the film in front of the source of light. They projected their first set of films in Paris in 1895 (Figure 2). By 1896 even Edison, who had not been particularly interested in developing a projection system, had joined forces with Thomas Armat to come up with the Vitascope. The claw of the Lumière brothers became obsolete with the incorporation of the Maltese cross, a mechanism which created intermittent movement by holding the film for a moment before the light source and then releasing it so the next image could move into place. The first public showing of this closest ancestor to modern projectors occurred in New York on April 23, 1896. By this date, the motion picture as we think of it — a photographic image projected on a screen and viewed by an audience — had become a reality.

The first films, lasting only about a minute, simply showed anything that moved: scenes from ordinary daily life (people walking, a train entering a station, workers taking lunch) alternated with the extraordinary, such as staged performances of jugglers, acrobats, and clowns. From the beginnings of film there were also those filmmakers who wanted to capture real life on the screen and there were those who wanted to create an "artistic" or imaginary world on the screen. Even the Lumière brothers, who were primarily interested in photographing daily life and objects, made a few short films which had a little narrative action: a practical joke being played on a gardener, a card game which ends with the classic accusation of cheating and the upended table and scuffle. These short narratives, however, still depended on representing more or less what might be seen in the real world.

By the turn of the century, longer lengths of film proved possible and the

★ 2   Although the Lumière brothers chiefly produced short films of everyday occurrences, their first program of publicly projected films included fictional narratives. This scene comes from THE HOSER HOSED, a slapstick physical comedy from 1895.

narrative powers of the motion picture began to emerge just as viewers were becoming jaded and bored with the new art. Seeing a film of the real world in motion was somehow no longer enough. After all, one could look around one and see the real world in motion. Georges Méliès, a professional theatrical magician in France, became fascinated with the possibility of doing tricks and creating illusions with the camera. Not only could films visually tell little invented stories, but they could also show us things that couldn't possibly happen in real life. In short pantomime films, Méliès used the camera mechanism to create mysterious disappearances and reappearances of his characters, to dissolve one image into another, and to duplicate images in the same frame through masking, double exposures, and superimpositions. Yet another Frenchman, Ferdinand Zecca, employed fast motion and slow motion in his fantasy films, usually culminating in a comic chase. Filmmakers now had the mechanical equipment and the imagination to alter reality if they chose, to defy gravity, to play games with time and space. The two greatest assets of the film medium had been discovered — its ability to *record* and its ability to *create*.

THE MOBILE CAMERA

In all these films, however, the camera never moved from its firmly rooted position on a tripod, no matter whether the subject was recorded or created, whether it was a train pulling into a station, a scene from a famous play, or a skeleton coming to life and dancing. All of the action and all of the bodies of the players were visible in the frame. The frame was treated almost as a stage and the camera like the eyes of the theatergoer who had the best orchestra seat. Although it seems like the simplest of ideas in retrospect, someone had to think of moving the camera. To do so, one would have to be thinking cinematically, not theatrically. The physical limitations of the stage were not relevant to this new and mechanical medium.

Although a **close-up** appears as early as 1898, and more notably in Edwin S. Porter's *The Great Train Robbery* (1903), close-ups (i.e., placing the camera close to the subject) did not become commonplace until D. W. Griffith began to use them regularly at the Biograph Studios between 1908 and 1912. It was Porter, however, who established the basic foundation for the editing of narrative film. To build suspense and drama in *The Great Train Robbery*, Porter broke away from the traditional dependence on single locations and "real" time. He introduced **crosscutting** (also called **parallel editing**), which not only added tension and excitement to the dramatic action but also brought to cinema its own time: for example, shots of the outlaws riding away are intercut with a shot of the stationmaster being discovered bound and gagged by his daughter, events which are happening at the same time. Porter is also credited with using the first insert of a close-up: a gun being fired directly at the audience.

D. W. Griffith, the first great filmmaker, refined a number of Porter's innovations and recognized their implications for narrative film. He changed the position of the camera within scenes as well as between them, attempting to create more dynamic angles from which to view the action. For example, in *The Lonely Villa* (1909) the camera is placed so that the diagonal movement of the robbers is emphasized as they enter; this is more visually dramatic than if the camera had viewed their entrance straight on. Griffith composed his actors into groupings, using cinematic space more dramatically than it had been used before. For example, the farmers in *A Corner in Wheat* (1909) are not found simply in the center of the frame (Figure 3, Figure 4). Their asymmetrical arrangements and movements emphasize their relationship to their environment in visually interesting images. Griffith also experimented with the use of shadows and highlights. Finally, by the time of *The Birth of a Nation* (1915), now usually acknowledged as the first film masterpiece, Griffith had liberated the camera from its fixed position during individual shots. In short, Griffith's greatest contribution to the art of film

★ 3 In this scene from A CORNER IN WHEAT (1910) D. W. Griffith
broke with the tradition of placing the actors in the center of the frame.

was to make the motion picture camera almost as important as human actors
in developing a narrative through exposition and drama; the camera no
longer merely recorded a story — it interpreted the story through perspective, movement, and visual emphasis.

From World War I until the end of the cinema's silent era in 1927, all
of the techniques for capturing and manipulating the image developed by
Griffith were extended and refined by movie makers all over the world. The
silent cinema, a cinema which depended almost completely on the image,
became a supple and powerful medium with which to tell stories and to
document life. From the United States came the great silent comedies characterized by breakneck action, brilliant pantomime, and names like Mack
Sennett, Charlie Chaplin, Buster Keaton, Harold Lloyd, Harry Langdon, and
Laurel and Hardy. A great many dramatic films, too, followed the imaginative
and epic standards set by Griffith's *Intolerance* (1916); directors such as Eric
von Stroheim, Cecil B. De Mille, and Ernst Lubitsch brought sophistication
as well as spectacle to the screen. And finally, there were certain key performers of the silent period who became stars and helped to shape the film
industry into what we know as Hollywood and the studio system. Abroad,
silent cinema developed along parallel lines, although there was some di-
vergence in the growth of national cinemas.

FURTHER EXPRESSIVE TECHNIQUES

In Germany, filmmakers effectively explored the expressive capabilities of the
camera, of lighting, of highly stylized and artificial sets and acting. Robert
Wiene's *The Cabinet of Dr. Caligari* (1919) used angular sets (architecturally

Don't blame us
the
...se in wheat
...esponsible

Owing to the
advance in the
price of flour
the usual 5ᶜᵗ loaf
will be 10 ᶜᵗ'ˢ

★ 4   Griffith displays composition in depth in this shot from A CORNER IN WHEAT.

impossible in the real world) and heavy shadows to develop a macabre and horrific atmosphere for its tale of murder and madness; although in many ways visually unique, the film was also typical of the early German cinema's preoccupation with nightmarish themes conveyed by subjective and expressive images — what was to become the horror film. There were also German filmmakers who dealt with more realistic subjects but who did so expressively. In *The Last Laugh* (1924), F. W. Murnau dispensed with the common practice of using **titles** between shots and relied only on his images to communicate the narrative. He used a **subjective camera** at times: the audience sees the scene as the leading character does, for example, in a blur. He took his camera on location into the street and moved it down alleys and into buildings, through crowded apartments. In Murnau's hands, the camera became a mobile spectator of the action; special cranes, dollies, and elevators were built so that the camera seemed to have unlimited mobility. The point of view shifts instantaneously from that of one character to another and then to the third person, the dispassionate bystander. The images on the screen draw in the viewer so that he becomes a participant in the drama. Although German cinema's "Golden Era" was relatively brief (c. 1919–1925), its influence was far-reaching and long-lived. The German cinema illustrated to the world what could be expressed with light and shadow, with the sheer beauty of images.

While it is true that of all national cinemas the German film contributed the most to the development of the *image* within the frame, and that is what concerns us in this chapter, other countries' contributions should not be overlooked. The Russians, too, were bent on conveying meaning without the use of a great many titles to explain the action; in many films, the way in which the images were composed created dynamic and dramatic tension and the **high** or **low angles** from which they were shot told the audience how to regard the characters and situations. France also contributed to the growing sophistication of silent cinema. Paralleling changes in the other arts, French cinema was often highly experimental. The film frame was used as a canvas for cinematic **surrealism, abstraction, cubism.** The fluidity of the film images seemed perfectly suited to the rejection of realism and to the espousal of dream logic which characterized the surrealists and French avant-garde. Additionally, Abel Gance was attempting to expand the limits of the film image; he experimented with projection on a screen that completely surrounded the viewers and made films which used **split screen** images and which used multiple screens, the forerunner of modern wide screens and **Cinerama.**

Film technology both preceded and followed the constantly increasing sophistication and artistry of the camera work of the silent cinema. In some cases, certain technological developments had to occur before certain artistic aims could be realized; in other cases, necessity became the mother of invention. One example of how technology influenced the quality of the image, and therefore its artistry, involves **film speed.** Most of the silent **film stock** (unexposed film) was relatively **slow-speed** (the slower the speed of the emulsion, the more light is needed to capture an image), and it required wide-open **lens apertures** to record an image at all. By 1933, however, Eastman Kodak had come out with their Plus X film, which was faster than previous stock. Thus smaller apertures could be used, which meant that more of the background in a given image could be kept in as clear a focus as was the subject in the foreground. The filmmaker of the late 1930s, then, through **deep-focus cinematography** was able to convey more complex spatial relationships between characters and objects than he was able to before this technological advance.

Perhaps the most important technological advance which influenced the film image was the addition of sound to the cinema around 1927. Initially, that

★ 5 Busby Berkeley's most significant contribution to the musical film
was his original use of cinematic space for the stating of dance numbers.
Even when a dance appeared to begin on a stage in a theater, it would soon
expand through a change in camera angle to some huge area which could
only exist on a sound stage. There, the camera could provide everything
from underwater shots to bird's-eye views of the figures in the dance. In this
number from GOLD DIGGERS OF 1935 (Busby Berkeley, 1935), white
grand pianos move about in a black space to form geometric patterns which
are viewed from a variety of angles.

influence was not a positive one and many critics and filmmakers felt that
motion pictures had taken a giant step backwards. Because the earliest microphones were extremely inefficient, requiring actors to stay within close range
of a mike hidden on the set, the once fluid and mobile camera of the late
silent period became rooted to one spot. Then, too, camera noise presented
another technical problem, which was at first solved by placing the camera
in a bulky soundproof booth, further curtailing the camera's mobility. The
very novelty of sound itself robbed the image of its expressive possibilities: the
emphasis was on dialogue, talk, on lips moving synchronously with the words
on the sound track. Although there were notable exceptions, from the first
sound feature — The Jazz Singer (Alan Crosland, 1927) — through the early
Thirties, movies had lost a great deal of their ability to move. Eventually, how-

11

ever, wheels were added to the sound booths, allowing for limited camera movement. And, in 1931, a soundproof housing (a **blimp**) for the camera alone was perfected and the camera was once again free to move about. By that year, the image on the screen became as flexible in the hands of artists like René Clair in France and Ernst Lubitsch and Rouben Mamoulian in the United States as it had been before 1927. (See Figure 5.)

The next major addition to making the screen image both more expressive and more realistic was color. Although it is a remarkable fact that some films were colored as early as 1908, the means available were so clumsy as to have little commercial impact. At first, films were actually hand-painted, frame by frame. And there was an unwieldy, mechanical process called Kinemacolor. The only fairly widespread use of color prior to the 1930s was in films which were printed on tinted stock; certain specific colors came to have conventional meanings: red was used for violent or passionate scenes, blue for night sequences, yellow for daylight. Technicolor in its original state was developed in 1916 and 1917; at that time it was a two-color (red and green) process, hindered in its commercial use by the fact that it was extremely expensive and not very attractive. Although a few films using the process were actually made and distributed during the 1920s, Technicolor did not become widely used until a more effective process was developed and until its cost was greatly reduced. The perfected three-color Technicolor process, in which three reels (one each of red, blue and green film stock) were synchronized in the same camera, photographing the same subject at the same time, was available by 1932. But it took a while for the film industry, happy and content with the success of sound, to try the new film. Although a few features were made in Technicolor well before 1939, it was the release of Victor Fleming's *Gone with the Wind* and *The Wizard of Oz* in that year which brought the process full public and industrial approval. From this point on, it became a matter of artistic as well as of commercial choice whether to make a film in color or not. Color was still considerably more expensive than black-and-white stock, and it was still difficult to modulate the **color saturation** so that it was artistically in agreement with a particular film's mood and tone. For these reasons, during the 1940s and early 1950s, color was primarily used in "star" vehicles and in lavish musicals where rich color values seemed important and appropriate. Today, of course, it is black-and-white film which is a novelty and which is generally used for very specific atmospheric reasons. Since the 1960s, color has been accepted as the norm for films dealing with all sorts of subject matter; it is used not merely as a means of dressing up the film image so that it is pretty, but as a powerful visual element capable of creating meaning.

Although Abel Gance had experimented with the use of three screens to enlarge his epic film *Napoleon in 1926*, it took the onslaught of television (a huge threat to the Hollywood box office by 1950) to bring about the develop-

★ 6 The aspect ratio (the relationship between the height and
width of the motion picture image) of early silent films was
nearly 1 to 1. To expand the width and create a more epic vista,
Abel Gance experimented with a triple screen (top) for his
film NAPOLEON (1926). But it was not until the fifties that the
wider image became commonplace. Systems such as Cinerama
(middle, HOW THE WEST WAS WON, 1962), Cinemascope,
Todd-AO, and 70mm film have given way to the current
standard, approximately 1.85 to 1 (bottom, WHAT'S UP, DOC?,
1972), considerably wider than the 1.33 to 1 used during the
thirties and forties.

ment and use of various wide-screen processes. If television was smaller, then movies would be bigger. The early 1950s saw the introduction of Cinerama in 1952, but the process required a special theater and equipment. It did, however, animate the flagging film industry into investigating other ways in which the screen could be widened (Figure 6). The development of the **anamorphic lens** (which squeezed the image during shooting but widened it during the projection process) led to **CinemaScope** in 1953 and other variations. Three-dimensional film (3–D) was attempted as well, but the audience and theater owners soon tired of the gimmick; it was necessary to wear special glasses to unify the two projected images into one image, giving the illusion of three dimensions. A third kind of wide-screen process was developed for commercial use on a large scale in 1955; the process simply used wider film, 65 or 75 millimeter instead of the traditional 35 millimeter. All of these processes were designed to lure television viewers away from the tiny image in their living rooms, but they also caused filmmakers aesthetic headaches. Composing images and moving the camera for the wide screen was not like composing images and moving the camera for the smaller screen. The space had to be filled differently and movement had to be adjusted as well. It wasn't until 1955 that the wide screen was used effectively in such films as Elia Kazan's *East of Eden,* Nicholas Ray's *Rebel Without a Cause,* and George Stevens's *Giant* (released the following year).

Today the standard screen size is approximately 1 unit high to 1.85 wide, considerably wider in proportion to its height than it had been up to the early 1950s. Most films, however, still keep the action in the center of the frame so that subsequent showings on television will be less of a problem. Most Cinerama theaters have converted to regular screens and 3–D has been resurrected on occasion, primarily for its "camp" value. At the present time, there is considerable interest in **holography,** a process which makes images appear three-dimensional and uses *no* screen. A recent science fiction film, *Logan's Run* (1976), used holographic effects, but the process required special projection equipment and extremely few theaters were able to show their patrons the spectacular effects. Unless holography can be used at little additional cost to the exhibitor it probably will remain, like 3–D, a novelty.

The historical development of the mechanisms and techniques used to capture the image and to project it on a screen has bequeathed to today's filmmakers nearly total control of how the projected image can look. Today's equipment is light enough and portable enough for location shooting. Incredible advances have been made with special effects cinematography since the success of Stanley Kubrick's *2001: A Space Odyssey* (1968). The range of camera movement, lighting, the choice of film stocks and lenses, seems endless. Through the choices made available by an ever-developing technology, the filmmaker is able to create the mood, the tone, the images to express the idea he wants to convey.

1
★ *SPACE IN THE CINEMA*

If we were asked to define movies, we might first think of a rectangular space filled with moving images and surrounded on all sides by darkness. Although sounds are an essential part of the cinematic experience, the projected picture is paramount. What we see dominates our perception — whether it is a representation of actual objects (houses, trees, people, animals) or nonrepresentational forms (colors, textures, lines) or a combination of the two in animated films. The first element of cinematic space, then, is the **frame:** that rectangular area which is bounded on all sides by darkness and which contains the projected screen image. In certain abstract or nonrepresentational films, which chiefly represent visual patterns, this space — the frame — is used as a two-dimensional canvas; the image has length and breadth, but there is no attempt to achieve the illusion of depth. In the documentary film and the story film the frame usually attempts to represent all three dimensions. In the abstract film we look *at* the space and what is happening in it; the frame functions like the frame of a painting, separating real space from artificial space. In the documentary and most story films, we look *through* the frame into a space which appears to have depth; the frame functions like the frame of a window, letting us see out into a world which seems to continue beyond the frame's boundaries, which merely focus our attention. Despite their differences, however, and excepting some recent experiments with holography (a process that without a camera makes a three-dimensional picture), all motion pictures consist of a projected series of images occurring within the space of a finite frame. This is the cinematic space to be discussed in Chapter 1.

★★★ The Image

> There is no short cut to photographic skill; to master it requires not only
> theory but intensive practice. Lens, light, material, subject, composition,
> angle, and the pattern of movement provide a thousand and one pitfalls for
> the unwary. The ablest painter, sensitive as he is to a single canvas, is
> helpless to control the ever-shifting, mobile canvas of the motion picture.
> Josef von Sternberg[1]

THE REAL WORLD AND THE REEL WORLD

In the beginning was the picture, not the word. Man's eyes saw before he
could name the objects he beheld. He drew before he could write, and
his first written language in most cultures was composed of pictures —
Egyptian hieroglyphs, American Indian pictographs, Chinese ideograms
— all visual patterns in space. In the beginning of cinema, too, the picture
came first. One of the cinema's various names is "motion pictures" or
"movies" — pictures that move. Before the turn of the century, when
inventors all over the world were trying desperately to perfect a device
to make pictures that moved, that pictured the vitality and dynamism of
everyday life in the real world, they were striving not for the word but
for the image.

The most important single element of a film is the flow of images,
pictures which fill the space on the screen or frame. Imagine sitting in a
theater watching a film when suddenly the projection bulb burns out.
The sound track continues, but the screen is blank. Nothing. It is no
longer the movie experience. If one reverses the conditions of this mis-
hap, however, and the sound system fails but we can still see the film
on the screen, a movie experience is still possible (or at least would be
possible if the audience paid attention instead of stomping and cheering
to wake up the projectionist). Movies used no **synchronized sound** until
1927, about thirty years after their birth, and yet the filmmakers of that
soundless era — D. W. Griffith, Erich von Stroheim, Charles Chaplin,
Sergei Eisenstein, F. W. Murnau — were able to tell their stories successfully without dialogue or **sound effects,** and sometimes without any
printed titles at all. Even today, a film lives primarily in those images
which fill the rectangular space of the frame.

What is the least that is needed to produce a motion picture? A motion
picture camera, unexposed film, a light source which is reasonably intense, and a subject for the camera to photograph. The Lumière brothers
in 1895 used no more than this. Their camera was set on a tripod (to
keep it steady) and pointed at the workers in the Lumières' factory who
left work at the end of the day and walked in front of it, or at a train

coming into a station and halting to allow passengers to get on and off. The camera remained stationary for these *actualités*, as they were called; the entire scene was shot in one continuous sixty-second movement of the film through the camera. There was no **editing,** no reshooting. But simple as they were, these brief bits of film, when projected on the screen, amazed audiences with their faithful and even frightening reproduction of the real movement of real people and objects in the real world.

Audiences today, of course, are more sophisticated. We have seen more complex cinematic achievements and would quickly tire of such simple motion picture fare. Yet Andy Warhol, the pop artist, made a film in almost exactly the same manner as did the Lumières; completed in 1963, it was called *Sleep* and was what experimental filmmakers call, appropriately enough, a **minimal film.** *Sleep* showed a man sleeping for six hours — or, rather, it gave the illusion of a man sleeping for six hours. For, in fact, the camera recorded three hours of the sleeping subject which, of course, included changing reels, and then those three hours of sleep were repeated to double the length of the film. Nonetheless, Warhol's film is remarkably like those films made by the Lumière brothers; in intent, it is a return to the one-shot movie of early film pioneers and it is, as well, an exploration of the question: to what degree can a movie be simplified and reduced and still be a movie. *Sleep* in some ways is even more simple than the earliest films, for it lacks an active and moving subject; whereas the early filmmakers looked for those subjects which would fill the screen space with movement, Warhol sought out subjects that were primarily static. (*Empire*, another film by Warhol, is a single shot — for eight hours — of the Empire State Building.) But the basic similarity between Warhol's work and that of the early filmmakers is there: the camera, mounted on a tripod, remains stationary and any movement within the frame comes from the subject; the camera also runs continuously until all the film is exposed, thereby producing a movie which consists of only one **shot.**

The Lumière films initially delighted audiences with their ability to capture any aspect of the real world in screen space, but Warhol's modern films outraged or bored their audiences. We are no longer excited by the camera's ability to present us with images of daily life. In its own way, *Sleep* presents an almost too perfect reproduction of reality. If you had been seated in the same spot as the camera, if you never let your eyes wander from the sleeper, you would have seen the same thing the camera saw, in color rather than black and white. But this close approximation of reality when projected on the screen is not interesting or entertaining. It is not art, only a sort of lifeless life. Life and art are two quite separate things. Now imagine, the very same camera setup, the very same subject. But let's edit these six hours of film down to one minute. Let us see what a person who seems to be sleeping soundly looks like when that seemingly static and slow activity is compressed into sixty seconds. Such a film might show a remarkable amount of tossing and turning, revealing that six hours of sleep may be a very active business. This would constitute an attempt at art — the intervention of the human mind, transforming the raw material of reality into something which is of a different order from everyday life. This process of transformation underlies all that we call art: a block of marble becomes a statue; canvas and acrylics, a painting; instrumental sounds, a symphony; or, more to our purposes, people and objects, a film.

Real life consists of people and objects and animals in motion through continuous time and space; film in its most basic form seems to include the same things. What, then, distinguishes the experience of watching a real live action (let's say a dog trotting down the street, sniffing at trees, lifting its leg, and continuing on its way) from the experience of watching that same action captured on film and projected before us on a screen? The most important difference is that when we watch this action on the screen, we are no longer sharing time and space with the dog. We are three-dimensional beings, sitting in a space we call a theater at a specific time during the day or evening. The dog, on the other hand, is a two-dimensional image, walking in a two-dimensional street contained within a two-dimensional rectangle which is contained within the three-dimensional theater in which we sit. Furthermore, the very fact that this dog has been isolated from a context — we do not see the other side of the street, or the upper part of buildings — and presented on a screen for our attention makes the dog's behavior something special, something shaped by the cinematographer. The dog may be walking and doing its doggy business on a sunny day which unfolds before us — as we sit in *our* time, which happens to be evening. The movie world seems real, but it is separate from our world.

A strange phenomenon occurs, however. Perhaps for the very reason that our bodies are disconnected from the events happening before us, we can more strongly focus our attention and sympathy on that event. While our bodies are seated in a chair in a particular theater at a particular time, our hearts and minds are set free from the distractions of the real world, and the emotional and intellectual elements of our being are greatly stimulated and excited by the images on the screen. That dog, which we may have seen hundreds of times in real life and casually dismissed, becomes, onscreen, through the power of the motion picture image, an object of immediate concern and importance. Where is the dog going? Why is he stopping just there? Isn't he a charming/amusing/

ugly/dirty/incredible/old/young dog! Or: why is the film showing us this dog now in just this way and from just this point of view? What is the larger meaning attributable to this image and how does it connect to the images that came before it and to those which will come after it? What communication is taking place between the image and the viewer? Or, to phrase it yet another way: what has the filmmaker done with the image of a simple everyday action to transform it into art?

We can begin to answer this last question by first taking a look at the physical process of capturing the image. A statement of the process is simple: light, passing through a lens, strikes a light-sensitive emulsion on a strip of celluloid. In most cases the emulsion on that first strip of celluloid captures a negative impression when it is processed, and therefore another strip of film must be exposed and processed to produce a positive print. It is the positive print which is projected on the screen.

THE EYE AND THE CAMERA

Strangely enough, motion pictures are only possible because of a flaw in human vision; we are all victims or beneficiaries of **persistence of vision.** This means, simply, that the retina of the eye retains an image of what we see a fraction of a second after the object is removed or the light goes out or we shut our eyes. We've all had the experience of this phenomenon; after looking directly at the sun, a large white or yellow spot will still remain on our retina as we look elsewhere, or even if we close our eyes. Because of persistence of vision, when a series of pictures is projected on a screen, our eyes blend the individual instances of movement together and we see what appears to be continuous movement.

Both motion picture cameras and projectors depend on the same principle for their success. Each image on the strip of celluloid must be taken when the film (though not the object being photographed, of course) is still. Otherwise the image will be a blur. Each little photograph must also be still when projected. If the film slips off the **sprockets** and slides freely through the **gate,** we see nothing but a blur. The projector has a device which stops the film frame for an instant, and then opens a **shutter** to allow the light from the projector's bulb to pass through the still photograph and project it on the screen. Then the shutter closes, the film moves down and the next individual frame is in position. The shutter opens again and we see an image on the screen, an image which seems to come smoothly and continuously, though in fact twenty-four separate frames are taken or projected each second (that is, for sound film, silent film speed varied). Between each projection of a frame on the screen and

★ **1-1**　The cartoon flip book illustrates the illusion of motion which makes the motion picture possible. Separate still pictures showing increments of a continuous motion are viewed by the eye individually just as with any still picture, if one flips the cartoon book very slowly to see each frame separately. When the still pictures follow each other more rapidly, however, the eye cannot distinguish the separateness; if one flips the book rapidly, the motion appears continuous.

the subsequent one, the screen is totally black, but because of persistence of vision we do not see this darkness at all.

The ability of the eye to blend together specific instances of stopped motion into the appearance of fluid motion can be demonstrated with a cartoon flip book (Figure 1-1). Here a series of drawings represents the movement of the limbs or face or body of the character. Because each drawing differs slightly from the one before and after it, when the pages of the book are flipped one at a time at a fairly rapid pace, the eye will see continuous movement. A deck of cards held in one hand and thumbed with the numbers and faces toward the eye will also show this effect; the spots will appear to move. The series of drawings in a cartoon flip book, by the way, is similar to the series of drawings used to produce animated films. Each increment of change in a facial expression, or in the movement of a body, must be represented in a separate drawing. Then each of these drawings is photographed by a movie camera which has been adjusted to photograph one frame at a time rather than to mechanically shoot twenty-four frames per second. But the rate of projection stays the same, twenty-four frames per second, and so the series of pictures conveys movement. On the other hand, in ordinary — or live-action — shooting, as long as the button is depressed, the movie camera photographs its individual still pictures at the rate of twenty-four frames per second. The end result for animated or live film is the same: no matter at what rate those thousands of small still photos were recorded on their strips of celluloid, projected at twenty-four frames per second they will present the illusion of motion.

There is one exception to this general condition which might be mentioned here: the **freeze frame**. Although the process of cinematography and the process of projection are exactly the way they've been described, the illusion which results from the projected image is of non-movement. Such an effect is called the "freeze frame" because it appears that a single frame has been frozen in place in the projector and motion has stopped. Actually, although the viewer has the illusion of non-movement, the film is still moving through the projector at the rate of twenty-four frames per second. It doesn't seem that way because each of those twenty-four frames (or, let's say, forty-eight frames if the image is frozen for two seconds) is exactly alike, having been duplicated in the laboratory in an optical printing process.

★★★ **Tone**

> A director may often say to a lighting cameraman that he didn't much care for yesterday's rushes, and that he thought the mood of the lighting was a bit *too* gay or *too* sinister. But he can only talk in general terms like that and he can only talk about the past. He can't make criticism of the moment because the moment is unintelligible to everyone on the floor except the lighting cameraman. It's even unintelligible to the camera operator or another cameraman coming on the set, because he doesn't have in his head all the technical facts of film stock and aperture and he hasn't seen each of the lights coming on in turn.
> Douglas Slocombe[2]

Given the present machinery, the mechanical process of capturing the image is quite simple. Artistically, however, it's extremely complicated. The cinematographer must try to photograph not only the physical objects indicated by the director, but he must also try to capture the particular emotional effect or atmosphere desired. We, the viewers, not only see images, but we feel, say, pity or terror or joy. This aspect of the images we see on the screen can, perhaps, cumulatively be called the **tone** of the film. The tone of a film relates physically — visually — to the "tones" or shadings of the actual images we see. The images in a musical, for example, are almost always bright, the images in a horror film generally dark. These distinctions, of course, are extremely broad; as we shall see, tone is usually a subtle accumulation of various elements, dictated much more by the overall effect produced by the quality of the image than by any one element in the image. Tone is the sum of what we see in the total image and, finally, in the total film (Figure 1-2). With the proper combination of, for instance, film stock and lighting, a sense of anxiety can be produced with color images such as appear in Michelangelo Antonioni's *Blow-Up* (1966), Ingmar Bergman's *Cries and Whispers* (1972), and Robert Altman's *Three Women* (1976). On the other hand, a sense of dreamy romance can be depicted in the cool, quiet, dark images of Ingmar Bergman's *Smiles of a Summer Night* (1955); a musical comedy can keep its lightness though shot in dark, somber or muted color as in Joshua Logan's *Paint Your Wagon* (1969); and, as Mel Brooks showed in *Young Frankenstein* (1974), even a sense of uproarious comedy can be

★ **1-2** The tone of a film like THE THIRD MAN (Carol Reed, 1950) is dark and brooding. Most of the action takes place at night, in darkened interiors, on mist-laden streets, or in the depths of the sewers. The strange and dank atmosphere is created as much by the expressive use of light and shadow as by the nature of the place. Lit from behind, figures in the tunnels of the sewer cast ominous shadows.

conveyed through the use of black-and-white film which parodies expressionist lighting. The choices which the cinematographer must make as he attempts to visualize concretely the inner vision of the director are almost infinite.

FILM STOCK

First the filmmaker must decide whether to shoot the film with black-and-white or color stock. The effect of using one or the other will be important to the final and cumulative tone of the film. Until the late 1950s, color was used primarily for musicals and historical films. At that time it might have seemed tonally inappropriate to use color stock for a film dealing with serious subject matter simply because past usage had caused the viewer to associate color with frivolous and lavish spectacles. Today, of course, color is used for everything from serious, thought-provoking films like *Seven Beauties* (Lina Wertmüller, 1975) to murder mysteries like *Farewell My Lovely* (Dick Richards, 1975) to grim films about contemporary problems like psychosis and violence such as *A Woman Under the Influence* (John Cassavetes, 1974) and *Taxi Driver* (Martin Scorsese, 1976). To be sure, the actual physical tone of the color is carefully controlled and modulated so that it can be used expressively in ways that were not possible years ago.

Michelangelo Antonioni used color in his *Red Desert* (1964) to express not only the emotional state of his main character but also to communicate the incongruities inherent in modern industrial society. In this, his first color film, Antonioni put his characters in drab clothing, which blends into background walls and fog and landscapes of industrial waste, while factory vats, pipes, and industrial paraphernalia are vividly painted in primary colors. The contrast between the drab and the colorful suggests the ascendance of machinery over man, of object over subject.

This same growth of aesthetic sophistication resulting from advances in technology and tools can be seen in the way contrasting film stocks have been used in the same film. As early as 1939, in Victor Fleming's *The Wizard of Oz*, black-and-white film stock was contrasted with color for specific aesthetic reasons. Although the contrast is certainly not subtle, it is totally effective in communicating visually the difference between Dorothy's drab Kansas and the world she finds "over the rainbow," a world filled with witches and magic slippers and Munchkins and a trio of improbable friends. More subtle in its aesthetic effects, yet equally powerful, is *Butch Cassidy and the Sundance Kid* (George Roy Hill, 1969), which moves between color and monochromatic sepia-tinted stock. The color sequences, contemporary in mood and tone, involve us with the characters on an immediate emotional level which convinces us to join the characters in their — and the film's — present tense. Conversely, the sepia sections (which are often combined with freeze frames) remove us from the characters and remind us of old photographs in old picture albums, daguerreotypes dusty with time, their subjects long dead. This tension between our immediate engagement and our sense of nostalgia is created, to a large degree, by the shift in film stock; a technical element which might not seem important nonetheless creates emotional responses to the film.

The cinematographer (usually working in collaboration with the director) must also make choices when he uses black-and-white film. For instance, a **high-speed,** or **fast, film** (one which needs less light to capture an image) will produce a **grainy, high-contrast** image: the blacks will be very black and the whites very white, with very few shades of gray in between. Because such film is — or has been — used by newsreel cameramen to record the events of the day in on-the-spot coverage, it produces a newsreel effect — that is, our sense of the actuality of the image is heightened. Although the association between fast black-and-white film stock and immediate reality may be weakening because movie theaters no longer show newsreels, and because color film and videotape bring us immediate events clearly and on television, modern filmmakers may still choose to authenticate their content and their images by using such a stock. Even if the viewer has never seen old, grainy newsreels, the grain and contrast in the stock still has a link with the grainy photos that daily appear in newspapers.

An interesting example is *The Battle of Algiers* (Gillo Pontecorvo, 1966). The film begins with a printed message, informing the audience that the film they are about to see is fiction. None of the footage is compiled from newsreels. Yet within a minute or so after the beginning of the movie, we have forgotten the message. What we see before us looks like a newsreel, like film shot hastily by a reporter whose life might be in danger and who had no time for composing his shots carefully. The images we see in the film are grainy and high-contrast, the camera is frequently hand-held, there are no known actors (Figure 1-3). We *feel* we are watching a documentary filmed on the spot during an actual historical event, even though we recall somewhere in the back of our minds the printed disclaimer at the movie's beginning, even though we *know* we are watching a fiction film. Such is the power of the images we see as the action unfolds — and some of that power is attributable to the choice of film stock.

Just as contrasting film stock can be used in sophisticated ways within the same color film, contrasting black and white stocks within the same film can heighten drama and show two distinct temporal or spatial worlds. Time and space, for example, are fluid in *Wild Strawberries* (Ingmar Bergman, 1957), a film whose central character is an elderly man who, though functioning in the present, has nightmares and fantasies and who visits his past through memory. If the filmmaker had to tell us verbally of each change in time and space, the film would bog down. Instead, Bergman uses different film stocks to signal to the viewer that the elderly man is no longer in the "present," but in a dream or a memory. High contrast for the nightmare sequence makes us aware that we are in a dream, and it also helps us to feel the terror of the protagonist. An image rich in light, full of details communicated in infinite gradations from very black to very white and all shades of gray in between, illuminates (literally and figuratively) the scenes of the protagonist's past. A moderate, though somewhat somber, contrast is used to depict his melancholy, pedantic, and empty present. In *Wild Strawberries* the choice of film stock is the starting point for the effects which the viewer will recognize in the finished film.

Robert Enrico also combined different black-and-white film stocks in his short film *An Occurrence at Owl Creek Bridge* (1961). In the opening sequence a man is being prepared for a military execution at dawn. The film stock is **low-contrast**, everything appears poorly lit (as it would just before sunrise), somewhat fuzzy. The scene has the look and feel of late autumn and the chill of winter approaching. The texture and grain of the images are somewhat reminiscent of old Civil War photographs taken by

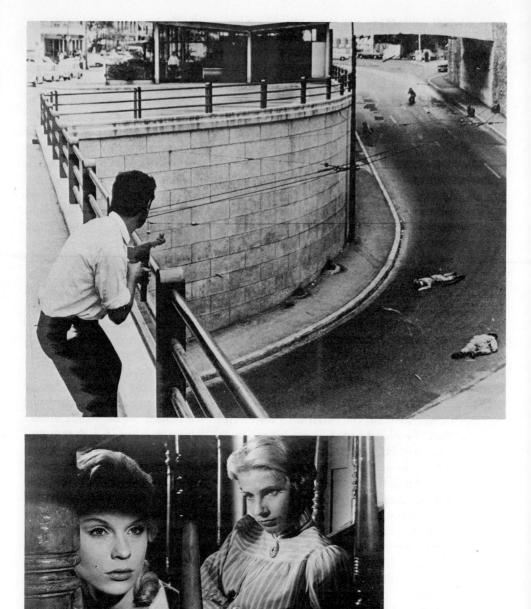

★ **1-3** The choice of black-and-white film stock affects the tone of the image. In THE BATTLE OF ALGIERS (1966), Gillo Pontecorvo used high-speed, high-grain stock to give the look of on-the-spot newsreel authenticity to his fictional treatment of the Algerian struggle for independence (top). Ingmar Bergman used a similar stock in WILD STRAWBERRIES (1957) for the old professor's nightmare, but he switched to a fine grain, low contrast stock (bottom) for the old man's memories of his adolescence.

Mathew B. Brady — and this is appropriate, for the film takes place during that period. In the film's next sequence, in which the man appears to have escaped his captors, Enrico uses a richer, fuller film stock, a slow-speed film which captures the image with exactitude and clarity. This sequence has bright highlights, sparkles with a feeling of life, and has the look and feel of warm spring with summer approaching. The very clarity of the image in this sequence somehow makes the man's escape much more "real" than the earlier, relatively lifeless, military sequence. Near the end of the film we perceive that the escaping man only lived the escape in his mind in the instant before he died. We see him hanging, and we are abruptly jerked back to reality — partly by the film stock, which is that of the beginning of the film, with its November mood. The evocation of tone, as well as the credibility of the various segments, is created in great part by the choice of film stocks.

LIGHTING

Having made a selection of film stock, the cinematographer's next expressive tool for producing the tone of the final image is **light**. The amount and kind of light used will depend upon the particular film stock chosen and, of course, the effect the director wants the film to have. The original properties for which the film stock was chosen will be amplified or subdued by the appropriate selection of light. In *The Battle of Algiers*, for example, the extremely bright quality of the Mediterranean sun brings out the high contrast inherent in the film stock. The light of the Swedish sun in the outdoor scenes of *Wild Strawberries*, however, is less intense, therefore moderating the tone of the final image.

Obviously the use of outdoor light imposes certain restrictions upon the filmmaker. He must wait upon the weather and the time of day. If he wants long shadows, he can only shoot in the morning or late afternoon. If the day is too overcast, he may not be able to shoot at all, unless he resorts to **floodlights, reflectors, filters,** and **sunscreens** in order to alter the available natural light.

In interiors, however, modification of the final image through effective lighting takes place most strikingly. Films designed to strike terror create their chilling, spine-tingling atmosphere with selective lighting. Two small **pin spots** focused on the eyes of Count Dracula make us believe in the intensity of his hypnotic strength and sensuality. Flickering shadows playing on the dungeon wall as Fritz, the hunchback, threatens Frankenstein's monster with a torch, are purposefully eerie. Alfred Hitchcock uses the harsh light from a naked light bulb to add to the terror of the dénouement in *Psycho* (1960) (Figure 1-4). A lone woman descends into the darkness of a creepy old house's fruit cellar and turns on a single light bulb, which reveals the figure of a woman sitting in a chair, her back to the camera. When the chair is wheeled around, we and the female protagonist are looking at a mummified body. The woman screams and knocks the overhanging light bulb so that it swings crazily about overhead, changing the direction of the light source from moment to moment, an effect which is in sympathy with the situation and which is disorienting and disquieting to the viewer.

★ **1-4** Shadows and harsh lighting create the emotional response associated with horror films. This scene (left) from Alfred Hitchcock's PSYCHO (1960) was lit by a single bare bulb which swayed back and forth, throwing light and dark alternately on the mummified figure. Above, the flickering shadows caused by the torch create a sense of oppression and doom in James Whale's FRANKENSTEIN (1931).

The effect of light in the horror film is obvious to all observers. But in other films it is perhaps more difficult to spot the subtle effects produced by what might be called "normal" lighting. We see a scene in a living room: sofas, chairs, tables, a couple of lamps, people talking or reading the newspaper. Everything is clearly visible. Somehow we feel that the two table lamps with their 100-watt bulbs are the actual source of illumination for the scene, just as they would be in our own living room. Actually, just out of camera range, there are **spotlights** and floodlights with thousands of watts of illuminating power carefully placed — above or below, in front or behind, obliquely — so as to produce the illusion of normal room lighting. Even lighting this comparatively simple scene requires great skill and knowledge. Imagine, then, the more difficult lighting assignments: creating the effect of early morning or late afternoon on the set when, indeed, actual sunlight may be unavailable; making a room look as though it is lit by candles, gaslight, crystal chandeliers — or a single naked light bulb; lighting the face of an actor to emphasize those physical characteristics which complement the character he is playing. Or, in fact, actually using gaslight or candlelight or firelight to illuminate the set sufficiently well to capture the image with the control usually made available by artificial lighting (Figure 1-5).

Though the interplay between light and shadow is most noticeable in black and white films, it is also crucial to color films. Whether filmed in black and white or color, a romantic heroine is often **backlit** to create a halo effect on her hair. Filters and gauzes, placed before the camera, soften and diffuse light so that what appears on the screen seems hazy, distant, soft and muted. In *Bonnie and Clyde* (Arthur Penn, 1967), there is a marked difference in tone when the film shows the Barrow gang returning to Bonnie Parker's home to visit her mother; because the light in the scene is diffused by lenses, filters, and gauze, the interlude seems like a dream, unreal, thereby foreshadowing the impossibility that the Barrows will ever escape their present lives. The diffused, though seemingly natural, lighting of *McCabe and Mrs. Miller* (Robert Altman, 1971) lends the entire film a tone which overwhelmingly communicates the fleeting nature of life and the pastness of the past; through the lighting, the film creates a nostalgia for the film's "living" characters in such a way that we also are aware of them as long dead.

In color films, light can also be effectively controlled within the camera itself or in the laboratory when the print is developed. Overexposed or underexposed color film (too much or too little light reaching the film stock) can guide the viewer's response to the image. If a filmmaker wants us to feel the heat and dryness and blinding sun of a desert, he may overexpose his film in the camera so that it looks bleached, washed-out,

★ **1-5** To capture a photographic image, enough light must strike the emulsion to effect a chemical change. Low light conditions, as in this scene from BARRY LYNDON (Stanley Kubrick, 1975) where candlelight is the only illumination, are extremely difficult assignments for the cinematographer. In such cases the film stock must be overdeveloped or "forced" in the laboratory to reveal a visible image.

parched. In the laboratory development process, many cinematic tricks can be performed with light. Using black-and-white film in 1922, F. W. Murnau, for example, wanted to produce a ghostly image in his horror film *Nosferatu*; to convey the eerie quality of a "phantom coach," he not only used speeded up motion but also a **negative image** which was inserted in the film amidst all the positive footage. Today, we can see the fascinating effects of color negative images in a film like *2001: A Space Odyssey* (Stanley Kubrick, 1968).

The specifically selected use of light can add, then, to the meanings of an image; it can cause us to respond emotionally and physiologically. Soft or harsh lighting can manipulate the viewer's attitude towards a setting or a character. In *Tom Jones* (Tony Richardson, 1963), for example, the scenes of English eighteenth-century country life on Squire All-worthy's estate seem to glow with warmth and a languorous richness; they are softly lit and diffused enough to make the green countryside seem al-

★ **1-6** The lighting in Orson Welles's CITIZEN KANE (1941) often undercuts or modifies the viewer's perceptions of a scene. Leaning over the table to ceremoniously sign the "Declaration of Principles," Kane's face slips into shadow, darkening the mood of exuberance associated with his pledge to help the downtrodden.

most dewy. On the other hand, when Tom is evicted from these idyllic surroundings and forced to make his way in a hostile London, the scenes of that city are harshly lit and the images appear cooler, either more forbidding or more brittle. The color, then, helps the viewer subconsciously to equate the country with warmth, honesty, and natural vitality, and the city with coldness, corruption, and artificial gaiety.

This kind of contrast in lighting works just as well in black and white. *Dr. Strangelove; or, How I Learned to Stop Worrying and Love the Bomb* (Stanley Kubrick, 1964) is a classic example. Because of the differences in the lighting in the various locations of the film, the characters seem to inhabit different worlds, and the possibility of their communicating with each other is virtually nil. The "maddest" characters in the film — the psychotic General Jack D. Ripper and the totalitarian paraplegic Dr. Strangelove — are lit as if they inhabited an old 1930s Universal Studio horror film; their faces, made grotesque by shadows, emerge from blackness. On the other hand, the military base from which the General issues his insane commands and the interior of the B–52 bomber which is attempting to carry out his attack plan on Russia are both lit with the flat and gray style reminiscent of 1950s war movies. The disparity in lighting styles visually underscores the impossibility of communication between the men in the B–52 bomber and the top brass in the War Room of the Pentagon. They exist in two separate worlds.

Of course, lighting effects need not be so obvious as a clear contrast in styles. The lighting of a character throughout a film may evolve

★ **1-7** Shadows also complement the activity of the dialogue and action in CITIZEN KANE. When Kane silences Susan Alexander's protests about her career, his shadow moves across her face as though blotting out her personality.

slowly, shaping our responses. In *Citizen Kane* (Orson Welles, 1941), for example, the lighting of the central character changes slowly as the film progresses. The face of the youthful and idealistic Charles Foster Kane is fully and evenly lit so that it appears attractive, soft, without shadows. At one moment in the early part of the film, however, Kane's change of character is literally "foreshadowed." As he is writing a "Declaration of Principles" (which he will later betray), his face is in complete shadow while the faces of those watching him can be clearly seen (Figure 1-6). As Kane's idealism fades, and as he becomes a more complex and less comprehensible figure, his face is seen more and more frequently in partial shadow. As he becomes finally an enigmatic cipher, more inscrutable in his motives and actions, so does the light reveal less and less of him to the audience. (See Figure 1-7.)

★★★ ## Composition

The camera is only an accessory to the human eye and serves principally to frame — to include and to exclude. Within the frame the artist collects that which he wishes us to share with him; beyond the frame is placed what he considers of no value to his thought.
Josef von Sternberg[3]

Composition is the arrangement of people and objects within the space of the film frame. Even if the camera remains perfectly still, that rectangular space within the frame can be filled in many ways. It may show us people and things arranged in pleasing and harmonious relationships, or it may show discordant relationships. They can, as well, be arranged in such a formal way that the viewer is aware he is watching not real life, but a movie which has been artificially constructed — or they can be arranged so randomly and spontaneously that the viewer almost forgets he is watching a film and instead feels as though he were looking through a window into the real world. Composition, then, is a tool that helps the filmmaker to create and communicate meaning (Figure 1-8).

COMPOSITION IN THE FRAME

When Michelangelo Antonioni composes a shot, he frequently shows us the feelings his characters have towards each other not by the dialogue they speak but through their position in the frame. In a scene in *Eclipse* (1961), a young, ambitious stockbroker is trying to locate his latest amour. She is clearly visible to us on one side of the screen, but a huge marble pillar stands between them so he can't see her, a pillar which holds up the roof of the stock exchange in Milan. The lack of connection between these two people is visually suggested by their physical separation in the frame as well as by the specific representation of the world of finance.

John Ford is famous for spacious westerns, with scenes where the sky fills nearly two-thirds of the frame. Although Ford's essentially optimistic themes stress the positive aspects of taming the wilderness into a civilization, many of his **long shots** dwarf the characters and their creations, such as wagons or houses, showing them as small and inconsequential against the awesome breadth and power of nature. The vast landscape emphasizes the heroism and the fragility of their attempts to civilize the wilderness.

On the other hand, the *lack* of space and spaciousness can be used for aesthetic and thematic effect (Figure 1-9). In films as separated by history and theme as Carl Dreyer's *The Passion of Joan of Arc* (1928) and Ingmar Bergman's *Persona* (1966), close-up shots of faces are a major portion of the footage. The viewer, forced to observe in close-up the planes and angles, the hills and valleys, of the human face removed from context, becomes somewhat dislocated in space. The sudden strangeness of what we usually take for granted in real life helps to make us receptive to the intense inner life of the character. *The Passion of Joan of Arc* deals with the mystery of saintliness, with the transfiguration of a peasant girl

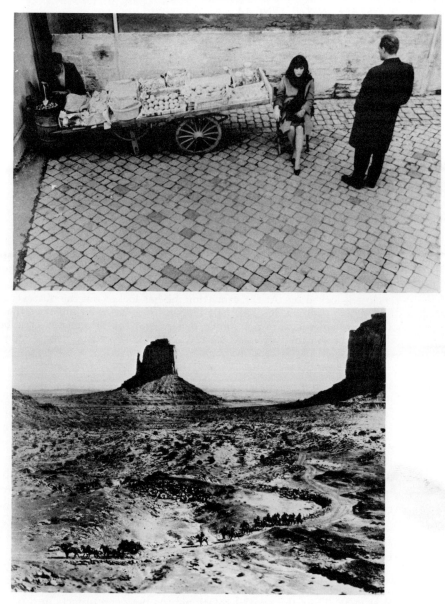

★ **1-8** Composition — the arrangement of objects in the frame — can indicate relationships between people and people, people and place. In the top picture from Antonioni's RED DESERT (1964), the man and woman are separated from each other, and from the fruit vendor. Having the main subjects in the shot stretched across the top half of the frame heightens the sense of anxiety and dislocation. In the bottom photo, from John Ford's STAGE-COACH (1939), the human characters are dwarfed by the setting. They seem to be intruders in the wilderness.

★ **1-9** The complex information contained in the visual images of a film
is illustrated in this shot from François Truffaut's 400 BLOWS (1959).
Photographed through the wire grid, the reform school boy appears trapped,
enclosed, locked up. At the same time he has locked out the observer: his
folded arm position, his face half hidden by the sweater indicates that.
The eyes, however, are not simply defiant, but full of anxiety. Thus both
the subject and the way in which the subject is revealed by the composition
combine to create the total message.

into a figure who will transcend time. It is, therefore, appropriate that
Dreyer shoots so much in close-up, that he angles Joan's head in the
frame so that it bears some resemblance to Christ's attitude on the Cross,
and that he lets us gaze for long periods of time at her eyes, the "window
to the soul." Bergman's *Persona* deals less with spiritual matters than it
does with the mysteries of the psyche, with those qualities which define
insanity and those which define normality. Bergman's decision to dislo-
cate the viewer from an environment, to fill the frame with close-ups,
causes the viewer to feel psychologically disoriented and disquieted himself, to feel the actual claustrophobia of being confined with one or two
beings in an ill-defined but nonetheless restricting space.

The position of actors in the frame is only one aspect of composition;
every object visible in the final shot will be part of the composition of
that shot. Thus the spatial relationships between objects and people and
between objects and objects are extremely important. In *The Lady Vanishes* (Alfred Hitchcock, 1938), for example, the heroine and hero are on
a train seated in the dining car with the film's villain. We know, but they
do not, that the villain has filled the couple's after-dinner drinks with
poison. We view much of this scene through the brandy glasses which
occupy the foreground of the frame. The liquor glasses, the largest ob-

★ **1-10** By placing objects in the foreground plane and having the characters in a background plane, in a sense Hitchcock has created a close-up within a medium shot. As long as both planes are in focus, the relationships between the two can be revealed. In the above shot from THE LADY VANISHES (1938), tension results because the viewer knows that the villain (on the left) has drugged the drinks, but the hero and heroine (not visible in this frame) do not.

jects in the frame because they are in the foreground, dominate the smaller figures, making clear the power of the poison and unnerving the viewer (Figure 1-10). The relationship of people to the objects which surround them and the relationship of objects to objects is, in fact, the very theme of Jacques Tati's amazing comedies. Using relationships within a single image, Tati communicates the complexities of human life with minimal dialogue. In his *Playtime* (1967), for example, a busload of tourists have come to Paris to see the marvelous city. What the audience directly sees of the city is all angular and modern, all chrome and steel and glass. One sees the old Parisian landmarks like the Eiffel Tower or Sacre Coeur only when they are reflected in the windows of the bus or in an occasional glass door. The implication is that romantic Paris can be experienced only in juxtaposition with modern transportation and modern architecture.

COMPOSITION OUT OF THE FRAME

It may seem strange, in considering composition, to discuss the space which exists offscreen, out of the frame. After all, because it is not part of the image we cannot see anything in it. And yet **offscreen space** does exist as part of many films, particularly those which, striving for realism, want the viewer to feel not as though he is looking at a painting, a piece of art quite distinct from life, but rather as if he were peering through a window at life itself.

Since the seventeenth century, the proscenium arch has traditionally defined theatrical space in the live theater; the stage, framed by the arch, contains the play. Each member of the audience views entire actors from top to toe, from a singular vantage point, the seat he happens to be occupying. Of course actors exit to the wings, but we scarcely think of a world offstage unless it is evoked by an actor onstage. The sense of space in film is different. Although it can show — in a long shot — the entire bodies of all the characters, it can also show in the frame, only parts of actors — heads only or feet only, or an eye only — incomplete images, images which are not whole unless the viewer mentally or emotionally fills them in, using the offscreen space as a larger canvas. The incompleteness of the image *in* the frame causes the viewer to continue the image *out* of the frame into offscreen space. Although examples of this **extended image** occur as a matter of course in most films, a dramatic example exists in *Citizen Kane.* The scene begins in Kane's campaign headquarters after he has been defeated for a gubernatorial race because of his involvement in a scandal. In the background Kane's best friend and campaign manager, Jed Leland, stands surveying the wreckage of posters and confetti on the floor. We see Leland's entire figure, but suddenly, along the whole left side of the frame, a dark shape emerges. It is a trousered leg, but because it is in the foreground it is gigantic in comparison with Leland, who is in the background (Figure 1-11). A conversation occurs between Jed Leland and the owner of that leg. Obviously, it is quite ridiculous to think of a leg having a conversation; we know from his familiar voice that Charlie Kane is conversing and that the leg is merely part of him. Without really thinking about it, we fill in the rest of Kane; we know he continues as a physical body beyond the rectangular confines of the frame. If we acknowledge his spatial reality outside the frame we are also acknowledging that the world of the film continues beyond the frame. Such extended images can be used for aesthetic purposes which complement the subject or theme of a film also. Akira Kurosawa's *Yojimbo* (1961) concerns an unemployed samurai who becomes involved in the petty larceny of two rival families in a small town. Each family attempts to employ him to destroy the other family. The samurai needs money, but he has no love for either of the families and does not trust them. He proceeds to manipulate both clans until they end up destroying each other. The samurai is viewed by the camera both as a down-at-heel, scruffy opportunist and also as a godlike man impatient with cruelty and

★ **1-11** Offscreen space is created by nearly all shots in films. Since the camera can move left or right, up or down, any shot implies that the world view within the frame continues beyond the boundaries of the frame. This is particularly clear when only a portion of an object or person is included in the frame. Here in CITIZEN KANE (Orson Welles, 1941), Kane's legs are visible in the frame; we assume that his body continues outside the frame.

pettiness. The characterizations developed in the film suggest that the samurai is both dynamically real and remarkable, whereas the members of the two families are like inconsequential puppets or scurrying insects. The composition of frames in *Yojimbo* helps create and then confirm these characterizations. In many scenes, the camera peers over the shoulder of the samurai, who fills the screen's foreground with half his head and half the upper part of his torso while he and the viewer look down the street to see the little figures of the warring families. The samurai's body extends out of the image, conferring on him a spatial reality which goes beyond the frame; the corrupt townspeople, contained within the frame, seem less real. Other scenes, too, show that the pettiness of the families and its full representation in screen space is no accident. While we again peer over the shoulder of this samurai whose vitality extends beyond the frame, we see as he does through an opening in a wall: in the building across the way, one of the families is placating a petty official from another town. It is as if we are actually watching a performance on a stage, so small are the figures and so contained in the rectangular opening in the wall.

★ **1-12** Objects within the frame can be used to isolate certain elements of the frame, by creating a change in the aspect ratio. Normally the rectangular shape of the frame emphasizes the horizontal, the horizon of the everyday world. In this scene from DIARY OF A COUNTRY PRIEST (1950), Robert Bresson has framed the priest in a doorway, emphasizing the vertical. In effect, he has modified the normal frame to create one which is higher than it is wide. Since the priest is concerned with the problems of salvation, heaven, and hell, using such framing often in this film makes the viewer aware that there is no horizontal escape for the young man.

Another and even more subtle way in which offscreen space can be created and communicated relates to certain kinds of composition within the frame. Robert Bresson's *The Diary of a Country Priest* (1950) concerns the anguish of a young priest who is in spiritual turmoil. The black-and-white film is extremely austere in the way it is lit, in the way the camera moves, and in its spare compositions. But the young priest seems consistently framed within the screen space by vertical planes (Figure 1-12). He is seen through the vertical bars of an iron gate, caught in the vertical darkness which is created by an open doorway, and so on. His face or his body, imprisoned by verticals, is discomfiting to watch. It seems almost as if we were trapped also, for it requires an effort of will to make our eyes move laterally across the screen. More often than not, our only release from the confines of the entire film frame is vertically oriented; we are made visually aware that escape lies upward or downward out of the frame. Since the film deals with the notion of religious grace and faith and humility, it is appropriate that our attention be directed upward or downward, that the space of some sort of heaven or hell be implied offscreen by what we see in the frame.

★ **1-13** The close-up limits the field of vision to a specific subject, forcing the audience to see what the filmmaker thinks is important. In addition, as in this still from Ingmar Bergman's PERSONA (1966), the close-up will abstract the subject from a context.

VIEWPOINTS

When we discuss **viewpoints** in a motion picture we are talking about two things: the apparent distance from which the camera records the subject, and the angle from which the camera records the subject. Again, as with all cinematic elements, choice will affect communication and meaning; from what apparent distance and from what angle we see what we see will determine part of our response to the subject being filmed.

The composition of the frame in a motion picture is similar to the composition of a still photograph. The screen is, after all, a two-dimensional rectangle within which the images of the photographed objects appear. Somehow these objects should be organized in that rectangle so that they all relate to the final or total effect desired. Two characters, let us say, are together — or they are separated. But in addition to this relationship, the camera's distance from the subject can also be significant. The filmmaker can choose to move the camera closer to the subject in order to block out or mask material he does not wish the audience to see. Or he can move the camera closer to the subject to concentrate our attention, focusing it more intently on the subject (Figure 1-13). We call this

★ **1-14** Medium and long shots show a subject within a context. In this shot from THE MAGNIFICENT AMBERSONS (1942), the viewer is made aware of the relationship between the characters and the nineteenth-century world they live in.

★ **1-15** The extreme long shot emphasizes the background since the subject is usually seen from a distance. In such views the subject appears lost in the context, at the mercy of larger forces. In this scene from D. W. Griffith's THE BIRTH OF A NATION (1915), the protagonist is swallowed up in the confusion and din of a battle.

shot a close-up (for example, a shot of a face) or an **extreme close-up** (for example, a shot of an eye), depending on the distance between the camera and the subject. Reversing the process, the filmmaker can choose to place the camera far away from the principal subject, forcing the viewer to see the surroundings in which the subject is located and the relationship between that subject and his surroundings (Figure 1-14). We call such a shot a long shot or an **extreme long shot** (Figure 1-15), depending on the distance between the camera and the subject. And, of course, somewhere between is the **medium shot** (for example, showing the upper half of a figure), with the camera fixed so as to incorporate most of the subject and some of the subject's surroundings. No definitions can distinguish exactly between these shots, just as no one can distinguish exactly between late afternoon and evening, but the distinction between day and night is clear, and so is the distinction between an extreme close-up and an extreme long shot.

In the early days of film, producers familiar with stage presentations felt that movie audiences had paid to see the whole actor, not just isolated parts of him. Although there was an extremely exciting close-up in Edwin S. Porter's *The Great Train Robbery* (1903), in which an outlaw's gun was fired directly at the camera, it was D. W. Griffith who realized the aesthetic and narrative implications of the close-up. In many cases it could reveal more than the posturing of a whole body. The close-up of Mae Marsh's hands in the courtroom scene in Griffith's *Intolerance* (1916) is a most powerful testimony to her anxiety. Griffith also knew that the long shot could be used effectively for both spectacle and significance. The battlefield filled with antlike soldiers swarming through thick clouds of smoke in *The Birth of a Nation* (1915) shows us not only the action on a grand scale, but it also shows us visually the futility of war, the way in which man is reduced to insignificance against the larger backdrop of nature and time.

The use of different lenses will also change the perspective of a shot. Although the camera may still be the same distance from the subject, the image it records will be altered depending on the lens in use (Figure 1-16). A **telephoto lens,** for example, is used to photograph Benjamin running to stop the wedding of the girl he loves in *The Graduate* (Mike Nichols, 1967). We see him running towards the camera, but the telephoto lens distorts the perspective, foreshortens the image, and creates the impression of a treadmill. Benjamin is running as fast as he can but seems to be getting nowhere. A **wide-angle lens** will produce the opposite effect: the background will appear farther away, but the person moving towards the camera will grow in relative size more quickly than with a normal lens (Figure 1-17). In numerous scenes in *Citizen Kane*,

★ **1-16** The choice of lens will change the spatial relationships within the image. In a telephoto shot the background planes will be compressed and will appear closer to the camera. Any figure moving towards or away from the camera will appear to make little progress, as in these shots from AN OCCURRENCE AT OWL CREEK BRIDGE (Robert Enrico, 1961). Such shots emphasize the intense but futile effort of the figure as he moves towards the camera.

★ **1-17** The wide-angle lens, on the other hand, makes background planes appear to recede from the camera, to be farther away. Any figure moving towards or away from the camera will appear to cover the ground rapidly. In this scene from CITIZEN KANE, Orson Welles dominates the group as he moves forcefully, in a stride or two, from the back of the room to the front. He appears to cover a relatively large distance with ease and agility.

★ **1-18** Depth of field describes the area in front of a camera lens within which objects are in focus. The depth of field in the shot on the left is relatively narrow: only the letters from "R" through "N" are clearly in focus. In the shot on the right, the depth of field is quite large: except for the first match every object from in front of the camera to the back wall is in focus. This is sometimes referred to as "deep focus." Generally, the more light available to film, the greater the possible depth of field. (Photos by Rob Wilkie)

Kane walks towards the camera from what appears to be the far corner of a room. As he approaches the foreground he becomes so much larger, so quickly, that it is impossible not to feel the dominance of his physical being and therefore his character. In other words, the figure of Kane is created not only by Orson Welles's performance but also by the cinematographer's choice of distance and lens.

The selective use of **focus** is another element of perspective and viewpoint (Figure 1-18). The camera may focus on a subject and record an image in which everything is clear and discernible, whether the subject is near or far in the frame; we say such a shot has a wide **depth of field** and is an example of deep-focus cinematography (Figure 1-19). The camera may, by changing its focus, blur an object in the foreground where our attention is normally placed, calling our attention to something clearly defined in the background of the frame; such a shifting of focus from foreground to background or vice versa is called **rack focus.** Or the camera may totally blur or distort our vision of the subject or it may present us with such clarity of vision that it seems we are looking through an incredibly powerful microscope.

A filmmaker will select these effects achieved by focus and **focal length** not for their novelty or oddness, but for their expressiveness within the particular film. Therefore, cinematographer James Wong Howe used a **fisheye lens** to distort those images in *Seconds* (John Frankenheimer, 1966) in which the film's protagonist is bound and

★ **1-19** The way in which "deep focus" or extended depth of field can show relationships between background and foreground planes is nowhere more evident than in this shot from CITIZEN KANE. While Mrs. Kane signs guardianship of her son over to Mr. Thatcher at a table in the foreground, and Charlie's father hovers ineffectually in the middle distance, young Charlie is visible through the window playing innocently in the snow. Thus the free-spirited boy is consciously present in the viewer's consciousness as we see his mother put in motion the series of events which will deprive him of his innocence and freedom.

gagged and subjected to an operation which will end his life. In *An Occurrence at Owl Creek Bridge* (1961), Jean Boffety photographs leaves and dewdrops and insects in extreme close-up, combining vivid clarity with rack focus not simply to reveal the aesthetic beauty of nature and its patterns, but to convey the intensity with which the protagonist sees (or thinks he sees) the world around him.

The angle from which the subject is photographed also dramatically affects the viewer's response to what he sees (Figure 1-20). If the camera is placed about eye level with the subject, the viewer sees what seems essentially a neutral, objective — or, we might say, comfortably familiar — shot. If the camera looks down on its subject from above in what is called a **high-angle** shot, the subject is diminished physically and seems small and vulnerable. If, on the other hand, the camera looks up at its subject from below in what is called a **low-angle** shot, the power, stature and strength of that subject tends to be increased. When the escaping protagonist of *An Occurrence at Owl Creek Bridge* is caught in the rapids of a river and carried downstream, the high-angle shot of him makes him seem particularly small and vulnerable. Conversely, before the cattle drive begins in *Red River* (Howard Hawks, 1948), the camera photographs each of the major characters from a low angle as they sit astride their horses; they appear confident and powerful and we visually know that they are "tall in their saddles."

★ **1-20** When the camera is tilted on its axis so that normally vertical lines in the image appear slanted either to the left or right, ordinary expectations of a stable world are frustrated. Such shots are often used in mystery and suspense films to create a sense of unease in the viewer — as in Carol Reed's THE THIRD MAN (1950).

By selecting a particular position from which he views the subject, the filmmaker allows the viewer to see the subject only in the particular way he has decided is best and appropriate. In this sense, camera angle allows the filmmaker to function like the narrator of fiction who *tells us about* the characters; he is able to move freely in time and space, to observe anything and everything and, indeed, to editorialize or comment visually on the events and characters presented to the viewer. By using camera angle combined with editing, he is even able to convey to us how one character is seen by another character. In *Citizen Kane*, Susan Alexander is dominated by Kane until the moment when she finally decides to leave him. In almost every scene in which the two appear, Kane is photographed from below waist level, from a low angle. He appears taller, larger, more dominating because of the camera's stance. Susan Alexander is invariably photographed from above, the high angle revealing her own sense of weakness and subservience (Figure 1-21).

Occasionally the filmmaker will use a **subjective viewpoint,** attempting to show a true first-person point of view (the "I" of fiction) by photographing not only *what* a character sees, but also *how* he sees it (Figure 1-22). Many images in *Downhill Racer* (Michael Ritchie, 1969) could be visible only from the skier's vantage point: visible in the lower foreground are the ski tips themselves; the image swoops around corners, leaps over bumps, skids across ice patches. We feel and see as though we *are* the skier, actually feeling what he feels as he plunges headlong down the steep race course. Similarly, shots taken from the

★ **1-21** A "normal" shooting angle is approximately eye level with the figures. High angles — looking down on a subject — tend to diminish the subject. On the other hand, low angles — looking at the subject from below — tend to emphasize the power and towering stature of the subject. In these shots from CITIZEN KANE, Welles looms large even though he has just lost an election, whereas Susan Alexander appears small, even though she is yelling aggressively at Kane.

★ **1-22** The subjective camera shot presents what is seen by a character, as if the camera lens were actually the person. In Michael Ritchie's DOWNHILL RACER (1969), the camera is mounted on a skier who actually skies down a course, and the viewer experiences the dizzying speed and thrills of the downhill ski racer. (Here we see the camera being attached.) The intimate identification that takes place between viewer and character adds intensity to a film like this. But the subjective camera, if overused, can be confusing or draw too much attention to the camera.

driver's viewpoint in *Grand Prix* (John Frankenheimer, 1966) are often powerful and seem real enough to make one lean in his seat as the racing car careens around turns. Less spectacularly although more substantially, we share the vision of Travis Bickle as he — and we — look through the windshield of his cab in *Taxi Driver* (1976); thus, for various moments during the film, we are linked to, *become*, a psychotic and paranoid consciousness locked in the protective interior of a taxicab. This kind of subjective viewpoint is often particularly successful in portraying a character's abnormal state: the effects of drugs, alcohol, visions, fantasies, and dreams. And, on occasion, the subjective viewpoint can be used to compound drama and suspense in novel ways (Figure 1-23). During the scenes in *Jaws* (Steven Spielberg, 1975) in which the shark cruises toward potential victims, subjective shots give us the shark's-eye view. The viewer is torn between his natural inclination to sympathize with the potential victim of the attack and his enforced subjective viewpoint, which makes him see through the eyes of the shark. His perceptions are physiologically linked with those of the "villain," while at the same time his emotional concerns are for the human being he is ostensibly going to attack.

Subjective shots are used to some small degree in most films. But when the viewpoint is used for too great a length of time, it not only becomes obvious and gimmicky, but it also produces an effect opposite to what was intended. Instead of making us identify ourselves completely with the person through whose eyes we are seeing, we tend to become distanced from the character — because we cannot see him. Certainly, there have been interesting attempts at creating films told entirely in the first person; *Lady in the Lake* (Robert Montgomery, 1946) made us see solely through the eyes of its protagonist, and the only time we ever saw him was when he looked in the mirror. (Perhaps the problem with such a filmic viewpoint is that if *we* see through the

★ **1-23** Alfred Hitchcock successfully involves the audience by making them identify with both the protagonist and antagonist. Here, in STRANGERS ON A TRAIN (1951), we see through the eyes of a murderer as he is transfixed by the reflection in a woman's glasses, the image recalling for him (and for us) the murder he has committed.

character's eyes, we *become* the character and should, therefore, see *ourselves* in the mirror.)

Cinema's strength as a narrative medium frequently lies in its flexibility of viewpoint and perspective. That is perhaps why most films seem shot from the stance of an omniscient narrator, one who is able to move back and forth, in and out, over and under, to adapt quickly to any change in action, mood, or thought, to slip in and out of the minds of its various characters, all to the benefit of the total film.

★★★ **Movement**

> . . . this pursuit of the subject by the camera has brought me some of my most thrilling moments, both in my own films and in those of other directors. . . . Needless to say, if the technique is to be perfect it must be imperceptible — as is true of all techniques. The audience must not notice that the camera is positively dancing a ballet, subtly passing from one actor to another. A sequence of this kind, if it is to succeed, must be like an act in itself, and this without forgetting the background, which is particularly difficult to cover because the ground is littered with lighting material.
> Jean Renoir[4]

MOVEMENT IN THE FRAME (SUBJECT MOVEMENT)

The complexity of composing the image of the motion picture frame becomes clear when we realize that some or all of the objects being photographed can be in motion. This motion can be lateral (from right to left or left to right), vertical (up and down in the frame), directly toward or away from the camera, diagonal, or in any direction in between. And we are just speaking here of the movement of the subject, without considering the added complications of camera movement.

Ordinarily a still photograph will have the object of most interest toward the center of the frame, but whatever its position, its relationship to the other objects in the frame will always remain as they were when the photo was snapped. On the other hand, an object in the center of a movie frame is free to move about, to alter its relationship with other objects. For example, imagine an actress moving from her position in a chair in the center of the frame to the left, where she gazes at a portrait hanging over the fireplace. Her relationship with the objects in the room has changed. Moving physically closer to the portrait makes us feel she is emotionally closer to the portrait, or at the very least, more intensely engaged with observing the portrait. We have learned something about the character without words.

When there is more than a single moving object or person in an image, the direction of the movement of each in relation to the others can also convey information nonverbally. Do characters move together? Do they move in and out of the frame? Do they seem to be at odds in their movement? The more movement there is in an image, the more complex deciphering the image becomes.

MOVEMENT OF THE FRAME (CAMERA MOVEMENT)

Most silent filmmakers moved the frame of the image by physically moving the camera *between* shots, but a few, like D. W. Griffith, experimented with moving the camera *during* the shot. In *The Birth of a Nation* (1915), he shot the ride of the Klansmen by mounting the camera on a truck moving just ahead of the oncoming horsemen. Consider the difference between an image produced by such a **trucking shot** and that produced by a fixed camera (Figure 1-24). With the trucking shot (more commonly called a **tracking shot**), the image of the horsemen appears continuous, relentless in the center of the frame, while at its edges surrounding objects slip by in a blur. With a fixed camera the objects at the edge of the frame would be constant while the horsemen would grow larger if they were headed straight for the camera, or they would speed past in a blur of motion if they were moving laterally. Each choice — to move the camera and thus the frame or to fix the camera and the frame — will produce its own effect. Griffith actually used both a static and a moving camera in his film, as well as subject movement in the directions cited, so as to give a composite impression of the Klan:

★ **1-24** D. W. Griffith expressed the movement of the Ku Klux Klan riding
to the rescue in THE BIRTH OF A NATION (1915) with a combination of
static camera shots showing the horsemen riding obliquely towards the
camera (above), pan shots as the horsemen ride past the camera, and trucking
shots with the camera mounted on a truck moving down the road in front
of the oncoming Klan (below). In the trucking shot the subject remains
stationary relative to the frame as the background flows past in a blur at
the edges of the frame.

they were relentless, speeding swiftly, and growing larger as they
moved towards the rescue of the film's sympathetic principals.

The way in which the camera moves — in, out, across, and around —
and the angle at which it photographs its subject — high, low, eye-level,
tilted — is of paramount importance to the effect the film will have on
its audience (Figures 1-25, 1-26). When the camera moves in toward a
stationary subject, the subject is intensified as it grows larger in the

frame. In such a forward **dolly** or tracking shot, seeing through the eyes of the camera, we move toward the subject — sometimes against our will. The movement of the camera towards the subject can produce great anxiety, as we are dragged along to see something we'd perhaps rather not see. The forward movement of the camera in Alain Resnais's *Night and Fog* (1956) impresses upon us the physical sense of numbers as it tracks forward in empty concentration camp dormitories and we sit in constant fear of what will be revealed to us next; the forward movement in *Psycho* (1960) takes us deeper and deeper into the terror of Norman Bates's home and psyche until we find the secret in the fruit cellar; and *Jaws* (1975) moves us unwillingly forward as the shark — and we — gain momentum toward our next victim.

Conversely, when the camera recedes from a subject, the subject becomes smaller, less significant in the frame (Figure 1-27). The camera itself can move backwards in a tracking shot, or the camera may remain stationary and a **zoom lens** may be used. This movement away from the subject is a dominant practice of Stanley Kubrick's *Barry Lyndon* (1975). Starting with a close-up of various characters, with an emphasis on the film's nominal "hero," Kubrick slowly zooms back to reveal the vast surroundings which they inhabit. The movement is a kind of ironic chuckle, debunking the romantic and beautiful images of lovely-looking people who are involved in intense dramas of love and dueling and war, by showing, as it takes us away from them, how small human beings are.

The movement of the camera when it rotates, on the pivot point of the tripod, across the subject matter is called a **pan.** The pan can be graceful and leisurely, allowing us time to appreciate the subject it is moving across, or the pan can flash across the subject so rapidly (a **flash pan**) that the image blurs and creates in us the feeling of speed and dizziness. The movement of the camera on a dolly circling completely around a subject reveals all aspects of the subject; besides being a notable technical achievement (where do all the cables and equipment go?), it creates a sense of omniscience in the viewer.

The speed of camera movement also influences the total image and the way we react to it. The camera can move slowly in or slowly out or it can move rapidly. A gradual dolly shot (the camera moving forward or backward on a wheeled platform) is not nearly so startling to the eye as is a quick zoom. If the filmmaker wishes to make camera movement relatively "invisible," that is, not consciously noticed by the viewer, the movements will generally be smooth, unless they reflect the subjective viewpoint of the characters. Those films which wish to call attention as much to the process of filmmaking as to the film's subject, may choose then, quick and disorienting camera movements.

Dolly right   a.

Dolly right   b.

Dolly back, right   c.

Dolly left   g.

Dolly forward   h.

Dolly forward   i.

Pan left   m.   Stop   n.

★ **1-25** Jean Renoir has been hailed as a master of mise-en-scène filmmaking. He
himself has said, "Another of my preoccupations was, and still is, to avoid fragmentation. . . . A sequence of this kind, if it is to succeed, must be like an act in itself,
and this without forgetting the background, which is particularly difficult to cover
because the ground is littered with lighting material." [5] The establishment of an
actual space and the creation of shifting relationships within that space during the
course of a shot in which the camera continually moves is exemplified in this
single shot from GRAND ILLUSION (1937). In the middle of the Allied prisoners'
Follies, it is announced that a French town lost to the Germans a few days earlier
has been retaken by the French. A young British POW who has been acting the
part of a girl removes his wig and begins to sing the French national anthem. The
camera tracks backwards, panning slightly to the right to show the men on stage
who are also now singing. As the camera continues to move back, Maréchal leans
forward menacingly toward the pit. Continuing backwards, the camera picks up the
object of his attention: two German guards, who begin to move left. The camera
pans left with their exit for a moment. Then it picks up the first row of the men in
the audience who have risen to sing. The camera then tracks along the first row of
singers back to the pit orchestra. Then, panning slightly to the right, it picks up the British soldier for a moment (coming full circle both literally and figuratively). And, finally,
it tracks back and pans left in order to frame the first row of singers, but from such a
position that we see towards the back of the auditorium and take in the entire audience
of Allied prisoners singing patriotically. The camera holds till the shot ends.

Dolly back   d.

Dolly back   e.

Stop, tilt down   f.

Dolly right   j.

Dolly forward   k.

Dolly back, pan left   l.

OVERHEAD VIEW

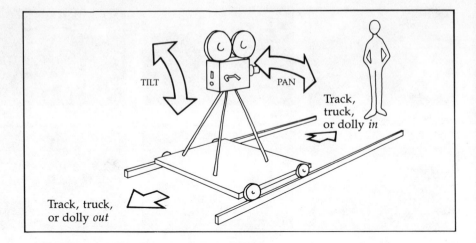

★ **1-26** Camera movement will change the relationship between the subject and the background, discover new elements in a scene, add to the illusion of reality by moving about in a space, and affect the viewer's feelings by the speed of the movement. Slow movements tend toward the lyrical, melancholic, or the inexorable, while swift movements may seem comic, adventurous, exciting, or terrifying.

The speed at which the camera moves in relation to the speed and direction of a moving subject also contributes to the effect and meaning of the image. The camera can move in a direction parallel to the moving subject and at the same rate of speed; this parallel movement (a tracking shot) creates a great sense of motion without calling attention to the camera itself, as the background whizzes past the subject held securely in the frame. If the camera movement does not parallel the subject movement, our attention may be called to the camera itself. And such a shift in our attention may be artful. In *An Occurrence at Owl Creek Bridge* it is necessary that the audience's emotional identification with the protagonist be disengaged gradually, so that by the time the viewer finds out that the escape was all a fantasy and that the protagonist has really been hanged he will not feel tricked by the film. Thus, towards the beginning of the last part of the film, we are shown the escaped man running towards the camera. After a moment, the camera begins to track slowly backwards. The man stumbles and falls, but the camera keeps tracking backwards, a movement we don't notice until it stops about ten yards down the road from the man. Suddenly jolted, we are less conscious of the protagonist than we are of the camera. The device is used to diminish our emotional identification with the hero and to start to prepare us subtly for his death.

★ **1-27** Camera movement away from a subject tends to diminish the subject as its size relative to the frame grows smaller. In this scene from Stanley Kubrick's BARRY LYNDON, the duel between Lyndon and the Captain becomes more and more meaningless as the camera pulls back away from the action. Movement towards the subject, on the other hand, tends to magnify the importance of the subject.

Camera movements in general fortify our sense of actuality. For instance, if, in the frame, we see a seated actor who then stands up, walks to his left through a doorway and down a hall, and the camera follows his movements in a continuous shot, we are more likely to believe that the room and the hall are in a real house and not on a studio back lot.

One of the characters in Bernardo Bertolucci's *Before the Revolution* (1964) says, "A **360 degree pan** is truth in cinema." What he means is if a camera in the center of a room rotates on its tripod in a complete circle, we will see the entire room; all four walls will succeed themselves in our field of view and they will be physically connected, as real walls are. From pictures you may have seen of typical shooting sessions in operation, you will realize how difficult this particular illusion is to create. Somewhere behind every camera there are technicians, lights, reflectors, microphones, props, and cables. When a director uses a 360 degree pan he is going all out to create the illusion of reality, to allow us to feel that we are simply an invisible observer standing in the middle of a real room in the middle of someone's real world.

One does not *have* to go to such lengths, however, to create such a sense of reality. Almost all camera movements convey some degree of this sense. For example, take our actor sitting at his table. He may be reading a newspaper and drinking a cup of coffee. If the camera moves away from the actor and pans to left or right to show us the objects which surround him and fill his life — his furniture, his walls, his ceiling, his floors — we get a sense of a whole real world which the actor inhabits. Think of the opening of Boeldieu's death scene in *Grand Illusion* (Jean Renoir, 1937), the pan and track across all the objects which cause us to remember moments in the relationship between Boeldieu and Rauffenstein.

Items which were outside the frame when we first see an actor become visible as the camera moves, giving us the sensation that they were there all the time and there is a spatial continuity surrounding this figure we are watching. He inhabits, we are forcefully led to believe, a world which is similar to ours in this respect, and this belief reinforces the illusion that what we see on the screen is as real as the world we live in. The frame is stretched and extended by the continuous movement of the camera and it again functions more as a window than as a container.

This particular effect of camera movement is most noticeable in outdoor shots. A man and a woman are picnicking on the grass. We sense that just outside the frame of the image we see on the screen, the world of physical reality exists. The camera tilts upward showing us the trees overhead, then sky and clouds and sun. The camera moves slightly to the right or left of the couple, and more trees, more grass become visible. We no sooner see a little brook flowing past the couple than we "know" those drops of water will eventually reach the sea and that the trout which flashed didn't know it was in a movie. In other words, we are aware of elements of the image which extend beyond the limits of the frame.

But a filmmaker may wish to reverse this illusion of reality, to break the spell, to call the viewer's attention to the fact that he is watching a *film* of real life and not real life itself. Jean-Luc Godard frequently interrupts the continuous flow of images in his pictures with the insertion of **title cards,** as in *My Life to Live* (1962). In *La Chinoise* (1967) he actually allows the camera which is photographing an actor to pan slightly to one side to reveal a mirror in which the camera and cinematographer are visible. The camera taking a picture of itself taking a picture of itself! Whenever such devices are used, the filmmaker clearly wants to jar us out of our customary response to the images on the screen, to make us think about ourselves and our immediate relationship to the events, characters, and themes being presented in the film as well as our passive acceptance of the filmed image as "reality" (Figure 1-28).

A filmmaker can effect another sort of break with the illusion of reality by varying the camera speed. We are all aware of the way some

★ **1-28** Cinematic space can sometimes bear no resemblance to any space in the real world. In George Lucas's THX 1138 (1970), the setting for this examination of government repression in a future "utopia" appears to have no physical boundaries; white-clad people wander about in a white empty space uncircumscribed by walls or a visible horizon line.

silent filmmakers used faster than normal motion to get extra laughs in chase sequences, but high-speed action has also been used to heighten suspense or to portray panic. In the silent version of *The Phantom of the Opera* (Rupert Julian, 1925), the frightened crowd disperses from the opera house in **fast motion.** Though fast motion is seldom used in contemporary films except occasionally for comic effect, **slow motion** continues to fascinate filmmakers. Despite the overused television ad image of young lovers running towards each other in slower than normal motion, this technique retains its validity as a visual metaphor for romance. The lyric and romantic quality of slow motion was amply demonstrated in *Elvira Madigan* (Bo Widerberg, 1967). On the other hand, slow motion is not used for romance by Sam Peckinpah, who, in *The Wild Bunch* (1969), used it to amplify violent, grisly death. The paradoxical balletic grace only made the effect grislier.

In addition to slow or fast motion, filmmakers have on occasion dispensed with motion altogether by freezing a single frame on the screen. There is no finer example of a freeze frame than the last shot of François Truffaut's *The 400 Blows* (1959) in which the young boy running from his pursuers is stopped in mid-stride at the edge of the ocean. He is trapped in time between the sea and his pursuers. Because motion is so essential to the screen image, when the motion suddenly stops, the viewer is forced to reflect upon the lifeless, still image frozen there on the screen which only seconds before was full of life and movement.

Finally, how the camera is mounted will also affect the movement of the camera and thereby the image. In the early days of cinema, the camera did not move at all but was mounted on a tripod to hold it steady. Today, cameras can be mounted on almost anything to achieve special effects and yet still capture the image. A camera mounted on a track or **crane** or dolly (a low platform that rolls on casters) will capture a steady, fluid image. However, if the filmmaker wants to create a sense of immediacy or of chaos, or the feeling that the viewer is directly participating in the action, the camera may be hand-held; this produces a jerky, bouncing, unsteady image which seems to respond physically to the events around it. This, of course, is a form of the subjective shot, like our earlier example in which a camera was mounted on a skier. Similarly, a camera mounted on a car can give the viewer the sense of being the subject; we see what the driver sees as he careens around corners and through traffic, chasing someone in what seems an impossible and nerve-racking pursuit in *The French Connection* (William Friedkin, 1971).

It should be apparent by now that what we *see* on the screen, though it may seem simple and straightforward, is achieved only by a complex pattern of choices made by the filmmaker who controls cinematic space. He must combine the appropriate choices of each element (film stock, lighting, composition, movement, and camera angle) to produce the particular and unique image which will best reveal his meaning or tell his story. One can learn the mechanics of making motion pictures in a day, but it takes understanding and feeling to produce beautiful and profound images which move an audience in the theater and linger in the memory long after the viewing experience is over.

All of these filmic elements discussed thus far are visible to the viewer, taking place during a shot, imparting a certain style, character,

★ **1-29** Most camera movements are visible to the viewer. During a shot, the frame appears to move relative to the subject within the frame. This is clear even when the subject is moving. But another kind of movement is invisible. It takes place *between* shots, rather than within a shot. This movement is detected as an abrupt change in area covered by the frame. In the courtroom scene here, the area visible in each successive shot becomes dramatically smaller, and the subject correspondingly larger, as the camera is moved closer to the witness box between shots. Here camera movement becomes a function of editing when the separate shots are linked in a logical order.

Second shot

Third shot

Fourth shot

CAMERA POSITION FOR FOURTH SHOT

CAMERA POSITION FOR THIRD SHOT

CAMERA POSITION FOR SECOND SHOT

First shot—Long shot

Second shot—Medium shot

Third shot—Close-up

Fourth shot—Extreme Close-up

and tone to the image. But another kind of movement is invisible. It takes place *between* shots rather than within them. We recognize this movement through the abrupt change in area covered by the frame. For example:

First shot: Courtroom from the back of the room showing the judge, bench, witness stand, spectators (long shot)

Second shot: View of bench, judge, witness stand, witness, attorney (medium shot)

Third shot: Witness's face and chest (close-up)

Fourth shot: Witness's hands playing with tear-soaked handkerchief (extreme close-up)

Camera movement took place *between* each of these shots (Figure 1-29), but this movement was not visible on the screen. This process of linking separate shots is called editing. The same group of shots could have been combined into one shot rather than being fragmented into four; a camera on a dolly could have begun the shot from the back of the room and slowly moved towards the witness stand until, in a single continuous shot, all the details of the scene would have slipped past the edges of the frame, leaving only the hands and handkerchief in close-up. Each of these ways of showing the same content would produce a slightly different effect. The single shot will appear smooth, slow, but steady (and perhaps relentless) as the setting surrounding the witness disappears. The four-shot sequence will compress time, providing information to the viewer quickly. Which will have the greater emotional impact? This will depend on how the shot or the editing strategy fits into the whole film, how it relates to the plot, the theme, and the rhythm of the other sequences. There is no rule that states that camera movement during a shot is better than the camera movement between shots, although theories of film art have been advanced emphasizing the primary importance of one or the other of these editing strategies.

NOTES

[1] *Fun in a Chinese Laundry* (New York: Macmillan, 1965), p. 322.

[2] *Screen Education Yearbook 1967*, p. 37.

[3] *Fun in a Chinese Laundry*, p. 310.

[4] *My Life and My Films* (New York: Atheneum, 1974), p. 157.

[5] *My Life and My Films*, p. 157.

Historical Overview: The Development of Editing

BEGINNINGS: MÉLIÈS, PORTER AND GRIFFITH

In the earliest films, running time and screen time were identical. The film consisted of one shot, starting when the camera was turned on (say, as a train entered a station) and ending several seconds or several minutes later when the camera was turned off (say, when the train came to a halt). Time was continuous, unbroken from beginning to end. Similarly, the film was projected as a single shot. In short, the first films of the Lumière brothers, Edison, and others made no use of the cinema's ability to manipulate time and space.

Even though the amazing Georges Méliès did not literally film a scene in segments, cut the segments apart, and glue them together again in some new kind of order and chronology, his films show his recognition of the relationship between running time and screen time. Thus, Méliès contributed a great deal to the beginnings of the art of film editing. He was the originator of "in the camera" editing. He found that after filming the end of one scene, he could crank the film backwards a number of frames and then begin shooting the new scene over the end of the old. This transition, called a **dissolve,** is still used today, although now it is done not in the camera (except in Super 8mm) but in the laboratory. Méliès also discovered the **fade** (in which the image darkens slowly to black before a new scene is introduced) and **double exposure** or **superimposition.** He was able to create trick appearances and disappearances of objects and characters by stopping his camera in the middle of a scene, adding or removing the object or character while keeping the camera and setting exactly as it was, and then starting to film again: this effect — now known as **pixilation** — manipulated time for the audience watching the finished film. They saw what appeared to be continuous time even though

Méliès, by stopping the camera for a moment and then starting it up again, had really cut a piece of time out of the film by not recording it. Despite his expertise with this cinematic trick, Méliès never realized the implications such a technique had for the development of narrative cinema. His charming story films joined scenes in the camera chronologically. Thus, Méliès's greatest contribution to the development of the art of editing was something he himself never fully exploited. In 1899, in his *Cinderella,* he filmed twenty different scenes, but they were all joined together in the camera in chronological order. What he did by using so many scenes, however, was to create the *potential* for their rearrangement.

Edwin S. Porter, an American who had become Edison's head of production, experimented with actually cutting up shot footage and reassembling it in novel and unchronological ways. In *The Life of an American Fireman* (1903), he created the first **simultaneous time** in the cinema by telling the same story twice, once from outside the burning building and once from inside. For example, we get a shot of a fire truck arriving at the burning building and then a shot of a woman and child inside the building. The audience understands, of course, that the two scenes take place not one after the other, but at the same time (or nearly the same time). Porter also used what has come to be called a **stock shot,** footage already available which can be spliced into the film and used for another purpose than the one for which it was filmed, joining together two pieces of film from separate sources to make what appears on the screen to be a coherent dramatic action taking place in the same space and time. Running time and screen time would no longer have to be the same, although, of course, a filmmaker might choose to make them the same.

Towards the end of 1903, Porter's *The Great Train Robbery* was released to popular acclaim. Again, Porter used simple **cuts,** simply splicing one piece of footage to the next. Each scene was photographed from a single camera position and was complete in itself. We have seen that this crosscutting or parallel editing had been done in *The Life of an American Fireman,* but what makes it critical to the development of editing is that in *The Great Train Robbery* Porter manipulated three separate units of the action (the interior of a telegraph office, a dance hall, and a changing exterior) to create not only simultaneous time but also suspense; each edited scene was not resolved immediately, but all moved to a climax of resolution in which a gun battle brought outlaws and posse together. *The Great Train Robbery* also ends with one of the first close-ups ever seen on the screen, an image of a gun aimed and discharged directly at the camera. But this close-up is used simply as a sort of cinematic punctuation mark, an exclamation point to finish the film. It is not an integral part of any scene and, in fact, the catalogue describing the film indicated that the shot could be used at the beginning or end of the film — or both!

Although Porter exploited editing, and in these films manipulated time so that running time and screen time were not identical, he seemed not to fully understand what he had done. His later films do not take advantage of some of his own discoveries. It took D. W. Griffith — the first conscious artist in the cinema — to sense the power and impact of both parallel editing and close-ups and to advance and refine their use.

Like many directors at the beginning of the twentieth century, Griffith did much of his own editing. During his stay at the American Biograph Company (1908–1913), turning out two or more pictures a week, he had ample opportunity to develop new ways of constructing scenes through the judicious use of long, medium, and close shots. Besides realizing that the camera was not cemented to a spot equivalent to a front-row center seat in a theater, at the editing table Griffith joined these various shots to create a dramatic and visually interesting scene. This kind of editing in the narrative film is relatively unobtrusive and has often been called **invisible editing** because the viewer, primarily involved with the narrative, is not aware of the process of editing. Griffith's **intercutting** (inserting, for example, medium and close shots to heighten emotion or to show details which would be lost in a long shot) is the basis of most editing even today.

Griffith also discovered that the length of shots on the screen and the rapidity with which one shot replaces another created a sense of variety or heightened suspense. In *The Lonely Villa* (1909), for example, he crosscuts between three separate simultaneous actions (the bandits battering at the door outside the villa, the mother inside guarding her children, and the father speeding to the rescue from a distant point), but he added to what Porter had done previously by shortening the length of each shot as the three dramatic units moved to convergence in a climax. By shortening the length of each shot as he cut back and forth among the three activities until the rescue occurred, Griffith accelerated the rhythm of the film, increasing the dramatic momentum. Griffith thus introduced what has become the convention of the last-minute rescue. He used this same kind of editing at the climax of *The Birth of a Nation* (1915), Griffith's and the cinema's first acknowledged masterpiece. (The racial prejudice in *The Birth of a Nation* made it a highly controversial film, but our concern here is with Griffith's mastery of narrative editing.) But in *The Birth of a Nation* he went further, controlling the various elements of *two* last-minute rescues. In one, the Ku Klux Klan rides to the rescue of a family who are being attacked by the black militia; in the other the Klan arrives in the nick of time to save the horrified heroine from a fate "worse than death" — a forced and miscegenated marriage. By 1916, when Griffith filmed *Intolerance,* he was no longer content to crosscut or parallel-edit two last-minute rescues together (with their respective single dramatic units combined and crosscut); in *Intolerance* he juggles four periods of history (ancient Babylon, Christ's Judea, Renaissance France, and early twentieth-century America), each using another as a **cutaway,** and each period having within it its own last-minute rescues created by their internal parallel editing. Griffith also began in *Intolerance* to use the close-up *within* scenes to great dramatic effect, for instance, a close-up of a woman's hands distressedly clutching a handkerchief was cut into a courtroom scene to indicate the character's tension and anxiety. A shot thus inserted into a scene is called, not surprisingly, an **insert shot.**

Griffith also practiced the cutaway shot in an attempt to translate verbal metaphors into visual terms. For example, in *Way Down East* (1920), he cuts away from the heroine to a shot of two white doves billing and cooing. The doves obviously represent her unphotographable inner thoughts: she is in love. The Russians extended the range possible with this technique. Impressed with *Intolerance,* the Russians studied Griffith, theorized about the implications of his editing, and (lacking raw film stock) actually edited and reedited old pieces of film footage so as to explore the possible combinations of shots and their potential meaning.

THE RUSSIANS AND MONTAGE

Perhaps the first theorist of editing was Lev Kuleshov, a young filmmaker who in 1920 established the Kuleshov Workshop. He assumed that editing was the primary way in which the cinema communicated. Kuleshov's experiments are now famous; he intercut an actor's unchanging, expressionless face with a bowl of soup, a woman in a coffin, and a child with a toy — and audiences applauded the subtle changes in the actor's expression as he supposedly reacted to all three. Kuleshov thus demonstrated that the meaning of a shot was not inherent in that shot but stemmed from its juxtaposition with other shots. Editing freed the cinema from a dependence on real time and space and allowed it to create a new geography, new time, and impossible people. It could, for example, create a believable city from streets existing in several cities.

Three other Russian filmmakers and theorists went on to develop and use in their own films the editing principles Kuleshov had demonstrated. These three, Dziga Vertov, Sergei Eisenstein, and V. I. Pudovkin, were also three of the greatest filmmakers of the silent cinema — and, perhaps, of all time. While Kuleshov was conducting his workshops, Vertov was making **compilation films** of available footage, attempting various combinations of shots for various effects. He scorned the melodramatic, professionally acted story film, finding everyday life more exciting and "truthful" than contrived and acted drama, but despite this documentary approach he considered editing (the manipulation of time and space) and various other uniquely cinematic devices (like fast, slow, and **reverse motion**) crucial to film's ability to reveal life to the viewer. Vertov's imaginative use of the medium culminates in his *The Man with a Movie Camera* (1928), in which he uses photographed bits and pieces of everyday life — stores opening for business, people playing sports, machinery revolving, trolley cars moving — like phrases in a musical composition, editing them together according to mass, motion, and action to create a composite portrait of Russian society in the late twenties. He was finally less of an influence on traditional cinema than he was on avant-garde or experimental filmmaking. Pudovkin and Eisenstein were the two Russians who exerted the greatest and widest influence on the development of editing. They both felt that editing was the cornerstone of film, the basis for all cinematic meaning, although they disagreed as to how that meaning was best created.

Pudovkin, who after seeing Griffith's *Intolerance* abandoned his career as a chemist and entered Kuleshov's workshop, believed shots were like building blocks and that meaning resided in an accumulation of details that naturally arose out of the story. For example, in *Mother* (1925), Pudovkin juxtaposes shots of a crowd going to liberate political prisoners with a shot of the spring thaw's effect on a river of solid ice, the blocks of ice breaking off and churning in the water (Figure 1). Although the second image has a metaphorical value, referring to the crowd freeing the prisoners, it is also literally relevant since there is a river in the story and the season actually is spring.

Eisenstein, on the other hand, did not believe that images of the story were the only building blocks or that their juxtaposition necessarily had a slow, cumulative effect. He also saw no reason why metaphoric images also had to be literally relevant. Thus in his first film, *Strike* (1924), he intercut the final massacre of workers and children with shots of cattle being slaughtered in a slaughterhouse. The metaphor is clear, but the slaughterhouse has not figured in the film before. Eisenstein, disagreeing with Pudovkin's theories of editing, theorized that meaning was created not through an accumulation of separate images, but from the clash or attraction between images and the elements contained in them (composition, movement, idea). Thus in *October* (1928) — also called *Ten Days That Shook the World* — Eisenstein intercuts shots of the provisional leader Kerensky with shots of a mechanical "golden" *objet d'art* peacock. The viewer therefore "sees" Kerensky as foolish, trivial, and as vain as a peacock. However, Eisenstein also expanded the range of meanings possible through juxtaposition of images — beyond the simple verbally inspired metaphor. In *Potemkin* (1925) he constructed, entirely through editing, or as he called it, **montage,** an epic of the Russian revolutionary spirit. Screen time is expanded and contracted as actions are broken down and reassembled into separate rhythmic units; screen space in image after image becomes a dynamic field of motion which can then be juxta-

★ 1 These two shots from MOTHER (1925) illustrate how Pudovkin used montage. He linked the scene of the uprising of the workers to the breaking up of ice after a long, cold winter. What differentiates Pudovkin's "organic" montage from Eisenstein's montage of conflict, is that Pudovkin found his images within the context of his narrative. The workers' uprising is taking place in the spring, and the bridge upon which the ice is breaking is the same bridge the workers must cross to free the political prisoners. Thus the two images are connected in narrative time and space.

posed with a contrasting or parallel motion in the following image. A sailor who has just witnessed the serving of rotten meat to the men breaks a plate upon which is inscribed "Give us this day our daily bread." The action is heightened and emphasized by expanding the time of the incident: the action is photographed several times and edited together as a series of chronologically overlapping images. In the famed sequence on the Odessa steps, the meaning of the event — a massacre, by Cossack troops, of civilians friendly to the mutinous crew of the battleship — is powerfully communicated by the interaction of motion in the various shots as well as by the expansion of time (Figure 2). The soldiers' boots march relentlessly down the steps, moving from the upper left-hand corner of the frame to the lower right. Intercut between this repeated image are shots of objects and civilians moving up the steps in the opposite direction to the Cossacks, of groups of civilians huddled together, and of the wild dispersement of multitudes in all directions. Each is visually linked to the others — round shapes are followed by round shapes, movements across the frame are followed by similar or opposed movements — yet at the same time the content is amplified and charged with an intensity of feeling that is the product of the "collision of images" on the screen: the combination of diverse images in this way has created intellectual and emotional meaning not inherent in any one of the images alone. What Eisenstein assumed in his theories of montage editing was really an aesthetic extension of the political idea of dialectic: thesis plus antithesis equals synthesis. The basic premise upon which Eisenstein's early theories of editing was based is $A + B = C$, or image A juxtaposed with image B equals in the mind of the viewer image C, a totally new and synthetic image which is not really there on the screen.

Throughout the rest of the 1920s the silent film developed and refined the two kinds of editing upon which Soviet cinema was based: the dynamic and visually exciting use of juxtaposition through collision of images (the Eisensteinian montage), and the less jolting, more organic, accumulation of images which supplied emotional depth through detail as well as metaphor (Pudovkin's "building-block" editing). However, the smooth transitions from long shot to medium shot to close-up (Griffith's invisible style) become the staple of the popular and commercial cinema around the world and was perfected, in different ways, by both American and German filmmakers.

SOUND AND EDITING

The arrival of sound in 1927, however, soon created new problems for filmmakers and editors. Sound and pictures now had to be matched. In the first successful sound process, a phonograph disc recorded the sound while the camera photographed the action. Because little or no editing of the **sound track** was possible, the film editor was confined simply to editing the movie so that it would match the recording. Little innovation in the use of sound was possible. Another system was developed in which sound was recorded on movie film as a series of photographed light impulses which, during projection, could be turned back into sound. By 1930 sound-on-film had all but replaced the disc system. A new technique with **optical sound** film had given back flexibility to the film editor: the optical sound track and the photographed action of the film were recorded on separate rolls of film, and each could be edited separately and then matched together in the final print. The development of the sound Moviola editing machine in 1931 made this process relatively simple, and soon filmmakers were no longer emphasizing "talking heads" but were exploring the possibilities of sound editing, of

★ **2** In the Odessa Steps sequence from POTEMKIN (1925), Eisenstein edits his material largely on the basis of changes in directional flow of the subjects. Above left, the movement of the soldiers is towards the lower right corner of the frame. Above right, the soldiers at the top are moving down in opposition to the woman at bottom center who is moving up. On the facing page, in the close-up of the woman carrying her child, the camera is tracking backward up the steps. At far right, the woman is moving diagonally toward the lower left corner of the frame (top), though in fact she is walking *up* the steps; and the camera tracks along with the baby carriage moving *down* the stairs (bottom) but *up* toward the upper left corner of the frame. Throughout the sequence Eisenstein alternates between directional flows to create the sense of confusion and terror in the crowd and the steady, sure purpose of the soldiers.

contrasting or paralleling visual imagery with music and dialogue and sound effects.

1930 also saw the introduction of the **optical printer,** a machine which could make fancy optical editing such as the **wipe** and dissolve with incredible ease compared to similar "in camera" editing which had been practiced in the early days of film. From 1931 to 1935, wipes (when one scene appears to push the next scene off the screen as if an eraser were being moved across a blackboard) were all the rage. Diamonds, triangles, and flip-flops can be seen in many films of the period. In 1932, **edge numbering** (also called "rubber" numbering) was introduced as a method of making the editing of sound and picture and picture and picture a simpler, more efficient procedure. Now an editor could match up numbers, and the picture and sound would be in perfect synchronization. Because of the increased mechanical ease of editing, many of the films of the mid-thirties contain far more shots than those of the first years of the sound era.

Originally, all editing was done by hand. Each piece of film footage was physically cut and spliced by someone hired for that specific and tedious job. A special print of all footage that might possibly be needed in the final assembly of the film was made, called a **work print.** If it was cut and spliced incorrectly — that is, not to the director's or producer's satisfaction — new pieces of work print had to be made. Today much of the work in editing is done mechanically. New technology makes the job of actually cutting and joining together film footage easier and faster. In 1962, the guillotine splicer was introduced and revolutionized cutting. The splicing tape no longer needed sprocket holes as did the film, for the new machine made its own; splicing thus became more economical and much faster, liberating the film editor to change and experiment more. The latest development in editing technology is a device which transfers the photographed footage to video discs stored in a large computer. These are viewed at will on a small television screen and the editor can electronically mark the footage where he wants to cut; then the edited material can be played back to see how it works. If the editor and the director wish to make further changes, the image is simply electronically erased and then electronically reedited. This whole process can be done many times without actually cutting the work print, saving both the time and money required by the older method.

Because a variety of sophisticated technology is available today, filmmakers can arrange all the visual and sound footage to their satisfaction. They can superimpose, dissolve, fade in, fade out, **straight-cut,** and rearrange images and sounds in millions of possible combinations. They can go forward or backward in time, slow up an action, speed up an action, or remove unnecessary material in order to best convey the meaning and emotion which is the heart of every motion picture.

2

★ *TIME IN THE CINEMA*

Many art forms take place in time: dance is movement in time, music is sound in time, drama and prose fiction are actions in time. The moving image in film is an image in time, and — unlike the experience of looking at painting and sculpture — the experience of viewing a film requires the viewer to be in some way aware of the flow of time. This "flow of time," however, is not a simple thing, for there are several different kinds of time in the cinema.

Each film has a **running time,** an exact number of minutes during which it will occupy the space on the screen. Thus, running time is the time it takes for all the frames in the film to move past the lens of the projector at twenty-four frames per second (or sixteen to twenty-two frames if the film is silent). This time can range anywhere from a few seconds for an experimental short to many hours for some less than commercial narrative and documentary films. The original uncut version of Bernardo Bertolucci's *1900* (1977) has still not been released in the United States because its length — about six hours — created exhibition problems. Even the four-and-a-half hour version shown here has had difficulty finding a large audience. Louis Malle's *Phantom India* (1968) runs six and a half hours, but it comes in the more acceptable form of a seven-part documentary.

Running time describes the length of the film, but **screen time** describes the time represented by the actions or events *within* the film. The running time of *2001: A Space Odyssey* (1968) is less than two and a half hours, but the screen time spans millions of years of human evolution. On the other hand, although the running time of *An Occur-*

★ **2-1** Japanese filmmaker Kenzo Mizoguchi uses what appears to be a continuous tracking shot to collapse time in UGETSU (1954). Actually, there are invisible cuts as the camera moves to the left, leaving the potter and his ghostly bride in a room, and then picks them up an instant later in a hot spring bathing. The camera pauses. Several lines of dialogue take place. Then the camera moves to the left slowly through some trees and then moves out onto a tilled field, where it again picks up the couple, this time having a picnic. The meaning of this tracking shot is quite clear. This must be a dream or a fantasy because it would be impossible in real life for the two people to run around behind the camera and get to the hot spring before the camera, if it were a single continuous pan, and of course the picnic takes place in the daytime, whereas the pan began at night.

rence at Owl Creek Bridge (Robert Enrico, 1961) is around a half-hour, most of the screen time of the film represents only a split second.

Finally, much more subjective and less controllable than either the running time or the screen time of a specific film, there is *psychological time*. Psychological time describes the viewer's sense of the pace and rhythm of the film, in other words, how long the film *feels*. A film running only five minutes may feel much longer, or a long film might seem as if it were really quite short. We may feel that a film is swift because we are interested, or slow because we are bored, but we may also be responding to the way the film is constructed.

Although a film's running time is precise and specific (unless, of course, the film has been damaged or there are various versions of a particular movie in release — for example, movies edited for television), both screen time and psychological time can be manipulated in an almost endless variety of ways (Figure 2-1). When separate shots are joined together to represent an action, the time of that action can be compressed or expanded. For example, a shot showing a character entering an airport in New York can be joined to one showing him leaving an airport in California, thus compressing his trip. Or several shots of the details of a character involved in a car accident may be joined together to expand the action. Through this joining together of separate pieces of film, the process called editing, we can be made aware of simultaneous actions and sequential actions; we can enter a character's mind, we can see the past, we can be dislocated from any sense of "real" time and transported to a place where time seems not to exist or where it seems to operate in ways that defy logic. And the kinds of transitions the filmmaker uses to move us from one shot to another are also the result of choice; the editing may move us abruptly from one time to another or it may bridge time gracefully and slowly. All these manipulations of time, of both screen and psychological time, are the result of editing.

Editing, the joining together of separate pieces of film footage by various techniques to form an entire and cohesive film, establishes the order and rhythm of a movie. This chapter, examining the role of editing, will first deal with the simplest form of putting the shots together to form a coherent whole and will then go on to examine the more complex techniques which are used to create different sorts of time. Finally, it will examine the three major schools of editing.

★★★ **Manipulation of Time**

> Kino-Eye is the overcoming of time, a visual bond between chronologically separated phenomena. Kino-Eye is concentration and decomposition of time. Kino-Eye is the opportunity to see the processes of life in any chronological order and at any speed.
> Dziga Vertov[1]

Although we can isolate three time schemes which operate and intersect during the course of viewing a film — running time, screen time, and psychological time — there is yet another kind of time involved in the motion picture process, a time which almost never plays a specific role in the finished film. This is **shooting time.** Shooting time represents not only the time when the camera is actually recording the actions in front of it (including any retakes), but also the total number of days required to collect all the footage deemed necessary so that the director and editor of a particular film may have some choice of shots when it finally comes to assembling the finished print. Shooting time, therefore, also includes setup time for camera and lighting equipment, for building the sets, for preparing the performers, for travel to locations — in other words, for all those processes in front of or behind the camera which go on from the beginning to the end of shooting.

As might be imagined, shooting time is expensive time, and to keep it to a minimum, filmmakers will arrange to shoot all the scenes taking place in one location or all the scenes using the same performers at the same time. Thus, all interior scenes which take place in a certain room will be shot on the same day whenever possible, even though these scenes will appear at different points in the completed film. Thus, the simplest and most basic manipulation of time demanded of the editing process is to rearrange the shot footage, the selected pieces of shooting time, into correct screen time. The breadth of choice the filmmaker has in selecting various shots from all the footage available is called the **shooting ratio;** a 1 to 1 ratio indicates that the filmmaker used all the film that he shot; a 1 to 10 shooting ratio indicates that the filmmaker used one foot of film in the finished movie to every ten feet of film that was shot. Once this footage has been selected, the various pieces of film shot at different times and in different locations must be physically joined together in the appropriate order so that shots become coherent **sequences** and **scenes.**

The footage can be joined so that the transition from one shot to another on the screen is gradual, as in the dissolve (when one image appears to dissolve into another), or gradual but flamboyant as in the wipe (when the edge of the new image appears, like a windshield wiper, to push the old image offscreen). The images can be joined so slowly that there appears to be a large gap of time between the end of one and the beginning of another, that gap represented by the blackness on the screen between shots as the first image fades to black and the second eventually fades into view. Created in the laboratory, these kinds of editing transitions are called **optical effects.** Because these devices have been long used in certain contexts, they have conventional meanings. The dissolve, the wipe, and the fade out/fade in normally indicate fairly long gaps in screen time.

The film editor who wanted to show a small gap in time between two shots, say a few minutes or less, would most normally join the film together with a **direct cut** between two shots of the same character, for instance, which differed in some way from each other (a long shot and a medium shot taken from another angle). A direct cut is a simple splice between two pieces of film and is conventionally neither particularly disturbing to the viewer nor particularly visible since it usually occurs on a movement and has become so much an integral part of what might loosely be called "cinematic grammar." The direct cut is performed at the editing table rather than in the laboratory; so are its variations, the **impact cut** and **disorientation cut.** But where the direct cut is almost invisible, the impact cut is startling and the disorientation cut is downright unsettling. Let us imagine, for example, a direct cut between a long shot of a city skyline and a medium shot of the Statue of Liberty: without even really thinking about the fact that the two shots have been joined together, we place ourselves and the story in New York City. Now, imagine an impact cut between a long shot of a city skyline and a close-up shot of a bronze torch from which the camera pulls back to a medium distance to reveal the Statue of Liberty; at first, our response to the second image is likely to be momentarily confused and we are aware of having been somewhat dislocated — but when the camera pulls back we readily and easily place ourselves and the story in New York City. Finally, let's imagine a disorientation cut: we see a long shot of a New York City skyline followed by a medium close-up of what appears to be the Statue of Liberty against a blue sky but is then revealed (through camera movement) to be a small statuette placed on a bureau against a painted blue wall. Now we are startled and disoriented to the point where we cannot be sure where we are precisely: are we in New York City? somewhere else? what relationship did the skyline have to this statuette in this room? There is yet one other kind of splicing together two separate pieces of film within a scene, which is very noticeable. This is called a **jump cut.** Rather loosely used today, the term was coined to describe the abrupt editing used by the French filmmaker Jean-Luc Godard in his film *Breathless* (1959). For example, in *Breathless*, during a conversation between the protagonist and a cab driver, the background outside of the cab changes, several times, indicating that a number of shots have been edited together, but the flow of the conversation implies that the scene should be continuous. The editing does not seem to serve any purpose and it calls attention to itself; the viewer wonders whether the print on the screen is in bad condition or whether the filmmaker is playing with the viewer's tendency to believe that the film image is *reality* when it is, always, a film image subject to manipulation.

Whether optically, mechanically, or electronically effected, all of these ways of linking separate pieces of film are editing devices. And whether the transitions from shot to shot are abrupt or gradual, they all manipulate time in some fashion. Indeed, except for the rare instance of a one-shot film, or a film shot entirely on a single roll of film, in which there has been no "in-camera" editing, every film uses at least one of these devices; separate shots are linked together to make a film.

Time is always being manipulated through the editing process. If nothing else, the time it takes to move the camera *between* individual shots is missing from the finished film — that is, a portion of the shooting time never gets on film. But even so, the editor, by reassembling the footage of the action at the editing table, can give the impression of an uninterrupted flow of events in screen time — if that is the desired effect. By carefully matching up separate pieces of film (for example, matching a shot taken from the street of a cowboy pushing open the saloon door with a shot taken from inside of the cowboy coming through the door), the editor can produce the illusion that screen time and running time and shooting time are all the same length. The temporal effect produced will be similar to that of an action filmed in one **take** and unbroken by editing. This kind of matching up of shots by the editor is often done in musical films for dance numbers. Part of the pleasure of watching expert dancers like Fred Astaire or Gene Kelly or Cyd Charisse on the screen is derived from their endurance. True, many of the dance numbers are photographed in one take to preserve temporal and spatial unity, but many other dances are best captured from a number of angles, that is, in separate shots. Then editing is used to join these shots, but it is made as invisible as possible so that the viewer may still marvel at the dance's duration and the dancer's lengthy defiance of gravity and exhaustion. Thus, one of the major — though unsung — manipulations of time in the cinema is the reconstitution of ordinary consecutive time (usually in a single scene) so as to give the appearance that screen time, running time, and shooting time are exactly alike.

COMPRESSION OF TIME

By far the most frequent manipulation of time in the movies is its compression. Indeed, Hollywood commonly uses the word montage to connote a sequence which compresses large hunks of time (months, years) into seconds by rapidly linking separate shots with various transitional devices. There are very few narrative films whose screen time is supposed to be the same as their running time — that is, in which the events on the screen are supposed to be ninety or so consecutive minutes in the life of the characters. Two notable exceptions, however, are

★ **2-2** Fred Zinneman's HIGH NOON (1952) is one of the rare fiction films in which screen time (the time of the story) and running time (the film's durational length) are nearly identical. Screen time is about an hour and a half and the film is only a little shorter. Most films compress weeks, months and years into a two-hour running time.

High Noon (Fred Zinnemann, 1952) and *Cleo from 5 to 7* (Agnès Varda, 1961), both of which come remarkably close to making screen time and running time equivalent. As the title of *Cleo* indicates, we are invited to observe the activities of the heroine from five o'clock in the afternoon to seven o'clock in the evening, a two-hour period during which she waits to find out the results of a biopsy, meets a soldier, conducts business and career affairs, and, in general, provides the viewer with an opportunity to see a cross-section of her life. Actually, although the film is supposed to cover two hours and although it even attempts to authenticate its "real" time by using notations at the bottom of the screen (Cleo: 5:03–5:07), the movie's running time is only eighty-six minutes. *High Noon* gets a bit closer to the mark. The story begins approximately at 10:30 A.M. screen time and lasts until shortly after noon, covering slightly over ninety minutes; the actual running time of the movie is eighty-five minutes (Figure 2-2).

Generally, screen time in most narrative films is far longer than running time, compressing days, weeks, or even years into an hour or two. And the same is true of most documentary and nonfiction films — for although there is a concerted attempt in certain types of nonfiction film such as **cinema verité** or "uncontrolled" documentary to preserve "real" time and space by not editing within sequences, those sequences themselves are finally edited to other sequences and the time *between* the sequences is not often specified or identifiable. Usually, it is only the **abstract film** (designs, patterns of light) which has no relation to the "reality" of the external world and common notions of time and space; thus, the abstract film is often easily able to erase distinctions between screen time and running time. What takes place on the screen (which is the only place and space where it is able to take place) occurs exactly in the time it appears to take place.

Compression of time in the movies most obviously takes place *between* scenes, between cuts or dissolves or various transitional editing devices. Thus, in *Citizen Kane* (Orson Welles, 1941), Charles Foster Kane ages from childhood to maturity *between* two shots: the first shows him as a child opening a Christmas gift from his guardian, Mr. Thatcher, whose voice says, "Merry Christmas, Charles," and whom he answers with a dispirited "Merry Christmas . . . ." There is a quick direct cut — linked by Thatcher's voice continuing — to an image of Thatcher caught in mid-sentence dictating, ". . . and a Happy New Year" in a letter to Kane, who he indicates has now reached adulthood. All those years disappear between two shots linked by a direct cut. The entire life of a character from birth to death, the history of a nation, of a world, all can be encompassed in a single two-hour film by the filmmaker's omission of material between one incident and another. We simply do not see whatever the filmmaker decides is unimportant to the movie.

The compression of time is not limited to the time between sequences or scenes. By means of editing it can occur *within* scenes as well. In "real" life, it takes, say, eight seconds for a man to climb a given flight of stairs. But in "reel" life that time can be compressed to increase the pace of the film or to remove irrelevant dramatic material. If climbing the stairs is not dramatically essential to the film's plot, the filmmaker may show us the character starting up the stairs in one shot and then cut directly to him entering a room in which important dramatic action will take place. We automatically recognize — because of the logic of the situation and our past movie experience — that the room is somewhere at the top of the stairs. A character's entire plane trip to Africa can be compressed into seconds. We see her board, we get a shot of the plane in midair, we see it land at the Nairobi airport. We may not even see that much; the character in one shot can indicate through dialogue that she is going to Africa shortly, and in the next shot she will be there.

Another sort of compression of time within a dramatic sequence can occur when the editor repeatedly cuts away from one piece of action to another piece of action. Thus, in a chase sequence in which shots are alternated between a fleeing bandit and a pursuing posse, each time we return to the bandit from the cutaway shots of the posse, we see an indication that time has passed — in one shot we see the bandit galloping down a road, in the next he is crossing a river, in the next his horse has dropped a shoe. Likewise, during each cutaway to the bandit, the posse has been moving in time: the first shot shows the posse stopped at a crossroads, attempting to read the trail, the second shot shows them galloping across a previously unseen terrain, and the last shows them waiting in a grove of trees — until the bandit comes riding into the shot and their custody. In each shot — whether of the bandit or the posse — we see that time has elapsed and space has been covered since the previous shot.

Most filmgoers today are visually "literate." They have been trained (partly by television commercials, which have offered viewers a cram course in rapid editing) to understand visual images much more quickly and with fewer explanations than movie audiences of previous decades. Films from the thirties through the fifties used, in their montage sequences, very obvious visual and aural clues to provide the viewer with information about the compression of time. The montage sequence depended heavily upon the transitional device of the dissolve to show the viewer that a relatively long period of time was passing. In *The Grapes of Wrath* (John Ford, 1940), for example, the Joad family's odyssey to California is conveyed by a montage which uses dissolves of various highways but gives the viewer a visual/verbal clue by showing road signs which indicate a movement west; since movement in space indicates a movement in time as well, the viewer has a sense of the long trip even though the montage sequence compresses the trip's actual time. *Citizen Kane* uses many such time montages. Charles and Emily Kane's years of marriage are compressed into a montage which, through a series of rapid pan dissolves, shows the changing relationship between Charles and Emily at the breakfast table; visual cues are abundant: the characters' clothes change, the hairstyles change, and the newspaper headlines change (Figure 2-3). In the same film, Susan Alexander Kane's unsuccessful operatic career is compressed into a montage of dissolves which link newspaper reviews, backstage and onstage shots, shots of audience reaction, and close-ups of Susan and a dimming stage light. Audiences of the period were also used to what has since become a a.

b.

c.

d.

e.

f.

★ **2-3** One of the most brilliant examples of time compression occurs in the breakfast sequence in CITIZEN KANE (Orson Welles, 1941). In two minutes of running time, several years and the disintegration of Kane's first marriage are revealed in quick cuts and short swish pans. The last shot of the sequence finds Kane's wife sitting far away from him and reading the opposition newspaper.

g.

h.

i.

j.

k.

l.

cliché — the pages of a calendar (either monthly or yearly) blowing off the screen in some sort of temporally induced wind, or the autumn leaves falling off a tree, then dissolving into its spring bloom and summer ripeness. Such clues to the passage of time, though obvious, can be charming; in *Meet Me in St. Louis* (Vincente Minnelli, 1944), the period atmosphere of the movie is enhanced by the seasonal paintings which divide the film into four parts and also compress its time.

A more subtle form of time compression can occur when **reaction shots** (the camera cuts from the speaker to a person reacting to the speaker) or close-ups of a character speaking are used to mask the passage of time while they also serve as transitions. Two people light up cigarettes and pour themselves drinks. The editor cuts to one person speaking, then to the other. Back and forth the shots alternate, with an occasional shot of both people together (a **two-shot**). The actual running time of the sequence is perhaps thirty seconds, but when a medium shot occurs we see that the cigarettes have been smoked and the glasses are empty. We have a sense that the conversation was long enough to account for this visually demonstrated passage of time, whereas in fact it wasn't. This method of compression also works effectively when, for instance, two characters have a conversation in the front seat of a car as Humphrey Bogart and Lauren Bacall do in *The Big Sleep* (Howard Hawks, 1946): all it takes is a series of shots linked by direct cuts which alternate between two or three people in a conversation and — providing there are visual clues to suggest it — the audience will sense that a longer time has passed than actually has. If such a conversation was filmed simply as a single two-shot or **three-shot** with all the participants in one frame, the effect of time passing would not work at all; screen time and running time would seem equivalent.

EXPANSION OF TIME

Screen time can be expanded as well as compressed. An action that takes, say, three minutes of running time may take only one minute of "real" time. This expansion of time can be accomplished either by intercutting a series of shots (either small portions of the whole action, which are inserted into the main action, or shots of some other simultaneous but related action) or by filming the action from different angles which can then be edited together with cuts or dissolves so as to extend the length of what might have otherwise seemed a brief action.

The example of the man climbing the stairs can again illustrate the expansion of an action through the use of insert shots which are intercut as details of the main action. Let us say that the act of climbing the stairs is important to the film (it is a horror film and there have been strange noises coming from the attic) so that the director wants to create suspense by expanding the actual time it takes to climb the stairs in "real" time. All the editor need do to expand time in such an action is to intercut details of the character's journey up the stairs — shots of a hand clutching the banister, wind blowing through bare trees in an exterior shot, a foot on a creaking step, a view of the blackness at the top of the stairs, a flickering candle held in the man's other hand, a cloud passing over the moon. In this way, intercutting can protract and expand the actual time an action may take to perform. A classic example of this kind of expansion, in which separate shots of details are cut together, is the shower murder sequence in *Psycho* (Alfred Hitchcock, 1960). The real time of the murder might be about ten seconds; the actual running time is about forty-five seconds, but in psychological time it seems a great deal longer. Hitchcock used seventy-eight separate shots to convey the murder, revealing its separate parts rather than showing it in one continuous shot.

The cutaway to a completely different action is in some ways similar to the insert shots of details within an action. Cutaway shots serve to compress time, but they can also extend time. Imagine in a film that burglars are attempting to open a safe and we watch them drill and drill. Then there is a cutaway to a policeman patrolling outside the building followed by a direct cut back to the burglars still drilling. Such crosscutting serves to extend time, creating suspense as the viewer anticipates the resolution of the action.

The second method of expanding time in a scene is to film the action from multiple angles and then to cut together (or dissolve) these different views of the same action; we see the action repeated in the finished film, but the repetition is emphatic and dramatic, giving us a sort of God's-eye view of the action — as well as extending either running time or psychological time. Sometimes this method of extending time can be combined with slow motion, as in the climactic shoot-out in *The Wild Bunch* (1969). Or it can be used to create anxiety and suspense when it uses complementary camera composition and involves a perilous activity. In *An Occurrence at Owl Creek Bridge* (Robert Enrico, 1961), for example, the main character has supposedly escaped from hanging because of a faulty rope and has plummeted downward from the bridge into deep water below. We are shown, from a variety of camera angles which are cut together, his underwater struggle to free his bound hands and to take off his heavy boots and to rise to the surface. The man's progress seems incredibly slow in terms of psychological time, so much so that it feels as if it would be impossible for someone to remain underwater so long and still live; when the man surfaces and lets out a gasp for air, the audience tends to gasp also. What is fascinating is that the running time of this edited sequence is only ninety-seven seconds. What makes psychological time seem so much longer is not only the number of cuts in the sequence, but also the composition of the individual shots. In most of the shots, the protagonist is shown in the lower third of the frame or moving laterally rather than vertically. Every time it seems as if the man is about to reach the top of the frame (and the water's surface), there is a direct cut to another shot which shows him again submerged in the lower portions of the frame. The editing of the various angles of his attempts to surface conveys to the viewer physically and visually a monumental struggle which then seems to last much longer than it actually does. Indeed, the entire film in which this sequence occurs demonstrates the expansion of time dramatically. About a half-hour in running time, the bulk of *An Occurrence at Owl Creek Bridge*'s screen time consists of the split second in which a character is hanged and passes from life to death.

SIMULTANEOUS TIME

Editing can be used not only to expand or compress time, but also to convey to the viewer a sense of simultaneity. The viewer understands that separate actions linked together are occurring not one after the other but simultaneously. How do we know that events or shots are taking place at the same time as each other? The conventional clue is that there is no *progression* of shots. Instead, into the main action to which we always return (bank robbers patiently working on a safe), shots are inserted (a lookout, a police car); or shots are alternated with each other (the fleeing bandits, the pursuing posse) until there is a resolution — a shot which unites elements of the two separate shots or which reveals to us in some other way (through dialogue, perhaps) how the two events we've been seeing alternately relate dramatically to each other. Much of our sense of cinematic simultaneity has been learned from our past cinematic experience. When we see certain editing patterns on the screen, we feel we are watching simultaneous time.

Inserts
Imagine a scene which takes place in a Western saloon. The first shot is a long shot, an **establishing shot** which gives us a sense of context. Let's say it shows a group of players involved in a card game. The long shot cuts directly to a medium shot of one of the players who wipes his

face with a bandanna and then moves to put it in his pocket. That shot cuts to a close-up of another man looking at his cards. The next shot cuts to a close-up of another man lighting a cigar. That is cut to a medium shot showing all the players around the table. The close-up shots just mentioned supply us with details already broadly established in the opening long shot. They make us aware of individual pieces of action occurring within the time span of the dramatic scene. They can seem to indicate pieces of simultaneous action (all the players do what they do at the same time), or they can suggest sequential action (the players do what they do progressively as we see them do it). Distinguishing whether the inserts are simultaneous or sequential is often difficult and is in part dependent upon information supplied by the situation of the story and by the conventions of the editing. Insert shots are just that — they are inserted into a larger context and are details plucked from it. The insert is perhaps the most invisible form of editing because it is so expected, particularly when it gives the viewer close-ups of a character's facial expression.

Parallel Editing or Crosscutting

Parallel editing or crosscutting, we saw, can be used to compress time or expand it, but it can also be used to keep the viewer conscious of two or more separate actions taking place at approximately the same time. Parallel editing or crosscutting is most often used to create a sense of suspense, because neither action is resolved before we cut away from them. Such editing alternates between events which are happening at the same time in different places; each scene therefore serves as a cutaway for the other.

In Alfred Hitchcock's *Strangers on a Train* (1951), for instance, parallel editing creates enormous suspense. The police suspect Guy, a professional tennis player, of murdering his wife, and they keep him under surveillance. Guy knows who the real killer is, and he knows that during a tournament at Forest Hills, the killer is at that moment attempting to implicate him further. It is imperative then, that he finish the set quickly and go after Bruno, the murderer. Crosscut with scenes of the tournament, in which the match seems to take forever, we see the killer on his way to an amusement park to plant incriminating evidence — Guy's initialed cigarette lighter — at the murder site. Accidentally, he drops the evidence down a sewage drain and tries to retrieve it. We see both scenes, each given equal importance, and each serving as a cutaway for the other; the shots cut back and forth at an accelerating pace (that is, each shot is briefer than the one before it) until the suspense is almost painful. Parallel editing creates this suspense not only by showing the viewer a series of unresolved shots but also by allowing the viewer an omniscience that the characters themselves do not have. Further, alternating those shots at an accelerating pace creates a forceful and rhythmic momentum. It is, therefore, no accident that such parallel editing is so often used at the climatic moments of action films; it is the stuff of which chases and last-minute rescues are created.

Split Screen (Multiple Images)

Parallel editing, of course, does not actually show the viewer simultaneous events simultaneously on the screen. But filmmakers have tried to show simultaneous activities on the same screen at the *same* time. The screen may be split in half or thirds by two or three separate moving images which occur simultaneously and side by side. **Multiple images** (sometimes repeated shots of the same action, sometimes contrasting images) may appear simultaneously on different parts of a single screen, dividing the screen into two or more segments.

Although the split screen had been used by D. W. Griffith in *The Birth of a Nation* (1915) and Abel Gance in *Napoleon* (1926) — Gance used three screens and three projectors at intensely dramatic moments, flanking the center screen image with supplementary images — the use of multiple images stayed in its experimental stages until the New York World's Fair in 1964. The wealth of split-screen short films exhibited there influenced subsequent commercial theatrical features, but except for its exploitation by television the split screen or multiple image is still somewhat neglected as a major expressive device.

Perhaps the best use of the split screen is in Richard Fleischer's *The Boston Strangler* (1968), the semidocumentary story of a schizophrenic murderer. The use of split screen is appropriate not only because it communicates the simultaneity of a big city manhunt, but also because it is a perfect visual metaphor for the split personality of Albert De-Salvo, the Boston strangler. About 35 percent of the film uses multiple imagery. Often the various images simultaneously shown on the screen substitute for the conventional sequential montage in which shots of action (for example, events taking place at the same time in various parts of a city) are dissolved or cut together to convey simultaneous activity. For example, one multiple-image sequence communicates the rounding up of all known sex offenders in Boston, while another shows the simultaneous efforts of women all over the city to take precautions against the murderer. In other episodes, the multiple imagery substitutes for parallel editing or crosscutting, showing us simultaneous events leading progressively toward a dramatic resolution. Moreover, because the split screen offers a visual "overload" of stimuli, it helps to convey the sense of panic caused by the strangler. But the split screen is also used to create emotional conflict in the viewer, to create a tension between two opposing feelings which duplicate — to a degree — the schizophrenia of the film's central character. At one point, early in the film and before we have seen DeSalvo's face on the screen, the audience is visually forced to identify with the killer and his victim simultaneously. We watch multiple images of buzzers and microphone speakers in an apartment building and we hear the voices of an elderly lady and the killer who is posing as a plumber. A hand-held camera shot then takes us up the stairs, duplicating for us the subjective, murderer's-eye view as he climbs toward the victim, and we simultaneously watch, in another and smaller image, an elderly woman getting ready to open the door.

A more recent example of split screen is the 1975 Academy Award–winning documentary *The Great American Cowboy* (Keith Merrill), which used the technique to communicate the violence and excitement of rodeo life. A cowboy eases onto the back of a bucking horse; the gate is opened and the screen splits into two, four, or more images of the same action photographed from different angles. Multiple images also show different cowboys on different horses, but all of them plunging and rearing wildly. Thus, the split screen not only can show the same action from slightly different perspectives, but can also emphasize the relatedness of similar actions actually performed at different times. Moreover, the split screen is well suited to conveying the excitement and frenzy of certain activities. Watching more than one image simultaneously places a demand on the viewer because of the uncommon quantity of visual stimuli, but it also may lead to an intensification of the viewer's attentiveness.

Superimpositions and Dissolves

Superimposition places two or more images on the screen directly over each other. A related device is the dissolve, in which the two images appear directly over each other only momentarily before one of them dissolves away leaving the other alone — and clear — on the screen. Both superimposition and the dissolve can be used to show simultaneous time. A superimposition of the heroine putting on lipstick before a dressing table mirror, for instance, and the hero knotting his tie before another mirror would convey simultaneity because of their related activities and our knowledge that they were preparing for a date. Similarly, a sequence connected by dissolves in which an image of a woman sleeping is dissolved into a milkman putting bottles near a door which is dissolved into a paperboy putting a paper in front of an apartment door which is then dissolved into a man sleeping would tend to convey to the viewer a sense of simultaneous time. Although both dissolves and superimpositions are less clearly able to communicate simultaneous time than parallel editing, insert shots, and multiple imagery, they are occasionally used because they tend to establish a lyric or languorous mood which may be more suited to the subject matter than the abruptness of cutting or the overloaded excitement of split screen.

★★★ Subjective Time: Dream, Fantasy, Memory, and Perceptual Distortion

We customarily assume that what is happening before our eyes on the screen is happening in present time. And as each action passes, it leads inexorably to the next and the next and the next, establishing a forceful sense of both continuity and chronological progression. We know that what has come before our eyes is now past, and that what will occur next before us is the future — and that what we are actually watching is the "now," the present. Through editing, however, all of the "normal" chronological time schemes can be rearranged to create a sequence out of chronological order.

How long is a dream? a fantasy? a thought? a memory? a drugged or drunken perception? We don't measure such occurrences of mind and feeling and perception by time — though, obviously, they occupy time in some fashion. Within a film, subjective time arises from a filmmaker's attempts to convey the interior of a character (and sometimes the filmmaker's own interior as well).

In literature, the kind of rambling, digressive, and highly personal associative thought processes in which we constantly engage may be revealed by a literary technique known as "stream of consciousness." With film, such mental and emotional processes as dreams, fantasies, memories, and distorted perception must be conveyed visually. And the spectator must be able to distinguish these interior processes from the more objective narrative of other portions of the film.

Until recently, a dream sequence in a movie was almost always introduced by conventional transitional devices. We usually knew who the dreamer was and when and where he or she was having the dream. The filmmaker provided us with a narrative context, such as a character preparing for bed, or eyelids becoming heavy, and also provided us with certain conventional editing devices that signaled a dream was going to occur: the sleeper would dissolve into the dream as if waves were undulating across the screen, or a whirlpool would be superimposed

★ **2-4** In the opening sequence of Fellini's 8½ (1963), the rope tied to the dreamer's leg, pulled by two men on the beach, brings him to the ground; instead of crashing to his death, he wakes up in his hotel room. Prior to that moment, no fictional "real" present time has been established.

over the sleeper and we would know we were descending into the vortex of a deep sleep. And, after the dream was completed we might see the dreamer, so we would know we were back in present screen time. The dream itself would be visually different from the rest of the film, either in its style or its content. A dream might be seen as through a veil or on tinted stock. More elaborately, in *Spellbound* (Alfred Hitchcock, 1945), the dream sequence, designed by Salvador Dali, mirrored the surreal artist's style and strange perspectives and thus drastically differed from the rather flat style of the rest of the movie.

Today, filmmakers are far less likely to signal a dream clearly as a dream. In fact, the movement into or out of a dream sequence may be disjunctive, and the editing may depend on disorientation cutting. In Federico Fellini's *8½* (1963), for example, the movie begins with a dream, but we do not know this at the start. We see an unknown man caught in a traffic jam in the claustrophobic interior of his car. He crawls from the auto and suddenly floats over the silent line of cars to the end of a tunnel and then out above a beach and ocean. We see a rope attached to his leg, and then, as if he were a kite, he is pulled down to the beach by two men and falls toward the sea (Figure 2-4). Although we may have a hunch that what we are watching must be a dream, we cannot know for certain until a character (in this case, a film director, Guido Anselmi) awakens from it. The imagery is certainly strange, but until Guido awakens no ground rules have been laid for the viewer and it is difficult to know precisely whether we are watching a surreal experimental feature or a dream or a fantasy. An interesting indicator of the audience's uncertain response to the opening of *8½* is its reaction to the fact that the opening sequence is silent until its midpoint; usually a rustling begins in the audience, and first-time viewers tend to look over their shoulders at the projection booth, as if there were something wrong with the sound system.

Like dreams, fantasy used to be signaled to the viewer by certain visual and aural clues. A classic example of a visual signal is the change from black-and-white film to color film as Dorothy half dreams, half fantasizes her journey to Oz in *The Wizard of Oz* (Victor Fleming, 1939); a classic aural signal is the *pocketa-pocketa* sound which signals the beginning of Walter Mitty's fantasy life adventures in *The Secret Life of Walter Mitty* (Norman Z. McLeod, 1947). In the musical film *On the Town* (Stanley Donen and Gene Kelly, 1949), one of the sailors daydreams about the girl whose picture is on the "Miss Turnstiles" sign in front of him; the sign image dissolves into the image of the girl herself and a dance number begins, taking place in a nonspecific space (the entire background is yellow and all the props are highly stylized). After the number's completion, this space is dissolved back into the yellow background of the "Miss Turnstiles" sign and the image of the girl's face.

Today, fantasies or daydreams are not signaled so obviously, probably because many artists, psychologists, philosophers, and laymen now believe that fantasy and reality are not separate things, or to put it a little differently, that fantasy is a part of reality. Whatever the reason, the viewer is expected to understand, by means of the content and the context and the dream logic of fantasies, when he is watching a daydream and when he is watching a supposedly objective reality. Sometimes the filmmaker goes out of his way to confuse "reality" and fantasy, since we live as much in our minds as we do in the external world. Fellini's *Juliet of the Spirits* (1965), for example, scarcely separates fantasy and dream from reality. The protagonist, Juliet, a housewife whose husband has lost interest in her and who seeks some kind of confirmation of identity, has visions which are peopled with characters who are no more strange than the friends and neighbors and relatives in her "ordinary" life; it is therefore difficult to distinguish between a fantasy and a party, between a spirit and a spiritualist.

Like dreams and fantasies, memories are linked to a specific character in a film. Someone has to remember — and therefore memory is (or can be) highly subjective. What the viewer sees on the screen is not an objective depiction of the character's past, but a depiction of the past as it is remembered and re-created by the character. In Ingmar Bergman's *Wild Strawberries* (1957), the protagonist's memories of his childhood are treated subjectively. The elderly Isak Borg walks through his own past as a ghost. He attempts to explain himself, but no one sees him.

Other cinematic signals, such as slow motion, impact cutting, strange angles, changes in lighting, also can indicate that the viewpoint is that of a character in the present remembering his own past. If we simply get a **flashback**, without some such distortion, we usually assume that the scene is objectively (rather than subjectively) presented. Perhaps the quintessential demonstration of the subjective nature of memory is Akira Kurosawa's *Rashomon* (1951), a film in which four different characters recall vastly different versions of an attack by a bandit on a husband and wife traveling through a forest; each character remembers what reflects favorably upon himself, and even the most "impartial" of the characters (an observer of the action rather than a participant) is suspect because of his biases (Figure 2-5). Spectators who watch *Rashomon* come away from the film less secure in their relationship to "truth" and "objectivity."

One other kind of subjective time in the cinema is securely attached to a particular character. If a character has been drugged, or is drunk, or is in a state of semiconsciousness, we often witness images in which the content is distorted — the camera has assumed a first-person relationship with the character and thus has taken on his distorted perceptions. This active participation by the camera occurs chiefly when a character is in some abnormal physical state; if a character is merely dreaming, fantasizing, or remembering, although the content of what we watch may be strange, illogical, or distorted, the image itself is usually not distorted. A physical abnormality that affects the character's perceptions, however, such as intoxication, is almost always portrayed through the use of a subjective camera distorting what the character sees. Thus, in *Murder My Sweet* (Edward Dmytryk, 1944), when private eye Philip Marlowe is beaten up and drugged, his return to consciousness is conveyed through camera distortions which turn ordinary objects in a room into nightmarish and nameless shapes. In *Vertigo* (Alfred Hitchcock, 1958), an ex-policeman who suffers from a fear of heights, experiences vertigo or dizziness; the camera demonstrates his distorted perception and fear of falling by tracking in and **zooming** out simultaneously.

All of the mental processes discussed thus far have been linked to specific characters. If what we see is a dream, then we shall discover the sleeper; if what we see is a memory, then we shall see who remembers. But occasionally, a filmmaker will create a dream without a dreamer — or with no one identifiable dreamer. In 1929, for example, surrealists Salvador Dali and Luis Buñuel made *Un Chien Andalou*, in which there is no real reference point (Figure 2-6). The film starts out with a title, "Once upon a Time," then shows a man smoking and sharpening a

★ **2-5** Prose fiction has often made use of multiple narrators who tell different versions of the same event. Akira Kurosawa, the Japanese director, used the same technique in RASHOMON (1951). A woodcutter, a bandit, a lord, and his wife each relate what happened one day in the woods. The audience sees each of the told tales as if it were an objective filmed story, but after seeing all four versions, the truth of the events remains ambiguous.

razor, a cloud passing over the moon, the man slitting a woman's eyeball with the razor and then a title which says, "Eight years later," and cuts to a young man riding a bicycle. All of the actions we see could be in the subconscious mind of a character, they could be a dream; but then there are none of the comfortable conventions of the movie dream: no dreamer awakens from a nightmare, perhaps falling out of bed, but restoring himself and the viewer to the real world and to chronological and decipherable time. In *Un Chien Andalou* nothing is clarified, and the time we see pass before us on the screen remains ambiguous.

Memory, too, can become detached from a specific character. In *Last Year at Marienbad* (1961), directed by Alain Resnais, present, past, and

★ **2-6** Some films never present a normal time scheme against which a dream or fantasy can be measured. In UN CHIEN ANDALOU (1928), surrealists Salvidor Dali and Luis Buñuel present what might be a dream, but there is never a dreamer who wakes up — and time itself is mocked by intercut titles.

future merge until the distinction between them is meaningless and time is seen as the merely arbitrary creation of a subjective consciousness. The film never clearly establishes a sense of present time or place. Characters with letters for names move about in a resort hotel; they meet and play games in which the outcome seems predetermined; they walk about the halls and grounds, sometimes not even casting shadows in bright sunlight — as if time were no longer measurable by the revolution of the earth around its axis. Scenes are repeated, conversations and monologues seem to be without meaning. Shot follows shot, but no chronology is established. The entire film could be a dream, a memory, a fantasy, but it is never clear whose mind or what state of consciousness or subconsciousness we are witnessing.

In all of the subjective states that the cinema conveys, the nature of time is ambiguous, unspecific. An elaborate fantasy that occupies the screen for sixty minutes can occur in a split second. Or the fantasy may occur while one is doing something else — Walter Mitty has a literally fantastic adventure as he drives his car to the station. The running time, of course, is measurable, but the screen time of a subjective sequence is rarely specific. Thus, although transitional editing devices usually locate the narrative in a specific time and place, they also can do exactly the opposite, creating a non-time and a non-place, the playground of the unconscious mind.

★★★   **Objective Time: The Flashback and
the Flash-Forward**

The previous pages have discussed some ways in which the cinema can signal and convey to the viewer subjective time, time which is not precisely measurable within the narrative. But, of course, it can also signal and convey **objective time,** time which we understand is a minute or a day or a week or a year. A case in point is the flashback; a flashback is a memory — or seems to be. Like a memory, it is connected with a specific character. And, like a memory, it recalls the past. Finally, like a memory, how long the remembering of the past takes within the film story is unclear, ambiguous.

Yet flashbacks differ from the subjective presentation of the past. Usually there is an element of impersonality in the flashback, a particular character may be doing the remembering, but the memory that we see on the screen is an objective fact — what really happened rather than the way one character remembers it. For example, in *Casablanca* (Michael Curtiz, 1942) we don't regard the flashback of the love affair between Ilsa and Rick as anything but what actually happened between them, so that when we speak of a "flashback" we are speaking of an objective flashback; what might be called a subjective flashback we call a "subjective memory."

The objective nature of the flashback may be in part derived from its formal structure. Until fairly recently, in most films the flashback, like the dream, was obviously signaled. The audience nearly always knew when a flashback was going to occur through visual and aural clues. The present image would usually blur or dissolve, and often, to make doubly sure the viewer knew what was happening, a character would say something like "It all comes back to me now . . ." and then the image would come sharply into focus or a new image would emerge from the dissolve and we would see the character usually looking appreciably younger and immersed in the action being remembered.

In *Casablanca,* for example, Rick, the owner of a café in Casablanca, is drinking after hours when the first flashback occurs. He has seen Ilsa earlier in the evening and the narrative has established that they knew each other during the German occupation of Paris. Rick, trying both to forget and to remember Ilsa, tells Sam, the pianist, to play a song Ilsa had asked for earlier in the evening. The song, appropriately enough entitled "As Time Goes By," obviously has specific meaning for the couple. As Sam begins to play, a close-up image of Rick is dissolved into a shot of the Arch of Triumph, thus, taking us out of Casablanca and to Paris. There is a cut to Rick and Ilsa riding in a car, obviously in love. After establishing the lovers' relationship to each other and their history as a couple, the flashback ends with a medium shot of Rick standing in front of a train about to leave Paris, being prompted by Sam, the pianist, to board it. The shot dissolves, the figure of Rick being replaced by a bottle of whiskey sitting atop the bar. We are back in Rick's Café.

Although it is Rick who nominally "remembers" his and Ilsa's past in Paris, we believe what we see is the narrative truth — and uncolored by Rick's nostalgia or bitterness or love. What makes the flashback, even when it is attached to a specific character, seem so objective? The curious difference between a flashback and a subjective memory is the establishment of time and narrative logic *within* the sequence. Most often, once the transition is made to a previous time in a flashback, the time sequence of the remembered material is chronological, adheres to the usual laws of cause and effect, and all in all is consistent with the rest of the film in which the camera acts invisibly as an omniscient third-person narrator. That is, watching a flashback, the viewer generally watches a continuous and consecutive series of actions which give the illusion of "present" and real time. When the sequence is over (the flashback sequence may be composed of a number of smaller units which still progress forward in time), we dissolve or cut back to the real present of the film, established at the beginning of the film's main action. Sometimes entire films are flashbacks, surrounded by bookend-like moments of "present" time. *Double Indemnity* (Billy Wilder, 1944), *Kind Hearts and Coronets* (Robert Hamer, 1948), and *The Man Who Shot Liberty Valance* (John Ford, 1962) are for most of their duration flashbacks. In the first, a dictaphone confession of murder listened to by an insurance claims agent takes us back into the past; in the second, a man awaiting execution writes his memoirs, which take us into the past in a series of flashbacks; and in the third, an elderly U.S. senator tells a young newspaperman the "true" story of a shootout, which leads into the flashback. What is interesting about films which are primarily flashbacks is that because the past occupies so much screen time, it starts to become the film's present time; we tend to forget we are watching something that has already happened rather than something which is happening.

The only time that flashbacks can be interpreted as more subjective than objective is when their narrative content is at odds with other material in the film. In *Rashomon* (1951) we get four flashbacks of the same event, each attached to a different character, and since the four flashbacks differ, we understand that each one is the subjective account of its particular character. And in *Citizen Kane*, although the flashbacks appear objective within themselves, the characters who begin the "reminiscences" all reveal such highly subjective feelings about Charles Foster Kane that the viewer ends up taking each flashback as subjective rather than as objective.

The **flash-forward** is a much less common movement in time than is the flashback. The flash-forward, unlike the flashback, usually doesn't belong to anybody. (The only exceptions are clairvoyant characters, like those in Nicholas Roeg's *Don't Look Now* (1973) or characters who are able to "time-trip," like Billy Pilgrim in *Slaughterhouse Five* (George Roy Hill, 1972). The flash-forward is therefore primarily a device connected with the camera as an all-seeing and all-knowing eye whose extraordinary vision the viewer is allowed to share. Although a filmmaker such as Alain Resnais, who views time as an entirely subjective entity, can link the flash-forward to the consciousness of his main character in *La Guerre Est Finie* (1966), films like *They Shoot Horses, Don't They?* (Sydney Pollack, 1969) and *Easy Rider* (Dennis Hopper, 1969) insert flash-forwards for dramatic emphasis, a cinematic forewarning which will also disorient and jolt the viewer. In *They Shoot Horses, Don't They?* and in *Easy Rider*, the flash-forwards gave us an intimation of the climax. In *They Shoot Horses*, the flash-forwards show Robert on trial for something (we find out at the end it is for shooting Gloria at her own request) and they are filmed through what seem like blue filters so that their eeriness and disjunctiveness is more disturbing; in *Easy Rider* the flash-forwards reveal in tiny and somewhat incomprehensible units the violent death of the hippie cyclist. These flash-forwards are not premonitions which belong to the film's characters; rather, they are insertions by the filmmaker/narrator, and so once they are understood they are seen as being objective.

★★★ **Achronological Time**

AMBIGUOUS TIME

Within the context of a well-defined time scheme — either clearly subjective or objective — sequences may occur which are ambiguous in their temporal relation to that time scheme. Take for example, a sequence of dissolves and superimpositions used in *Tom Jones* (Tony Richardson, 1963) (Figure 2-7). We see Tom and Sophie Western walking in a country landscape in various combinations of shots superimposed and dissolved with images of trees and flowers. In what time do these images take place in relation to each other? Are we seeing simultaneous time or continual time or no time at all? We know from the context of the

★ **2-7** A sequence of superimpositions and dissolves can convey a sense of ambiguous time. In TOM JONES (Tony Richardson, 1963) Sophie Western and Tom are shown in a courting sequence which implies that young lovers lose track of time.

narrative that Tom and Sophie are spending — specifically — one afternoon together, but the visual sequence does not let us know whether minutes or hours are passing. Obviously, the aim of the dissolves and superimpositions was not to convey precise information about time, but rather to set up a romantic, lyrical mood. **Ambiguous time** is most often communicated through dissolves and superimpositions.

UNIVERSAL TIME

There is another kind of purposely achronological time which may be called **universal time.** It is created consciously by the filmmaker who wishes the images in the film to take on a universal quality.

★ **2-8**   Though the narration in THE PLOW THAT BROKE THE PLAINS
(Pare Lorentz, 1936) describes a historical progression — from the settlement
of the plains in the nineteenth century to the Dustbowl of the 1930s —
the images of tractors moving back and forth across the land, plowing,
harrowing, reaping, are temporally unspecific. They exist in achronological,
universal time, conveying the notion of many tractors doing this work
over and over again, year after year.

Documentary films, particularly those made in the 1930s, frequently
sought to create universal time. In Pare Lorentz's *The Plow That Broke
the Plains* (1936), for example, we are shown images of farm machinery
working huge Midwestern fields (Figure 2-8). Plows and harvesters
move back and forth in a series of alternating shots: a group of machines moves across the screen from left to right, in the next image
from right to left, and so on. They are never the same machines in the
same field. Although the film begins with a map of a specific geographical area — the Great Plains — its purpose seems to be to transcend a
specific place and a specific time so that the migrating victims of the
drought and wind which helped create the Dust Bowl are explained to
the public not in geographic or historical terms, with which not everyone might identify, but in terms of man's unchanging, universal qualities. Thus, although the film seems to deal with a specific locale and history, the images and narration do not emphasize them. The narration
describes, in a most general and simple way, the process of a booming
agriculture depleting the land, which then becomes vulnerable to erosion
and the ravages of the elements. Because the images as edited lack landmarks and chronology, what we see takes place not so much in, say,
Kansas in 1935, as in a universal time and place. By emphasizing the
idea rather than the particular chosen example (this is not farmer Smith

plowing his Kansas field, but this is the Farmer plowing the Field — the symbol of any farmer in any field), a sense of universal time is created.

Two techniques help the filmmaker to rob time of its specificity: first, the use of a great deal of editing, which links images together in separate shots so there is little sense of context against which time can be measured, and second, the use of a large number of close-ups and/or shots which are not defined by their backgrounds. *The Plow That Broke the Plains*, for instance, rarely shows us a human face which we can inspect and identify as a particular, highly individual human being; faces are shot in shadow or are not held on the screen for long. The movie also shows us many close-ups of useless or old farm machinery lying on parched ground, objects to which people are no longer attached and which are no longer defined by their activity. Those objects exist in time, but it could be any time. And they also exist in space, but as there are no reference points, it could be any space. Further, the idea of an action becomes important beyond the specific action depicted in the shots. Shots of moving tractors cut to shots of moving tanks, similar shapes and similar directions. The idea conveyed through the montage — that grain and tanks are both weapons of war and are both equally important to the war effort — far outweighs the specific content of the individual shots.

Although perhaps the most obvious examples of the editor's creation of universal time can be found in the heavily edited documentaries of the 1930s from America and Great Britain, where the emphasis is on man's universal struggle to endure, examples can also be found today in subtler documentaries. Even the documentary filmmaker Fredrick Wiseman creates universal time. This sounds odd, because one of his primary methods is to present extremely long sequences of activity with no interruption by editing or commentary; real time and real space seem to be captured in the sequence and preserved, minimally controlled by the filmmaker. A Wiseman documentary like *Titicut Follies* (1967), his first film, exploring the world of a mental institution, or *Meat* (1977), recording the various activities in a slaughterhouse and packing plant, seems hardly the place to find universal time. And yet it is there — between the sequences. *Titicut Follies*, for example, begins with a strange variety show in which the participants seem ill at ease, unnaturally stiff. The film ends with the show as well. In between, sequences show us men in an institution for the criminally insane being abused by guards, amusing themselves in the exercise yard, being interviewed by staff personnel, being led through the motions of a birthday party by volunteers, doing in fact all that they do and what the camera has been able to record in the given time it was there. Each sequence preserves its own

★ **2-9** Carl Dreyer in THE PASSION OF JOAN OF ARC (1928) places his central character in a universal time. Frequent close-ups of Joan against bare white backgrounds eliminate temporal clues suggestive of a specific time and place.

temporal and spatial continuity. The screen time and running time within sequences are usually the same. Space is unbroken by editing as the camera moves to change perspective. And yet there is absolutely no establishment of an overall time scheme for the film. Does all this footage come from a typical week? A day? What time relationship exists between the variety show and the events shown after it? By leaving the time between sequences undefined, unspecific, Wiseman takes extremely particularized events and makes them emblematic of such events at mental institutions everywhere and at any time. While preserving the integrity of each specific sequence, because of the film's overall atemporal or timeless editing structure Wiseman is also able to create universality.

Although universal time is suggested chiefly in documentary films, fiction films also occasionally suggest it. A primitive example of an attempt at universality exists in the parallel editing of D. W. Griffith's *Intolerance* (1916), which attempts to link four widely separated periods of history and to emphasize what they had in common. Moreover, *Intolerance* used one image which is indeed universal in its spatial and temporal ambiguity: linking the different periods is the image of a woman rocking a cradle, prefaced by the title "Out of the cradle endlessly rocking, ever bringing the same joys and sorrows." In the shot itself the cradle is covered with roses, a strong beam of light shines from above on the woman, and three shadowy figures (the Fates) sit in the background. This image exists in no particular time and in no particular space.

Because the close-up tends to exclude the identifying and specific elements of space and time, fiction films which depend heavily on the close-up are able to suggest universal time. Carl Dreyer in *The Passion of Joan of Arc* (1928) not only gives us a Joan who is alone and in close-up in the frame, but he also purposely removes background clues suggesting a particular time, using instead white backgrounds for his close-ups (Figure 2-9). The effect creates a sense of timelessness, of non-time, of universal and eternal time. We are not only watching the story of a particular woman engaged in a particular religious and political struggle at a particular time in history, we are also watching the struggle between faith and doubt which can take place at any time and anywhere. Many of Dreyer's films, as well as those of French filmmaker Robert Bresson, attempt through editing to create images which deal with eternal and timeless states of the spirit.

★★★ ## Visual Rhythm

Running time is absolute. We can use a stopwatch to count the seconds of every shot in a film, in every sequence, in every scene; added up, the result will be the running time of the movie. Screen time is also absolute, although we may occasionally have difficulty deciphering it. Usually, however, we can figure out from the dialogue, from visual clues, from knowledge we bring to the film, how long the story or narrative is supposed to be; we can tell if it takes place in a year or ten years, three days or three weeks. Psychological time, which is subjective, might be thought to all a matter of opinion, or of feeling, but in fact most members of the audience will probably agree that a given film is light or swift or steady. Psychological time is usually created chiefly by the rhythm of the editing and by the pace of motion within the frame. The rate at which the film is edited, the kinds of editorial transitions, the number of shots in the entire film, and the length of each shot will impart a visual rhythm, a pace, to the whole film. This rhythm and pace will not only contribute to the mood of various sequences, but will also influence our perception of the entire film. The way we feel a film (rather than clock it or understand it) is similar to the way we feel a piece of music, and both depend on their rhythms to induce those feelings.

What makes a film exciting or lyrical or fast or slow? The editing might be called the heartbeat or pulse of a film. If images dissolve into each other, the mood produced may be lyric, romantic, graceful, and certainly somewhat leisurely. A dissolve from one image into another takes more running time than does a direct cut from one image to another. A sixty-minute film edited primarily in dissolves and fades will seem slower and possibly longer to the viewer than a sixty-minute film which is edited primarily in direct cuts. The number and pattern of dissolves, fades, direct cuts, impact cuts, disorientation cuts in any given film will partially determine its overall rhythm and pace, and that will in turn determine psychological time, or, to put it a little differently, it will determine the viewer's response to the film's content.

For example, Richard Lester's *A Hard Day's Night* (1964) was edited so as to achieve a hyperactive rhythm; it greatly depended on impact and disorientation cuts which were admirably suited to its anarchic and ebullient subjects, the Beatles. When the film was released, it left audiences exhilarated and breathless. Today, however, *A Hard Day's Night* seems much slower than when it was first released; the Beatles retain their charm, but the pace seems almost sluggish. The editing rhythms of the film have not changed, of course, but the audience's sense of them has changed; we have learned to see more quickly, and the techniques which were used so originally in Lester's film have now become commonplace.

★★★   ## Meaning Through Editing: Montage

In front of me lies a crumpled yellowed sheet of paper. On it is a mysterious note:

"Linkage — P" and "Collision — E."

This is a substantial trace of a heated bout on the subject of montage between P (Pudovkin) and E (myself).

This has become a habit. At regular intervals he visits me late at night and behind closed doors we wrangle over matters of principle. A graduate of the Kuleshov school, he loudly defends an understanding of montage as a *linkage* of pieces. Into a chain. Again, "bricks." Bricks, arranged in series to *expound* an idea.

I confronted him with my viewpoint on montage as *collision*. A view that from the collision of two given factors *arises* a concept.

Sergei Eisenstein[2]

Montage — the juxtaposition of separate images — is one way of creating meaning in the cinema. Originally, the word *montage* was used simply; borrowed from the French language by the Russian filmmaker and theorist Sergei Eisenstein, it literally means "mounting" and was used to signify the physical act of editing, the cutting and splicing of one piece of film to another. However, the word has undergone an interesting and somewhat confusing evolution. Refined and qualified by Eisenstein himself, it has come to be associated with the Russian principles of editing, principles which stress combining images so that they will produce an idea. The word has also been used to describe a certain kind of editing common in the German silent cinema: sequences were constructed primarily with dissolves, and their aim was less to create intellectual meaning than it was to create mood. In Hollywood, the word has been used generally to describe sequences which compress time, no matter whether they do so by cutting or dissolving.

All of these definitions of montage share a common denominator; they all imply that meaning is not inherent in any one shot but is created by the juxtaposition of shots. Simply and dramatically, this basic principle of editing was demonstrated by an experiment conducted by Lev Kuleshov, an early Russian filmmaker. He intercut images of an actor's expressionless face with images of a bowl of soup, a woman in a coffin, and a child with a toy. Audiences who saw the film praised the actor's performance — they saw in his face, emotionless as it was, hunger, grief, and affection. They saw, in other words, what was not really there in the separate images. Meaning and emotion, then, were created not by the content of the individual images, but by the relationship of the images to each other. Alone, his actor's expressionless face is expressionless, his bowl of soup is just a bowl of soup; shown in relationship to each other, however, the shots will communicate a man's hunger to the viewer.

MONTAGE BY COMPOSITION

The composition of shapes and masses in the film frame can be used to link one image to another. A relationship can be established between two shots emphasizing either their similarity or dissimilarity in composition.

An example of a relationship established by shots with a similar composition can be found in Eisenstein's *Strike* (1924). One image shows us a close-up of a man's hand dangling a child whose body, precariously angled on a diagonal plane, fills the major part of the frame. Another is composed similarly, although its subject seems to have no relationship to the image of the child: a cow's head, filling most of the frame, is also angled diagonally and a man's hand has just finished cutting its throat. Because the composition of both shots is similar, the shots are linked together by the viewer who looks, then, for the meaning of the juxtaposition of such seemingly different content. The relationship emerges: the child is being slaughtered in a massacre of strikers by police, much as an animal is slaughtered in a slaughterhouse.

The relationship of shots based on diametrically opposed compositions is best illustrated by those numerous scenes in westerns or war movies in which we get an image of the "good guy" on screen left followed by an image of the "bad guy" mirroring the previous shot on screen right, or the army of one group advancing from screen right and the army of its enemy advancing from screen left. This opposition of composition in such an exact manner again makes the linkage of the two shots meaningful. Not only does such a juxtaposition make physical the notion of conflict between opposites, but it also implies — particularly when there is accompanying movement — that the two opposing forces and masses will eventually converge in the frame.

MONTAGE BY MOVEMENT

Since few shots in a film are static, composition alone rarely provides the basis for linking two images. Usually similar movement or opposed movement is combined with composition, providing another element which can provoke associations between two separate images. This directional flow from image to image can indicate a great deal.

A montage sequence in *The Graduate* (Mike Nichols, 1967) compresses time, as usual, but it also creates meaning through the similar movement of its central subject in the juxtaposed shots (Figure 2-10). We see Benjamin jumping into his family swimming pool, then Benjamin jumping into bed with Mrs. Robinson in a hotel room, then Benjamin idly floating in his pool on an inflated rubber mattress, then Benjamin in a similarly relaxed position and movement in the hotel bed. In one juxtaposition of two shots within the montage sequence, the direct cut comes in mid-motion; Benjamin begins to roll off of the mattress into the pool and the shot is changed in mid-motion to pick up and complete the action of the dive into Mrs. Robinson's bed. The montage communicates not only the recreational aspects of Benjamin's summer but also the feeling that Benjamin's affair with Mrs. Robinson is as idle and emotionally casual as his time in the family pool.

Opposition of movement within a montage sequence, like similarity of movement, can also tell us a great deal. At the beginning of Alfred Hitchcock's *Strangers on a Train* (1951), for example, we are introduced to the two central characters feet first: we literally see their shoes and watch them walk before we ever see their faces. Besides the differences in their personalities indicated immediately by their contrasting taste in

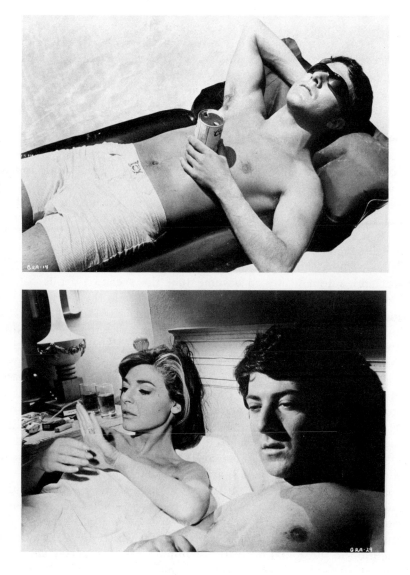

★ **2-10** In THE GRADUATE (1970), Mike Nichols punctuates a sequence showing the affair between Benjamin and Mrs. Robinson with an example of cutting together two similar motions. Here he alternates between Benjamin relaxing in his family's pool and lounging in bed with Mrs. Robinson in a hotel room. Later, we see a shot in which Benjamin comes out of the water onto the float in the pool cut to another shot which appears to continue that movement as he slides onto Mrs. Robinson in the hotel bed.

footwear (one pair of shoes is sober and plain, the other pair flamboyant and decorative), we sense a difference between them because the physical direction of their movement is opposed. They each get out of cabs which have arrived at a train station from contrasting directions and they each walk toward the train, on which they will finally meet, from opposite directions. And, again, because in their respective shots they move toward center screen from opposite directions, we have a clear sense they will converge and eventually come together in the same screen space. Which is, of course, what happens: the two sit down across from each other in a club car, their feet accidentally touch, and the story of two men and a "crisscross" murder begins. Hitchcock's editing here is formally in tune with the structure and theme of the film.

Editing by this kind of directional flow must be carefully controlled so that the viewer is not accidentally misled. When we see one shot in which a man on horseback is galloping from left to right and that is followed by a shot of another man similarly galloping from left to right, we tend automatically to assume that the second rider is *behind* the first rider and that the action we are watching in the linking of the two shots is a chase of some sort. If the second character is not really following the first, the spatial resemblance is misleading and the editing is probably faulty — unless of course, the filmmaker purposely misled us for some reason.

Contrasting screen movement can also be used to mislead the viewer. In *The Man with a Movie Camera* (1928), for instance, Dziga Vertov crosscuts between a fire engine racing across the screen from right to left and an ambulance racing across the screen from left to right; each shot is accelerated — or shortened — as the two are alternated. There seems to be only one possible conclusion to this montage in which parallel editing also gives us a sense of simultaneous time: the two vehicles are on a collision course. But Vertov simply cuts away from this sequence to other unrelated shots and the two vehicles never crash; their movement toward each other — created by artificial means, Vertov seems to say — is never resolved. In a film which did not pay so much attention to the actual processes of filmmaking (for Vertov shows us the camera, film editing, and so on), we might be inclined to think the editor had made a careless mistake. But Vertov is likely to be poking a little fun at the expectations of the film audience. Throughout the film — which is a virtual textbook of editing technique — motion is used to link shots together. Spinning wheels on machinery are linked to other spinning objects. Some movements are contrasted, others are similar. In one particularly fascinating sequence, Vertov shows us, by juxtaposed shots, spectators watching athletes perform. Although we do not see the

★ **2-11** Dziga Vertov intercut a rotating spindle in THE MAN WITH A MOVIE CAMERA (1928) with other shots of rotating objects to develop a pattern, a visual harmony, based on a particular motion and enforced by repetition.

spectators in the same shots as the athletes, because of their eye movement and reactions we link the following shots of the athletes to them and assume that the spectators are actually seeing the action. This in itself is not unusual; most editing makes the viewer assume the existence of an action he hasn't really seen on the screen. What is strange, however, is that the spectators blink their eyes, move their heads, in what we consider normal time, in natural lifelike motion — but the athletes move in slow motion. Vertov not only juxtaposes shots to create action, he juxtaposes the dimensions and movements of time as well.

MONTAGE BY REPETITION

So far we have been talking about repetition of composition and/or motion, but not repetition of the image itself. On occasion, however, an editor may choose to repeat a shot exactly as it appeared on the screen before (and may appear again).

If an exact replica of a frame (a single image) is juxtaposed next to its original, we are watching a freeze frame, an image which stays the same even as the film travels forward through the projector. We do not, of course, get the editorial effect of repetition, for we seem to see only one image for an extended period. To get the editorial effect of repetition, we must *perceive* that the repeated image is repeated; only when we perceive the repetition is a different meaning created. The freeze connotes time stopped and is emphatic, whereas repetition tends to convey a sense of a cyclic unit, to indicate an action gone through again and again. Repetition of images, as distinguished from freeze frames, requires the juxtaposition of different shots intercut with a repeated image. The effect of this repetition can be soothing or anxiety-provoking; it can function to *unify* disparate images, or, because it destroys normal time, it can function to *shatter* images connected chronologically. In Vertov's *The Man with a Movie Camera*, for instance, the repetition of a rotating machine spindle (Figure 2-11) between shots of different objects

109

★ **2-12**   Tension can be created by the timing used for alternating two images. In a sequence from AN OCCURRENCE AT OWL CREEK BRIDGE (Robert Enrico, 1961), the crosscutting between the husband and the wife is set to music with the image of each having a distinct number of beats. The repetition of the pattern signals the viewer that something is wrong, that the scene is too artificial to be real.

which are rotating, creates a pattern, a rhythm, a visual harmony because the image of the spindle draws all the other shots together and cements them into a unified sequence. In *An Occurrence at Owl Creek Bridge* (1961), on the other hand, we are disturbed by the repetition of several shots within a montage sequence. Telephoto shots of a man running towards the camera are juxtaposed with shots of a woman moving down plantation steps and then laterally across the screen. Because the man, who is running toward the camera (and the woman), is shown repeating the action from the same point in space, the viewer increasingly senses that what he is watching is a fantasy or dream — which, in fact, it turns out to be.

MONTAGE BY RHYTHM

Let's imagine a series of shots consisting of three two-second shots, one three-second shot, and then two one-second shots. This pattern could be repeated once, twice, three times, thus creating a rhythm or pattern. Then another pattern might be created and repeated. In some abstract films this rhythmic alteration of shots is synchronized to music, as in the animated design sequence to Bach's Toccata and Fugue in D minor in Walt Disney's *Fantasia* (1940).

The intrusion of such rhythmic editing into an unrhythmic context occurs at the climax of *An Occurrence at Owl Creek Bridge*. Some shots are repeated, and a very formal rhythm between shots is used in conjunction with rhythmic music on the sound track. The result is very disturbing; it immediately tells the viewer something is unnatural or wrong, and it finally severs the viewer's identification with the escaping protagonist. We get crosscutting between a head-on telephoto shot of the protagonist running — but seeming to make no progress — toward his wife (and the camera), and a normal-lens shot of his wife moving in slow motion laterally to greet him (Figure 2-12). Each of the images of the protagonist lasts for five bars of music, and each of the images of the wife — except the last one — lasts for seven bars. Further, the cut from the wife to husband occurs on the first beat of the musical bar, but the cut from the husband to wife occurs on the last beat of the fifth bar. The formal rigidity of the rhythm makes viewers aware of artifice and withdraws them from too intimate a connection with the characters, so that the protagonist's death will come as a proper narrative conclusion to the film rather than as a cruel joke on them.

MONTAGE BY CONTENT: DETAIL AND METAPHOR

All the juxtapositions between shots thus far discussed have had one thing in common: visual resemblance of the images (whether composition, movement, or repetition) connected them into a unit or sequence. But there is another basis for the juxtaposition of images: their content, what their subject is, what they're about.

Juxtaposing images with related content (for example shots of factory workers and shots of smoke stacks) creates meaning as the shots accumulate. This accumulation of juxtaposed shots — for instance, a close-up of an ashtray full of cigarette butts, following a long shot of a man smoking at his desk — also helps create a sense of duration, a sense of a sequence being built up from separate images bit by bit, rather as if the images were building blocks. This sense of the montage sequence being constructed detail by detail was first articulated by the Russian filmmaker V. I. Pudovkin, who not only made films but who also wrote about film and explored film theory. Pudovkin was not in modern terms a "realistic" filmmaker (he did not think that editing should be either invisible or linked solely to notions of natural time and space), but the traditional Hollywood film nevertheless has relied heavily on his method of creating meaning through the invisible accumulation of separate images.

Suppose, for example, a filmmaker wishes to show us commuters catching a train in the morning and wants to suggest with his images that the men hurrying to work are all alike, that their lives are uniform, and that the mass rush for the train is an indication of the lack of individuality in modern life. These are *ideas* we are supposed to draw from the imagery, but ideas cannot *literally* be photographed. Of course he could *tell* us this on the sound track, or he could add titles to his picture. But if he does not want us to be aware of his presence outside the movie, and if he wants us to concentrate on and be absorbed in the story, the filmmaker will suggest these ideas to the viewer by editing together appropriate details from the scene. After establishing the context in a long shot (people appearing on the station platform), he probably will create a montage sequence out of close-ups of objects in the scene itself, and through them he will attempt to establish uniformity.

He may juxtapose many images of briefcases, newspapers (perhaps all of them the *Wall Street Journal*), similar gray flannel suits, and close-ups of faces with the same expression. These images in quantity and in juxtaposition will indicate to the audience the sameness of the commuters, yet all of these images arise naturally out of the entire scene and the context of the characters' daily life.

Is there another way to communicate the same idea? Is there another method of editing which can convey the commuters' lack of individuality? Instead of accumulating details over a period of screen time, the filmmaker could create a quick and economical visual "metaphor" — which, although it would lack realism and would probably call attention to the filmmaker and his manipulation of images, would certainly get the idea across visually. This kind of juxtaposition of images relies on linking shots in which the content is absolutely unrelated one to the other — except by an idea. An example of this editing approach — and one which brings us back to our commuters — exists in Charles Chaplin's *Modern Times* (1936). In the film we see a shot of commuters descending into a station. The next shot shows us a flock of sheep pushing each other into the depth of the frame, in the same movement seen in the previous shot. This juxtaposition of images which are completely different in photographic content and context causes us to understand the metaphor: the commuters are like those sheep, mindlessly following each other. Of course, the image of the sheep does not arise naturally from the established context; there is no flock of sheep at the station. The image springs from nowhere in the world of the film and is certainly not realistically placed, yet the juxtaposed images quickly and effectively convey the idea to the viewer.

This kind of montage was first practiced by Sergei Eisenstein, a contemporary of Pudovkin and like him both a filmmaker and a theorist. The two men were friends but disagreed strongly on editing practice. While Pudovkin believed images of the details of the narrative were building blocks whose accumulation led to meaning, Eisenstein saw images as more like Chinese or Japanese ideograms, which, by juxtaposing unrelated word pictures (such as "eye" and "water"), create a new idea and a new word (such as "crying"). Eisenstein applied this principle to cinematic images. Two images — quite unlike in content — could be juxtaposed to create a new image, an idea in the mind of the viewer. He called this collision of unrelated images **intellectual montage** (Figure 2-13). A classic example of intellectual montage is the juxtaposition of shots in Eisenstein's *Potemkin* (1925) after the sailors on the battleship open fire on the town of Odessa to retaliate for the city's massacre of those citizens who were sympathetic to the sailor's plight. A shot of the

★ **2-13** These three shots from Eisenstein's STRIKE (1924) demonstrate intellectual montage. The shot of the animal being slaughtered is inserted into the sequence of the workers being massacred by the Czar's troops. The viewer is presented with an idea: the workers are being slaughtered as if they were cattle.

battleship's cannons firing is followed by a shot of the target, cupids on a theater; in turn, that shot is cut next to a shot of a shell bursting against the gates of the theater, filling the screen with smoke. This shot is followed by a series of three separate cuts of sculptured stone lions: the first is shown at rest, the second has its head raised, and the third is upright with a snarling expression on its face. The film then cuts to another shot of the theater gates and smoke, which thins enough to show that the theater has been destroyed. What is notable here is that the stone lions have no context in the sequence; they are placed within it because they create an idea by comparing or metaphorically equating the sailors' angry fire and rebellion with the awakening of a previously passive animal and its arousal to rage. The metaphor is enriched by Eisenstein's decision to show us *stone* lions awakening. He suggests not only the ultimate kind of arousal from a state of dormancy (shots of a real lion would do that) but also that the very stones of the city are incited to sympathetic anger with the mutineers.

A visual comparison or "metaphor" to convey an idea to the viewer may, of course, be too obvious, or, on the other hand, it may be obscure and confusing. It can also be used for comic effect. In Chaplin's *The Gold Rush* (1925), the "little tramp" visually changes on screen from a man into a human-size chicken (Figure 2-14). The tramp, shuffling his feet to keep warm, seems to his starving companion to be a chicken scratching the ground; therefore, the little tramp *is* a chicken in the image. A visual metaphor is created.

Less comically but just as simply, Dziga Vertov in *The Man with a Movie Camera* creates an instant metaphor and communicates a complex idea by juxtaposing an image of an eye opening and an image of the aperture of a camera lens widening (Figure 2-15). This is the central metaphor on which he bases the entire film (and also his writings about

★ **2-14** Chaplin, like other silent film directors, resorted to literal visual imitations of verbal metaphors. When his starving partner in THE GOLD RUSH (1925) looks at Charlie strutting around the cabin and hallucinates that he is a chicken, a dissolve shows us a strutting Charlie in a chicken costume.

the "Kino-Eye"), but he also juxtaposes other images with these, for example the lifting of a retractable shop-front covering as the owner starts the business day, the opening of window shutters, and the opening of the slats of venetian blinds to let in the morning sunlight. Thus, not only does he show us metaphorically that the camera is an eye, but he also extends the metaphor so that a city, its inhabitants, and a camera all awaken to movement and the happenings of a day together.

Although this kind of intellectual montage reached its peak during the days of silent cinema and has been used to a lesser degree since, modern cinema does regularly use the juxtaposition of images to create in the viewer's mind what is not really there — photographed — on the screen. The lessons of Lev Kuleshov's editing experiments showing an expressionless face are still in use: the meaning of a shot is not necessarily inherent in the shot but in the juxtaposition of shots.

One can see this principle in action whether one looks at a film as old as Eisenstein's *Potemkin* or as young as Alfred Hitchcock's *Psycho* (1960). In the Odessa steps sequence in *Potemkin*, for example, Eisenstein juxtaposes images of boots, guns, horrified faces, and various objects, and the result is a massacre which remains violently imprinted on our minds, but which we do not really see in its entirety on the screen. In *Psycho*, Alfred Hitchcock constructed the shower murder sequence out of a montage of seventy-eight separate short shots. A close examination of the sequence reveals that the murder weapon, a knife, never touches the

115

★ **2-15** A superimposition occurs when two different shots are printed one atop the other. In THE MAN WITH A MOVIE CAMERA (1928) Dziga Vertov superimposed an eye on the camera lens to create a visual metaphor: the camera lens is an eye.

body — and that the body is not necessarily the body of the actress who plays the victim. Yet when we watch the movie, we are convinced that we have seen a violent and bloody murder.

Although this kind of editing seems especially suited to the world of movie melodrama, it is also employed in ostensibly realistic films which will occasionally juxtapose two images that reveal an idea not inherent in either of the two shots shown separately. For example, a recent partisan documentary, *Hearts and Minds* (Peter Davis, 1975), has a sequence in which a shot of General William Westmoreland glibly discussing how cheap life is to the Oriental is juxtaposed with a shot of a small Vietnamese boy crying uncontrollably at a relative's graveside. Earlier propaganda films also used this kind of montage — whether they were the product of Axis or Allied filmmakers. In the German *Triumph of the Will* (Leni Riefenstahl, 1934), shots of Hitler's airplane descending are juxtaposed with shots of majestic clouds and church spires; in the American *Why We Fight* series (Frank Capra, 1942–1945), shots of children playing in some American suburb are juxtaposed with staged shots of Japanese and German children playing with war toys.

Filmmakers eager to convey a "message," whether in a fictional or documentary film, usually employ montage more frequently than do other filmmakers. In this way, not only can they manipulate time and space through editing, they can manipulate the very content of their images and control the meanings of their films.

★★★   Meaning with Minimal Editing:
Mise-en-Scène

> The search after composition in depth is, in effect, a partial replacement of
> montage by frequent panning shots and entrances. It is based on a respect
> for the continuity of dramatic space and, of course, of its duration.
> André Bazin[3]

Mise-en-scène, a French phrase, was originally a theatrical term meaning "to put in place." (A stage director in France is called the *metteur
en scène*.) While montage achieves meaning through the relationship
between shots, the juxtaposition of separate images, mise-en-scène
achieves meaning through the relationship of things visible *within* a
single shot. The filmmaker who uses montage imposes his art on the
reality he photographs; the filmmaker who uses mise-en-scène tends to
respect reality and to preserve space and time as much as is possible.
The montage filmmaker regards photographic images as raw material
from which art is constructed; the mise-en-scène filmmaker regards
photographic images as raw material in which art is found.

Clearly, only the extreme filmmaker adopts one approach so fanati-
cally that he never uses any of the devices of the other. Most filmmakers edit and move the camera, create and record, impose meaning
and find meaning. Yet, these two poles of cinematic philosophy and
practice should be analyzed for their implications. The mise-en-scène
filmmaker minimizes editing or fragmenting a scene into separate units
because he is interested in showing reality. Thus, he tends to avoid those
cinematic devices (such as Eisenstein's stone lions that seem to rear up)
which call attention to themselves and to the film as film. Editing, one
of those devices, is not "real"; it brings form and order to that which
is formless and chaotic and spontaneous: life. On the other hand, the
montage filmmaker is not concerned with how obvious a film seems,
because his aim is not to objectively capture reality but to interpret and
subjectively express it, he is not so concerned about concealing the artistry and artifice and techniques of filmmaking. The meaning and texture of a mise-en-scène film is primarily created by context; the film
appears realistic and the filmmaker invisible. The meaning and texture
of a montage film is primarily created by frequent editing; the film appears more expressionistic and the filmmaker's presence is more obvious.

The mise-en-scène filmmaker prefers to find meaning in his shot
rather than to create it from separate shots. But how is that meaning
achieved and where is it found in any single shot? The spatial relation-

ships between people and other people, between people and objects, between objects and other objects are what conveys meaning. Thus, the composition within the mise-en-scène shot is extremely important, whether the shot is static or the subjects move or the camera moves or both subject and camera move. All of these variables can change the meaning of a single shot without the intervention of a single cut.

Consider, in Jacques Tati's *Mr. Hulot's Holiday* (1954), a comic shot in which the camera is static and the subject moves. Mr. Hulot, sitting in a canoe in the ocean, is barely discernible in long shot; we watch the canoe slowly fold up on him as the prow and stern rise from the water and close on the gentleman, quietly gulping him down. What makes the scene (of one shot) so funny is that we can see the man in relationship to his environment: he is being defeated by both the man-made contraption and the sea. Watching the action in a single take also emphasizes the inexorability of the forces marshaled against him.

Movement becomes the important element of the impressive mise-en-scène of the beginning of Orson Welles's *Touch of Evil* (1958), in which both the subject and the camera move. A three-minute shot, in which relationships between people and objects and place are constantly shifting, starts with a close-up of a time bomb planted in an automobile. The camera then introduces us to the hero and heroine, and moves above the mazelike confusion of an unknown place and the distortions of night and neon to come finally to a stop (followed by the film's first cut) as the bomb explodes and the car is consumed in flames. Besides conveying a wealth of information central to the narrative, the restless and inquisitive camera (which is constantly seeing things from new perspectives) mirrors the film's thematic emphasis on the search for concrete answers to a complex and puzzling mystery, a complex and puzzling person, the complex and puzzling issues of morality, public and private.

In order to reveal spatial relationships within the frame during the length of a shot, there must be room as well as time. In a mise-en-scène film, the ideal distance of the camera from the subject will emphasize space. Therefore, the basic unit of a mise-en-scène film is the long shot showing a figure or object and its surroundings. The close-up and even the medium shot usually exclude too much of what makes up a spatial context. In addition, in order to allow enough time for the viewer to perceive and understand the spatial relationships within the frame, the basic temporal unit of the mise-en-scène film is the **long take,** a shot lasting, say, at least several seconds. If a shot disappears too quickly from the viewer's field of vision, the shifting and changing relationships in the frame will be harder to grasp.

THE ILLUSION OF REAL SPACE:
THE LONG SHOT

The long shot, in which both subject and background context are clearly visible, accentuates the notion that the space within the frame is the same kind of space that the film viewer inhabits. The space within the frame is continuous, as it is in our daily lives, and this continuous quality is heightened and "authenticated" the longer the shot is on the screen and the more the camera follows the subjects around in it. The moving camera within the context also helps to define the space and to create depth, again qualities associated with space as we know it outside the theater. Thus, the long shot and the moving camera strengthen our belief in the reality of the actions going on within the frame.

Contrast the use of the long shot and moving camera with the shorter and more static shots in Walt Disney's animal adventure films. The frequent cuts fragment real space. Instead of a long shot showing us, within the frame, a bear chasing a raccoon, we may see in one shot the image of a bear about to attack. Then there is a direct cut to a raccoon looking startled. Then a direct cut back to the bear starting to run and a direct cut to the raccoon running. The edited sequence continues alternating between separate shots of the two animals. Although we are offered the illusion of a chase between the bear and raccoon, we know that this particular chase might never have really taken place. The running sequences could have been filmed at different times and in different places; the bear and the raccoon might have been introduced only in the cutting room.

On the other hand, if we watch *Nanook of the North* (Robert Flaherty, 1922) we see Nanook wait before a hole in the ice in which he's speared some unseen animal and we watch him move backward, pulling in his line, only to be dragged sprawling to the hole again and again until he and some Eskimos who have joined him in the shot, after what seems like an interminable struggle, finally pull in a huge seal. We know from the shot not only that we are watching a documentary, but that we are watching Nanook actually catch the seal before our eyes. Everything happens in the one frame, in the one shot, and it is evident that the editor has not manufactured the situation. (Or, rather, it *seems* evident that there was no trickery; in fact the seal hunt was staged, but the long shot makes it look thoroughly convincing.)

Even in films which make no attempt to be faithful to the usual behavior of the external world, the use of the long shot and the moving camera may make the space within that otherwise fabricated world seem real. A prime example of the creation of real space in an other-

wise unbelievable world would be one of Busby Berkeley's dance numbers. Rationally, we know that no space exists outside the film set
equivalent to the space of a production number like "Dames" in the
movie *Dames* (Ray Enright, 1934). During part of the number, girls
wearing white organdy gowns and Ruby Keeler hairdos and masks
swish their skirts and pose on a piece of 1930s architecture which looks
like a combination of stairs and treadmill. What is so surreal about the
number is not only its depiction of duplicate women by the multitude,
but also the incongruity that such an unreal subject is being photographed by a camera which moves and inhabits and *authenticates* what
should — by all rights — be an *unreal* space. We know by the camera's
creation of depth and its movement that such space existed — if only on
a movie set. But that it existed anywhere is mind-boggling and awesome.

THE ILLUSION OF REAL TIME: THE LONG TAKE

If there are no cuts in a scene, if the scene is recorded in one continuous
take and is in fact one shot of at least several seconds, then the viewer
must accept the idea that screen time and running time are the same.
Combined with the long shot, the long take creates an overpowering
sense of real time, of the viewer's witnessing a real event, the sense
that there's been no trickery. Time has not been manipulated in the
editing room. It is, like the space in a long shot through which the
camera moves, continuous, unbroken.

What also makes the long take "authentic" is that it is not inherently
dramatic; there is (as in real life) time wasted with little happening, and
when actions happen, they seem to happen spontaneously. Editing can
impose drama on actions, removing what seems dull or simply unessen-
tial. But the preservation of continuous time in the long take makes the
shot resemble time as we experience it in our daily lives. Continuous
time in film, like continuous space, authenticates the action in the
frame.

Again, the long take is chiefly associated with the documentary film.
We could look again at Nanook catching the seal in *Nanook of the
North* and appreciate the scene for its duration as we did for its distance and creation of context. A more recent example is Fredrick Wiseman's *Welfare* (1975), an almost three-hour documentary which is
based on the pain inflicted upon both the film's subjects and the film's
viewers by interminable time. One funny and moving and sad and horrible confrontation between an elderly welfare client and the building

★ **2-16** The long take, giving the sense of real time, adds a sense of reality to dance sequences. Most Ginger Rogers and Fred Astaire dances, like this one from SWING TIME (1936), were primarily filmed and presented as one continuous take, allowing the viewer to marvel at the stamina and perfection of the dancers' artistry. We would be less admiring if we thought that a two minute dance was made up of the best snippets of dozens of hours of filming.

security guard goes on for fifteen minutes or more. The two men insult each other, trade witticisms and sarcasms, affirm their isolation and yet meet on some emotional ground without even knowing it — and all in real time.

The long take, however, like the long shot, can also be used in an unreal context. The space can be faked, but the action within it can still be authenticated by duration. This authentication of an action in an unreal space is particularly important to films in which the talents of a performer are showcased. The dance sequences in a Fred Astaire and Ginger Rogers musical, for instance, must exist as much as possible in real time or the viewer has nothing to marvel at (Figure 2-16). The reality of the space that Rogers and Astaire inhabit in *Top Hat* (Mark Sandrich, 1935), for instance, is patently unreal; the cardboard and plywood bridges of its Venice bear no relationship whatsoever to the Italy where Benito Mussolini was in power. But time in the dance sequences must be real or we cannot see the talent we have come to admire. What is the magic of Astaire and Rogers? That they dance together flawlessly in time, that they defy gravity and match each other's steps in time. We would admire the dancers far less if we thought that a two-minute dance was in fact made up of the best fragments of dozens of hours of filming. Watching fine dancers in a musical film is akin to watching a long-distance race. We all can dance, we all can run — but we know that we can't dance well enough long enough without making some horrible mistake and we all can't run well enough long enough without falling down or stopping from exhaustion.

The long take may do more than authenticate reality (as in the documentary) or create a temporal reality within an unreal space (as in the performance musical). Vincente Minnelli in *Meet Me in St. Louis* (1944) projects a romantic, fluid movement and mood in the scene when Judy Garland and Tom Drake turn out the lights in the house after the party. One continuous take, the whole scene has a gentle, suspenseful quality; we wonder whether the journey through the house and the increasing darkness will end in the couple's first kiss. If this long take had been pieced out of many separate shots, the rhythm and smoothness of this almost dancelike courtship would have been greatly deemphasized.

★★★   ## Invisible Editing

> If a film is well edited, one is never aware of cutting from one shot to another.
> Reginald Mills[4]

The long shot/long take sequence employs no cuts; all the variations within the one shot are achieved through the camera. It is almost impossible, however, to make a film without editing. Even those documentaries which seem the most uncontrolled by the filmmaker, the most spontaneous, must edit each long shot/long take sequence to another long shot/long take sequence. And the narrative fiction film seems to need editing even more than does a documentary. Although there have been experiments with fiction films using minimal editing, the exception tends to prove the rule. An interesting example is *Rope* (Alfred Hitchcock, 1940), an attempt at the illusion of a one-shot film. Apart from the first shot of the film, the locale is a single apartment; the film was shot in ten-minute takes and every time the film had to be replaced, the camera would move in to focus on a dark object like a man's jacketed back so that the change of film would be masked. The viewer's eye detects no break between the takes. All the camera movements were rehearsed for days in advance of shooting and the resultant film is a feat of technical expertise that has never been matched.

Invisible editing, for the most part, means unobtrusive editing. When cuts go unnoticed by the viewer there is an illusion that the material has not been manipulated; generally, the principle behind such invisible and discreet editing is for the editor to cut on an action (for example, a person begins to turn towards a door in one shot; the next shot, taken from the doorway, catches him completing the turn), because if the viewer's eye is absorbed by the action he will not notice the movement of the cut itself. Although this kind of editing has become associated with Hollywood, it is probably accurate to say that today the vast majority of narrative films — no matter where they are made — are edited this way.

This kind of invisible editing is, in fact, not so much unseen as disregarded. We have seen so many films use these devices, always for the same purpose, that we don't notice them any longer. When, for example, we see a close-up of a character's face looking offscreen and there is a cut to a landscape, we instantly know from past movie experience that the particular editing sequence means that the character is looking at the landscape. We read this meaning into the juxtaposition so unconsciously that we are not even aware that the two shots have been edited together.

Other similar conventions which, by now, have created their own invisibility because they have been widely used, are the editing patterns based on the establishing shot, the medium shot, and the close-up. Usually a filmmaker shoots what is called a **master shot,** a long shot that contains the entire dramatic action of the scene. This is not what the audience will usually see on the screen in the finished film. We may see part of the master shot (called an establishing shot in the finished film because it places the characters and the action in a context) — but inserted or edited into this master shot are various medium shots and close-ups. In the finished film, for example, we may see a long shot of a wagon train wending its way, slowly and painfully, across a desert. Intercut with our view of the whole may be a medium shot of a particular wagon and a close-up of a particular face or a particular wagon wheel. The filmmaker will shoot these insert shots after he has shot the master shot. In the editing process, these insert shots and the master must be put together to convey some dramatic emphasis or emotional nuance. Our response to all this editing, however, is likely to be unconscious and the editing process is likely to seem invisible.

Invisible editing, then, creates dramatic or internal realism: what we are watching is happening uninterrupted by *obvious* references to the presence of the camera and the participation of a godlike editor, manipulating pieces of film. Since the obvious juxtaposition or contrast of images is an artistic effort which calls attention to itself, filmmakers who wish to achieve a realistic rather than an obviously artistic effect tend to emphasize the narrative and action either by simply understood editing conventions or by using as little editing as possible. They authenticate the space and time of their cinematic worlds chiefly by using the long shot and the long take and/or invisible editing.

Editing — how the bits and pieces of a film are put together — always conveys some kind of information about the film and its intent. If it is natural and unobtrusive, it tells us to watch the other filmic elements, to watch the plot unfold, to find significance in the dialogue, to notice the lighting and the composition; these are the main carriers of meaning. If, on the other hand, the editing calls attention to itself, it has something particular to announce: these images juxtaposed in this particular way have a special relationship to each other, are saying something important.

We have been discussing editing in a fairly narrow way, specifically defining it here as the ways in which pieces of film — images — can be joined together and to what effect. These images can be joined in the laboratory (with dissolves and fades), found and joined by the camera within one shot (mise-en-scène), or spliced together on an editing table (montage). Speaking broadly now, we can say that editing is the creator of *all* the relationships in a film; it is the relationship of what we see to what we see, of what we hear to what we hear, and, finally, of what we hear to what we see. Editing shapes the whole film, generating meaning from the relationship of all of the parts.

NOTES

[1] "The Vertov Papers," translated by Marco Carynnyk, *Film Comment* 8, no. 1 (Spring 1972): 48.

[2] *Film Form* (New York: Meridian Books, 1957), p. 37.

[3] *What Is Cinema?* (Berkeley, University of California Press, 1967), p. 34.

[4] "Film Editors Forum," *Film Comment* 13, no. 2 (March–April, 1977): 24.

Historical Overview: The Development of Sound

SOUND AND THE SILENT FILM

The first motion picture audiences were fascinated less by little stories or fantasies than they were by images of real life, captured and moving before them on the screen. Therefore, it is in some ways natural that from its very beginnings, the moving photographic image has been in search of the accompanying realism of sound. The two major problems which had to be solved before sound film could be produced were those connected with **synchronization** and amplification; yet even at the birth of the motion picture, sound was in attendance.

When William Dickson first demonstrated his moving-picture machine to Thomas Edison in 1889, he also played a phonograph cylinder of his own voice which roughly matched the film's flickering images. By 1894, Edison had issued a number of short films with accompanying phonograph cylinders for the home market, but these cylinders were more a curiosity than a commercial success. Thus, Edison's Kinetoscope went into peep-show parlors as a silent entertainment. However, after projection of the filmed image became standard practice, several French companies matched their films with voice recordings on cylinders and discs. Although these worked fairly well in a very small hall, the fidelity was poor and the volume extremely low. As the popularity of the cinema grew, and theaters became larger and larger, discs and cylinders were abandoned because there was no way of amplifying the recorded sound.

By 1900, live musical accompaniment had become the aural mainstay of the silent cinema. As anyone who has sat through an otherwise totally silent movie screening can attest, something is needed to camouflage the sounds of the projector (which, in the early days of cinema, was frequently in the same room

125

as the audience rather than in a separate projection booth) and to muffle the noises of the audience itself. The very first public screenings of the Lumière brothers' films in 1895 used piano accompaniment, and it was soon discovered that music could actually enhance the viewing experience. Music — loud or soft, lively or mournful — accompanied the images and the story much as it does today. It added emotional undertones to the scenes on the screen, it cued the audience and moved them transitionally from one scene to another, and it provided sound effects.

Thus, nearly every picture house or "palace" had live music of one sort or another ranging from a rickety upright piano to a full-size symphony orchestra. In France, one of the first original musical scores was written for a film (Le Film d'Art's *L'Assassinat du Duc de Guise*) in 1908 by the famous composer Camille Saint-Saëns. In America, as early as 1909, the Edison Company distributed a guide for instrumental accompanists called "Suggestions for Music." This practice gave rise to the creation and development of **cue sheets** indicating where in a given film certain kinds of music creating certain kinds of rhythms and moods might be played, and recommending certain pieces which the accompanist might choose to follow. With the longer and more prestigious films, the musical accompaniment became more elaborate. Following European example, in 1915 D. W. Griffith commissioned and co-wrote with Joseph Briel a compilation of symphonic themes for his epic *The Birth of a Nation*; the music was arranged for a seventy-piece orchestra, and when the film opened in the larger cities such was the accompaniment. Throughout the silent period, film studios supplied musical scores and cue sheets for their movies, which local musicians could follow.

Sometimes the orchestra supplied sound effects as well as music, with most of the responsibility falling on the shoulders of the percussionist, whose array of noisemaking instruments became larger and larger. Larger picture palaces added thunder sheets (metal sheets which could be rattled) and an assortment of other sound effects devices placed behind the screen; there, the sound effects personnel would watch for various signals to cue them into the noisy activity of supplying the footsteps, doors closing, telephones ringing, and dogs barking that would enhance the realism of the film viewed by the audience out front. Even smaller theaters could provide a clanging, buzzing, trilling aural experience for their patrons with the Mighty Wurlitzer theatrical organ, which could duplicate a host of nonmusical sounds through its intricate series of pipes and air-operated percussion devices.

The human voice was not forgotten either. Many nickelodeons in large cities employed a person (*der Spieler*) who would read the titles out loud for the immigrants in the audience who were unable to read English. Sometimes the reader would provide a continuous narration to help make the story more comprehensible. And occasionally actors would be hired to stand behind the screen and speak the dialogue for the characters seen on the screen by the audience. But all of these attempts to add the human voice to the moving picture image were too unwieldy and impractical to become successful, and by the time of World War I audiences and filmmakers had arrived at a mutually understood set of visual conventions to make up for the absence of spoken dialogue. What sometimes appears to us as bizarrely exaggerated dramatic performances in silent films is, in fact, a kind of visual code which audiences of the time understood and responded to. Some audience members also became adept at lip-reading, so much so that film stars had to watch their language and say lines appropriate to their film characterizations.

EARLY INVENTION

Progress towards the sound cinema such as we know it today began with the invention of a device which solved the problem of amplifying recorded sound. No matter whether the sound is recorded on a cylinder or disc or on the film itself, if it cannot be heard by a theaterful of people it can hardly be considered part of a film. Therefore, Dr. Lee De Forest's invention of the selenium audion tube was as crucial to the development of sound cinema as it was to the development of the radio. De Forest's invention was patented in 1907, but the possibilities of the application of the audion tube to sound film went unappreciated for twenty years. Although various crude methods of synchronizing **sound-on-disc** with images on film had been demonstrated and exhibited sporadically since 1889 (and with some success in recording musical scores, which need not be finely synchronized with the images), the emergent film industry did little to link De Forest's solution to the problems of amplification with a sound-on-disc process.

Sound cinema might, then, have been a commercial reality as early as the first decade of the twentieth century. But neither the country nor the film industry was ready for anything so novel. When an occasional exhibitor demonstrated sound-on-disc musical accompaniment to motion pictures, audiences felt shortchanged; they felt that they were being given music secondhand, rather than live and performed expressly for them as they watched the film. The industry, too, was not highly receptive to the idea of sound film. First of all, any conversion to sound would cost a great deal of money. The early moguls in the business would not only have to convert their production equipment, but would also have to pay to convert their movie houses to accommodate sound films. There was little incentive for the major figures in the industry to embrace the possibilities of sound; after the First World War, movie patronage was booming and profits were large, and sound — untried, technically tricky, and expensive — seemed an irrelevant novelty.

Not until the film industry felt the competition of home entertainment produced by the radio and the phonograph did it feel pressed to develop the
sound film.

By the end of World War I, in Germany Josef Engle, Joseph Massole, and
Hans Vogt discovered a method of recording sound directly onto film. Their
"Tri-Ergon" **sound-on-film** process was based on the principle of the oscillo-
scope, which turns sound into light impulses. These light impulses could
then be recorded on the film **emulsion,** after which the light was converted
back into sound by a device which "read" the light images as they passed
through the projector. After the war, De Forest also invented a process based
on the same principles. He developed a photoelectric cell which could
translate sound into light. The light was then photographed as a series of
bars of varying shades of gray and black on the celluloid. By placing this
pattern of bars on a thin strip next to the film's sprocket holes, image and
sound could be locked into one synchronized unit. Thus, both the Tri-Ergon
process and De Forest's "Phonofilm" process eliminated the problems inherent in synchronizing two separate machines — a projector for the film and
a phonograph for the sound.

By 1923 De Forest was exhibiting short subjects in his Phonofilm process
at various theaters around the country. But these song and dance numbers
by vaudeville stars (including Eddie Cantor) were treated simply as a novelty.
For the reasons previously mentioned, Hollywood was loath to rush into
sound filmmaking and exhibition, although they did supply a few sound-on-
disc short subjects to those theaters which had the facilities necessary. Finally,
in 1925, Bell Laboratories (Western Electric) perfected a special turntable
for 17-inch discs, discs large enough to hold sound for an entire reel of
projected film. They called the system "Vitaphone" and attempted with little
success to interest various large, successful film studios in buying it. But
Warner Brothers — new, little, and aggressive — gambled on Vitaphone;
unlike their more successful and complacent competition, Warner's had nothing to lose. They purchased the rights to the system and kept the name
Vitaphone.

In August of 1926, Warner's released a program of various sound shorts
which used the new sound-on-disc process. Also included was the first
sound-on-disc feature, *Don Juan* starring John Barrymore, with a synchronized
musical score. Audience response, though favorable, was neither ecstatic
nor indicative of the effect the Vitaphone process would have on the entire
film industry the following year when Warner's released *The Jazz Singer*
(Alan Crosland), starring Al Jolson (Figure 1). Perhaps Jolson's personality
captured the imagination of the public, or perhaps it was the *songs,* a change
from mere accompaniment; there were, in addition, a few words spoken by
a performer on the screen. Whatever the reasons, when *The Jazz Singer*

★ 1 Al Jolson in THE JAZZ SINGER (Alan Crosland, 1927). This film opened on Broadway in October 1927. Though sound had been technically possible from the beginning of the decade, the box-office success of the film made Hollywood invest in "talking pictures."

opened on Broadway, October 6, 1927, it immediately captured the fancy of the moviegoing public. This "first" sound feature was not in sound except for four singing or talking sequences; the rest of the film depended on titles. But because of the enormous impact this film had on the history and production of film, *The Jazz Singer* might as well have been the first sound feature (*Don Juan* was) or the first "all-sound" feature, which in fact was the unmemorable *The Lights of New York*, released in 1928 by Warner's as a follow-up to *The Jazz Singer*.

THE MOVIES TALK

The Jazz Singer moved Warner Brothers ahead of its competitors, who quickly followed the leader by rushing into sound production. Unreleased films which were essentially silents, either completed or currently in production, were hastily altered by adding sound segments. Within a year nearly every film "talked" to audiences in those theaters that were equipped to hear them, while silent versions of the same films were distributed to theaters which had not yet converted to sound.

129

★ **2** At first, sound recording techniques required that the camera be placed in a soundproof booth (the large box in the right middle background), thus making camera movement virtually impossible. (Notice the large microphones hanging from the ceiling in the background.)

Early in 1927, William Fox of the Fox Film Corporation (eventually to become 20th Century Fox) purchased the rights to the German sound-on-film Tri-Ergon system and then added to the system the process developed or "borrowed" by Theodore Case, a former associate of De Forest's. Thus in 1927, the year *The Jazz Singer,* the Vitaphone sound-on-disc film, was released, William Fox released the first largely distributed sound-on-film newsreel. 1927 also saw the inauguration of the popular Fox Movietone News series which, using the Fox-Case process, played to packed houses with its synchronized pictures and sounds of Charles Lindbergh's triumphal return to America after his transatlantic solo flight in May of that year. The sound newsreel became a fixture in movie houses for many years — until television in the 1950s made theatrical filmed news out of date before it could reach the theaters for exhibition. The following year, 1928, brought the public the first sound cartoon, Walt Disney's *Steamboat Willie,* in which an imaginative mouse makes musical instruments out of various farm animals. During the next several years, sound-on-film systems appeared all over the world and competed with the sound-on-disc system, and by 1930 the practicality of the sound-on-film system had won out and the Vitaphone disc system was retired.

The new technological miracle of sound film, though appreciated by filmgoers who started pouring back into the theaters to see anything that "talked," caused a great many headaches for the filmmakers. To record the sound and the image at the same time, even though they were recorded on separate machinery, the camera had to be placed in a soundproof booth so that its noise could not be picked up by the unselective microphones. And, since the studios wanted all-talking films (since they presumed that was what the public wanted), the flexible and dynamic moving camera so brilliantly developed in the silent era had to be immobilized. The camera remained stationary because it was too bulky to move in its housing, and static medium shots became the standard for films in which the performers simply talked and talked and talked. The filmmaker's composition of his shots was also greatly affected. Actors could not move about the set because of the position of the microphone; like the camera, they were immobilized, generally forming close groupings so all could be heard (Figure 2) .

Critics and film artists, regarding sound as an enemy of art and the imagination from which it sprang, announced the death of the cinema. Sound not only immobilized the camera, but also fostered a literalism that seemed to destroy all the poetry and nuance of the silent cinema. In Russia, three leading filmmakers, Eisenstein, Pudovkin, and Alexandrov, published an apprehensive and cautionary "Joint Statement on Sound Film." In their statement they deplored the consequences of sound's being used unimaginatively as a mere accompaniment to moving lips and suggested that the future of the sound film lay in its attempts to create aural **counterpoint** to the visual image.

Such critical concern was prompted by the talkiness and the static quality of films made during the first two or so years after sound was introduced. But as early as 1929, the more creative filmmakers began to experiment with ways of overcoming the limitations sound had placed upon them. In Hollywood, a number of fine filmmakers developed what were to become standard techniques of sound cinema in an attempt to realize their films visually as well as aurally. Rouben Mamoulian, for instance, used two microphones for a single scene so that his performers could stay at the dramatically proper distance from each other rather than having to huddle together inappropriately so both would be audible to the traditional single mike. Thus, his *Applause* (1929) instituted the use of **multiple-channel** sound recording and of **soundmixing,** the latter a process whereby multiple recorded tracks are balanced with each other to finally form a single and selective sound track. Mamoulian also shot a great deal of the film silently so that the camera could again move; the sound was added afterwards through the process which is called dubbing or **postsynchronization.** Ernst Lubitsch, a director who had made a reputation in the silent cinema for his sophisticated comedies, also added sound to many scenes in his *The Love Parade* (1929) *after* they had been shot. Lubitsch was particularly creative in his imaginative use of silence and in his ability to create an integrated and rhythmic balance of sound and image in his films. Again recording the sound after the image was shot, King Vidor created wonderful atmospheric effects with selective sound effects in his *Hallelujah!* (1929); to a chase sequence in which a character runs through a menacing swamp, Vidor added postsynchronous bird cries, panting, the sound of twigs underfoot not only to create realism but also to heighten the suspense. Abroad, other filmmakers were also learning how sound could be manipulated artistically. In Great Britain, Alfred Hitchcock used a subjective sound track in *Blackmail* (1929), which was added to what had been shot as a silent movie; words which have special significance to the heroine are amplified and reverberate according to their emotional importance. And in France, director René Clair, at first an outspoken opponent of sound films, used the new element unrealistically to create humor and irony in *Sous les Toits de Paris* (1929). The experimentation and success of these innovative filmmakers set the standard for what could be achieved by adding sound not at the time of shooting, but afterwards through dubbing and postsynchronization.

Although by 1931 techniques which could suppress track **noise** were developed, making feasible the dubbing of dialogue, postsynchronizing dialogue was a great deal more difficult than postsynchronizing music and sound effects. The sound Moviola editing machine perfected in that same year, however, facilitated the matching of sound and picture. And by 1933, the mechanics of mixing multiple postrecorded sound tracks without any loss of quality had been refined enough to allow filmmakers to use an amalgam of simultaneous sounds in their films. Thus, after 1933 continuous background music became common because the quality of the several combined tracks — music, dialogue, sound effects — could be selectively controlled. By the midthirties, meaningful and expressive sound on film was also common.

Sound film brought about the end of the silent cinema. And those who mourned the passing of the silent movie had some just cause — even after creative filmmakers demonstrated that sound could be used artistically. The silent film had created an international language; it was a form of communication which was able to speak to everyone, albeit silently. Once the movies could talk, the cinema became less international and more dependent upon language and those processes still used today to effect a translation: dubbing and **subtitling.** Yet, if the sound film was responsible for the death of silent cinema, it was also responsible for the birth of several new film genres, notably the musical and the gangster film. Without sound, there could hardly be a musical film. And though films about crooks had been made since the earliest days of filmmaking, the rise of the gangster film owed as much to sound as it did to the newspaper headlines of the day. The aural effects of machine guns, screeching tires, and slangy dialogue provided the genre with an immediacy and excitement the silent film lacked. Another change that sound caused in the thirties was in the comedy film. Before the sound film, comedy was physical, visual, the great comic artists like Chaplin and Keaton using their bodies and screen space to make people laugh. Sound changed the emphasis from physical to verbal humor; although physical comedy remained, it was integrated with verbal comedy, and the combination gave rise to different sorts of comic stars like the Marx Brothers.

Sound has become the norm in cinema. Silent films are generally thought of as primitive or experimental. Most all of the basic sound hardware used today has been available since the mid-thirties, which already seems like a very long time ago. The only fairly recent technical additions to the sound process are **stereophonic sound,** developed in 1952 to accompany Cinerama's wide screen, lightweight and portable **magnetic tape** recorders, more sensitive and selective microphones and mixing equipment, and — most recently — **flatbed editors,** TV tape transfer editing systems, and the **Dolby stereophonic sound system.** Among them, Dolby sound is perhaps the most important, for it has made multiple-channel sound film nearly as inexpensive to produce and exhibit as standard optical sound film. How these new developments in sound recording, editing, and projection will affect the artistic use of sound in films is not yet entirely clear, although both the expressive and the realistic possibilities of multiple-track stereophonic sound systems are already beginning to be exploited.

3
★ *SOUND IN
THE CINEMA*

Movies have always been heard as well as seen. After their initial
demonstration, even those films we refer to as silent were projected
commercially along with some sort of sound, usually live musical accompaniment. Nevertheless, something was still missing. Those images
which appeared so lifelike on the screen were mute. People moved their
lips and "spoke," dogs "barked," doors "slammed," telephones "rang,"
but these screen images of people, animals, and objects were themselves
silent. Music and sound effects might well up from a Wurlitzer organ,
a pit orchestra, or a lone piano, in an attempt to cover the silence, but
such sound — no matter how effective — was separate from the film
and from the artistic control of the filmmaker. And though the film's
title cards were under the control of the filmmaker and actually *in* the
movie, titles tended to break up the flow of images. The sound film
changed all this.

The process of creating a rich, complex, and meaningful sound track
is as complicated as creating rich, complex, and effective images. The
artistic choices are many, and the technology to achieve a desired effect
is readily available. Each filmmaker must decide whether to use performers whose voices are as suitable to their characters as are their
physical characteristics, or whether to **dub** in voices of other actors with
more suitable voices. He must also decide what sort of background
sounds and special effects are desirable. And he must choose the kind
of music suitable to his film, and decide how much of it to use and
where to use it. Finally, he must consider the possibility of using silence

expressively. All these sounds must then be recorded successfully, and the various sound tracks must be mixed and balanced with the necessary emphasis in order to produce the desired effect. In short, sound in the cinema is never something that is simply there as it is in real life. Rather, it is yet another element which must be worked with and controlled to create an imaginative cinematic work.

Dialogue, narration, sound effects and music are the sounds of cinema. Chapter 3 will investigate and examine both the physical process and the artistic potential of sound in the cinema.

★★★ **The Process**

> We used an 8-track system and it's really unmixing rather than mixing sound. We'd just put microphones on all the principals and hang them out the window and stick them in the clock and under the doorbell and wherever we want a live sound. And they all go down on different tracks, pretty much the way music is done today. And in our musical sequences we had an additional 16 tracks. We didn't have to come back later and put in dead sound effects.
>
> Robert Altman[1]

The early attempt to synchronize moving images with sounds recorded on large phonograph discs presented problems: if there was a break in the film and a few frames were lost, there was no way to make a corresponding correction on the disc; one could only add a few black frames to the film. The ideal solution to the problems of synchronization was to put the sounds on the film itself — so that if a splice became necessary, only a small portion of the sound track would be lost and the remainder of the reel would still be in perfect synchronization. After a few years in which both systems competed, the sound-on-film or **optical sound** system became standard. Today, sound may be recorded on tape (**magnetic sound**), but in most theatrical release prints the final composite sound track is optical. In the optical system, the desired sound — dialogue, background noise, or music — is captured by a microphone and converted into electrical impulses, which in turn are changed into light impulses. These impulses of light are then photographed on film similar to that used to photograph the image. Eventually, in the final print of the film, these impulses appear in the narrow space between the frames which hold the images and the **sprocket holes** which control the film's progress through the projector. During the projection process, this optical sound track runs past a light bulb (the sound reader) and the process is reversed: the light impulses are converted back into electrical impulses, which are then converted into the sounds we hear coming from the speaker. Thus, each sound projector has two light bulbs — one to project the visual image onto the screen and one to "read" the sound track. The most recent technological development replaces this optical sound track with a magnetic strip upon which the sounds have been recorded.

Though simple in concept, the recording of the sounds we finally hear in a released movie is a complex process. **Synchronous sound** is the sound in a film which is synchronized or matched to an onscreen source — an actor's lips, an axe chopping wood, a musician playing an instrument. (It may have been recorded after the image, but it nevertheless is called synchronous sound if the viewer perceives it as matched to the image.) **Asynchronous sound** is the sound in a film which is not synchronized or matched to any source visible onscreen at the moment — the sound of wind and waves when the image is of the interior of a ship's cabin, background music when no instruments are visible, any voice speaking when the lips are not clearly visible in the image, the sound of footsteps when the image shows only the upper body of the actor.

Although sound which is synchronous in the finished film can be recorded at the same time the image is being photographed (the sound recorder and the camera are electronically "in sync," running at the same speed), it can also be recorded **wild** (with a sound recorder alone) and then synchronized with the appropriate image. Sounds which are recorded wild and then dubbed in can vary from orchestral background music to lines of dialogue which actors have fluffed at the original shooting, from the sound of waves to the computer talk of a robot. And any of these sounds, whether recorded in sync or not, may be used as either asynchronous or synchronous sound in the final print. For instance dialogue which appears in sync in one scene in a film may be repeated on the sound track in a later scene in which the character may be "remembering" what was said earlier: the second use of the dialogue would be asynchronous.

The **sound mixer** works with a multitude of sound tracks — tracks of dialogue, tracks of natural and synthetically-created sound effects, tracks of the music selected for the finished film, tracks of the **narration,** if any — and it is his job to blend those tracks together at the right volume and with the right emphasis, thereby creating a unified sound track (composed of many different sounds) which is appropriate to what the film is trying to communicate.

★★★   The Human Voice

> Relatively few movie patrons become analytical enough to be aware of
> the voice as an independent medium of artistic illusion on the screen.
> Parker Tyler[2]

The storytelling arts have traditionally depended on words. Painting,
music, and dance can tell stories also, but their storytelling ability is
limited to simple narrative, high in emotional intensity but low in communicating cause and effect. Words are the most explicit, specific, and
commonly understood means of telling a story.

Even in its silent infancy, the motion picture needed words to exploit
its narrative capacities fully, to satisfy completely the demands of the
stories it wished to relate. Title cards supplied those words. But title
cards were no substitute for human **dialogue.** They interrupted the
rhythms of a film, stopping the action. If few cards were used in an
effort to maintain the film's visual rhythms and momentum, the film
might sacrifice complexity. If many cards were used, the film often became dull and inert when rhythm and momentum were sacrificed to a
complexity which was never animated by the visual images. It is true,
however, that certain films by gifted directors avoided excessive dialogue titles without sacrificing meaning and complexity. F. W. Murnau's
The Last Laugh (1924) had only one title, but it was able to tell the
story of its central character visually and to tell it well with the use of
a few verbal devices like writing on a wedding cake and a newspaper.

Generally speaking, however, as the cinema became an art form
which told stories and in which the interaction of human characters
dominated those stories, there was a need for some way of delivering
the voices of the actors to the audience. Although the silent cinema provided its audiences with music and sound effects of some sort, the means
by which some theaters attempted to provide human dialogue simultaneously with images were both ingenious and sadly ineffective; live
performers standing behind the screen were an unwieldy substitute for
the voices of the photographed personalities. But when synchronized
sound communicating the voice of the actor on the screen finally became a commercial reality in 1927, the movies were no longer silent and
title cards were replaced by spoken dialogue.

DIALOGUE

Dialogue can appear and function in all sorts of films: story films, documentaries, some experimental films, animated films. In most cases, dia-

★ **3-1** The characterization represented by the dialogue in a film and the voice and physical presence of the actor playing the part seem to merge, to become one. We may know somewhere in our minds that Al Pacino and John Cazale were speaking dialogue written for them by a screenwriter (Frank Pierson) in DOG DAY AFTERNOON (Sidney Lumet, 1975), but it is difficult to separate the actor from the character during the performance.

logue physically authenticates the speaker as an individual (whether human or cartoon animal) and continues to do so whenever we see that individual in the frame move his lips. Dialogue tends to confirm the audience's assumption that the image projected on the screen is that of a real person and not simply a character, an imaginary creation of the storyteller. Curiously enough, this confirmation of a character's reality works in animated films as well as live-action ones. For example, the voice of Bugs Bunny sounds the same each time we hear it, and each time we see the animated rabbit supposedly speaking, we hear the same accent, the same nuances of phrasing; indeed, we would easily be able to identify the voice as that of Bugs Bunny without its accompanying image. We may know from a cartoon's credits that Jim Backus is the actor responsible for the voice of Mr. Magoo, but when someone does an imitation of Backus's voice, everyone identifies the voice as belonging not to Jim Backus but to the cartoon figure of an impossibly nearsighted gentleman.

Although there are similarities, dialogue in the cinema is not the same as dialogue in drama. Dialogue in drama is the words that actors will say when they perform the play (this definition of dialogue also

applies to a film **script**), but it is also the words a reader may read un-
performed, without an actor present. Dialogue in the cinema, however,
is the words spoken by a particular human voice; it is both the words
and the voice speaking the words. Dialogue in drama can be interpreted
and reinterpreted with each performance of the play. Dialogue in cinema is what it is when we hear it; a subsequent viewing of the film will
reveal the same reading and interpretation of the words. Because the
words and the performer who speaks them are less obviously separable
in films than they are in theater (Citizen Kane is only Orson Welles, but
Hamlet is innumerable actors from Shakespeare's day to our own),
often the characterization represented by the dialogue in a film and the
human voice and physical person of the screen actor playing that character seem to merge, to become one. As far as the audience is concerned, there is little or no difference between the performance and the
performer, between the character and the actor (Figure 3-1). Sam Spade
sounds like and speaks like Humphrey Bogart; Humphrey Bogart sounds
like and speaks like Sam Spade.

In addition to establishing the speaker as unique, the dialogue in a
film will do what it has done in drama for centuries. It will tell what
must be told and provide the characters with a way of expressing their
motivations, past experiences, feelings, attitudes, philosophical ques-
tionings. For this reason, even if for no other, dialogue must be clearly
recorded so that the audience will be able to follow what is going on in
the character and in the film.

Dialogue which will appear in sync with an image of the actor's
lips is usually recorded at the same time that the image of the actor is
being recorded by the camera. This is the easiest way of assuring that
the words and lips are synchronized. But lines of dialogue which do not
have to be in sync (the actor is out of the frame, or is in long shot so
that we can hardly see his lips, or he is not facing the camera or not
moving his lips because the lines of dialogue represent internal thoughts)
can be recorded after the images are recorded. With sophisticated equipment, dubbing of actors' voices can be perfectly synchronized. Such
dubbing may be necessary because of a bad sound recording made while
the film was being shot or because the director wishes the actor to
change the reading of a particular line of dialogue or wants to add
something which wasn't there in the first place. Nonsinging performers,
for example, have often had a singer's voice dubbed in when the film
demands a song. And television's "moral code," which is a great deal
stricter than the cinema's, has frequently required the doctoring of a
movie's sound track to eliminate objectionable language. Modern methods of dubbing can easily alter Jack Nicholson's four-letter words in

The Last Detail (Hal Ashby, 1974) to more acceptable euphemisms like "damn," "crud," or "hell," and the resulting sound track will still give the impression that he is indeed saying the less objectionable words.

Most of the time, viewers hardly think about such postsynchronous sound — except, perhaps, in the case of television bowdlerization of a movie they have previously seen. But one kind of dubbing presents more obvious and difficult problems for both the editor and the audience: the dubbing in of one language for another. Shortly after World War II, in an effort to keep down production costs, the Italian film industry pioneered in dubbing entire films; today, they and other European countries are equipped to dub a film into any one of a dozen languages so that the completed film will have a broad market. This kind of dubbing also allows a film's director to cast performers who may not even be able to communicate with each other in the same language. The results of such dubbing are not always of the highest order; it is almost impossible to achieve absolutely perfect lip-sync from one language to another, and often the performer doing the dubbing for the actor on the screen is not able to give a performance equal in artistry to the original. These problems and the distractions they cause arise when any foreign film is dubbed into English. On the other hand, the only alternative — English-language subtitles — also causes problems and distractions. Subtitling clutters up the image, causes the viewer to do more reading than viewing, and often fails to translate adequately and communicate the complexity of the original dialogue; we obviously hear a lot more in a second than we could possibly read. Viewers who are irritated by out-of-sync lip movement and dialogue will usually prefer subtitled versions of foreign films; those who feel the subtitles interfere with the visual experience of a film will usually prefer dubbed versions. Many films are available both ways — *Story of O, Z,* Fellini's *8½,* Visconti's *The Innocent,* to name only a few — and sometimes both versions will play in the same city, particularly in larger metropolitan areas, giving the viewer a choice.

The decision to see a dubbed or subtitled foreign film becomes even more complex if one realizes that the original language in which a film was made is an element of locale, emphasizing the atmosphere of the region in which the film takes place or emphasizing the rhythms of a particular culture. Italian and German do not sound alike; their cadences are strikingly different. Actually *hearing* the differences in language helps the viewer to locate the film physically and to place it culturally and emotionally.

The notion that the sound of a voice can do more than merely relate the meanings of words spoken by characters visible on the screen can be extended to English-language pictures also. Certainly, the meanings of words are crucial to any film, for certain abstractions and ideas (like love, honor, and duty) are impossible to photograph. Very often characters in films will tell us the meaning of events in their lives. But, again, it is important to remember that dialogue is not the words alone; it is also the *sound* of those words being spoken. The very texture of a performer's voice also supplies a certain element of character, as much a part of the performance as is the actor's physiognomy, stance, gesture. All of the great film stars of the past (and to a lesser degree, of the present) had such distinctive voices that they could be and still are easily caricatured. The sincere and somewhat garbled drawl of Jimmy Stewart, the smooth, brusque and well-oiled voice of Clark Gable, the sinister and reverberant quasi-lisp of Boris Karloff, the clipped, impatient, and slightly grating voice of Bette Davis — all were as much a part of these performers' screen personae as the lines they had to say.

Finally, the viewer has to evaluate a film's dialogue not only in relation to the meaning of the words, but also in relation to how much dialogue there is in the film and how it is used. There is a great deal of dialogue in Howard Hawks's *Bringing Up Baby* (1938), for example, but because it is delivered at breakneck speed one doesn't feel the film is "talky." The breathless and seemingly incessant chattering of Katherine Hepburn's portrayal of a daffy yet shrewd socialite comically wears down the audience as much as it wears down Cary Grant's eventually exhausted paleontologist. Stanley Kubrick's *2001: A Space Odyssey* (1968) runs for 138 minutes, yet there are only 43 minutes of dialogue in it and that dialogue is incredibly banal. The banality of the dialogue, however, always seems to come as a bit of a shock, for the long periods of verbal silence in the movie lead the viewer to expect that if someone opens his mouth to speak, what will be said will be important. Instead, the dialogue is intentionally insignificant. It is Kubrick's way of pointing out the inadequacy of man's responses to the exquisitely specific and complex technology man has developed and to the visual beauties of the universe around him. This way in which dialogue functions in a film is as important as the overt content of what it says.

NARRATION

Narration in film is the words spoken by a human voice, addressed to the audience, but not heard by the subjects of the film. Most often, narration is asynchronous, that is, the speaker is not seen on the screen addressing the audience as he speaks. Thus, narration is also referred

★ **3-2** During this shot from TOM JONES (Tony Richardson, 1963), we do not hear the voices of the performers we see. Rather, we hear an omniscient narrator who is never seen. The narrator comments on the action and the characters with an amused, slightly condescending tone of voice, which creates a conspiracy between audience and narrator. This allows the audience to distance itself from the follies and foibles of the orphan, first found in Squire Allworthy's bed.

to as **voice-over,** particularly when it is used in documentary, news, and commercials. Although most viewers tend to associate narration with the documentary or non-story film, narration is used widely in all kinds of film and for all kinds of purposes.

In *Tom Jones* (Tony Richardson, 1963), for example, an omniscient narrator — who is never seen and who takes no part in the action — speaks to the audience and comments on the action and characters with an amused, slightly condescending vocabulary and tone of voice; indeed, he functions like the authorial voice in the Henry Fielding novel from which the film was adapted, a voice which creates a conspiracy of intelligence and superiority between the narrator and the audience (Figure 3-2). Like the storyteller who begins "Once upon a time . . ." the narrator leads us through the story as an ally and friend, and also as a presence who exists in our present temporal frame of reference. A film which is narrated is a film in which *past* events are being recalled or structured; the narrator already knows how the story turned out, how the documentary will make its point. It is no accident that a film's narrator almost never speaks in present tense.

In fact, because a narrator *now* is telling us what happened *then,* many films structured around flashbacks use narration. In these instances, the narrator *is* a character in the film but a character who has already experienced what we are about to see; the entire film is there-

★ **3-3** Narrators are often found in films which are told in flashbacks. One
of the strangest examples is SUNSET BOULEVARD (Billy Wilder, 1950)
in which the narrator of the story is found dead at the beginning (we see his
body floating in a pool). Nevertheless, he narrates the story as the rest of
the film brings the action up to the moment where his body is fished out
of the pool by the police.

fore the means of bringing the viewer through time past into the character's present. In *Great Expectations* (David Lean, 1947), the central
character Pip speaks to us about his childhood from his present vantage
point as an adult. In *Murder, My Sweet* (Edward Dmytryk, 1944), we
are at least aware that the detective Philip Marlowe has survived the
events we are about to see. But in an ironic and impossible reversal of
that surety, the narrator of *Sunset Boulevard* (Billy Wilder, 1950) is
dead from the film's beginning — since we see him shot *before* he
brings us up to the present and the flashback ends (Figure 3-3).

Besides providing a tidy flashback structure for the story film, narration by one of its characters also reveals that character to the viewer.

In *Badlands* (Terence Malick, 1974), Holly — the narrator — tells us as much about herself as she does about the events we witness in this film of two teenagers who in the 1950s go on a killing spree for no particular reason. Her language is so artificial and unoriginal that the sadness and smallness of her aspirations are revealed when she says to us: "Little did I realize that . . . ." When she tells us how her boyfriend murdered her father, her tone is as unemotional as it is when she talks about her life in high school or the lovers' drive through the Dakota Badlands. And she also reveals a chilling and quiet aberration by what she chooses to emphasize as important and what she chooses not to mention at all as we hear her voice comment on events which we are watching. A similar revelation of the discrepancy between what we in the audience see as important and what the character chooses to emphasize is used in the diary sequence narrated by the psychotic character of Travis Bickle in *Taxi Driver* (Martin Scorsese, 1976).

When the narrator is also the film's central character, then, there may be a counterpoint between the narrator's perceptions and the perceptions of the audience watching the event. But this is not the only function of a character's voice-over narration. Like counterpoint, the agreement of the narration with the visual event can also function meaningfully. In Robert Bresson's *The Diary of a Country Priest* (1951), the tortured young priest of the title delivers his innermost thoughts to the viewer through his narration as he composes his diary. As we see his pen write the words, we hear him think the same words in an emotionless voice. In one sense, this is the cinematic version of the theater's soliloquy: the character is not addressing another character but rather is thinking to himself in a moment we are privileged to be able to hear. This kind of "private" narration is one way film represents interior dialogue, the mind thinking, talking to itself. But in Bresson's film, such narration serves an additional dramatic purpose. *The Diary of a Country Priest* attempts to deal with matters of the spirit through the physical images of film; it attempts to convey to the viewer the mystery and wonder of divine grace, the irreconcilable separation of the earthly from the spiritual. When the priest writes in his diary and we see and read the words on the page we also hear his voice saying those words; the written words are confirmed by their spoken repetition, and yet as we see and hear them they tell us nothing about the priest's tortured soul. The movie's insistence that we have been told and shown all there is to know makes us doubly aware that we have been told nothing at all.

We are, of course, much more consciously aware of narration in the nonfiction film than we are in the narrative film, perhaps because most viewers have been exposed to "teaching" films in school in which information was conveyed by a narrator and illustrated by the film's images. The refinement and increased portability of sound equipment have made voice-over narration almost obsolete, but it was formerly common in documentary films when sound could not easily be recorded on location. Voice-over narration strongly influenced the viewer's attitude toward the images he was seeing. The voice of Westbrook Von Voorhis, narrator of *The March of Time*, the news series which originated in the 1930s was aptly called "the voice of God." The voice of a documentary narrator can be male or female, loud or soft, emotional or unemotional — and because it is a human voice, it will speak through its tone, timbre, and inflection as well as through the words it utters. Two versions of the documentary film *Nanook of the North* (Robert Flaherty, 1922) provide an interesting example of how a narrator can affect the meaning of the visual images his voice accompanies. *Nanook* was made as a silent film about an Eskimo and his family, but some circulating versions shown to schoolchildren have substituted a narrator and sound track for the film's original titles. The sound version of *Nanook* is condescending in both the commentary and the tone of the narrator's voice. The Eskimo is made quaint and primitive, his skills are regarded as curious, and his accomplishments are minimized by overstatement. The silent version, however, allows us to view Nanook relatively uninterpreted. The titles give us information, and occasionally they editorialize, but when we *see* Nanook, what we see speaks for itself and is not qualified by the attitudes and tone of someone else's perceptions.

Narration can also serve yet another purpose, an aesthetic one. A continuous sound track in which a narrator speaks to the audience throughout the film can unify what would be otherwise fragmented and disconnected visual images. This is a particularly effective function of narration in compilation films, which are composed of materials from diverse sources: historical footage from archives, paintings from museums, clippings from newspapers, sections of newsreels, footage taken in the present by the filmmaker to augment the collected materials. Edited together, all this film might seem disjointed and arbitrarily chosen. Space and time are constantly shifting within a compilation film. The narration binds the film and creates a cohesive whole, for the narration takes place in continuous time. This unifying function of voice-over narration can be used to great emotional effect, as in Alain Resnais's *Night and Fog* (1955). This short film about the Nazi extermination camps alternates relatively static footage of black-and-white archival materials with moving-camera footage in color showing the empty camps as they were when the film was made. The method of the film is contrast: black-and-white images are contrasted with color ones,

★ **3-4** Sound can be used to substantiate the solidity of the image. Though the set used to represent the Thatcher Memorial Library in CITIZEN KANE (Orson Welles, 1941) was made of plaster and painted canvas, the hollow-sounding voices and the reverberating slam of the vault door made it seem to be made of stone and steel.

static images are contrasted with images from a nervous, moving camera, death is contrasted with life, the present is contrasted with the past. The one element in the film which unifies and finally reconciles these opposites is the narration. The narration brings the past into the present, animates the dead into a connection with the living, and enables viewers to connect and reconcile their own often conflicting emotional responses to the film's images of the holocaust.

★★★ ## Sound Effects

SYNCHRONOUS SOUND

When an object in the frame (say, a door) reveals itself by its sound (a slam or a creak) as well as by its visual presence, we are convinced that the object is real and not constructed of cardboard. Of course, in actual fact, the door frame visible on the screen may be constructed of extremely lightweight material, and closing that particular door would result in a sound which bore little resemblance to the sound of a real door closing. The sound technician, however, can dub in the sound of a real door closing, and because it is synchronous with the image, the audience is convinced of the substantiality of the door it sees, and by extension, of the film's physical world (Figure 3-4). Though we take this ordinary function of synchronous sound for granted, its contribution to the illusion of reality is crucial to films which are fantasies such as *Star Wars* (George Lucas, 1977); in a visual setting which bears little resemblance to the world we know, synchronous sound effects authenticate fantastic objects and fantastic places (Figure 3-5). Current develop-

★ **3-5** Sound is an important device for creating the illusion of reality in such fantastic films as STAR WARS (George Lucas, 1977). The sounds created for various pieces of machinery and the robots convince the viewer by their appropriateness. For instance, C3PO's voice began as an actor's voice, but then it was altered electronically to make it seem more metallic.

ments such as Dolby stereophonic sound have further increased the illusion of reality through the use of **multiple tracks** and dynamic **sound perspective.**

Like dialogue, synchronous sound which seems to emanate from objects onscreen may be recorded at the time of shooting the film or it may be dubbed in later. Either way will create the illusion that what is heard is the natural sound made by the machine gun, the waterfall, the car engine, the door.

Synchronous sound not only contributes to realism; it can be manipulated to create atmosphere, meaning, and emotional nuance. The sound mixer can emphasize an onscreen sound, such as a telephone ringing, so that it becomes an extremely urgent call or, on the other hand, a call that is simply part of everyday existence and background noise. Even in the most ordinary circumstances, the sound track of a film must be blended for dramatic effect or merely for clarity; this blending and emphasis and clarity are achieved not by the microphone which recorded the sounds but by the sound mixer. Although modern microphones are extremely sensitive and are able to pick up sounds from a selected and specific location, so that on-location recording has become more common than it once was, the microphone is still not able to dis-

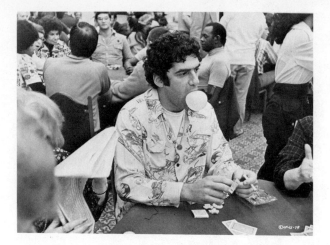

★ **3-6** Robert Altman uses his sound tracks to authenticate his characters. In crowd scenes such as this one from CALIFORNIA SPLIT (1974), the dialogue of the main characters around the card table overlap with each other and this in turn is blurred by the voices and noise from other players in the casino. The audience has to work hard to pick out the important dialogue just as they would if they were there in person.

tinguish between what is dramatically important and what is simply part of the background sound. Turned in a specific direction, it will listen impartially to everything it hears (Figure 3-6). Like a microphone, the human ear picks up everything in its range, but the brain focuses selectively, picking out important sounds and ignoring others even when they are heard at the same volume. The sound mixer functions as the brain behind the microphone, selecting and focusing on only those recorded sounds which are dramatically relevant to the scenes with which they will be synchronized. Therefore, just as the filmmaker uses **lighting** or framing to call attention to important visual elements of his composition, the sound mixer arranges the sound track to call attention to a specific object within the frame with which the sound is synchronized. For example, if a family appears in a shot watching TV when the phone rings, the sound mixer can heighten the sound of the phone and reduce the sound of the television set.

ASYNCHRONOUS SOUND

Much of what has been said about synchronous sound effects can be applied to asynchronous sound effects, those whose source is not visible on the screen. If, for example, we see a face in close-up but hear thunder, we have asynchronous sound. Asynchronous sound extends the

★ **3-7** Asynchronous sound — sound that does not come from any visual source in the image — provides a way of counterpointing the primary meaning of the image. In LE MIL-LION (René Clair, 1931) the actors are seen fighting over a coat which contains the winning lottery ticket, while the sound track contains crowd noises and officials' whistles from a rugby match.

filmmaker's freedom in ways which synchronous sound does not. Synchronous sound, after all, chiefly gives us more of what we see. If, for instance, a train appears onscreen, it gives us some sort of train sound no matter how subdued. But by using asynchronous sound, let's say the sound not of a train but of someone screaming, a director may shock the viewer or create a surreal world. René Clair in *Le Million* (1931) shows his actors fighting over a coat containing a lottery ticket, while we hear the sounds of a rugby match (Figure 3-7).

Because asynchronous sound need not be in sync with anything onscreen, it allows the filmmaker great freedom. He may introduce a sound which has just the right emotional nuance for his drama, even though this sound is not really related to the images. In a scene, for instance, showing a couple having a heated argument and then suddenly silently and angrily confronting each other, the filmmaker might choose to introduce the sound of an ambulance, increasing in volume as it nears and decreasing in volume as it races off (unseen in offscreen space). Because of the viewer's associations with ambulances — their urgency, their connection with someone's misfortune, their piercing and whining sound which is both commanding and plaintive — such a sound asynchronous with the image will enhance the dramatic tension on the screen and comment implicitly on the couple's painful and precarious relationship.

Asynchronous, wild sound effects (and human voices, to a lesser degree) also complement the image in another way: they extend the world beyond the confines of the frame. They help to make the film frame seem less like a container for the action than like a window which reveals to the viewer only a portion of the world which continues beyond the window's limits. We may, for instance, hear traffic noises although the camera is focused on an interior setting; the previous example of the offscreen ambulance siren heard while we are watching an action set in a confined interior is pertinent here. What is created is not only an off-screen sound accompaniment which is emotionally suitable to the action of the couple arguing, but also the illusion of a world extended beyond the limits of the rectangular screen, a life going on outside the field of the camera's vision. Though we may be watching the safari guide and the client's wife making love in his tent in the corniest of adventure films, our notion that they are really in the middle of the African plains and not on a sound stage is created by the careful addition to the sound track of insects chirping and buzzing, monkeys chattering, and an occasional lion roaring. The constant clickety-clack of wheels on rails encourages us in our belief that Cary Grant and Eva Marie Saint are actually on a real train in *North by Northwest* (Alfred Hitchcock, 1959) and not on a cutaway mock-up produced by the prop department. Even when we don't really believe in a film's contrived story, we often do believe in the authenticity of the same film's place. Because sounds from a multitude of unseen sources fill up our lives, asynchronous sound must be audible in a film character's life as well, if the filmmaker wishes us to feel that what we are seeing and hearing is credible.

★★★   **Music**

> To comprehend fully what music does for movies, one should see a picture before the music is added, and again after it has been scored. Not only are all the dramatic effects heightened, but in many instances the faces, voices, and even the personalities of the players are altered by the music.
> Dmitri Tiomkin[3]

BACKGROUND MUSIC

Background music — at first the piano or organ played for silent films — has long been used by filmmakers to add emotion and rhythm to their pictures. From travelogues to westerns to serious dramas, music has complemented the mood of countless scenes, to such an extent that certain kinds of musical passages are instantly recognized by the audience as fitting certain kinds of films or certain parts of films. We are all familiar with "chase" music, circus music, western music, and Oriental music, and with the strains of ukuleles playing as the sun sets on another visit to some island paradise. No horror film would be complete

★ **3-8** John Williams is one of the best-known composers and conductors of film music today. His credits include JAWS (1975), STAR WARS (1977), CLOSE ENCOUNTERS OF THE THIRD KIND (1977), and SUPERMAN (1978). Even though he writes music specifically for each film, the symphonic structure of his work has made it possible for the music to achieve popularity independent of the film.

without ominous bass notes or sudden piercing shrieks of strident violins. Science fiction films are often accompanied by synthetic and atonal music or by music which grandly evokes the vastness of a universe. Lyrical passages underscore romantic love scenes and sad melodies in a minor key evoke the nostalgia of love lost.

Background music may be more distinctive and noticeable than its name suggests, so much so that an audience may, after seeing a film, always associate the selected music with the visual images which accompany it. If you have seen Stanley Kubrick's *2001: A Space Odyssey* (1968), when you hear Richard Strauss's "Also Sprach Zarathustra" you recall Kubrick's images. Sometimes, too, a particular composer of film scores has such a distinctive style that anyone who has seen a number of films accompanied by his music will feel (if not actually identify) something familiar about what he hears (Figure 3-8). The late Bernard Herrmann was just such a composer. Herrmann created music totally in keeping with the various films he worked on, giving all of them an added suspense and psychological depth; yet despite the appropriateness of his music to each film, an identifiable and evident similarity exists between the music of *Citizen Kane* (Orson Welles, 1941), *The Day the Earth Stood Still* (Robert Wise, 1951), *Psycho* (Alfred Hitchcock, 1960), and *Taxi Driver* (1976), to name but a few of the films which he scored. Sometimes, background music will become so recognizable that the associations with the film in which it was used will be left behind. Marvin Hamlisch adapted Scott Joplin's ragtime music as background to *The Sting* (George Roy Hill, 1973) and the score was so successful that not only did it win an Academy Award but it also stimulated a new interest in ragtime music. And, finally, certain background music is accentuated at the beginning of a film or at its end by including

151

a voice-over song which picks up the major themes in a movie. Such music — for example, the title song for *The Way We Were* (Sydney Pollack, 1973) — may become so popular itself that one can hardly consider it background any longer.

Generally, however, background music, whether composed for the film or taken from already composed sources, is not meant to be noticeable. Rather, background music is conceived of as a relatively inconspicuous support for a film's images, evoking time and place and mood. For example, the sprightly harpsichord music played as background in *Tom Jones* (Tony Richardson, 1963), helps locate the viewer in the eighteenth century, carrying with it associations of the polite and structured society of that era. Because the music is often played at breakneck speed, it also creates a light, tongue-in-cheek, comic climate which supports the **tone** of the film. Background music may contradict a film's images, for example, the ironically gay zither melodies which accompany Carol Reed's *The Third Man* (1950) or the ballad which accompanies the world blowing up in Stanley Kubrick's *Dr. Strangelove* (1963). Background music, however, chiefly complements the image rhythmically, tonally, atmospherically. Thus, a chase sequence will be accompanied by lively, suspenseful, action music; a love scene, by violins that swell in harmony with the rising and falling dramatic action.

Background music may also have more specific narrative functions. Through repetition it can link shots, scenes, and sequences. For instance, a certain musical theme may be played early in a film when a particular character appears on the screen, or it may be associated with a particular situation — a lover's tryst, for instance. The character or the situation can then be evoked later in the film by repeating the musical phrases. Background music can also foreshadow a change in mood, signal to the viewer that there will be a dramatic shift in the plot. For instance, the music played during a happy family reunion scene may change into a minor key — usually associated with gloom and foreboding — just before there is a knock at the door. The viewer immediately senses that the visitor will bring bad news, even though he may not realize that it is the background music which has affected his feelings.

The invisibility of background music is one of its most important characteristics. For background music is, of course, often unreal. Music will begin with the credits (or before), underlining and amplifying the content of the film. But it will always be music which does not originate from any onscreen source; it is asynchronous sound. In this sense, the use of background music in, say, a western, is incredible, illogical, patently unreal. The wagon trains actually crossing the prairies were never accompanied by 101 strings playing a stirring epic melody. Although such music may be dramatically and emotionally credible, it is best that it function in the background unless the filmmaker is consciously striving for an unusual effect.

FOREGROUND MUSIC

There are other ways to bring music into films, however, which are credible and dramatically plausible. For example, characters may be in a room with a radio, a television set, or a stereo set. Although some of this music may arise from offscreen sources and thus be asynchronous sound, it may just as often be synchronous, arising from some image on the screen. Instead of using a score written for the film and played by an offscreen and unrealistically placed studio orchestra, a filmmaker who wishes to create a relatively representational film, a realistic movie, may instead place his characters in bars, in automobiles, in rooms in which there are radios, TV's, or stereos to provide atmosphere without betraying the film's realistic premises. *The Last Picture Show* (Peter Bogdanovich, 1971), for example, set in the 1950s, employs many songs of the time. These dramatically appropriate songs, which "happen" to come from the radio, atmospherically support the dramatic actions of the characters and also comment ironically upon them.

Most **foreground music,** however, is that performed by on-camera musicians and singers. Film musicals, of course, contain the greatest number of such performances. Whether an onscreen but subordinate orchestra is playing the absolutely necessary music so that Ginger Rogers and Fred Astaire can dance for us or whether Barbra Streisand and Kris Kristofferson are singing, music performed onscreen is the main attraction in the musical film.

There are two primary conventions for such performances: either the personality is a "performer" in a story about show business and thus will appear "onstage" or "in rehearsal," as in *New York, New York* (Martin Scorsese, 1977), or else the performer will simply be an ordinary person who must sing in the middle of a narrative to reveal his or her emotional state, as in *West Side Story* (Robert Wise and Jerome Robbins, 1961). Sometimes a character in a musical film will do both. In *Top Hat* (Mark Sandrich, 1935), for example, Fred Astaire plays a character who is a professional dancer and who is performing in a show. The number "Top Hat" is presented on a stage as part of the show, but most of the other songs and dances, such as "Isn't It a Lovely Day?" and "Dancing Cheek to Cheek," are done in the middle of the narrative simply because the characters feel like bursting out into song and dance. In a later musical, *Funny Face* (Stanley Donen, 1957), however, Astaire plays a character who is a fashion photographer, not a professional dancer; thus, all of his song and dance numbers occur as part of the story, not as the performances of a dancer.

In the popular revue films of the 1940s, a contrivance of the plot requires the main characters to attend an opera or a ballet performance or go to a nightclub where those in the audience would be treated to a musical performance by some famous opera star, singer, or swing band. The ways to get on-camera music into a film are many, some obvious and some devious. Although it is unlikely that any viewer would describe Robert Altman's *Nashville* (1975) as a musical, the director used the country and western music capital of the world — the city of Nashville, Tennessee — as a means of exploring life in contemporary America. All the music was performed on camera by actors representing country and western stars or would-be stars, and this music served to authenticate the film's physical world, to lend atmospheric support to the film's plot and its visual imagery, and to comment ironically on the characters and their actions.

Offscreen or asynchronous music can also be used in a way which calls attention to itself, which makes it part of the foreground in the audience's consciousness. Functioning almost like narration, it can lend rhythm and atmospheric support to major transitions, it can structure and cement images which may lack inherent continuity, and it can guide the audience in shaping its attitudes toward the characters or actions. Most asynchronous foreground music is vocal as well as instrumental, featuring songs sung by prominent singers who can hold the audience's attention. Such music occurs in *McCabe and Mrs. Miller* (Robert Altman, 1971), which uses the songs of Leonard Cohen. Because Cohen's lyrics are fairly complex, the music does not so much give voice to a character's feelings (like, say, Simon and Garfunkel's music in *The Graduate*); rather, it is a means of making the audience consider the characters and events from a distanced perspective. Thus, Cohen's "The Sisters of Mercy" functions paradoxically when sung over images of the prostitutes who have been brought to the mining town of Presbyterian Church; the song simultaneously supports the imagery and ironically contradicts it. Obvious, asynchronous foreground music serves another function in *Jeremiah Johnson* (Sydney Pollack, 1972), a quiet film which has relatively little dialogue and explosive action. Much of the visual imagery shows us Jeremiah, the "mountain man," riding his horse through fields of snow, moving from one place to another as he hunts, but neither interacting with other human beings nor finding himself in suspenseful situations. What might otherwise seem beautiful but dull footage is given meaning and atmospheric support by the film's theme song, "The Ballad of Jeremiah Johnson." As we watch Jeremiah go about his daily business of living, we hear in the present a song which turns the character we see into a legendary figure and thus places Jeremiah in the past. The song, therefore, not only tells us that the central character is important beyond his own time, but it also creates nostalgia: Jeremiah is dead and gone into history, and the present images of him we watch seem particularly privileged and precious.

★★★ ## The Artistry of Sound

> In the early period of talking pictures, while writing the film script for
> *Le Million*, I amused myself by making the conscience of one of the characters talk, or more exactly, sing. This innovation had a certain success and
> it was confirmed in the most flattering way: by the numerous imitations that
> were made of it. Some time later, I conceived the project of a film in which
> the entire action would be commented on in the manner of the "voice of the
> conscience" — that is to say, in which the thoughts of the characters would
> be expressed by sound, either according to or contrasting with the actions of
> the images shown on the screen.
>
> René Clair[4]

Like the images in a film, sound is edited or molded to suit the needs of the individual film. Sound can be used to emphasize or alter our visual perspective of a character or place, to transitionally bridge a cut, or to contradict the image or a previously established mood, and it can be used to establish the identity of a particular kind of film, such as a western or a gangster film.

SOUND PERSPECTIVE

The perspective (or distance) from which we hear sounds in a movie can affect our understanding of what appears in the frame and can affect our emotional responses to what we see. Voices or gunshots or music can be near or they can be far away; they can come from one speaker or, as with the new Dolby stereo system, from several so that they may appear to travel across the screen as their source in the image travels. Usually, sound perspective is created through the use of **selective sound** (some sounds are removed from the track, others are retained), or by a change in the quality of the sound (amplification is changed and/or the sound is distorted).

Selective sound obviously emphasizes some sounds (for example, a

★ **3-9** Distorted sound can often be used for aesthetic purposes. When the protagonist of AN OCCURRENCE AT OWL CREEK BRIDGE (Robert Enrico, 1961) seemingly escapes his bonds underwater and rises to the surface, he appears to see and hear the soldiers' reactions to his escape in slow motion. The slowed-down sound and images indicate the subjectivity of time.

watch or a bomb ticking) and omits others. Usually it tends to function subjectively, indicating how a *character* hears rather than presenting a "natural" **sound mix.** The selective sound track puts us physically inside the character we see on the screen, allowing us to feel as if we are participating in the action. In *Downhill Racer* (Michael Ritchie, 1969), a movie about ski racing, the sound becomes highly selective in the racing sequences. The sound track lets us hear only heightened sounds of breathing, skis scraping against icy snow, and a watch ticking away the seconds. These isolated sounds link the viewer to the central character, helping the viewer to experience the racer's intense concentration. Another instance in which selective and amplified sound creates subjective engagement with the film occurs in *An Occurrence at Owl Creek Bridge* (Robert Enrico, 1961). At first it appears we are watching an objective presentation of Union soldiers preparing to hang a Southern civilian, but boots striking the wooden ties of the bridge, the rope rubbing against a crossbeam, the sound of fabric as it is tied around the condemned man's legs to hold him secure, all sound louder than normal. The viewer feels uneasy, although he may not even be aware that his unease is caused by the discrepancy in perspective between the selectively subjective sounds he hears and the initially omniscient and objective images he sees. This amplification of sound adds to the tension generated up to the moment when the prisoner drops from the bridge and makes us identify ourselves with the condemned man even before we visually enter his consciousness.

The selective sound track can combine amplification with distortion to achieve an even more intense psychological subjectivity. The audience is not only linked with the protagonist but is also involved in the process by which other characters are dehumanized or objects are made unfamiliar. An obvious example occurs in *An Occurrence at Owl Creek Bridge* when the protagonist, who has just survived his own aborted hanging, surfaces from a prolonged underwater escape to hear pursuing soldiers on a bridge yell at him in what seems to be "slow-motion" sound (Figure 3-9). In keeping with the notion that under stress one's mind operates hyperactively, the technique connects us aurally with the protagonist, and also dehumanizes the soldiers, who sound like grotesques. One problem with distorting sound, however, is that the audience, rather than realizing that the sound has been purposely distorted, may think something has happened to the theater's sound system or the projector. Enrico guards against this misconception by recording the sound of birds at normal speed, and those sounds, unobtrusive as they are, provide the audience with a frame of reference. Another example of amplification and distortion occurs in *The Graduate* (Mike Nichols, 1967). The alienated Benjamin puts on his birthday present, a complete scuba diving outfit. As he walks down into the family swimming pool, having been coerced by his incessantly chattering parents to try it out, the water covers his face mask (the subjective camera places us in his position, looking out through the glass), and the sound track alters. The voices of the adults gathered around the pool thicken, distort, and finally disappear. All we hear is the amplified gurgle of the breathing apparatus which, in comparison with the previous meaningless and unpleasantly grating chatter, sounds peaceful and contented.

Amplification of a sound track need not be used solely to make the viewer identify himself with a character, to hear what he hears. It can be used more neutrally, less as a subjective device than as a dramatic one. In some films, an extreme long shot may show a couple walking along the beach or sitting high on a hillside; in contrast, we hear their voices "close up" so that their conversation seems exceedingly intimate, more so perhaps than it would if we were watching a close-up image where we would tend to take the match in perspective between image and voice for granted. Besides heightening intimacy, amplification can heighten excitement and drama. In an automobile chase sequence, such as the extensive one in *The French Connection* (William Friedkin, 1971), sounds of screeching tires, shifting gears, metal cracking against metal, are often amplified to increase the dramatic intensity of the visuals.

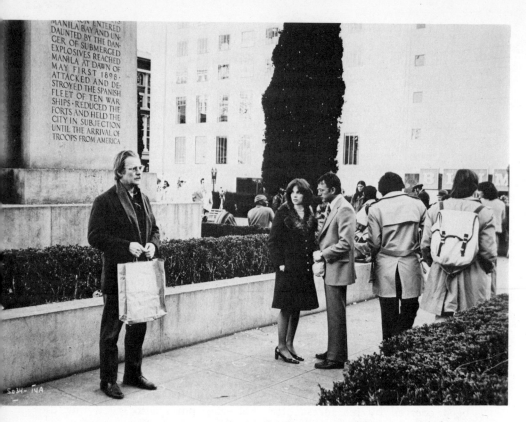

★ **3-10** The entire range of sound selection, amplification, and distortion is demonstrated in THE CONVERSATION (Francis Ford Coppola, 1974). The film shows how a surveillance company cleverly records a couple's private conversation as they talk in the middle of a busy plaza: as we hear snatches of conversation that only the man in the left foreground could be hearing, we come to realize that the man has a microphone in his hearing aid and a tape recorder in his shopping bag. The film shows not only how sound can be manipulated technologically, but also how it can be interpreted — or misinterpreted — by the human consciousness.

The entire range of sound selection, amplification, and distortion is itself demonstrated in a film which shows the recording and manipulation of a couple's conversation obtained as they talk in the middle of a busy plaza. *The Conversation* (Francis Ford Coppola, 1974) not only shows us how sound can be manipulated technologically, but also how it is always finally interpreted — or misinterpreted — by a human consciousness (Figure 3-10).

THE SOUND BRIDGE

Sound can be used not only to complement or contradict the content of the visual image, but also to bridge the gap often caused by the abrupt juxtaposition of disparate images. The **sound bridge** is an effective transitional and artistic device which can connect two or more differing images, helping the audience to realize that some connection between them is intended. We have already seen how, for example, continuous narration can create continuity between images, say, of airplanes bombing a ship and of infantrymen advancing on land, collected from various archival sources, to make a compilation film. And we have mentioned that music, too, can bridge images unconnected in time.

The first device, narration as a transition, is commonly used by the documentary film. Its most flamboyant transitional functions are best illustrated by examples from films made during the 1930s and 1940s, but the technique in more circumspect forms is still used today. Pare Lorentz's *The Plow That Broke the Plains* (1936) and *The River* (1937) both use continuous narration to link images which were filmed at different times and in different places. Both films show us images which are essentially abstract, contextless: close-ups of rusted farm implements lying on parched ground, drops of water dripping slowly from a twig. But the narration, with its temporal continuity, its single voice, and its rhythmic cadences, links these images.

The second device, the use of music to effect the transition between images that are not inherently connected, is extremely common. The music accompanying a scene begins to change to a major or minor key, or we hear a musical **motif** connected with a character we will see in the next scene. A song can link or unify images which, though edited together, have little spatial or temporal relationship. In *The Graduate*, for example, there are several juxtaposed shots, alternating Benjamin on a rubber raft in his swimming pool and Benjamin in bed with Mrs. Robinson. Some of these are linked by motion (Benjamin dives into his swimming pool and lands in bed with Mrs. Robinson), but even these visually strong connections would seem extraordinarily contrived were it not for the smoothness and unification of the sequence provided by Simon and Garfunkel singing "The Sounds of Silence" on the sound track. The song bridges the spatial and temporal gap between the intercut shots and communicates a relationship. The total effect of the unified sequence (or montage) is that Benjamin drifting into an affair with Mrs. Robinson and Benjamin drifting in his swimming pool are equal activities — both for Benjamin and for us.

Dialogue and sound effects can also function effectively as sound bridges. A change of image, moving abruptly in time and space, can be bridged without confusing the viewer if the shift is softened by the use of continuous sound. In *Citizen Kane* (1941), the director used his previous radio experience with sound bridges to compress great periods of time, as when we see the young Kane glaring up at the torso of his guardian, who is saying, "Merry Christmas, Charles," and who finishes the phrase years later to the mature Charles in the next directly cut image: "and a Happy New Year." The direct cut from one image to an image of years later might have disoriented the audience, but because there is no pause on the sound track, the years are intelligibly connected. In the same film, a sound bridge unifies and compresses the unhappy and short-lived operatic career of Susan Alexander, Kane's second wife: her creaky rendition of an aria bridges the images of newspaper accounts of her tour, theater lights, audiences, and people running about onstage.

A sound bridge can also act as a foreshadowing device, preparing us for a change in mood, a flashback, a scene to come. In *An Occurrence at Owl Creek Bridge,* the escaping protagonist flees from pursuing soldiers, gunfire, and cannon shot. He finally comes to rest in an idyllic spot which visually conveys a sense of release, of life's beauty and value. The man moves forward in one shot to smell a flower. During the latter part of this shot, we hear a barely perceptible whistling noise which becomes louder and finally is recognizable in the next shot (effected by a direct cut) when a cannonball explodes. Thus, the ominous, almost unidentifiable sound we hear in one shot not only begins to make us uncomfortable, even though we are looking at an idyllic scene, but also prepares us for the next scene. We also are able to recognize the source of the sound a moment before the film's protagonist; as the sound becomes clearly audible and we realize what it is, we want to warn the protagonist to run from the danger before he is even aware of it.

SOUND COUNTERPOINT

When various elements of film are used simultaneously to contradict each other so that new meaning is created, we speak of counterpoint. Obviously, not every kind of contradiction between filmic elements deserves consideration as counterpoint. Sloppy filmmaking can also result in contradictions, but these contradictions do not result in a purposeful meaning or effect.

Because we cannot discriminate so easily with our ears alone, most counterpoint involving sound is not between sound and sound but between sound and image. But one fascinating experimental short, *Frank Film* (Carolyn and Frank Mouris, 1973), combines two voice tracks to accompany its animated collage of images. One voice track, presumably using the voice of the actual filmmaker, narrates an autobiography: Frank is being "frank," candidly telling us just how he came to be a filmmaker and how he came to make this particular movie. The autobiographical track moves along chronologically and coherently. Simultaneously, a second voice track (again using Frank's voice) rattles off a barrage of numbers and of nouns which more or less match the bombardment of quickly changing images of objects. The combination of both tracks with the visual imagery results in such an overabundance of stimuli that many people have trouble watching the film without discomfort, yet this method is perfectly suited to this particular film's subject matter, which combines several levels of consciousness and explores the ways in which an individual is bombarded and influenced by the visual and aural stimuli of his culture.

This kind of sound counterpoint — dialogue with dialogue — is unusual. The problem it presents is demonstrated by *Frank Film*, for it is extremely difficult to absorb both sound tracks and equally difficult to concentrate on only one sound track at a time when both tracks consist of a voice speaking language which is supposed to mean something. The effort to grasp the meaning of what is being said would produce an intolerable mental strain in a film of any length. The device has been used with some success, however, in a few isolated instances, among them in a film made during the early years of sound, *Gabriel over the White House* (Gregory La Cava, 1933). At the start of the film, a newly elected President, who has been revealed as a "party" man with absolutely no concern for the nation's economic problems, is seen playing on his office floor with his young nephew; on the sound track one hears the President and the child as they play. But one also hears, from a radio in the room, news about the dire unemployment rate, about a populist leader named John Bronson who has organized the people to fight for some kind of action to end the Depression and create jobs, about the grafters and gangsters who are taking advantage of Prohibition. Simultaneously, then, one hears the serious problems facing the country and the unconcerned chatter of the President as he plays with his nephew; the juxtaposition of these two dialogue tracks provides the viewer with information and with an attitude which neither track would be able to convey by itself. The most common counterpoint created by spoken language in a film is a great deal more simple and seems, as well, more realistic: in a given crowd scene — such as in a restaurant or at a party — various conversations will overlap, but the viewer tends to find that

★ **3-11** Music can be creatively juxtaposed with dialogue. Throughout THE
LAST PICTURE SHOW (Peter Bogdanovich, 1971), the actual instrumental
and vocal recordings of the 1950s add an extra dimension of irony. The
banal, sentimental lyrics of country and western tunes and romantic ballads
heard from radios in cars, barroom, or café, tell how life *should* be. Yet the
dialogue we hear from people trapped in small-town realities indicates a life
that is drab and harsh.

one conversation is dominant and more continuously audible although
key words which counterpoint that dominant conversation are heard
clearly arising from the more subdued babble of the other conversations.
Thus, the viewer need not divide his attention equally between separate
dialogues, and the illusion of spontaneous counterpoint will be effectively created.

Sound and sound, however, can be easily and creatively juxtaposed
when one of the sounds we hear is music and the other is dialogue. Such
juxtaposition is used frequently throughout *The Last Picture Show*
(1971) (Figure 3-11). Nearly everyone in the film listens to the radio
and so the sound of the fifties, the actual instrumental and vocal recordings of the times, provides an extra dimension of cinematic irony
to the sound track. We hear the banal, sentimental (and easily comprehensible) lyrics of country and western tunes and romantic ballads
tell us and the characters how life should be, and at the exact same instant we see the drab, harsh, complex life of the people trapped in
small-town realities.

Most often, we have said, the counterpoint is of sound and image, creating meanings which are not inherent in either by itself. What is created by such counterpoint is similar in many ways to the counterpoint created by editing two disparate images together so as to form a new "image" — an idea in the mind of the audience. Much as Sergei Eisenstein, the great Russian filmmaker, demonstrated that shot A + shot B = shot C, one could demonstrate that shot A accompanied by sound B = shot C. In fact, Eisenstein experimented with this principle in his first sound film. In *Film Sense* he explains how he used Prokofiev's music in the making of *Alexander Nevsky* (1938). At times the film was cut to the music; at other times music was written to match the already edited footage. But in every case there is a unique blend between the music on the sound track and the images on the screen. As the armies of Russia battle the Teutonic knights across the face of Lake Neva, the music swells and soars heroically. When the heroine searches for her wounded comrades in the dark night after the battle, the music is appropriately somber.

The difference, of course, between editing together two disparate images and editing together a disparate sound and image is that one image comes after the other but the sound and the image occur simultaneously. The economy, clarity, and comparative subtlety of such counterpoint of image and sound makes it a favorite device of contemporary directors who find the traditional counterpoint of image and image too unwieldly and heavy-handed.

Federico Fellini, for example, creates ironic counterpoint in *8½* (1963). Against images of elderly men and women shuffling slowly in long winding lines towards the fountains of a spa where mineral water is being dispensed, Fellini juxtaposes the sounds of a brisk orchestral arrangement of Wagner's "Ride of the Valkyries" on the track. As the camera pans we discover that the music is being played by a band meant to entertain the elderly spa guests. The contrast between the heroic, dynamic music and the slow-moving image — the feeble, the elderly, the ill — produces a sharp sense of discrepancy between man's aspirations and his realities.

Stanley Kubrick is another filmmaker who frequently creates an ironic counterpoint between image and sound track. In *Dr. Strangelove* (1963), Kubrick begins the film (and its credits) with a shot of two Strategic Air Command B–52 bombers in midair, one refueling the other. On the sound track, however, one hears not the complementary sounds of droning engines but a saccharine instrumental ballad, "Try a Little Tenderness." The counterpoint between the utterly different content of these two cinematic elements creates an entirely new meaning, one inherent

★ **3-12** The creative use of sound can also mean the use of silence. As the young boy in Ingmar Bergman's THE SILENCE (1963) walks up and down the deserted corridors of a hotel in some foreign city, his loneliness is underscored by the total absence of sound.

neither in the image nor in the sound by itself: the B–52's are not re-fueling, they are copulating. The sound track forces us to regard what we watch in an entirely new way. Kubrick again uses music as an integral and highly important element of *A Clockwork Orange* (1971). The film follows the adventures of Alex, a violent hoodlum in a futuristic society. Although music is used in ironic counterpoint to the images it accompanies in many scenes, perhaps none is so shocking as the one in which Alex brutally beats up a writer and sexually assaults his wife — while he sings "Singin' in the Rain" and tap-dances in his stormtrooper-like boots, punctuating his performance with the painful thud of kicks.

One other way in which sound and image can be used in counter-point in a film is by the juxtaposition of an image and silence (Figure 3-12). Just as the freeze frame in a moving picture frustrates the expectations of continuous, lifelike movement, so does the sudden absence of sound in a sound film frustrate our sense of the reality of a given situation. Because we are so used to hearing while we watch a movie, the selected use of silence can provoke odd and self-conscious responses from us. In some contexts, silence can also intensify our attention, making us focus more tightly on the image. The lack of sound can also cause us to feel apprehensive, dissociated from reality, which is never without some noise. Continued for a long period, cinematic silence becomes almost tangible and extremely discomforting. Thus, an absence of sound over images of a great deal of activity (which, therefore, should produce a good amount of sound) will subvert their activity and their seeming reality.

SOUND CONVENTIONS

A convention is commonly defined as a general agreement on usage and social practice. For example, policemen wear a standard uniform, and we cover our mouths when we yawn in public. In the arts, too, there are agreements: when we see *Julius Caesar*, we agree that these Romans will (for our benefit) speak in English. Thus, a convention in film might be the established use of a particular camera movement joined with a particular content. For example, in 1930s and 1940s films, the camera moves upward and away from embracing lovers, which indicates that they are about to do something together which we have agreed not to watch. The dialogue pattern in a particular sort of movie and the musical or sound accompaniment to a specific kind of dramatic activity, such as the playing of the "March from Lohengrin" to announce the entry of the bride at a wedding, are examples of sound conventions.

We have become so accustomed to hearing some sound conventions that pointing them out may seem unnecessary, and yet it is *because* we take conventions for granted that they need to be examined. Dialogue patterns can be conventional. Think, for example, of how we expect the snappy cadences and hyped-up, super-fast delivery of newspaper reporters, how, in fact, a slow-speaking reporter would surprise if not disturb us by his unconventionality. In contrast, in a western we expect characters to talk slowly, ungrammatically, and even painfully so that self-expression tends to resolve itself in action rather than words. Slang, though now widely used in many sorts of films, was first associated with the early sound gangster films, and it is still a convention of movies with urban settings rather than rural ones (Figure 3-13). Certain contemporary films use ambiguous or purposely uninformative dialogue which has come to communicate the nature of its speaker or relationships between speakers far better than it communicates its own subject matter. For example, in *The Manchurian Candidate* (John Frankenheimer, 1962), the characters played by Frank Sinatra and Janet Leigh meet for the first time between cars on a speeding train. The conversation between the two is made up of ordinary phrases — "Let me light your cigarette"; "I love train travel, don't you"; "I used to know a man once who . . ."; and so forth — which are less meaningful in their content than in what they reveal about the characters. The rhythm of the phrases spoken establishes Janet Leigh's calming influence on the psychologically disturbed Frank Sinatra.

Music and sound effects have also been used conventionally. Again, the most obvious use is the most taken for granted. It is conventional that music accelerates for a chase sequence, that it becomes louder to

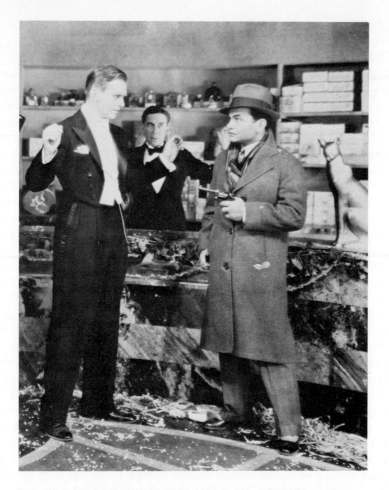

★ **3-13** Certain sounds identify certain films. Slang, though first associated
with early sound gangster films, is now used in many sorts of films. But
the screech of tires on a getaway car, the rattle of tommy guns, the wail of
a pursuing siren will always signal a crime film. Edward G. Robinson's
distinctive snarl will always be associated with the ambitious hoodlum he
played in LITTLE CAESAR (Mervyn Le Roy, 1930).

underscore a dramatically important action, that its tempo or pitch indicates whether or not a particular action demands special attention from
the viewer. Less obvious are the ways that music and sound effects function to take us back in time by repeating an already established motif or

by using echo and distortion to indicate that something unusual — perhaps a flashback — is going to occur. Music in musicals appears out of nowhere, coming up slowly under a dramatic scene so as to lead us gently into a song or dance number which finishes in a crescendo as the image fades or the characters freeze for a fraction of a second to indicate the end of a scene.

Even the tonal quality of a film's entire sound track may be a convention. A fiction film made today but set in the 1930s may imitate the imperfect sound recording of early on-location documentary filming. Just as the more obvious sounds added to exotic and historical fictional subject matter create an illusion of authenticity of place (jungle sounds in a safari picture, the clank of spurs and snuffling horses in a western), so in a contemporary film the intentionally sloppy sound track can add the illusion of authenticity and on-the-spot immediacy. Originally, because on-location documentary sound recording was less selective than it is today, an unselective and unpolished sound track was normal for films which recorded on location. If a film was being shot in an actual office, the sound recorder would not only pick up the voices of the principals, but also the peculiar complex of sounds in an office, such as the noise of typing down the hall, people scurrying about off-camera, and also the "buzz" or "feedback" that a microphone will pick up in a place that sound technicians call "live." (In a "live" space, any sound made simply keeps bouncing around in the space, setting up a nearly omnipresent reverberation, rather than being absorbed. A correctly constructed and draped sound recording room, which absorbs sounds, is called "dead.") All these sounds authenticate the reality of place and time in a documentary film. Whether filming and recording in a factory, on a ranch, at a press conference, or out on the street, the documentary filmmaker was not technically able to refine on-location recording until the 1960s. The very limitations of documentary recording set up a tradition, a convention: sloppy sound equals immediacy, honesty, a certain measure of objectivity. Feature films adopted the use of sloppy sound tracks to authenticate their contemporary settings and content. Ironically, even current documentary films made on location, though technically able to achieve a clear and clean sound track, often purposely do not clean up their sound tracks because the less professional they sound the more they are accepted as realistic.

There is another way in which sound (dialogue, sound effects, and music) can communicate in a film. A particular sound or combination of sounds can evoke a whole cluster of associated thoughts and feelings from other films or from ordinary life. Lines such as "I wouldn't marry you if you were the last man on earth!" or "You're not going up in a crate like that," after repeated use in many films, may become invested with greater significance than the mere words themselves convey.

Music may function similarly. The most obvious examples are national anthems which represent the qualities of their respective nations to anyone who hears the familiar tunes. The "Marseillaise" connotes France (the liberty, equality, and fraternity of the French Revolution) much as the "Volga Boatman" connotes Russia (brooding serfs, neurotic aristocrats). Musical instruments, similarly, may convey place: the sitar, India; castanets, Spain; drums, frontier America or jungle Africa. Sound effects, aurally accompanying the specific film we're watching at a given moment, may also evoke all the other films with similar sounds we've seen. The gangster film has its screeching of tires, its machine-gunning. The horror film has its creaking doors and stair risers, its ominously sudden and expressive moaning winds and claps of thunder. The science fiction film dotes on the sound of machinery, the clicking of circuits, the humming of computers.

Film, then, is an aural as well as a visual medium. The idea that "cinematic" is a term which should be confined to the visual elements of the cinema has surely been put to rest by the outstanding achievements of the sound film. Spoken dialogue and narration, by assisting the uninterrupted flow of images, give us the illusion that we are observing reality. They also contribute effective ambiguity, irony, and ideas to the film medium. Music, too, makes a contribution, extending or counterpointing what is expressed in the images we see. And sound effects not only add tone, mood, and tensions to film, but they can also authenticate a two-dimensional world confined by a rectangle of light beams so that it becomes extended far beyond the boundaries of the theater in which we sit.

NOTES

[1] Quoted in Connie Byrne and William O. Lopez, "Nashville," *Film Quarterly* 29, no. 2 (Winter 1975-1976): 15-16.

[2] *Magic and Myth of the Movies* (New York: Simon and Schuster, 1970), p. 1.

[3] "Composing for Films," in T. J. Ross, ed., *Film and the Liberal Arts* (New York: Holt, Rinehart & Winston, 1970), p. 234.

[4] *Four Screenplays* (New York: The Orion Press, 1970), p. 109.

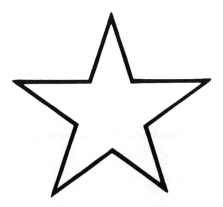

PART II CINEMATIC CONTENT: THE FICTION FILM

★★★ **Knowing and Understanding Film**

Cinema, film, motion pictures, movies — whatever the words, for most people they are synonymous with films that tell a story, a fiction about created characters interacting in situations which are plausible once the premise of the tale is established. Even a filmed story that is based on historical facts is in some degree pictorial or "made up," for characters may be omitted or added, time may be condensed, and in any case only a selection of happenings is reproduced on the screen. The basic assumption of a story is that even if it didn't actually happen, it could have happened, or at least we are willing to suspend our disbelief and pretend it could have happened.

The story, then, is the content of a fiction film. Yet it is important to recognize that we cannot actually see some of the attributes of the story which we nevertheless apprehend. We may *see* actors performing actions, but we *understand* characters and *know* they are in a plot. We may *see* a person working in a factory, but we *understand* the conditions of such labor and *know* that the film is taking an attitude toward those conditions, showing us, for example, the dignity of labor, or the tedium of factory work.

This kind of understanding and knowing usually takes place while we are watching a film; we understand automatically who, what, where, and why. But there is another kind of understanding and knowing that takes place after we watch a film; we may have to think about what we have seen to understand it. The film's theme may not be clearly stated, the filmmaker's ideas may be begging for interpretation. Or reflection about a film may bring an understanding of the film's place in history, its relationship to other films by the same director, or to other films of a similar type. We may discover its connections with a film movement or recognize certain characteristics shared by films made in the same country. Thus, both while viewing a film and afterwards, we can understand and know cinematic content and see how the formal elements have worked together to create that content and communicate it.

What is communicated in fiction films varies tremendously. Stories range from outrageously fantastic tales about Martians to highly realistic representations of small town life in the midwest in 1950. Some stories begin with the premise "Once upon a time...," while others offer the illusion of immediacy and presentness ("if you had been there, this is what you would have seen"). Story films can tell the life of a single character or of a group of characters; they can portray a few hours of a single day or they can span centuries.

★ GRAND ILLUSION (Jean Renoir, 1938), a realistic film, probes man's relationship with war and the illusions of heroism, class consciousness, and national pride. In GRAND ILLUSION, the passing of the pre–World War I world is symbolized by the death of Boeldieu (Pierre Fresnay) as von Rauffenstein (Erich Von Stroheim) looks on.

Some fiction films contain extremely fresh situations and characters, while others, relying on formula plots and stereotyped characters, seem to belong to a group of films, or a **genre.** Non-genre films, such as *Citizen Kane* (Orson Welles, 1941) usually attempt to individualize their characters and situations, thereby making them fresh experiences for the viewer. Formula or genre films, on the other hand, portray representative figures (such as the tough but decent detective) acting in conventional situations. The fiction film, whether a genre or non-genre film, can be more or less realistic in its setting, time scheme, and character motivations. Non-genre films, however, tend to have complex, ambiguous themes which challenge commonplace ideas, whereas genre films tend to deal in clearly delineated conflicts, usually between obvious good and evil. The pleasures of the non-genre film derive from its originality and its ability to surprise us. The pleasures of the genre film derive from its familiarity and its ability to meet our expectations in satisfying ways.

Our primary expectation of any fiction film, however, is that it will engage us. This loose requirement applies to nearly everything from Charlie Chaplin's attempts to defeat the pompous stuffed shirts and nasty villains he encounters in his travels to Jack Nicholson's symbolic

★ In THE SEVENTH SEAL (1956), a nonrealistic or more openly symbolic film, Ingmar Bergman investigates the age-old search for proof of God's existence through nonrealistic means. Death is personified and moves through the film as a character, seen here playing chess with the Knight (Max von Sydow).

journey through an exotic landscape in Antonioni's *The Passenger* (1975). Often we simply want to find out what happens next. Will Harold Lloyd make it to the top of the skyscraper? Will Lassie come home? What new dangers lurk in the deep? Sometimes our involvement is with something less active or less physically represented. Is America's insensitivity to the plight of the poor the result of her emphasis on material success? Is God really dead or just turning his face away from the world? In the finest examples of the filmmakers' storytelling art, the audience will be interested both in what happens and in what the happenings add up to. Thus, in a masterpiece like *Grand Illusion* (Jean Renoir, 1937), one is simultaneously concerned with what will happen next to Marechal and Rosenthal after they escape from the castle in which they were held prisoners of war, and with a consideration of the brotherhood of man set against the insanity of war.

Aspects of the fiction film are presented in three chapters. Chapter 4 will deal with genre films, Chapter 5 with film movements, and Chapter 6 with the non-genre narrative film.

★★

Historical Overview: The Development of the Fiction Film

Man has been telling stories ever since the first hunter returned to his cave and pantomimed the way in which he'd spent the day. Perhaps he gestured about the big one that got away, or the long and exhausting struggle he'd had before he finally killed his quarry. Perhaps even before there was a vocabulary of words sufficient to the event, man may have drawn pictures in the dirt to aid his audience's understanding of the personal drama he described. Eventually, of course, words, pictures, and body movements were used in a variety of combinations to tell stories. Painting and sculpture, drama, oral and written tales, and music and dance were all available to early storytellers.

EARLY STORYTELLERS: HOLLYWOOD AND THE SILENT FILM

With the invention of cinematography in the late nineteenth century, man had a new medium through which to tell stories, a medium which literally could combine the tools and techniques of painting, music and dance, pantomime, drama, and literature, and which could reach and affect a mass audience. But the idea of using the motion picture camera and projector for narrative purposes was not developed as immediately as one might think. Those men who invented the motion picture were not artists, were not concerned with the fanciful or "unreal" aspects of the medium. Instead, they were men of science and industry, inventors and tinkerers who were chiefly concerned with capturing on film the physical world in which they lived. Even though the Lumière brothers frequently staged rather than simply observed little bits of action — *L'Arroseur Arrosé* (*The Hoser Hosed*, 1895), in which a boy steps on a gardener's hose to stop the water from flowing until the gardener looks down the nozzle, getting squirted in the face, must be the first filmed comedy — the brothers relied mainly on observed scenes from real-life situations to fill out their catalogue of offerings — a train arriving at a station, workers leaving the factory, and so forth.

It was Georges Méliès, a magician and theater operator involved less with the scientific than with the magical and fantastic, who first consciously realized the narrative capacity of the new medium. He had seen the Lumières' first projected screening at the Grand Café in Paris in December of 1895, and as an entertainer and showman he instantly recognized film's potential for mass entertainment. Between 1896 and 1914 he made over a thousand short films, all of which told fantastic and miraculous stories. Having discovered that the camera could be stopped in the middle of an action and then restarted after the action was altered, so that during projection a scene would appear to be filled with magical transformations, Méliès was able to create "realistic" illusions in which actors' heads were severed from their bodies and then magically returned and people were transformed into puffs of smoke. Through the magic of animated sequences and fabulous cardboard scenery, Méliès's characters could fly off to the moon or plunge deep into a fairyland world under the sea. It is not surprising that — unlike his more scientifically oriented predecessors, the Lumière brothers and Thomas Edison — Méliès was drawn to filming stories, short versions of childhood favorites like *Cinderella* (1899) and *Little Red Riding Hood* (1901) as well as literary adaptations like *A Trip to the Moon* (1901), *Gulliver's Travels* (1901), and *The Legend of Rip Van Winkle* (1905). But for all his delight in storytelling and for all of his discoveries about how to "edit" in the camera (he developed the fade-out, dissolves, double exposure, slow and fast motion, and **animation**), Méliès never transcended his own theatrical background or the narrative limitations of the stage and proscenium arch. All the action in Méliès's films was contained in the center of a static frame, and stories were related in a strict chronological order, one complete scene following another.

Edwin S. Porter, an itinerant projectionist who rose to head Thomas Edison's Kinetoscope operations, found the key which freed the new medium from the shackles of theatrical tradition. Porter, we have seen in Chapter 2, demonstrated that editing could manipulate time and space to create drama, suspense, and excitement in a way which would be impossible for the theater to duplicate. In 1903, he took pieces of film footage of various fire companies in action from the Edison files, shot several scenes to match this **stock footage,** and then edited the action together to make *The Life of an American Fireman.* For example, a shot of a fire truck approaching a building is followed by an interior shot of a woman within the building,

★ 1   Edwin S. Porter is credited with creating the first story film that took advantage of the camera's unique abilities. The close-up, parallel editing, camera movement, and subject movement towards the camera are some of the formal devices found in THE GREAT TRAIN ROBBERY (1903).

and we understand that although the second shot, of course, follows the first, the two episodes take place at the same time. Later that same year Porter made *The Great Train Robbery,* which went further towards refining the storytelling techniques that have become essential to the medium. Porter employed the parallel editing of two simultaneous actions taking place in different locations, the chase sequence, scenes shot from different camera angles, and the dramatic close-up.

Interestingly enough, Porter's techniques were more the result of happenstance and the particular filming conditions imposed upon him by the subject matter of *The Great Train Robbery* than they were the result of conscious discovery. The film tells the story of a gang of bandits who rob a train, are pursued by a posse, and are finally dispatched (Figure 1). Much of the action takes place outdoors in the "wild, wild West" of New Jersey, and this on-location shooting in rough terrain required that the camera be set up in positions other than squarely in front of the action. The camera also moves slightly at one point in the film to produce a brief and tentative pan shot which keeps the moving bandits in the frame. Further, characters are occasionally forced by the terrain to enter or leave the scene from behind the camera rather than from screen left or screen right, the cinematic equivalent of theatrical "wings." Porter's most important achievement, however, was in allowing the action of the story to dictate the narrative structure of the film. Cutting back and forth between the robbers and the posse is a natural way of telling the story and of satisfying an audience's equal interest in both groups as well as creating dramatic suspense. The chase is cinematic story material par excellence. Although Porter was the originator of the edited chase, he never fully realized that parallel editing — crosscutting — could be used anytime in film fiction, not just in a chase sequence. Unfortunately, most of his subsequent films returned to the traditional tableau format which preserved a strict theatrical chronology as one resolved scene followed another. Despite his lack of awareness of his accomplishment, Porter's popular little film clearly established the medium's potential for a distinctly cinematic narrative, a potential which was realized by the first master of cinematic art, D. W. Griffith.

Griffith, a Southerner, came to New York to make his fortune as a great dramatist, but ended up as the most remarkable film storyteller of his time. As a failed playwright, but fairly competent actor, he became a player for the Biograph film company. In 1908, with Biograph's promise that should he fail he would not lose his acting job, Griffith tried his hand at directing a movie and thereafter made two or three or more short story films each week, constantly experimenting with the camera's narrative capacity. It is intensely ironic that this man who had trained himself for the serious theater, and who was never an avid fan of cinema, should so brilliantly have modified the theatrical conventions practiced by other filmmakers of the period. Whereas other filmmakers tended to use the single static camera position for an entire film, exaggerated stage acting played to the balcony rather than to the more intimately located camera, and bright, flat, unimaginative lighting, Griffith moved the camera between shots, occasionally within shots, restrained the performers' gestures and posturings, and used dramatic lighting parallel to stage mood lighting. He also realized the selective nature of the medium, understanding that it was capable of isolating elements of the drama through the use of **irises** and **masks** and close-ups in a way unavailable to the stage even though the stage could do something like this with spotlighting. Although Griffith retained a great deal of the content of the theater — most of his films were nineteenth-century melodramas — he was able to tell his stories with an astonishing narrative forcefulness to a more intensely involved audience. Griffith's filmed stories had an energy, fluidity, and vitality which took advantage of the motion picture's ability to move.

This illusion of motion, of "movingness," is essential in cinematic form and in cinematic storytelling. It is not only that images on the screen move, but also that the audience seems to change location and perspective. Griffith could place an audience high on a hill overlooking the battle lines of the Northern and Southern armies and fill it with the sense of epic spectacle as he does in *The Birth of a Nation* (1915) and in the next shot bring the audience close to an individual act of heroism on the battlefield, isolating the details of human action necessary to build the audience's empathy with specific characters. Drama, of course, can change the scene too, but not with the rapidity of cinema. Moreover, cinema has an immediacy and specificity of time and place which drama does not possess. In *Henry V* an actor, speaking on behalf of Shakespeare, must apologize for the limits of the stage, saying, "Think, when we talk of horses, that you see them," and he goes on to say that the audience's imagination must go "here and there," but a film can show us horses and in a second can take us from France to England. The mobility Griffith found through editing meant that film stories did not need to be told like theatrical stories.

Griffith perfected parallel editing to increase suspense. He built up scenes out of shots photographed at varying distances and angles, thereby increasing the audience's involvement with the plot and the characters. He used objects such as the cameo of Elsie Stoneman that Ben Cameron holds tenderly in *The Birth of a Nation,* and small yet significant details (for example, having Mr. Jenkins, the factory owner, stoop to pick up a dime before looking in on the workers' dance in *Intolerance,* 1916) to reveal the emotional states of his characters, and he recognized that a slight change in a facial expression could give far more information than an exaggerated grimace. Aware that the cinema could span time with a cut and could authenticate an imaginary event with its images, he set his characters in significant social and historical contexts in order to establish the reality and the serious intent of his stories. *Intolerance,* a plea for an end to bigotry, combines four stories from four different time periods and places — an urban drama set in modern times, Judea in the time of Christ, the St. Bartholomew's Day Massacre in the Paris of 1572, and Babylon in 539 B.C. — and thus both captures the sweep of history and the meaning that history has for the individuals caught up in it. Griffith was not the first filmmaker to use the **epic** form nor the spectacular mise-en-scène (the Italian cinema developed the spectacular epic first), but he was the first to combine the epic and the personal. One example of many suffices to demonstrate Griffith's fluid movement from the grand to the lowly. During the Babylonian story, a feast for the ruling Prince Belshazzar is held amid the splendor of one of the largest sets ever constructed in Hollywood. Extreme long shots take in the cast of thousands of dancing girls and retainers, the whole whirling mass of people and bodies, garlanded and draped columns, huge statues of ancient temple gods, and all of this is viewed with a godlike omniscience by the audience. But Griffith particularizes the monumental scene by focusing in — via inserted close-ups and masking devices — on the simple and hard-fighting Mountain Girl and recording her reactions to the feasting surrounding her. Though commercially unsuccessful in its own day, *Intolerance* is a monument to the imagination and skill of the motion picture's first great storyteller.

While Griffith refined the narrative structure of epics and melodramas, others developed the art of pantomime and burlesque, taking specific advantage of film's malleable time and space. Thomas H. Ince, a **producer** who supervised every facet of the films in his charge, ran a tight studio, and his films were marked by taut construction, a direct narrative line, believable characters, and lots of action. Mack Sennett, another producer/director, covered the comic elements of storytelling with as much verve as Griffith covered the melodrama and Ince the adventure film. Sennett created the Keystone Cops, and he discovered visual **slapstick** and custard pies, bathing beauties and fast motion. He also found the actors that he needed for his kind of stories: Ben Turpin, Fatty Arbuckle, and, of course, Charlie Chaplin (Figure 2). The narrative structure of slapstick comedy depended less on coherence than on motion, less on nuance than on the ridiculously broad, and less on the development of character and intricacies of plot than on the use of physical space and cinematic time.

Essentially, then, by the start of World War I, storytelling in the movies had established its types and its forms, its production, distribution, and exhibition system. Hollywood was the place that produced epics, tearjerkers, westerns, and slapstick comedies starring famous screen personalities, films which were then shipped throughout the country to adoring fans who paid to see their favorite performers in action on the silent screen. Stories tended to be made to type and performers were usually cast to type. During and after the war, audiences went to films whose subject matter tended to reflect whatever was popular in pulp novels, theater, and vaudeville. Movies had become big business and producers had become the dominant force in Hollywood filmmaking, listening more attentively to the ring of the cash register than to the creative artist. The practice of giving the producer the right to "final cut" became an industry standard. Thus, if a **director** turned in a finished film which the producer didn't like, the producer simply recut it, shot extra footage if necessary, and changed the whole to suit what he thought was the public's taste.

This desire to please the public and thus to make money, rather than to develop the public taste, meant that some filmmakers had a great deal of trouble making films in America under the watchful eyes of powerful movie moguls. For example, director Erich von Stroheim was in conflict with producer Irving Thalberg over such issues as film length, adherence to a budget, and controversial themes. Von Stroheim's *Greed* (1923–1924), a meticulously detailed adaptation of Frank Norris's naturalistic novel *McTeague*, was cut by the studio head from its original length of nine hours to two hours. Even though one can see the brilliance of the film in this short version, it is not what von Stroheim intended. On the other hand, an

★ **2** Much of silent comedy depends upon exaggeration of emotion and broad gestures. Chaplin, however, often extracted laughs using exactly the opposite method. In THE GOLD RUSH (1925), while starving in the middle of a blizzard, he calmly polishes off a boiled shoe as if it were a rare gourmet treat served in a fancy restaurant, even going so far as to suck the last traces of food off the shoe nails as if they were chicken bones. The sequence derives its humor from the Little Tramp's straight-faced delicacy.

imaginative filmmaker like Charles Chaplin had no difficulty in pleasing the public, making money, *and* making art. For most of his career, these talents allowed him to make films with minimal interference from others.

EARLY STORYTELLERS: EUROPE AND THE SILENT FILM

Early in the 1920s other national cinemas arose to challenge the supremacy of Hollywood. Though each nation had its own distinctive cinematic character, all of the famous European filmmakers of the period shared the assumption that the cinema was an art equal to literature and was thus capable of treating the most serious, complex, and profound material with sensitivity, subtlety, and expressive technical daring. Film in Europe had never been regarded, as it was in the United States, simply as "lower-class" entertainment.

From Germany, perhaps the most innovative national cinema of those years between 1919 and 1925, films such as Robert Wiene's *The Cabinet of Dr. Caligari* (1919), Ernst Lubitsch's *Anna Boleyn* (1920), F. W. Murnau's *The Last Laugh* (1924), E. A. Dupont's *Variety* (1925), G. W. Pabst's *Joyless Street* (1925), and Fritz Lang's *Metropolis* (1927) stunned the world with their inventive camera work and serious subject matter. Often this inventive-

★ **3** Some German expressionist films employed realistic settings to tell stories that were closer to everyday life. Yet they were still able to use subjective camera and harsh shadow effects to add an eerie quality to the depiction of elemental conflicts. In VARIETY (1925), E. A. Dupont blended the real and the expressionistic in his story of jealousy and murder under the "Big Top."

ness and seriousness took the form of **expressionism,** in films that explored dream, nightmare, and psyche and that found their narrative shape determined less by action than by emotion (Figure 3). Sweden contributed two masterful and creative directors, Mauritz Stiller and Victor Seastrom, who, like so many of the German directors, were lured to Hollywood by large salaries and promises (not always fulfilled) of artistic freedom. In Denmark, Carl Dreyer (one original who was not invited to Hollywood) developed a cinematic style that also subverted traditional notions of what constituted the story film. Dreyer was fascinated with what a pared-down cinema, concentrating on close-ups and minimal but intense details, could communicate about the human soul; working in France he made *The Passion of Joan of Arc* (1928), a masterpiece which reveals the spiritual agony Joan underwent during her trial for heresy.

René Clair and Abel Gance, two French directors, also notably expanded the narrative limits of film storytelling. Clair's filmmaking ranged from the avant-garde (*Entr'acte,* 1924) to the farcical (*The Italian Straw Hat,* 1927), but he was consistently interested in telling a story visually through rhythmic editing. Gance, who was treated as badly as Erich von Stroheim, also experimented with various camera techniques and made an epic, *Napoleon* (1926), using a triptych screen which not only created the wide-screen effects we tend to associate only with Cinerama but also made use of multiple images.

The Russians, too, contributed to the development of film narrative — particularly following the Russian Revolution of 1917. Influenced by their careful study of D. W. Griffith's films (especially *Intolerance*), new Soviet filmmakers like Sergei Eisenstein, V. I. Pudovkin, Alexander Dovzhenko, and Dziga Vertov became masters of editing, expanding the possibilities of manipulating narrative time and meaning.

By the time sound was introduced in 1927, the movies had reached technical and artistic heights almost unimaginable. Yet, except for a handful of experimental shorts (made in France and the United States) and a few documentaries, the silent cinema was primarily a storytelling cinema, a narrative medium. The camera and the written title had combined with the pantomime of actors to create every conceivable kind of story, from the silliest and simplest of slapstick comedies to sophisticated farce, from the most familiar "shoot-'em-ups" to the most profound evocations of historical epochs, from trite melodramas to emotionally draining dramas of heroes and heroines caught in the grip of fate, and from cheap thrillers to exotic and expressionistic nightmare worlds. Based upon the structural principles evolved — if not always articulated — by Méliès, Porter, and Griffith, filmmaking in the 1920s, both in Europe and in America, achieved a consummate artistry which viewed today is still fresh, exciting, and moving.

SOUND AND THE FICTION FILM

The concept and structure of cinematic storytelling changed, however, with the advent of sound. Once actors could talk and be heard and music could be synchronized with the action, audiences demanded verbal as well as visual drama. People wanted to hear voices in conflict, in love, or describing what had happened or what was about to happen or what things meant; voices that could ponder out loud or tell snappy jokes or sing a song, cry out for help or plead for mercy; voices that could "tell" what it was all about or recite lines full of poetry and significance. The first years of talkies produced a spate of filmed plays and musical revues, and so total was the concern with sound that the camera again became a static observer seated front-row center. In effect, the camera was immobilized by the microphone. The technological achievement of realizing sound set back the cinematic art of storytelling.

However, within a year or so of the success of *The Jazz Singer* (1927), creative filmmakers began to discover and develop more effective means of using sound to enhance their stories. The use of **multiple sound tracks** and asynchronous sound originating offscreen made contemporary dramas seem authentic and real and immediate. Sound also allowed the filmmaker another element through which to create humor or pathos. And sound

★ **4** Sound ushered in the era of musicals: "All Talking, All Singing, All Dancing." Dick Powell and Ruby Keeler became stars, playing the love-struck couple in several Busby Berkeley musicals of the 1930s.

was extraordinarily economical; information could be conveyed quickly without unnecessary visual emphasis. Screenwriters and directors now had a choice: if they wanted to convey something to the audience, they could either show it or say it. By the mid-thirties the movies had become expert at the art of telling stories both aurally and visually.

Sound did have a great influence on what kind of stories got told. Musicals (Figure 4) and gangster films, for example, would not have been made in such great quantity without a sound-on-film process which could provide delightful songs and terrifying machine-gun blasts. And comedy changed drastically in its orientation and structure. Silent comedy depended on visual momentum, on broad and simple actions which snowballed in accelerating images until they left the audience laughing breathlessly. Although title cards occasionally made puns, the viewer's apprehension of the comedy primarily depended on the physical and the visual. Sound changed that. The images in comedy might seem ordinary — or at least normal — while the dialogue might snowball and accelerate. Funny lines were often more intellectual, dependent upon a play on words, or on class distinctions.

THE HOLLYWOOD FICTION FILM

Other technological advances since the 1930s (color and wide-screen processes, for example) have had relatively little impact upon the kinds of narrative films made and the way in which narratives are put together. The Hollywood staples — proven successful by box office receipts — were genre films: gangster films, westerns, musicals, adventure films, science fiction and horror films, "weepies," Biblical epics, costume dramas (Figure 4). Although enhanced by the addition of sound and color and wide screens, most of these genres were established in the days of the silent cinema and their storytelling patterns were not significantly altered by the introduction of new technology alone. One either has to look at certain non-genre films which used the new technology in an idiosyncratically creative way or at certain film movements (usually associated with a national cinema) which absorbed the technology as another tool through which new narrative patterns could be realized.

One such non-genre film which has had a tremendous impact on the art of contemporary cinematic narrative as well as on other aspects of cinematic art was Orson Welles's *Citizen Kane* (1941). The use of multiple flashbacks, overlapping narrative segments, and a film within a film created enormous complexity in what might have been a simply conceived, chronologically executed fictional biography of a powerful man. *Citizen Kane* was as innovative in its day as *The Birth of a Nation* and *Intolerance* had been in theirs. It liberated cinematic narrative from traditional time schemes and it demonstrated that films could be more complexly structured and still appeal to audiences.

During the second World War, Hollywood film stories were for the most part conservative and patriotic — and European cinemas, except for Germany's propaganda machine, scarcely existed. After the war ended, however, several interesting cultural and technological realities influenced the shape of film narrative, its substance and its form. In America, for instance, awareness of the effect of the war — for example, of returning veterans who would face psychological and employment problems, and of women who had been financially independent and gainfully employed — affected even what seemed the most escapist film fare. A genre (or, some maintain, a film style) appeared which has since been given the name, **film noir** (literally, "black film") (Figure 5). Stylistically the ancestry of these films could be traced to the horror films of the 1930s and early 1940s, films whose use of light and shade (*chiaroscuro*) had been imported with German directors and cameramen during the late 1920s and the 1930s. Thematically, their ancestry owed something to the gangster film, less Germanic and dark than American and urban. Film noir, however, was post-World War II,

★ **5**   Barbara Stanwyck, Fred MacMurray, and Edward G. Robinson appeared in
DOUBLE INDEMNITY (Billy Wilder, 1944), an early *film noir* — literally
"black film." In opposition to the traditional optimism of Hollywood films, the
film noir explored the seamy side of urban life in post–World War II America,
focusing on a corrupt and deceitful world.

focusing on the seamy underbelly of the urban world, the big city full of
corruption and deceit, a disillusioned world with few heroes and few if any
redeeming social values. True, most Hollywood films still echoed the
optimism about the future that has always seemed a part of American culture, but films like *Double Indemnity* (1944), *The Big Sleep* (1946), *The
Strange Love of Martha Ivers* (Lewis Milestone, 1946), *Out of the Past*
(Jacques Tourneur, 1947), *The Asphalt Jungle* (John Huston, 1950), and *The
Big Heat* (Fritz Lang, 1953) indicated a deep-seated pessimism which was
far more brooding and disturbing than those films which, like the intelligent
and narratively satisfying *The Best Years of Our Lives* (William Wyler, 1946),
dealt more overtly with postwar themes (Figure 6). After World War II
films in America began to mature in their thematic content; the emergence
of film noir signalled a trend towards psychological realism.

★ **6** Non-genre films in the realistic mode will often be about something most people consider relevant to contemporary life. THE BEST YEARS OF OUR LIVES (William Wyler, 1946), for instance, recounted the problems faced by three returning veterans of World War II, exploring their difficult readjustment to civilian life.

FILM MOVEMENTS

This move toward realism, dramatically evident in filmmaking in postwar Europe, was especially evident in Italy. Because Italian studios had been bombed and film stock was hard to come by, Italian filmmakers literally took to the streets to find their stories and to film them. Using natural locations, natural lighting, and nonprofessional actors as well as professionals, directors like Roberto Rossellini and Vittorio de Sica told stark, episodic narratives of ordinary people living ordinary lives in a war-torn country governed by a usually unfeeling and inadequate bureaucracy. This movement, called **Italian neorealism,** changed the shape of film narrative. Storytelling no longer needed to be neatly fashioned, tidily resolved, artificially constructed; narrative — in imitation of life — became more open-ended and less dramatically symmetrical. And because these films were financial

★ 7   Alain Resnais, a French new wave director, uses the fiction film to explore the relationship between memory and history, between what really happened and what we remember. In HIROSHIMA, MON AMOUR (1959), he contrasts the painful memories of two participants of World War II, a Japanese man whose parents died at Hiroshima and a Frenchwoman who had a love affair with a German soldier during the Occupation. Resnais uses film's ability to manipulate time to indicate the complexity of the problem.

as well as critical successes in the United States, Italian neorealism influenced the narrative traditions of American film.

Factors other than the war influenced a further change in narrative cinema in France during the 1950s. There, the champions of a "new" cinema were a number of young film critics who had studied and written about film history and particularly enjoyed the taut and dynamic Hollywood films made in the 1940s. François Truffaut and Jean-Luc Godard were the leaders of this group of new filmmakers, most of whom had grown up in the Paris Cinématheque, a film archive which showed films from around the world around the clock. Although each filmmaker who emerged from this group was an original and individual talent, all of the filmmakers were united by their desire to abandon — as well as often subvert — formal and conventional and boringly respectable stories usually adapted from novels or plays, and by their desire to make films which went to the center of contemporary concerns and dealt with them through contemporary forms. By the end of the 1950s, the films of what has since come to be called the **French new wave** (nouvelle vague) began to attract international notice. The new wave introduced many important directors, but perhaps Jean-Luc Godard and Alain Resnais exerted the greatest influence on film narrative: Godard because of his attempts to educate the viewer to the ideology behind the processes of the cinema, and Resnais because of his innovative explorations of time and memory (Figure 7).

A renaissance of British filmmaking occurred at about the same time as the French new wave films began to appear. The **British free cinema** movement began in the mid-1950s, reflecting the English artists' increasing concern with everyday life as lived among the middle and lower classes. Earlier, the narrative cinema (like the drama) had emphasized the upper classes and had tended to ignore social problems or to put them in comic form. But in the fifties British filmmakers began to fashion an original and gritty cinema, at first adapting other media for the cinema — a novel for *Room at the Top* (Jack Clayton, 1958), and a play for *Look Back in Anger* (Tony Richardson, 1959). Until the mid-1960s, when the movement seemed to lose its impetus, England exported films which combined social drama with innovative forms and touches of wry comedy.

Two other film movements which have further changed the shape of the fiction film have been the **cinema novo** of Brazil and the **new German cinema.** Although Brazilian filmmakers had long used film for political ends, especially to criticize governmental policies which favored the rich and ignored or exploited the poor, it was not until the 1960s that their films gained international recognition as bizarre and innovative combinations of realism, folk myth, music, fantasy, and social documentary which promoted, in allegorical fashion, revolutionary ideas. First recognized in the mid-1970s, the new German cinema is the most recent film movement. Although each filmmaker's vision is unique, the works of Rainer Fassbinder, Werner Herzog, and Wim Wenders all share a modernist aesthetic, an antagonism toward traditional cinematic narrative, and a critical attitude toward contemporary German values.

NEW DIRECTIONS

American film has chiefly continued to excel in traditional narrative forms. Although the work of filmmakers such as Stanley Kubrick, Robert Altman, Woody Allen, and Terence Malick indicate new directions in American narrative cinema (Figure 8), the basic shape of the Hollywood fiction film has remained relatively constant. Europe, except for the new German cinema, has not seen particularly drastic or significant changes in film narrative either. France, for example, now seems to export humane, domestic, bourgeois dramas and comedies, rather than the groundbreaking experimental and existential ones of the 1950s and 1960s. National cinemas, however, throughout the world still continue to pour energy and talent into the fiction film. Individual, beautiful, moving and intellectually stimulating works are still being made by those filmmakers who are now considered "old masters": Federico Fellini, François Truffaut, Ingmar Bergman, Luis Buñuel. And there are also original and exciting new talents beginning to emerge from the Middle East and Africa.

★ **8** Even though Stanley Kubrick began directing films under studio conditions, he is now in a position to control every aspect of his films. For instance, he adapted a Thackeray novel into a screenplay, which he then produced and directed: BARRY LYNDON (1975) is totally a Kubrick film from the casting, through the photography, the editing, to the choice of music. Here he is shown during the shooting of the film.

The ways of telling stories through film are many, and new forms of storytelling are important because they open up new possibilities and new choices for the filmmaker, but what is essential to narrative cinema is not new forms, not new plots, but great imagination in using what is available. It has been said, with some plausibility, that there are only seven basic plots and that all stories are simply variations of the seven whether they are told through literature, drama, or film, but the variations and adaptations which are suited to each generation's narrative needs are countless. Despite the sophistication of its culture, it is unlikely that even the most civilized of nations — or worlds — will ever lose its desire for well-told tales.

4
★ GENRE FILMS

The emphasis . . . is on a description of popular movies, viewed in sets
and cycles rather than as single entities. It is an approach that accepts
obsolescence and in which judgements derive from the sympathetic con-
sumption of a great many films. In terms of continuing themes and motifs,
the obsolescence of single films is compensated for by the prolongation
of ideas in film after film.
Lawrence Alloway[1]

Long the staple product of Hollywood, the genre film such as the western or the gangster film is different from other fiction films in that it
follows established narrative patterns, uses stereotypical characters, and
communicates through certain familiar images (**icons**). These images are
a sort of shorthand, compressing information about the story, characters, and theme into objects such as décor, costume, and topography.
For example, in a western the derringer (a small, easily concealed pistol)
indicates its owner's basically underhanded character. Or consider
clothing: both cowboys and outlaws wear loose-fitting and practical
clothing, indicating a free and open life-style, but people from the town
usually wear suits, vests, and ties to indicate their more restricted way
of life. The genre film also builds upon preexistent audience expectations: we go to see a "thriller," a "gangster" film. The experience of the
genre film is a familiar rather than a new experience and its satisfactions
are based on our previous knowledge of the **formulas** and **conventions**
in the films. Genre films are popular and comprehensible — and although
certain critics look down on genre films as escapist, mass, and mediocre
entertainment, audiences turn out in droves to see the likes of such

recent genre films as *Jaws* (Steven Spielberg, 1976), a horror film; *Rocky* (John Avildsen, 1976), a sports film; and *Star Wars* (George Lucas, 1977), a science fiction film. More sophisticated critics, recognizing that the popularity and comprehensibility of the genre film do not necessarily mean simplicity, know that some genre films are worthy of critical scrutiny. Contemporary filmmakers, too, recognize and exploit the audience's familiarity with genre films. Through parodies or reversals of familiar genres — such as *Blazing Saddles* (Mel Brooks, 1974) and *The Long Goodbye* (Robert Altman, 1973) — they have turned the genre film into a modernist, self-conscious, self-reflexive exploration of its own form and content.

★★★ The Definition of Genre

What, precisely, is a film genre? It is a film that belongs to a particular group of films that are extremely similar in their subject matter, thematic concerns, characterizations, plot formulas, and visual settings. Such a film somehow depends on these similarities for its very existence and for the satisfactions it brings the viewer. Some genres, such as the western, are easily recognizable; many points of similarity exist between films, linking them firmly into a group. On the most simple level, we know a western is a western because nearly all westerns are set on the American frontier from 1865 to 1900. Certain historical elements recur again and again in western films: we have seen, on many screens, images of the building of the transcontinental railroad, the U.S. cavalry defending a fort, the wagon train crossing the country. We have seen repeated images of the bounty hunter, the lawman, Monument Valley or the Great Plains, the roundup, the bunkhouse, the campfire, the Indians, the Western town with its board sidewalks and saloons and bank and general store. These visual elements help us to identify a western as a western, although all of them, of course, need not appear in any one film. In fact, unless the film is an epic (Ford, Hathaway, and Marshall's *How the West Was Won*, 1963, or Italian director Sergio Leone's operatic *Once upon a Time in the West*, 1969), the inclusion of too many conventional elements in a single film may result in an effect which is unintentionally comic.

King Vidor's *Duel in the Sun* (1947), for example, though it was expensively produced and was much publicized at the time it was released, today provokes howls of laughter or groans of disbelief from audiences who now are used to films which vary or break with at least some of the traditions of the western film. *Duel in the Sun* seems to go out of its

★ **4-1** Genre films are crafted out of formula plots, conventions, and stereotyped characters. Each film contains a selection from the pool of available elements. DUEL IN THE SUN (King Vidor, 1946), however, used far too many in one film and the effect is close to parody. Jennifer Jones played the half-breed "bad" girl and Lionel Barrymore, the domineering, independent rancher trying to stave off the coming of the railroad and civilization.

way to include as many of the conventional aspects of the genre as possible (Figure 4-1). The heroine, Pearl, is a half-breed. The protagonist and antagonist are brothers; one has become a "dandified," "civilized," "Easternized" lawyer who is genteel with ladies, and the other is still a wild, crude, irresponsible, stallion of a cowboy. Their father (a retired senator) owns a huge cattle empire and favors the toughness of his wild son over the refined manners of his other son. Their mother (a tired but strong-willed Southern belle) prefers the civilized qualities of her favorite over the animal crudity of the son she is sure will come to no good. Both sons confront each other over Pearl; one son wants to improve Pearl's mind, the other is more interested in her body. The railroad enters the picture, its construction threatening the ranchers' rangeland. There is a confrontation between the ranchers and the railroad crew, and the cavalry arrives from nowhere in the nick of time to prevent a full-scale battle. Pearl (whose half-breed "bad blood" has not been able to resist the advances of the "bad" son, although she does want her mind improved) and the "bad" son end up killing each other, leaving the "good" and civilized son free to marry an Eastern lady, who is not too sexy or too dark-skinned and who has turned up on the train, appropriately arriving from the East. *Duel in the Sun* is funny today not because it uses conventional elements, but because it uses too many of them too rapidly, too gratuitously, and too rigidly (rather than imaginatively).

★ **4-2** A western need not take place in the legendary past. As long as generic elements are present, the story can be set in the contemporary West. In LONELY ARE THE BRAVE (David Miller, 1962), set in the present, the traditional underlying conflicts between the individual who seeks the freedom of the frontier and the encroaching society that seeks to tame him are as clearly visible as they are in the more traditional western. In typical "formula" westerns, such as the many films cranked out in the Hopalong Cassidy series, good guys and bad guys are clearly drawn. The only unconventional element in this series was that Hopalong (William Boyd), the hero, always wore a black hat, and the villain (here, Robert Mitchum) frequently wore a white one.

Other western movies such as *The Wild Bunch* (Sam Peckinpah, 1969), *Little Big Man* (Arthur Penn, 1971) and *McCabe and Mrs. Miller* (Robert Altman, 1971) seem to break with tried-and-true formulas and **characterizations,** and yet they are still recognizable as part of the western genre because they retain enough generic elements to bear a strong resemblance to other films in the genre. An interesting example of this sort of departure from classic generic elements in a film which still remains a western is *Lonely Are the Brave* (David Miller, 1962). The film breaks with traditional convention in that it takes place in contemporary times, in a world full of freeways, appliances, cola drinks, and helicopters (Figure 4-2). After purposely getting himself into prison to help a close friend escape (a fairly conventional plot contrivance in the traditional western), the film's protagonist, Jack, himself escapes (his friend refuses) and is hunted down by a reluctantly admiring sheriff, his colorless assistant, a prison guard, and finally by an impersonal helicopter and its crew from a nearby military base. Jack is defeated not by gunshot in a final shoot-out on the dusty streets of a Western town, but by the wheels of a huge truck carrying bathroom fixtures cross-country on the blacktop surface of a modern highway.

Why is this film, so dependent upon its contemporary context, still a western? There are enough traditional elements in the movie to remind us constantly of other western movies that we've seen, and the **theme** of the film — the end of frontiers and the toll that progress takes on the lone individual — is basic to almost all movie westerns. Jack is a typical western hero: he hates fences and boundaries; he has rejected the stability of marriage and home because it would rob him of freedom and would force him to conform; his true home is the rapidly diminishing wilderness; his only property is his horse and gear; he cannot understand or abide by the bureaucratic and seemingly arbitrary rules of civilization. Then, too, the film's characters are engaged in relationships common to other westerns: Jack and his married friend have grown up together and are almost like brothers, but they have gone their separate ways and chosen dramatically opposed life-styles and relationships to society, each of which is ultimately incomprehensible to the other man (similar to Howard Hawks's more traditional Red River, 1948, and Rio Bravo, 1959); both men love the same woman and are both loved by her, although she has married the man who can provide her with the traditional female values of stability, a family, a civilized and social life (similar to the conflict presented in George Stevens's more traditional Shane, 1953); the prison guard is the typical bully and coward who wants to break the spirit of the hero and who regards Jack's confidence and strength as a personal accusation and threat (similar to a situation in Anthony Mann's more traditional The Tin Star, 1957); the sheriff and his deputy provide an almost vaudevillian representation of cool, leisurely efficiency and bumbling ineptitude (reminiscent not only of TV's Gunsmoke series but also of many Ford's and Hawks's westerns with drunken, aged, or gimpy sidekicks who act as dramatic foils as well as companions to the more virile hero); the sheriff's admiration for Jack's persistence and ingenuity creates a relationship between the two, and even though they have never met they become adversaries of equal strength (similar to situations in Sam Peckinpah's The Wild Bunch and Abraham Polonsky's Tell Them Willie Boy Is Here, 1970). Finally, the casting of Kirk Douglas as Jack evokes the traditional western, for Douglas has played many western heroes and even in the contemporary

★ **4-3** Setting plays an important part in the western. In addition to its function as a concrete image of the Frontier — the place where, both historically and imaginatively, civilization and the wilderness exist side by side — the wide-open spaces provide the cinematic space for unlimited, exciting action. Here Indians and outriders fight it out during an attack on the wagon train in HOW THE WEST WAS WON (John Ford, George Marshall, Henry Hathaway, 1962).

settings of *Lonely Are the Brave* he reminds us of the hero of the traditional western.

For a movie to be considered part of a genre, or of a generic tradition, then, it need not include *all* the conventions of that genre, but it should include *enough* generic elements to cause the viewer to associate it clearly and consciously with other films containing similar elements. These similarities of theme, **plot,** and characterization should also be quite specific. There are countless films built on the "boy-meets-girl, boy-loses-girl, boy-gets-girl" plot, yet all these films do not constitute a genre because the details, characterizations, and themes of the films may have no other points of resemblance whatsoever.

Not all film genres are as easily identifiable as are the western, the gangster film, and the traditional horror film, films that provide the viewer with a great deal of temporal and geographic specificity. Westerns take place in rugged open terrain, and because they generally are set between 1865 and 1900 the clothing and décor are fairly consistent from film to film (Figure 4-3). The gangster film generally takes place in a city, tends to occur in the 1920s and 1930s, and usually bases some of its material upon historical facts such as Prohibition and gang wars. The traditional horror film has developed its own topography, consisting of small English or Carpathian towns divided into moors, lone castle/fortress/laboratory and civilized manor houses and tiny inns.

Unlike these easily identified film genres, there are others which are harder to categorize. Is there such a genre as the adventure film, and what characteristics describe it? Is the war film a separate genre or is it part of the adventure film genre? The musical is a genre by virtue of its songs and dances, but beyond these does the musical have a certain kind of content which helps us describe it as a film grouping? Does the fact that people sing automatically make a film a musical? It is not necessary or desirable, of course, to categorize or pigeonhole groups of films merely for the sake of filing them neatly away. Rather, by attempting to find what links a particular film to others, we begin to understand that we gain satisfactions from repetition as much as we do from unique experiences. We also come to understand film tradition, a way of linking the art's past with its future.

FORMULA

Genre films are constructed from formula plots. The basic conflict of the story is familiar, and we know from past viewing experiences more or less how the story will be resolved. Thus, what happens in a particular genre film is predictable; we do not get *surprise* so much as *suspense* generated by small variations. We can relax and only pretend anxiety about whether the hero will live or die at the end of the movie. Different genres, however, tend to concentrate on different basic conflicts. From one genre to another, then, we get different episodes in the plot and different characters.

Consider, for example, the adventure film. The basic conflict presented in the adventure film — whether it is a film about a wild animal hunt like Howard Hawks's *Hatari!* (1962), a war movie like *Battleground* (William Wellman, 1949), or a survival movie like *The Poseidon Adventure* (Ronald Neame, 1972) — is the formation, from a random group of people, of a functioning mini-society which can accomplish a given task successfully. Because this is the central issue, all these films tend to concentrate on delineating different stereotypical characters (the coward, the braggart, the lover) and on the process whereby these individuals are tested and found to be useful or useless to the group and its single goal (Figure 4-4). Thus, the formula situations (a shipwreck, a jet plane in trouble, a platoon cut off behind enemy lines, a search for hidden treasure) provide a way to isolate and estrange the characters from civilized society so that their true natures may come to the surface. The characters represent a cross section of society ethnically and geographically (the Italian-American from New York, the black, the Texan), occupationally (the banker, the laborer, the farmer), and mor-

★ **4-4** Genre films use formula plots. The adventure film frequently brings together a group of people from different stations in life and places them in a situation of stress. In THE POSEIDON ADVENTURE (Ronald Neame, 1972), passengers on a swamped ocean liner are tested to see who wins and who loses, who lives and who dies, who is a coward or a shirker and who has the courage and skill to survive.

ally (the sniveler, the stoic, the sentimentalist) to indicate the democratic nature of group action.

Since the adventure film presents a model for a truly democratic mini-society in which each member is as good as his peers as long as the good of the group is his primary concern, the hero in the adventure film is not such a maverick as the hero in, let us say, the western. He begins as one of the victims of the initial and major crisis (e.g., the shipwreck) which starts the adventure early in the film. By virtue of his common sense, his knowledge of the goal to be achieved, his ability to organize — in short, by his ability to act decisively and in the group interest — he rises above his peers. Once the goal is achieved, the hero returns to his stance of ordinary man, a functional and average member of the larger society he has rejoined. He does not ride off into the sunset seeking new adventures and tests, but instead seeks refuge in the very society he has gone about recreating on a smaller scale.

Such is the adventure film, and certain formula scenes seem almost obligatory. When we see war movies or disaster movies, we recognize fairly early on which characters will do what, which will die early in the film, which will selfishly betray or desert the group, which will survive. We know that there will be scenes which will individually test the characters. We know that the film will be structured so that it will begin in a normal context in which people take themselves and their social roles for granted. We know that the characters will be in a situation in which a microcosm can be collected on some realistic pretext: on an airplane, in the random unit of an army, on a pleasure ship or railroad train, on a floor of an office building. We also know that after the characters have been shown to us in their civilized guise, a catastrophe will occur which will shut them off from contact with the larger society to which they belong. From that point on in the film, we expect small tests of courage and ingenuity and endurance, and we may even have a fairly good idea of who will fail and who will succeed, and of when and how they will do so — simply by the casting of various familiar actors and actresses in several kinds of roles. Certain performers tend to play parts which are repeated with minor variations from film to film. For example, Red Buttons offers the comic relief which is finally a sign of true courage, and Shelley Winters tends to die midway through the film, playing offbeat characters who sometimes are sacrificial victims to the gods of the catastrophe. Finally, the suspense in the adventure film, as in most other genre films, is less genuine than the viewer might at first think. We know, because we are familiar with the formula, that there will be survivors of the adventure and that they will rejoin the larger society at the end of the film. The suspense that is genuine in the adventure film is not about the outcome; rather, it is aroused by the small variations in characters and their reactions to the individual tests they must face.

The word formula, of course, denotes a repeated series of activities which result in a predictable end result. Certain formulas underlie specific genres — the natural catastrophe which tests a mini-group of individuals is the stuff of the adventure film, and the variations on the theme of opposing groups in the American West (settlers vs. Indians, ranchers vs. sheepmen, cavalry vs. Indians, and so forth) is the stuff of the western. But it is also true that certain formulas tend to be the communal property of all narrative film — in fact, of all narrative art.

For example, boy-meets-girl, boy-loses-girl, boy-gets-girl is one such formula, and another is that of the falsely accused person who must clear his name. Part of the enjoyment of watching traditional narrative films is our familiarity with such basic formulas, our recognition of the basic outline which holds together the innumerable small, fresh details that make the film different from the previous one with the same basic outline. Thus, when we watch a genre film, a pleasurable tension is created between the expected and predictable and familiar elements of formula and the unexpected variations of the specific film story we are watching.

CONVENTION

Whereas a formula is an entire structure or series of actions which results in a predictable and familiar end, a convention is a small, relatively separate unit of action in genre films. Conventions are the specific ways in which the formula plot (who did what, when and where, to whom) is translated into visualized action in a particular genre. The showdown gunfight between the protagonist and antagonist in the western, or the love duet between the boy and girl in the musical, are examples of such conventions. These conventional actions recur from film to film, sometimes even in remarkably similar detail.

Most westerns, for example, have a showdown gunfight between the protagonist and antagonist, and these fights are pretty much alike from film to film. The reluctant hero appears in the street, finally provoked to a showdown by the villain. The townspeople scatter and hide. There will be some interchange of terse dialogue, a challenge and acceptance of sorts. The villain must make the first move for his holstered revolver, but — like lightning — the hero draws faster and shoots down the villain.

Besides the gist of content of the convention — the chief thing that happens — there is also the way in which the content is treated, that is, the way in which the camera photographs it and the editor edits it. These, too, become familiar and predictable. Conventionally, in that shoot-out, there will be clear, sunny weather so that long shadows can dramatically enhance the action. There will seldom be any wind. A long shot of the street, usually from a high angle looking down, will give the viewer a clear idea of the spatial relationship between the two characters. This long shot will usually be followed by a series of cuts alternating between each of the men in medium shot and close-up, and these may be followed with a long shot of the townspeople scattering, and a few close-ups of eyes peering from behind windows. Then the cutting of close-ups between the two men will accelerate until the final close-ups show the faces of each, the hands reaching for the hips, the guns being drawn. Then there will usually be a long shot of the villain being struck by the fatal bullet and his fall to the ground. This is customarily followed by a high-angle long shot again revealing the town and letting the viewer see the townspeople and possibly the heroine rejoin the lone hero on the street. Variations, of course, are probable; the street may be larger or smaller, there may be fewer or many more witnesses to the showdown, there may or may not be a heroine, there may be shots inserted of the villain's henchman on a hotel roof waiting to gun down the hero before he can fire at the villain. Still, the basic convention in both content and form is clearly recognizable and satisfyingly familiar. This convention is almost never violated except purposely, for example, when a filmmaker parodies the genre or makes a consciously anti-genre film which attempts to subvert our expectations. Otherwise, certain aspects of the gunfight are always maintained: the hero never draws first, he never shoots his opponent from ambush, and he always triumphs in the end.

Although we are perhaps most familiar with the conventions of westerns, we recognize conventions in other genres, too (Figure 4-5). In the gangster film, the death of the protagonist usually shows him cornered, caught in some kind of trap and, unlike the ending of a western, there is no gun duel, no stylized interplay between protagonist and antagonist. Instead, the gangster is surrounded and gunned down. We are also familiar with the convention in a war movie in which the soldier gives his watch or some personal object to his girlfriend, wife, or buddy to "hold for him." We know as clearly as if it were spelled out in block letters that that soldier is never going to come back. Similarly, we expect a hysterical soldier in a war movie to wander out and get shot down or to be slapped across the face by the hero, who will be told by the revived soldier something along the lines of "Thanks, I needed that." All of these are conventions of content. But, as in the western, there are stylistic or formal conventions in other genres too. In science fiction films which feature giant mutations threatening giant cities, we expect alternating close-ups of people and creatures and then long shots in which the creature and an identifiable urban landscape are together. And in the musical, we have come to accept lovers singing to each other, cheek pressed against cheek and faces directed out towards the film audience. We tend to be more aware of plot conventions than of formal conventions (such as camera work), but both kinds of conventions are crucial to the genre film and to the pleasure we derive from watching variations on the familiar.

★ **4-5** A convention often found in the musical genre is that one of the lead couple falls hopelessly and secretly in love with the other. Here Polly (Ruby Keeler) has fallen in love with Brad (Dick Powell), a songwriter who lives across the court, in GOLD DIGGERS OF 1933 (Mervyn Le Roy, 1933).

ICONOGRAPHY

In *Little Caesar* (1930) a police lieutenant and two of his men visit a night-club run by gangsters. All three wear large hats and heavy coats, are grim and sardonic and stand in triangular formation, the lieutenant at the front, his two men flanking him in the rear. The audience knows immediately what to expect of them by their physical attributes, their dress and deportment. It knows, too, by the disposition of the figures, which is dominant, which subordinate. . . . These examples indicate the continuity over several decades of patterns of visual imagery, or recurrent objects and figures in dynamic relationship. These repeated patterns might be called the iconography of the genre, for they set it off visually from other types of film and are the means whereby primary definitions are made.
Colin McArthur[2]

An even smaller unit of the genre film is the icon, from a Greek word meaning "image," "likeness." Whereas formula refers to an entire structure or series of actions upon which an entire film is based (the essential plot and characters), and convention refers to a unit of action or episode within a formula which recurs from film to film, the film icon is a yet smaller element of the genre film. Certain costumes (cowboy clothes, evening dresses), certain objects (suitcases, pistols), certain landscapes (foggy moors, wide-open prairies), and certain performers (John Wayne, Red Buttons) instantly signify — simply by their presence — elements of plot which have not yet occurred, complete psyches and motivations in characters, and complex thematic associations regarding the content of the genre and with the past cinematic experience of the viewer.

An icon gets its meaning from its repeated use in many films. The round glass paperweight in *Citizen Kane* (1941), for example, though important in that film, is not an icon, because paperweights have not accumulated, in film after film, any special meaning. Similarly, the tune whistled by the child murderer in *M* (Fritz Lang, 1931) has no meaning outside of its appearance in that specific film. On the other hand, the sound of a creaking door tends to be iconic, conveying menace, dread, potential horror; it evokes all those moments of terror and all those dreaded figures from past horror films the viewer has seen. The same is true of a horse neighing or a dog howling in a horror film; within the context of the genre those sounds have come to signal impending danger, the presence of some otherworldly menace sensed by animals but not by humans. (In *Young Frankenstein*, 1974 — one of the funnier genre allusions uses neighing horses whenever a particularly evil house-keeper's name is mentioned, even though the animals are not near enough to such conversations to "overhear" them.) The sound of a machine gun with its rapid-fire rat-a-tat and its specific physical appear-ance in a gangster film communicates not only itself in the one particu-lar film, but also communicates the crudeness of gangsters.

Icons in the western genre, the gangster film, the traditional horror film derive many of their meanings from extra-filmic sources such as history and literature, as well as from film tradition itself. But as visual imagery, the icons take on added significance, emotional weight, and power, and come to communicate enormous amounts of narrative infor-mation to the audience. Consider, for example, the meaning generated by the handgun in the western. The Colt Peacemaker is the most popu-lar handgun used in the western film — and part of its cinematic appeal has to do with the fact that the shape of the Peacemaker is more pleas-ing than those of some of the other handguns of the period. Since the western hero is often a graceful figure concerned with self-defining style (the proper patterns of ritual behavior), it is appropriate that his weapon be graceful and stylish too. Thus, the handgun functions in the western

★ **4-6** Many performers have become icons, their mere presence in a film signifying more than just an actor playing a character. John Wayne played the same Westerner from John Ford's STAGECOACH (1939) to Don Siegel's THE SHOOTIST (1976), to the extent that the audience knows from the moment he walks onto the screen what he represents morally and dramatically. This image from Howard Hawks's RED RIVER (1948) includes Walter Brennan, who turned up time and again as a foil to the Wayne figure.

not only as a firearm, but also as a visual means whereby the film-maker communicates information about character to the viewer. Similarly, derringers and other small concealable weapons have accumulated cinematic associations which make them icons signifying deception, rascality, cowardice, and effeteness.

While the iconic significance of objects in genre films is often easily discernible because we notice *things* in movies, the more pervasive yet less noticed background can also function iconically. We expect a certain physical topography in the western (even if it is actually filmed in Spain or Italy), and that landscape conveys more than its physical self; it communicates a way of life with particular hardships, particular demands, it communicates certain unplayed dramas which have taken place in its "arena" in other movies or which will take place in the movie being viewed and in future movies (the ambush in the box canyon, the Indians appearing on the crest of a bluff, the stumbling descent of a horse through badlands). The city is more than a merely physical characteristic of the gangster film; it communicates from film to film a nightmare landscape, a cold, unnatural world, a world full of hiding places where devious transactions can take place in the shadows.

Finally, certain performers are iconic. They communicate not only themselves as recognizable stars, or as the characters they play in the specific film, but they also communicate a kind of character, a whole set of moral values, from film to film simply by their physical appearance in these films. John Wayne, for example, is an actor who is an icon. He need not have very many lines of dialogue in any given western movie for the viewer to understand, to almost intimately know, who and what the character is, what he believes in and how he will act in a given situation. Because Wayne played in so many westerns, becoming a star in John Ford's *Stagecoach* (1939) as a relatively young man and showing his age most poignantly as the cowboy hero dying of cancer in Don Siegel's *The Shootist* (1976), he accumulated so many lines of dialogue and so many repeated actions performed in similar situations that when he appears on the screen in a western he still communicates a whole set of ethics, a predictable range of behavior, a wonderfully familiar sense of a known character (Figure 4-6). It is hardly surprising that when he occasionally attempted to play roles other than western heroes (or World War II heroes, another and similarly successful forte) as he did in *McQ* (John Sturges, 1974), his films were not particularly well received.

★★★ **Types of Genre Narrative**

> One gangster film follows another as one musical or one Western follows another. But this rigidity is not necessarily opposed to the requirements of art. There have been very successful types of art in the past which developed such specific and detailed conventions as almost to make individual examples of the type interchangeable. . . . One goes to any individual example of the type with very definite expectations, and originality is to be welcomed only in the degree that it intensifies the expected experience without fundamentally altering it.
> Robert Warshow[3]

There are two major types of genre films, **comedy** and **melodrama**. **Tragedy,** in contemporary films, tends to appear in nonformula films rather than in genre films — although one might possibly argue that certain gangster films and some of the "weepies" or "women's films" in which the protagonist ends badly are both tragic *and* genre films. Undoubtedly, elements of the tragic are present in such films, but when the genre film draws to its conclusion, the audience has usually transferred its allegiance to society's notions of order, which dictate the elimination or punishment of those individuals who violate the norm, such as gangsters and women who seek independence and fulfillment outside the domestic pale. Tragedy (with its emphasis on the nature of a hero who opposes society) is alien to the ends of genre films, for tragedy demands that the easy resolution of genre films be abandoned. The genre film, by resolving its conflicts easily, almost as if it were a dream, does not challenge the audience's values, as tragedy does. It is this easy resolution in genre films that pleases and soothes the viewer.

GENRE COMEDIES

There are, of course, many kinds of comedy in film. There is physical comedy and there is verbal comedy and there is a combination of both; there are comedies which are harshly satiric, and there are comedies which are mild and gentle. There are comedies which are singular films, funny or satiric or bizarre but unique, unlike other comedies. And there are comedies which seem like familiar friends, which look and sound and feel like films we've seen before and will see again. These last films are genre comedies, and like all generic forms they share certain similarities of structure and content; their **formula plots** are recognizable, and so are their conventions and icons (although icons are less an element in some comedy films than are conventions).

Slapstick Comedy

The earliest comic genre (and perhaps the earliest genre of any kind of film) is slapstick comedy, a comedy based on physical activity (especially assaults) and accelerating momentum (especially chases). The silent motion picture derived this action-oriented comedy from burlesque, vaudeville, and music hall entertainment and brought it to a new height, especially with the slapstick comedies produced by Mack Sennett and the Keystone Studio (Figure 4-7).

Rational continuity and narrative continuity are *not* part of the formula of slapstick comedy. Indeed, the very lack of such coherence of logic and plot is part of the slapstick formula. Nor is there always the continuity provided by a single protagonist. A single character is usually the center of interest in most other genres, but as slapstick events slip from one to another, the events' initiators and victims change too. Types (rather than characters) move through the world, doing battle with whatever obstacles present themselves. These obstacles are either inanimate objects — food that won't stay on the plate, pianos that have to be moved through small spaces, doors that won't open or which swing back and forth inopportunely, cars that break down or break apart — or people who stand for the pressures of society — policemen, headwaiters, rich and/or pompous social figures. The episodic, almost musically connected, nature of slapstick comedy also determines that those

★ **4-7** Slapstick comedies contain certain conventions — the car chase, the pie fight, the dignified being undone. Mack Sennett's Keystone Kops films used such recognizable material. Physical reaction and pursuit will follow this phone call.

obstacles be varied, and that the desired goal be relatively unimportant. Sometimes, in fact, the goal is actually forgotten. We may forget, for example, that the protagonist is on his way to a new job because we are taken up with the comic adventures (an escape from a dog, an encounter with a drunk) that take place on the way.

The formula resides primarily in activity, in the commotion resulting from attempts to overcome obstacles and obtain goals, whether the film is an early slapstick silent like one of Sennett's Keystone Kops shorts or his *Tillie's Punctured Romance* (1914) or the more modern attempts at slapstick in films such as *It's a Mad, Mad, Mad, Mad World* (Stanley Kramer, 1963) and *Silent Movie* (Mel Brooks, 1977). Motion and its acceleration through performance, camera manipulation, and editing are the key characteristics of slapstick comedy — and the resolution of the "non-plot" occurs most usually through exhaustion. The car/train/motorcycle chase finally involves the entire city, including the fire department and all of the dogs that have escaped from the pound; the pie fight moves from the confines of a restaurant or bakery into the street and the world, but eventually the car collapses, and the pies give out.

Thus, the formula of slapstick comedy is based on an episodic structure in which highly undifferentiated character types (when one cop is outwitted, another appears) struggle with one another in situations which emphasize physical movement and accelerating momentum, and the conventions of the genre can be identified by such units of action as the car chase, the pie fight, the dignified being undone, and also by such formal devices as fast motion and the long shot (the latter crucial as a convention of slapstick because it shows crazy actions expanding spatially as far as they can go.

Romantic Comedy

Romantic comedy arises from the literary tradition which scholars call new comedy, a form (developed in ancient Greece and then in Rome) with a rigid structure: a male and female (naive ingenues) fall in love and must overcome various obstacles (usually at least one parent objects) so that they can be united in marriage; in the ancient plays, most often, the couple is helped by someone who is worldly-wise, especially a wily slave or adviser. Within the formula, certain conventions arise which play upon various sorts of reversals: mistakes of identity, of timing trysts and meetings, of male/female dress. A classic modern example of the new comedy (which also happens to be a musical), first written for the theater and then adapted to the screen, is *A Funny Thing Happened on the Way to the Forum* (the film version directed by Richard Lester and released in 1966).

Romantic film comedy can only rarely, of course, include wily slaves or even feuding families, but it nevertheless retains more than merely the spirit of new comedy. Feuding families are sometimes turned into family obstacles of quite another sort: one of the lovers (or both) is married, as in *The April Fools* (Stuart Rosenberg, 1969), or the couple is already married and has created its own obstacles based on sexual misunderstandings, as in *Wife vs. Secretary* (Clarence Brown, 1936). Often the wily slave has been transformed into an urban domestic servant in the person of a butler or a maid or has become a shrewd, wisecracking neighbor (either a bachelor or a spinsterish woman who keeps discussing her bad luck with men) or one member of an older and happily married couple.

A more far-reaching change in formula does away with the wily slave or adviser completely and allows one of the lovers to serve the dual function of naive ingenue in matters of love and wise and shrewd mentor in matters of life. Thus, one of the partners is usually more aggressive and more influential in effecting the desired outcome of new comedy — the marriage. Sometimes this role falls to the male; in *It Happened One Night* (Frank Capra, 1934), Clark Gable's newspaperman is the romantic protagonist who falls in love with Claudette Colbert's willful socialite, but he is also the shrewd educator whose knowledge of the world outstrips that of his romantic interest, and so he is able to teach her a thing or two and bring about their eventual union. Usually, however, it is the female romantic protagonist who performs the function of the wily slave, cleverly coping with the various obstacles placed in the couple's way (very often the obstinacy of the male) and bringing about the desired marriage. In *Bringing Up Baby* (Howard Hawks, 1938), for example, although Katharine Hepburn plays a scatter-brained ingenue who seems to be constantly getting herself and others into hopeless trouble, she is really an artful young woman going about getting her man and educating her naive paleontologist (played by Cary Grant) to an acceptance of the chaos inherent in life and to an acceptance of his love for her (Figure 4-8). In *Mr. Smith Goes to Washington* (Frank Capra, 1939), *The Lady Eve* (Preston Sturges, 1941), and *Ball of Fire* (Howard Hawks, 1941), too, it is the woman who is the aggressor and who, even when the male protagonist is in love with her and needs no persuasion, educates the male to the realities of life. It seems hardly an accident that the male protagonists in these films are idealists or are isolated by their single-minded zeal and their professions (paleontologist, small-town senator, rich snake enthusiast, and professor working on an encyclopedia) — and that the female protagonists are women whose occupations have taken them into the real world: the socialite who deals with people rather than with dinosaur bones, the Washington secretary who knows the ropes, the card-sharp con artist, and the stripper. Perhaps one of the chief pleasures of the romantic film genre (and one which explains its appeals to women *beyond* the supposed satisfactions to be found in the marriage or reunion at the end) is that it is a form in which it is safe for the female protagonist to wield power and to pursue goals in a way usually open in films only to male characters. Because the desired end of romantic film comedy is marriage and the creation of a family within an accepted social structure, the female aggressor can do no wrong, cannot be, perhaps, too strong or too threatening; further, the comedy and comic inventions of the romantic film comedy make it a decidedly closed film form, "safe" because it is distinctly separate from real life.

Whether the romantic comedy is a "screwball comedy" (like those films mentioned above) or whether, like many modern comedies, it can be subclassified only as a "Doris Day–Róck Hudson" movie like *Pillow Talk* (Michael Gordon, 1959), the film will end with a wedding — either onscreen or off (after the credits have ended). In all the films, whether the hero and heroine are ingenues or a married couple, an education will take place, obstacles will be overcome, and the couple will be united or reunited to affirm marriage, home, and the continuation of an institution

★ **4-8** In Howard Hawks's BRINGING UP BABY (1938), Cary Grant, and Katharine Hepburn played the "new comedy" roles of the naive ingenue and the wily slave. Though the wily slave is sometimes a male, often (as in this film) that part is given to the female. Katharine Hepburn appears to be a daffy, scatterbrained young socialite, but in fact she is a shrewd young woman overcoming all obstacles in her pursuit of her man.

crucial to society as we know it. Within the basic formula, many conventions signal the genre: the gallery of male suitors who surround the female, who are patently inappropriate mates, and who are made to seem asexual or ridiculously vain; the predatory female who stalks the protagonist but who loses out to the domestic potential and intent of the heroine; misunderstandings involving identity, intent, marital status; role reversals, fairly often including female impersonation when the male is caught in a situation in which he must don female clothing. The formal conventions of the genre include fast pacing: not only frenetic action, but also swift dialogue between hero and heroine, indicating their appropriateness for each other; their ability to match each other verbally or expressively indicates sexual and psychological compatibility. The conventional settings for the romantic comedy are interiors or obviously artificial exteriors (even the location shooting tends to clean up New York City by either the quality of the color or the editing), confirming the artificiality of the world of romantic comedy and enhancing its unthreatening aspects.

Musical Comedy

Although not every comedy with music is a musical comedy, musical comedies are readily indentifiable as a genre. In a musical comedy, most characters sing or dance, and those who do not, or who do so badly, are suspect morally, ethically, emotionally. In *Singin' in the Rain* (Gene Kelly and Stanley Donen, 1952), Lina, the silent movie star, has a horrible voice and must be dubbed by the newcomer Kathy; this is important to the plot, but it is also crucial thematically and it is a key to the genre as a whole, which sees good and bad characters in terms of their ability to entertain. Many films, of course, use a great deal of music either in the background or in the foreground, but if the music in these films does not serve to tell us *about* the characters, the films are not musicals.

The musical comedy is a kind of romantic comedy, and it is interesting to note that whereas the nonmusical romantic comedy has tended to replace one of the two naive ingenues of new comedy with a shrewder, more engaging protagonist, the musical comedy has often kept up the tradition of bringing two equally naive ingenues together. What a naive young couple might lack in audience appeal, however, can be supplied by music, dance, and spectacular sets. Thus, it is not important that Ruby Keeler and Dick Powell are fairly dull and saccharine and overly familiar and predictable in such films as *42nd Street* (Lloyd Bacon, 1933) and *Dames* (Ray Enright, 1934), or that Judy Garland and Mickey Rooney almost browbeat the viewer with their youthful enthusiasm in Busby Berkeley's *Babes in Arms* (1939) and *Babes on Broadway* (1941). And because of the return to the new comedy tradition of the naive romantic pair, often there is a return to a contemporary version of the wily slave or adviser: the character Donald O'Connor plays in *Singin' in the Rain* or the father figures in the Mickey Rooney–Judy Garland movies, or Eric Blore in the Astaire films.

The musical, of course, as a romantic comedy may also use the more contemporary treatment of the hero and heroine in which either one or both are knowledgeable rather than naive. In some ways, the Fred Astaire–Ginger Rogers musicals are equivalent to the romantic comedy in which two rather sophisticated married people are parted through a misunderstanding revolving around some sexual/marital matter and are finally reunited with a true knowledge of the depth of their relationship. Although in these musicals the couple begin the film as separate entities, in their sophistication and self-confidence they are much like the married couple in the nonmusical romantic comedy. Through dance rather than snappy repartee their emotional difficulties are resolved and their union realized. Their difficulties come from similar sexual/marital misunderstandings and involve mistaken identities and motives; one need only examine, for example, *The Gay Divorcé* (Mark Sandrich, 1934), and *Top Hat* (Mark Sandrich, 1935).

One of the major distinctive formulas of the musical comedy film is the "backstage musical" or "show business" plot. From the early 1930s through the 1950s (after which most movie musicals came from Broadway shows, which were never fond of the "backstage musical" formula), the putting on of a show was equivalent to the courtship of the film's central characters. The show's problems were clearly related to the conflicts between the romantic protagonists, and the final successful opening night, including the audience's applauding at the finished production, was equivalent to the romantic union of the protagonists. The show business plot, calling for production numbers in the finished show, in *Dames* allows the songwriter hero and the aspiring actress heroine to join together — through the show itself — to convince the disapproving and ridiculously prudish uncle that show business and their romance are really good clean fun. In *The Band Wagon* (Vincente Minnelli, 1953), the romantic difficulties between the characters played by Fred Astaire and Cyd Charisse are personal equivalents to the difficulties which jeopardize the show in which they both become involved. In *Singin' in the Rain*, the introduction of sound to the movie industry is paralleled by the introduction of Kathy (a singer as well as a dancer) into the life of silent screen idol, Don Lockwood; her emergence and replacement of Lina (the female star) is also the emergence of Don's commitment emotionally — and it is the emergence of a new form of entertainment, the sound film.

Several other musical formulas also are variations of the new comedy and romantic comedy formula. One variation is the musical biography, represented by films like *Night and Day* (Michael Curtiz, 1946) and *Funny Girl* (William Wyler, 1968); in both, there is less interest in biographical accuracy or completeness than there is in the film's presentation of music. Another variation, popular in the thirties and forties, was the "revue" film, a sort of grab bag of musical numbers, vaudevillian turns, forays into opera and ballet, all brought together under the very loose rubric of a "follies": *The Great Ziegfeld* (Robert Z. Leonard, 1936), *The Goldwyn Follies* (George Marshall, 1938), and *The Ziegfeld Follies* (Vincente Minnelli, 1946). And there have been numerous musical transcriptions of fairy tales and fantasy stories, most of them geared to children, although at their best they have appealed to audiences of any age. The paradigm of the formula may be *The Wizard of Oz* (Victor Fleming, 1939), but films are still made which use fantasy and fairy tale and combine the narrative with music and dance to create a wonderful and unreal world; one such recent venture was a musical treatment of Cinderella, *The Slipper and the Rose* (Bryan Forbes, 1977).

As in all other film genres, conventions abound, both of content and form. One can point (for content) to the conventions of the audition, the discovery of new talent, the initial dislike between the two romantic protagonists, and the culminating production numbers. Among the conventions of form, one can point to the almost obligatory romantic love duet, rhythm song (which is more important for setting up momentum and pacing than it is for its emotional content), comic song (generally relegated to the leading supporting player or players), and so forth. But there are also certain formal conventions that viewers are less aware of: the way in which screen lovers sing to each other and to us so that the emotion and intimacy between the principals is maximized but artificial enough so as to include the audience, and the way in which the long shot and the long take are used so that we marvel at a dancer's endurance and defiance of gravity in what seems an unbroken space and time, and the way in which modern musicals have minimized the dancer and maximized the dance by creating motion through editing rather than through performance. Icons are relatively few in the musical compared to those in the horror film or the western, but the nightclub or the stage itself in a musical is iconic, as are the dressing room and various other objects and places associated with the theater. And certain objects, though not icons, are used iconically: certainly, when a dance number is about to begin, we in the audience *know* that the mop in the corner and the dummy on the couch will become part of the choreography.

The musical, once the most popular genre, has suffered the greatest decline. Musicals are extraordinarily expensive to produce compared to other film genres and it is almost a contradiction in terms to think of a "B" musical — although there were "B" westerns and "B" horror films and "B" gangster films. True, one can point to the handful of fairly inexpensively produced "beach party" pictures, but most musicals cost so much that filmmakers came to rely on the musical that had already proven itself financially on Broadway: *West Side Story* (Robert Wise,

★ **4-9** Because musicals are so expensive to produce, most recent film musicals have been made from Broadway hits to insure an audience. CABARET (Bob Fosse, 1972) was made from such a source. The Broadway *Cabaret*, however, was adapted from an earlier stage play, *I Am a Camera*, which had been made into a nonmusical film in 1955 and was itself based on a collection of Christopher Isherwood short stories.

1961), *The Sound of Music* (Robert Wise, 1965), *Hello, Dolly!* (Gene Kelly, 1969), *Fiddler on the Roof* (Norman Jewison, 1971), *Cabaret* (Bob Fosse, 1972). These musical films have become classics, but their conventions and variations on formula are those of the musical theater rather than those of the musical film (Figure 4-9).

Musical film today greatly differs from what it used to be, perhaps because the musical film has borrowed so completely from the Broadway stage, or perhaps because musical entertainment is changing as a form no matter what its medium. Whereas once all musical films could be comfortably placed under the rubric of genre comedy, today there might well be a special classification for the musical melodrama, including such films as *Cabaret* and *Saturday Night Fever* (John Badham, 1977). Contemporary musicals do not always end in weddings; often, in fact, they end with death. Although they are filled with song and dance, they also

★ **4-10** Musical comedies take many forms. In the past it was traditional to create a fantasy world in which the character sang and danced and found "true" love. Sets frequently were clearly made of plaster and paint, as in the "Kissing Rock" number from Frank Borzage's FLIRTATION WALK (1934). More recent musical comedies have not only adopted more realistic settings (doing much location shooting) but, as in FIDDLER ON THE ROOF (Norman Jewison, 1971), the story line has come to grips with serious human problems, in this case anti-Semitism in Czarist Russia.

depict a world which seems much closer to the real world than were the artificial worlds of earlier musicals (Figure 4-10). The psyche of character is explored, motivations seem realistic, and the obstacles that the protagonists must overcome are real and — often — insurmountable. These are characteristics more common in melodrama than in comedy.

GENRE MELODRAMAS

In a comedy, the protagonist must overcome obstacles of one sort or another in order to achieve success, a success the audience is certain will be achieved. One way to allow the audience to relax and pleasurably feign suspense is to make certain that the obstacles facing the protagonist are never taken seriously by the film itself — and so are not taken seriously by the viewer. The comic hero's problem or conflict is never actually a matter of life and death — although on occasion it may pretend to be. For example, the audience *knows* that Harold Lloyd will not fall to his death while climbing up the side of the skyscraper, no matter how close he comes to losing his grip, simply because it is Harold Lloyd. Even if he slips and appears to fall out of one shot, in the next he will be saved by his suspenders or a convenient scaffold or an awning. The audience knows this because it is a convention of comedy that real death cannot exist in the comic world. Thus the suspense generated by Lloyd or Chaplin or Keaton's antics is only a feigned suspense. In effect the exaggerated obstacles in comedy, and the exaggerated solutions, distance the viewer from the plight of the comic protagonist. The activities are seen as outside ordinary experience. For instance, when a person loses his job in a comic film, he is often literally kicked out of the office; he will then not only regain his job, but be elevated to an executive position by producing some outlandish publicity stunt which will include wild animals or a stunt plane or a trip in a barrel over Niagara Falls.

Even minor breaches of etiquette are treated with exaggeration. The average viewer is likely to feel self-conscious and to act awkwardly in certain tense real-life social situations, but he is not likely to stumble and fall down several times and to douse himself with liquid and cover himself with spilled food as does the male protagonist in *The Lady Eve.* The exaggeration distances us from the comic hero's *feelings* and makes us look instead at the funny elements of the action itself. We laugh because the situation we are watching is removed from reality.

In melodrama, however, even though we know that the protagonist will triumph in the end or that a satisfactory solution will be found to the central conflict, we also know that the dangers which threaten the protagonist are truly life-and-death matters, are truly problems which are real and which matter to the audience as well as to the protagonist. Unlike genre comedies, genre melodramas include the potential for real mental and physical pain, suffering, and death: characters dodge bullets, not custard pies. In fact, it is because of this sense of the reality of physical danger that the hero's eventual triumph or failure matters.

It is possible to consider all melodramatic film genres as based on a single structure — although that structure can accommodate a wide range of variation. Much as we can place the romantic film comedy in the tradition of new comedy, we can place the genre melodrama within the context of the romance in medieval literature. The romance (not to be thought of chiefly as a love story) follows a basic pattern: a society is found to be in grave trouble and a hero must be located who has great

★ **4-11** One of the major plots found in the swashbuckler genre concerns the restoration of a proper and just authority to the throne. After being imprisoned unjustly, Errol Flynn escapes and turns pirate in CAPTAIN BLOOD (Michael Curtiz, 1935). Eventually he uses his powers to unseat the tyrannical governor of the island where he was held captive.

and special skills; he is charged with the task of saving the society by overcoming obstacles and solving problems, and he does so in a series of encounters which often culminate in one big struggle, at which point the society is returned to a state of harmony. Though we can clearly distinguish separate types of genre melodrama (the adventure film, the western, the horror film, the crime film), this basic romance formula can be found in nearly all of them. The few exceptions, such as the gangster film or the "weepie" in which the protagonists subverts the formula, are still based on the romance formula, though perversely as in a mirror image. Although each of the major genre melodramas contains plot formulas, conventions, and icons which distinguish it from another, the primary struggle of a hero who embodies good against the forces of evil pervades nearly all the melodramatic genres. The hero's eventual triumph ends not only in personal glory, but also in the resolution of social unrest (Figure 4-11). The harmony and rest at the end of the romance are common to all genre melodramas, from a classic western like *Shane* (1953) to the recent genre classic *Star Wars* (1977). In fact, *Star Wars* is truly classic in its adherence to the romance formula. The young Luke Skywalker is rather like the young King Arthur (even developing special skill with a futuristic version of Excalibur). Aided by a wise and humane magician akin to Merlin, Luke's struggle against Darth Vader and the forces of evil is not only personal but also social; the destruction of the Death Star is crucial to the salvation of the film's world. *Star Wars*, in fact, is so attuned to classical tradition that it simultaneously shares the characteristics of a number of genres: the adventure film, the science fiction film, the western, and the musical. Although the generic inclusiveness of *Star Wars* is, perhaps, atypical, it should be stressed that melodramas often overlap several genres. Although specific icons and conventions within the melodramatic formulae separate groups of films from each other, an overriding formula links them and, on occasion, allows us to consider a specific film as representative of more than one kind of melodrama.

Adventure Films

The adventure film is a broad and somewhat ill-defined genre. It can, however, be broken down into smaller groupings such as the "swashbuckler," the "war" movie, the "safari" film — and a group which might be called survival stories, including the recent "disaster" films. All of these sub-genres have more in common than one might at first think. The distinctions are chiefly matters of their particular topographies, recurrent objects, specific modes of costume, in short, their iconography. But beneath the abundant surface differences there are only two major variations within the adventure genre. One focuses on a solitary hero, the swashbuckler, and the other focuses on a hero interacting with a microcosmic group, for example a platoon in the war movie or a boatload of castaways in the survival film (Figure 4-12).

In the swashbuckler, the hero — at heart a good citizen and a member of society, and in no way an anarchist — has been turned into an outlaw because the society in which he lives has been corrupted from within: a tyrannical regent has bent law and order to his own selfish ends in Michael Curtiz's *Captain Blood* (1935) and *The Adventures of Robin Hood* (1938), or some social injustice puts the hero in an adversary position to the prevailing social order as in *Scaramouche* (George Sidney, 1952) and in the two sound versions of *The Prisoner of Zenda* (John Cromwell, 1937, and Richard Thorpe, 1952). The hero's role is to restore order to society, not to destroy it. Sometimes this restoration of order means actually restoring an absent (or kidnapped) ruler to the throne, sometimes it means the hero must remind the society through

★ **4-12** Though the adventure film is a broad genre, it can be broken into smaller more clearly defined units. THE ADVENTURES OF ROBIN HOOD (Michael Curtiz, 1938), starring Errol Flynn, is a classic swashbuckler — a subgenre comprising sword fighting and elaborate costumes. The war film is another obvious subgrouping. The scene above — a platoon pinned down in a foxhole — made familiar by much use, is from WAR IS HELL (Burt Topper, 1963).

his actions that it's time to reexamine its institutions and the people who have become responsible for them.

One of the most interesting conventions of the swashbuckler (and one which separates it from the other major adventure film variant) is that the hero is aristocratic. Although there are, of course, exceptions to this convention, it is recurrent enough to deserve consideration. In these costume dramas, the hero is at first set apart from the masses, either by virtue of his high birth or his profession. After facing evidence of the injustice of his society, he chooses to separate himself from alliance with the ruling order, and allies himself with the poor and downtrodden. The hero dramatically moves from aristocracy to democracy (although he is never so democratic as to lose his flamboyant individuality or special skills). Thus, Robin Hood merges with his band of merry men and stresses egalitarianism. Scaramouche becomes an actor, a member of a profession which absorbs all talent equally and which allows passage through all sectors of society. Captain Blood becomes a common prisoner aboard a slave ship and mixes with men he might not otherwise ever have come to know.

A related convention in the swashbuckler affects the heroine. She is always aristocratic and is always initially repelled by the crudeness of the disguised hero, unable to respond to his democratic approach. By the end of the film she has come to realize that moral value and social value are represented by spirit and intent and action rather than by the superficial trappings of title, wealth, clothing, and manners (conventional manners, that is — for the swashbuckling hero never lacks manners or style). Once the heroine has realized this and made a commitment to the hero in his democratic guise, he in turn is able to reveal himself and to reenter the aristocracy. Together, it is implied, the couple will recreate a better society, one which retains all the best of the old rules and which maintains the tried and true status quo (there are no real revolutions in genre films), but one which also will make sure that those old rules are being administered justly and benevolently.

The swashbuckler is especially interesting in its emphasis on the individual hero. In this it adheres to the romance formula. It shares, too, certain elements with new comedy and with musical comedy, because it usually ends with a wedding and the hero is defined as much by his physical expressiveness as he is by his good deeds. It is no accident that some of the directors who were particularly productive in making Hollywood musicals were also productive in making swashbucklers — and it is useful to see dance numbers and sword fights as similar in their function and structure. George Sidney, for example, directed musicals like *Anchors Aweigh* (1945), *Showboat* (1951), and *Kiss Me Kate* (1953) —

and swashbucklers like *The Three Musketeers* (1948), *Scaramouche* (1952), and *Young Bess* (1953). And Vincente Minnelli, the director responsible for many of Hollywood's best musicals, directed the musical swashbuckler *The Pirate* (1948). Indeed, in *Singin' in the Rain*, Gene Kelly plays both a song-and-dance man and a swashbuckling hero; the relationship between the two roles is made comically evident when the film-within-the-film Kelly is making, changes its title from "The Dueling Cavalier" to "The Dancing Cavalier." What links dancing and sword-play is not mere choreography; as physical activities they also have in common their emphasis on style. The dancer in the musical and the swashbuckler in the adventure film share a self-consciousness of their own artistry, and the viewer tends to judge their moral character on the basis of how well they physically perform.

Unlike the hero in most other adventure films (who takes himself and his function quite seriously), the swashbuckling hero, like the hero of a comedy, will often abstract himself from his actions and situation so he can evaluate or regard events ironically. Because he is often in disguise, in essence he is a performer giving a performance, partly for his own entertainment. Most contemporary audiences who are familiar with Richard Lester's remake of *The Three Musketeers* (1974) think of it as a spoof of George Sidney's version with Gene Kelly — and yet Sidney's film and its characters are as self-conscious and purposefully amusing as Lester's. Gene Kelly's d'Artagnan, for example, in the middle of a deadly serious duel will turn a particularly acrobatic somersault and land neatly in a stance ready to parry another thrust; it's done not only for the viewer's amusement but also for the character's. Thus, personal style and self-consciousness are as characteristic of the swashbuckling hero as swords, plumed hats, sailing ships, and caskets of jewels are characteristic icons of this sub-genre.

The second major variant of the adventure film can be called the survival film; its most obvious forms are the war movie and the disaster film. Grimmer than the swashbuckler, perhaps because it usually is more contemporary and less costumed and thus is less distant from the audience, the survival film nevertheless shares the basic characteristics of the adventure film and is strongly linked with the romance formula. The survival film's major emphases, like the romance's, are on the heroic triumph over obstacles which threaten social order and on the reaffirmation through individual action of predominant social values such as fair play and respect for merit and cooperation.

Survival films (including safari films as well as war movies and disaster epics) deal, as we saw on pages 195–97, with a microcosm of society rather than with society in its largest numbers. Isolation, in the survival film, allows society to test itself and its components in a circumscribed and easily identified arena, and it allows all the obstacles facing society to be represented by one large and dramatic obstacle. Groups are isolated in the desert in *The Sands of the Kalahari* (Cy Endfield, 1965) and *The Flight of the Phoenix* (Robert Aldrich, 1966), both downed in airplane crashes. An overturned ocean liner contains the microcosm of *The Poseidon Adventure* (1972), the top floors of an office building isolated by an unreachable fire contain the microcosm of *The Towering Inferno* (John Guillermin, 1974), the prison barracks isolate the American soldiers of *Stalag 17* (Billy Wilder, 1953), *The Great Escape* (John Sturges, 1963), and somewhat similarly the military prisoners forced to build *The Bridge on the River Kwai* (David Lean, 1957). In the war movie, in fact, separation into regiments or platoons creates a real and democratic microcosm embodying a wide spectrum of character types and ethnic groups, specifically organized to fulfill clearly defined objectives.

After initially presenting its various characters, its *individuals*, in a normal situation without life-and-death stress, the survival film separates those characters from the society as a whole and causes them to confront the problem of survival. The major portion of the survival film is spent watching the process by which the group becomes an effectively functioning unit, and this process is marked by emphasis on the various kinds of behavior available to the individual character types. The viewer, therefore, sees before him a range of personal qualities (courage, cowardice, humor, intelligence, selfishness, self-sacrifice and so forth), a range of ethnic, religious, and economic types (the Jew, Catholic, black, Native American, Chicano, rich snob, poor punk, and so forth), and a range of skills, either professionally acquired or amateurishly cultivated (the engineer, the electronics technician or radio "ham," the Olympic swimmer, the priest, the hunter). This breadth of social representation allows the viewer to watch a range of behavior, to see played out before him all the possible ways in which the average social being (like the viewer) might respond to a life-and-death situation in a group. Obviously, all the skills and qualities which help the group rejoin the larger society are considered positive; those which serve only the individual are seen as negative. In *The Sands of the Kalahari*, for instance, one of the characters is better able than any of the others to hunt and physically sustain himself in a wilderness setting, but he uses this skill to gain power over the other characters and to extort sexual favors from the film's one female character; it is fitting that at the end of the film, he is unfit to reenter the large society and he chooses to remain in the wilderness as "king" of a society of baboons.

One of the primary, if submerged, lessons of the survival film is that crisis creates its own democracy; all sorts of people from all sorts of backgrounds and practicing all sorts of professions (socially acceptable under normal circumstances or not, as witness the "hooker" in *The Poseidon Adventure*), are important and crucial and *worthy* if they expend themselves to benefit the group and to reaffirm the value of social order. In all survival films, some members of the microcosm will end up sacrificing themselves for the good of the group. In contrast, the "villain" in the survival film is usually the group member who is too concerned with personal welfare, or too intellectual to act swiftly, or too cynical, or too neurotic, and who thereby threatens the success of the group's goal of reuniting with the larger society. On the other hand, the hero of the survival film emerges from the small group because of his skills, but once the group reenters the larger society from which it has been isolated, he is ready to disappear into the crowd. He has none of the personal style and idiosyncrasies which mark the swashbuckling hero. In fact, personal style and idiosyncrasies are seen as undesirable qualities in the survival film, for they threaten the group and its goals in their individualistic, antisocial implications. Unlike the swashbuckler, the survival film is less interested in the lone heroic figure than it is in the ways in which individuals hinder or contribute to the creation of social order.

The Western

The western is the most clearly, visually identifiable film genre (Figure 4-13). Although it often shares certain characteristics with the adventure film (such as plots revolving around group survival, or conventions emphasizing personal style), it possesses its own specific landscape and geography, specific costuming, and, significantly, specific time — say, between 1850 and 1900. The western has a long tradition, but it has been the genre most responsive to changing thematic concerns despite — or possibly because of — its limited geography and time. There is a great difference in the notions of heroism displayed by films such as *Stagecoach* (1939), *Shane* (1953), *The Man Who Shot Liberty Valance* (John Ford, 1962), and *The Wild Bunch* (1969), and yet the topography and costumes and certain objects (guns, stagecoaches, barbed wire) have remained constant (Figure 4-14).

The basic situation of the western concerns the change in the frontier region of the United States from a wide-open territory in which an individual male could find self-definition (through acts of violence and crime or through the possession and practice of prized individual skills) into a civilized and structured society with its foundations in family

★ **4-13** From THE GREAT TRAIN ROBBERY (Edwin S. Porter, 1903) to the present, the western has been a consistently popular genre. Setting, formula plots, and icons of this genre have remained generally constant. Even though THE WILD BUNCH (Sam Peckinpah, 1968) takes place around the time of World War I — there are machine guns and early automobiles in it — the story of a group of men avenging the death of one of their own is very familiar.

stability and group effort. This change did, of course, actually take place in America from Colonial days up to the beginning of the twentieth century, but the movie western (following the tradition of the pulp novel) has focused primarily upon the last fifty years or so of the nineteenth century, a period which included the opening up of the Oregon Territory and the movement of wagon trains westward, the Gold Rush, the conquest of the Indian, cattle drives, and the beginning and completion of the transcontinental railroad. The iconography of the western film establishes the West as a place of deserts, wide-open plains, or badlands, full of wild Indians and equally wild and lawless white men, the former living in tepees, the latter in shantytowns, ruthlessly gouging the earth for gold, or buying up land and water rights for profit, setting up and running saloons with dance hall girls and gambling, or bounty-hunting from town to town. Everywhere in the western, justice or the lack of it has been embodied in the presence of the gun. Although ordinary townsfolk and peace-loving settlers and farmers and ranchers appear in the western film, the central figures of the genre are the gun and the men who use it.

The gun is to the Westerner what the sword was to the knight of the Arthurian romance. The weapon can be used by both good men and bad

★ **4-14** Though depending on repetition for its success, the genre film has always been responsive to changes in society. Thus the early western, for example, nearly always used Indians to represent a savage force facing the settlers of a hostile wilderness. In recent years, however, westerns have depicted the Indian with far greater sympathy. In CHEYENNE AUTUMN (1964), John Ford revealed the suffering and hardship of Indians forced to move to reservations.

men — but in the romance, the good man is just a little bit quicker and a little bit more accurate. His agility and accuracy, which combine to become a personal style, define his place in the film morally and socially. The protagonist of the western, or at least of the older western, lived by a code; he never shot a man in the back or drew first, and even in fairly recent films the protagonist never kills a man merely for sport. The gun is an extension of the man, a physical representation of power and individual style.

Other recurrent objects (or icons) of the western are familiar modes of transportation, each carrying its own significance, its own cluster of dramatic associations and potential action: the horse, the stagecoach, the buckboard, the wagon train, the railroad. Costumes, too, are iconic, although films have come a long way from the simple representation of the good guy wearing a white hat and the bad guy wearing a black hat. One can identify dramatic roles and patterns of behavior by the clothes characters wear: the tin star, the string tie, the low-cut dress, the high-necked dress, the holster, the various hats.

Like other genre films, the western ends with an affirmation of the prevailing social order. At the end of the traditional western movie, the lawless town has been cleaned up and women and children can walk the streets in security, and schools and churches will spring up as signposts of civilization; the hero, who has lived by the gun and used it to clean up the town, will marry the girl at the end of the movie or promise to return to her as Wyatt Earp promises to return to Clementine Carter in *My Darling Clementine* (John Ford, 1946). Or range wars and disputes between farmers and ranchers will be settled by a hero who has no place in the pastoral life that he has helped achieve, and he will ride off into the sunset, no longer needed, a melancholy, solitary, vestigial figure like Shane, the ex-gunfighter. The only other end for the man who has lived by the gun and used it to define himself is, of course, death; the death of the hero-gunfighter in a film like *The Gunfighter* (Henry King, 1950) is the death of a way of life which cannot in its extreme forms be integrated into civilized society. The western is, above all, a nostalgic genre, for it shows men with one foot in the wilderness (with all its associations of freedom and individualism) and one foot in civilization (with all its associations of constraint and social contracts). And, while the western nostalgically celebrates the individual determining his own destiny, it simultaneously celebrates the growth of civilized society. Watching the western genre, we may mourn the passing of the past and at the same time feel pride in the emergence of the future; the conflicts between the benefits and disadvantages of both the wilderness and civilization are balanced and resolved on the screen.

Fantastic Genres: Fantasy, Horror, and Science Fiction

Although it may be true that in some westerns, guns fire dozens of shots without being reloaded and that some heroic escapades stretch the limits of probability very thin indeed, the world of those genre melodramas previously discussed more or less resembles the world in which the viewer lives. For example, someone who leaps out of a window goes down, not up. Some genre melodramas, however, invent their own worlds in which patently "made-up" events occur and in which fabricated physical laws operate. These genres are the fantasy film, the horror film, and the science fiction film. While each of them has a great deal in common with the others, each is distinctive in the way it uses its fantastic premises (Figure 4-15).

Fantasy films, for example, often drawn from mythology and fairy tales, are generally not meant to seem realistic at all. They deal with patently impossible occurrences and beings and, in fact, revel in their use of special effects to create the impossible onscreen. The viewer is

★ **4-15** Some acts of heroism in the western and the adventure film frequently stretch the limits of belief, but to a large degree the world of genre melodramas resembles the world the viewer lives in. For example, when a person leaps out of a window, he goes down, not up. Fantasy genres, on the other hand, invent their own laws. Superman can, indeed, leap out of a window and fly in SUPERMAN (Richard Donner, 1978).

never asked by the film to believe in the armed skeletons who attack Jason in *Jason and the Argonauts* (Don Chaffey, 1963) or in the giant cloven-footed Cyclops in *The Seventh Voyage of Sinbad* (Nathan Juran, 1958); indeed, part of the enjoyment of such films is a recognition of the skills of the special effects technicians — for even children, the chief audiences for such films, are clearly able to distinguish between the real world and the world on the screen in which skeletons and Cyclopes roam. Although the special effects seem realistic on a surface level, the fantasy film does not pretend to be credible or to deal with the real world — and this emphasis on unreality separates it from its closest genre counterpart, the swashbuckler. Moreover, though the fantasy film often deals with the kinds of adventures and quests found in *The Odyssey* and in Arthurian legend, it deals less than any other film genre with the theme of the breakdown and restoration of social order. Because of the utterly strange context in which the adventure of the fantasy film's hero takes place, little emphasis is placed on the social effect of the hero's triumph. Even when the fantasy film is set in the present and is less flamboyant in its use of special effects — as in *The Red Balloon* (Albert Lamorisse, 1956), in which the viewer hardly thinks about the effects or editing required to construct the relationship between a little boy and an anthropomorphized balloon — the fantasy film genre, more than any other, removes its hero and his adventures from a social context. In its exuberant presentation of the unreal, its lack of social and moral relevance, the fantasy film is perhaps the most "escapist" of genres.

Both the horror film and the science fiction film, in contrast, are concerned with social and moral realities, even if they have been set in a fantastic context. Both genres, like more realistic melodramas, are concerned with the conflict between individual desires and needs and community desires and needs. The horror film's plot, for example, generally begins with a breakdown in the tranquil workings of a closed and traditional community. The moral breakdown usually involves an individual's Faustian rejection of man's limitations and of God's singular power, and it is manifested physically with the appearance of the monster whose very existence is an affront to natural and God-given physical law as well as a threat to the community (Figure 4-16). In *Frankenstein* (James Whale, 1931), man is guilty of trying to create life as if he were God — "unnaturally," by himself — rather than in the normal and "natural" and moral manner, within the social act of marriage and the establishment of a social unit, the family. Henry Frankenstein leaves his fiancée, his family ties, and his responsibilities to the community to bring forth his own "child," the monster, secretively, antisocially, and blasphemously. Both *Dracula* (Tod Browning, 1931) and *The Wolf Man* (George Waggner, 1941) are also physical manifestations of "unnatural" and antisocial impulses. Both the vampire and the wolf man threaten the simple moral universe of the films they inhabit. Thus, one of the chief themes underlying the traditional horror film (and even those contemporary horror films which attempt a certain psychological or surface realism) is the beast within man, that unreasoning, primal, sexual, and selfishly asocial being which may erupt through the thin veneer of civilized life and wreak havoc with all the good and moral social constructs upon which we have come to depend.

The horror film has readily identifiable conventions and iconography. In the films made in the thirties and forties, those conventions and iconography were more rigid than they are today, and some psycho-

★ **4-16** The monster in FRANKENSTEIN (James Whale, 1931) is seen in moral terms. The traditional horror film considers the desire for unlimited knowledge and power as sacrilegious, an affront to God and the natural order of things.

logical horror films now have given up graveyards at midnight, garlic and wolfbane necklaces and garlands, silver-headed canes and silver bullets, wooden stakes, coffins, rats, and cobwebs. Yet almost all horror films, old or new, depend on the conventions of darkness, creaking doors, sudden noises, and surprise. The thematic concerns of the genre, too, are still the same. Whether one is dealing with old films like *Frankenstein, Dracula* or *The Mummy* (Karl Freund, 1932), in which a fear of the irrational and bestial side of man actually takes a physical and monstrous shape and character, or whether one is dealing with modern films like Hitchcock's *Psycho* (1960), in which fear is manifested in the violence of a psychotic, or like *The Exorcist* (William Friedkin, 1974), in which the fear of the irrational and bestial is linked to the supernatural but is treated realistically, almost all horror films share the same basic themes.

Many horror films also share certain conventions (Figure 4-17). The creature — whether Dracula, Norman Bates, or the devil in a child's body — is at first hidden from the rational world, which cannot conceive of or believe in unnatural beings and events; thus, the creature can initially operate without interference. As long as no one believes in it, it can menace, enslave, or kill many victims. And those victims, in a convention characteristic of the horror film, are morally or sexually linked with the monster; they have some intimate connection with it and their deaths never seem as haphazard and random as the deaths caused by the creatures in a science fiction film. The hero of the horror film is almost never the young and inexperienced male romantic lead, but instead tends to be an older figure, perhaps a physician or a priest, someone established and experienced in the irrational aspects of life and less

227

★ **4-17** Contemporary audiences often find the horror films of the 1930s and 1940s not very frightening. Yet it is possible for a contemporary filmmaker to take stock formulas and restore them to power. George Romero updated the "ghoul" or "zombie" story in his NIGHT OF THE LIVING DEAD (1968) and established a nightmarish tone through the use of grainy black-and-white stock, high-contrast lighting, and makeup.

libidinally distracted than the young male lead. Because this older figure is familiar with both the empirical world and the irrational world, when rational weapons don't work he is able to resort to mysterious means to defeat the evil and unnatural creature. He uses the laws governing the unnatural against the unnatural creature — hunting the vampire by day to drive a wooden stake through its heart, exorcism, psychoanalysis. Usually, at the end of the horror film, the "children of the night" who threaten our civilized, social, moral everyday existence are subdued and society is returned to normal. The villagers can extinguish their torches, virgins can enjoy undisturbed sleep, people can go to motels and take showers again, and adolescent girls can learn about sex and profanity gradually — at least until the beginning of the next film in which the beast will erupt again.

Science fiction films, like horror films, often have creatures which threaten established order and society, but where the horror film emphasizes the moral and God-given order, the science fiction film emphasizes social and man-made order. The horror film tests the individual and his personal dealings with moral choice, but the science fiction film tests society and its institutions. The science fiction film is less about the conflict between good and evil in a closed community than it is about the workings of social institutions: government, the military, the public media, technology. The menace in the horror film is usually to the individual and the arena is usually small: a small town tucked away in the Carpathians, a tiny motel off an old highway, a bedroom in a Georgetown house. In the science fiction film, the threat is global and impersonal. While horror films are about the nightmare world which springs from within ourselves, science fiction films are about the terrors of the daytime world, a world in which logic and the light of reason are as fearsome as those dark corners and the beast within. Reason, having not only produced the anxieties of the nuclear age, has extended to its disturbing extreme, disallowing the good as well as the bad expressions of human emotion. *The Invasion of the Body Snatchers* (Don Siegel, 1956 and Philip Kaufman, 1978) is typical in its evocation of an alien invasion which turns people into "pods," unfeeling, unloving beings who look human but who all have the same bland and imperturbable expressions on their faces. Whereas the horror film deals with our fears of our mysterious spiritual and animal origins, the science fiction film deals with our fears of our reason, a reason that has created the unfeeling machinery of the contemporary world.

Science fiction films also have their conventions and icons, although the fact that they deal with limitless space and time tends to make the conventions and icons a bit less constant than those of horror films. Various icons such as the spaceship, the topography of the desert or the seacoast (found with chilling regularity in the low-budget films of the fifties), and the laboratory (clean and well lit, in contrast to the musty and sepulchral labs in horror films) often appear in the genre. And certain visual conventions such as the cool, flat, third-person distance of the camera from its wondrous subject matter (aliens, starships, planets in space, mutants) are also constant, if less obvious (Figure 4-18). Always, however, the concerns and emphasis of the genre are more social than moral. The "thing" which threatens the planet may be alien or may be the mutant result and by-product of man's tampering with atomic power, but whatever it is, its threat is impersonal and random; no Faustian scientist ends up in personal battle with a protagonist who represents his own darker side.

The fantastic aspects of the science fiction film, unlike those in the horror film, are meant to seem conceivable to the viewer. The laws which govern the world of science fiction are based on supposed fact, and they are regarded as extensions of the physical laws that operate in the real world. The films, in short, are meant to be credible in ways in which the horror films are not. Whereas the horror film confronts the terrors of the unknown with the laws and rituals of magic and religion, the science fiction film confronts the terrors of the unknown with the laws and rituals of science.

★ **4-18** Two kinds of images are contrasted in most science fiction films: (1) brightly lit familiar everyday scenes, like the laboratory and (2) the wondrous imagery created with models, makeup, costume, and special effects. These shots of a laboratory and the alien invader forces from William Cameron Menzies's INVADERS FROM MARS (1953) show the two types.

In the science fiction genre, therefore, science is the basis of both the problem and its solution. As "bad" science, it is private, elitist, involved with knowledge for its own sake rather than for social good, and it is often represented by an obsessed individual (the familiar "mad scientist") who speaks a private and undecipherable language. As "good" science, it is public, democratic, involved with knowledge which will be employed technologically for the good of society, and it is often represented by a team of scientists, or by a scientist-hero who speaks accessible, plain English. In *The War of the Worlds* (Byron Haskin, 1953), for example, we first meet the hero-scientist on a fishing vacation, where he wears grubby clothing, attends a small-town square dance, and talks "plain" English. Open, democratic, and cooperative activity leads to a positive solution in the genre, just as lonely, secret obsession and solitary hysteria (even in a crowd) is shown to be ineffectual, if not downright dangerous to the social order.

Although occasionally ambivalent about the uses of technology, the science fiction film emphasizes (through its use of special effects) the beauties of technology, the wonders of machinery which nearly transcends human imagination: the prim golden robot of *Star Wars* (1977) standing against a background of pale sand and sky, the fountain of lights that is the vast extraterrestrial spaceship of *Close Encounters of the Third Kind* (Steven Spielberg, 1977), the ambiguous and dark "monolith" of Kubrick's *2001: A Space Odyssey* (1968), the sleek and ascetic flying saucer sitting in the middle of Washington, D.C., in *The Day the Earth Stood Still* (Robert Wise, 1951).

Science fiction films, however, do not have to use a great many special effects, and they do not have to deal with spaceships and extraterrestrial creatures. Science fiction has come to include films which extrapolate from present reality in politics, social problems, medicine, human relations; thus, *Privilege* (Peter Watkins, 1967), *Wild in the Streets* (Barry Shear, 1968), and *1984* (Michael Anderson, 1956) treat alternative political structures, *Soylent Green* (Richard Fleischer, 1973) treats the problem of overpopulation and food supply, *The Terminal Man* (Mike Hodges, 1974) treats medicine, and films like *Charly* (Ralph Nelson, 1968) and *The Tenth Victim* (Elio Petri, 1965) treat problems in human relations. No matter what the time of the film (for science fiction can happen in the past, present, or future), no matter what the location (for the genre can take place in small-town America or in the middle of a galaxy), the films all have in common their attempt to astonish us, to cause us to wonder at the images we see. These images can be bizarre, like the Korova Milkbar with its sculptured nude drink dispensers in *A Clockwork Orange* (1971), or normally inaccessible to our human and physical perception, like the holistic vision of planets and moons in space in, for example, *Forbidden Planet* (Fred Wilcox, 1956), or such images can be ordinary and familiar like the shriveled stalk of celery and a misshapen tomato in *Soylent Green*. But because of the context, these images amaze us, fill us with wonder rather than fear. We tend to anticipate what we will see next — rather than, as in the horror film, dread what we will see next.

Antisocial Genres: The Crime Film and the "Weepie"

> In ways that we do not easily or willingly define, the gangster speaks for us, expressing that part of the American psyche which rejects the qualities and demands of modern life, which rejects "Americanism" itself.
> Robert Warshow[4]

Although all genre films end by reaffirming the value of unselfish devotion to the needs of society, a few genres flirt with the possibility that the desire to be different, to stand out from the group as an individual

★ **4-19** America's fondness for the antisocial individual as a heroic figure is quite evident in both gangster and western films. In the gangster film, the hero is the gangster himself, a man on the other side of the Law. Until recently, heroes in the western had to be reformed outlaws, not outright "baddies" like the group in THE WILD BUNCH (Sam Peckinpah, 1969). This tradition started with William S. Hart, who frequently played a criminal eventually reformed by the love of a good woman.

(Figure 4-19), to act out of self-interest, is heroic, if finally misguided and unprofitable. Although all genre melodramas end up by reaffirming the status quo and the predominant social order, two film genres de-emphasize group and/or community needs — until near the end of the films — and concentrate instead on the individual who dares to oppose the values of society. These two genres are the crime film (and within that genre, particularly, the gangster film) and the film that chronicles the struggle of a woman to find happiness, a kind of film which, for want of a better name, we shall call the "weepie." Both of these genres focus on individuals who, by choice, become social outcasts. Although, at first, these genres may seem worlds apart in their concerns, they are similar in their exploration of an independent and ambitious individual whose attempts at self-definition are both heroic and tragically anti-social. In both genres, the protagonists believe they are superior to so-ciety, and in both genres, they pay dearly for that belief — either by dying or by being socially isolated. And, although both genres end by affirming traditional morality, showing the viewer, in effect, that "crime does not pay" or that "women belong in the home," they also both

·spend most of their screen and story time on the progress of the individual who has dared to challenge the basic values of society.

The crime genre encompasses many variants. The gangster film, perhaps the most antisocial of all, was chiefly made in the 1930s in Depression America. Examples include *Little Caesar* (Mervyn Le Roy, 1930), *The Public Enemy* (William Wellman, 1931), and *Scarface* (Howard Hawks, 1932). But it has been resurrected from time to time and with great success in films like *The St. Valentine's Day Massacre* (Roger Corman, 1968) and *The Godfather*, Parts I and II (Francis Ford Coppola, 1972, 1974). The gangster film originally came out of the newspaper headlines of the 1930s, headlines referring to real gangsters like Al Capone and Baby Face Nelson, who became figures of mythic stature, headlines referring to Prohibition and bootlegging and bad economic news for the average citizen. On one level, the gangster film of the 1930s can be seen as an antisocial, if covert, response to a society which was not adequately serving the average citizen. The gangster film's basic plot generally charted the rise and fall of an individual criminal within the ranks of a criminal organization which closely resembled the corporate structure of business organizations. The film's protagonist starts, like a Horatio Alger character, green and raw on the bottom rung (often coming to the big city from a smaller town or from a rural environment), and through ambition, hard work, ingenuity, and perseverance he achieves success — defined in both the socially accepted world of big business and in the illicit world of organized crime, by becoming the head of the organization, the president or the "Big Boss." The socially approved method of achieving success is, in the gangster film, directed toward antisocial ends. Moreover, the hardworking, ambitious, ingenious gangster also demonstrates the vile side of Horatio Alger's work ethic; winning out over the competition means machine-gunning them, advancement means killing those who stand in the way ahead of you. The eventual success of the central figure of the gangster film, too, is unattractive, because once all the opposition has been eliminated, once the Big Boss's chair has been attained and secured, the only rewards of success left are isolation, loneliness and fear, for one by one the gangster's friends become his enemies (Figure 4-20). All that hard work, the gangster film seems to say, is for nothing, for emptiness or for death. In Part II of *The Godfather*, after Michael Corleone's final "business" success is ensured by the murder of his brother, and his wife and children are no longer with him, Corleone is shown in close-up, alone in the frame, isolated by all his massive effort. The other end of success in the gangster film is death; the gangster's rise to the top leads to his murder, either by an associate who emulates him or by the forces of the society. All in all, the gangster film deeply questions the basic value of success as Americans have defined it; it suggests that individual success (esteemed in our society) is inseparable from personal corruption. In the gangster film, it is not merely crime which does not pay — success itself does not pay. And, although the ending of the gangster film reaffirms legitimate society by bringing about the gangster's death or by focusing on his isolation, the major emphasis in the film is on this covert and subversive theme. The gangster is a heroic and tragic victim of his belief in a system which has no meaningful payoff (Figure 4-21).

The G-man film was an offshoot of the gangster film of the 1930s. An outcry that movies (as well as the other media of the times) glorified criminals resulted in implementing the industry's Hollywood production code in the mid-thirties, and so films which previously had centered on the gangster shifted their attention to the law enforcer who battled the gangster. Often little else was changed; the films contained the same crimes — and, in fact, some of the actors who had played the gangster-hero before the code, like James Cagney in *The Public Enemy*, now played the law enforcer–hero in films like *G-Men* (William Keighley, 1935). Despite the similarities between the gangster film and the G-man film, however, the one basic difference was crucial; the underlying thematic complexity of the gangster film, which questioned the value of success, was severely simplified.

Another variant of the crime film is the private eye or detective film. Again, the protagonist of the story is on the right side of the law — but, more interestingly than in the G-man film, he is sometimes only just on the right side of the law and his social morality is often hidden from the viewer until the very end of the film when he places his social responsibility above his personal desire. Thus, the morally ambiguous Sam Spade (played by Humphrey Bogart) in *The Maltese Falcon* (John Huston, 1941)

★ **4-20** Though there have been many changes in the gangster film since its inception, one of the consistent themes has been that the struggle to reach the top ends in loneliness or death. In each of these shots we see the young, ambitious protagonist at the beginning of his career. Edward G. Robinson in LITTLE CAESAR (Mervyn Le Roy, 1930), meets the gang for the first time. By the end of the film he will have taken complete control, but when he dies at the hands of the law, none of the gang members will be with him. Al Pacino in THE GODFATHER, parts I and II (Francis Ford Coppola, 1972, 1974) is protected by a friendly bodyguard in Sicily, where he is hiding out, but at the moment when he finally reaches the pinnacle of success, he will be alone, no longer able to trust anyone.

★ **4-21** One of the most famous moments in the history of the gangster film occurred in William Wellman's THE PUBLIC ENEMY (1931). James Cagney displays the extent of his irrational hostility by shoving a grapefruit into Mae Clark's face.

reveals himself as an adherent of the social code which says that a man has a responsibility to his partner even if he doesn't personally like him, and Spade turns in the woman he loves to the authorities. Spade ends by affirming the social structure. Even though he recognizes the arbitrariness and unfairness of society's codes, their abuse at the hands of the selfish on either side of the law, he also recognizes that without them there would be unbearable chaos. The private eye is in some ways comparable to the gunfighter in the western; like the gunfighter, he moves between two worlds: the world ruled by violence, personal desire, and the gun, and the world ruled by law, social needs, and sanctioned violence. And, like the gunfighter, the private eye is partly defined by his style, his cool responses, his resilience and readiness for the unexpected. Unlike the western genre, however, the private eye film more often focuses on the moral world of the protagonist. That world, urban and nightmarish, is peopled with characters who are not to be trusted, however attractive they may appear. This is as true of the lying Mrs. Mulwray (Faye Dunaway) in a recent film like *Chinatown* (Roman Polanski, 1974) as it is of the faithless Brigid O'Shaughnessy (Mary Astor) in the earlier *The Maltese Falcon*. The private eye must travel through this morally unstable landscape and escape with his principles intact; that is the best he — and the viewer — can hope for. Although the crimi-

★ **4-22** The *film noir* is set in an urban landscape: cheap apartments, dreary streets, warehouse districts, crummy dives. This landscape is a metaphor for the corruption, dishonesty, and conniving that takes place in a dog-eat-dog world where survival is the only value. In THE ASPHALT JUNGLE (John Huston, 1950), Sterling Hayden plays a small-time hoodlum who dreams of getting away from it all, escaping to the good life in the country. But he can't break free.

nals in the film may be apprehended in the end, the private eye film depicts a world whose foundations are crumbling.

Often, the private eye film is linked with a group of films identified by certain common themes and stylistic traits, called the *film noir*, that is, "black film"; *films noir* are visually marked by their nighttime imagery, urban landscapes, and thematic focus on ambiguously corrupt characters whose chief activity is double-dealing in a society which seems to have no redeeming members and no hope for a moral and civilized survival (Figure 4-22). Because the *film noir* was usually a low-budget film made in Hollywood in the 1940s and 1950s, it was generally shot in black-and-white. Today, however, hardly any films are made in black-and-white, and a contemporary *film noir* like *Chinatown* must create its aura of seedy decadence with color.

The caper film, chiefly concerned with executing an ingenious crime, on the other hand, is not particularly concerned with society; rather it focuses on process. In some ways, this variant of the crime film resembles the survival film (one of the two major forms of the adventure film). It chronicles a team effort to achieve a common goal — and most of the film focuses on the process of overcoming obstacles in the path of successfully robbing a train, or cracking a bank safe, or some such thing. Like the survival film, the caper film is interested in the ways members of the group respond to each other and to crises. But the isolation of the group in the caper film is self-imposed, and the group does not necessarily represent the larger society. Instead, the emphasis in the caper film is on the caper itself, on the human and mechanical processes involved in preparing the caper, in brilliantly overcoming the obstacles to success, and in finally attaining the goal: opening the bank vault, stealing the jewels. The caper film is a celebration of professionalism and process; it is akin to a "how-to" film: how to make a crystal set, how to throw a pot. It is no accident that one of the great examples of the caper film — *Rififi* (Jules Dassin, 1956) — has practically no dialogue; we and the criminals are intent on accomplishing the caper, and the very lack of human interchange recognizes the degree to which a human group has become a well-oiled machine. Since all the participants in the caper film are involved in a criminal activity, nothing in the film moves the group towards integration with the main body of society from which they have temporarily seceded. Because watching the caper film is so absorbing and generally pleasant and nonviolent, it is easy to overlook the fact that the viewer wishes for the success of an illegal enterprise; so much film time and painstaking effort (by the characters and the camera) is lavished on an illegal activity that the viewer would be sorely disappointed by a caper which wasn't finally "pulled off." In this sense, the caper film is antisocial in its thrust, although it tends to ignore the society of the world in which it takes place and is, therefore, often located in exotic places like Monte Carlo or indoors in what amounts to almost abstract space filled simply by chairs and a table spread with "plans." Sometimes, too, the films end with a rather whimsical affirmation of justice: while the caper itself is successful, the loot turns out to be fake or, after the caper, the participants are double-crossed, or the wind blows the money away.

Most crime films are set in a city, generally contemporary with the time in which the film was made. But some modern films have focused on the gangster of the 1930s or have attempted to remake the private eye film of the 1940s; examples are *Al Capone* (Richard Wilson, 1959), *Dillinger* (John Milius, 1973), the previously mentioned *Chinatown* and *Farewell, My Lovely* (Dick Richards, 1975). The urban setting of modern life — even when that modernity is placed back in the late 1920s and early 1930s — is filled with objects which have become iconically significant to the crime film: telephones ("candlestick" and coin phones), radios (and later television sets) spouting "news bulletins," machine guns, liquor stores, nightclubs, fast cars (particularly black sedans) with screeching tires, newspapers, murky bars and cigarette smoke, cheap hotel (and later, motel) rooms marked by their anonymity, and neon lights. Clothing, as well, has had a particular significance to the genre: the snap-brimmed hat pulled down so as to hide a character's eyes; the private eye's trench coat, its collar pulled up for protection against some all-pervasive dankness; the expensive suits and cashmere coats of gangsters who have reached the top, and the cheap flamboyance of the clothes their molls wear.

As previously mentioned, it seems a big leap from the crime film to the "weepie," that ill-defined genre of films made to appeal to female audiences. The "weepie," however, has a great deal in common with the crime film, particularly the gangster film. Both focus on an individual who dares to oppose the law which governs social behavior, charting that individual's initial naive optimism and ambition, the individual's rise towards what seems a desirable goal, and finally, that individual's fall and recognition that the goal carried with it the seeds of personal and social destruction. Indeed, if the gangster film shows the irreconcilable conflict between personal success and popular democracy in the predominantly male world of business, then the "weepie" shows the same conflict in the predominantly female world of the home. What is illegal in the "weepie" is the protagonist's desire to go beyond the socially approved limits of home and family — and when she succeeds, she must, like the gangster, pay dearly for her success, a success which is revealed as finally worthless and containing the seeds of her own destruction. In these films the woman's greatest crime is infidelity or its counterpart, "home-wrecking." But the crime of personal ambition — even to benefit her family — is almost as bad. We watch the female protagonist in the "weepie" in much the same way we watch the gangster: noting and even admiring that pathological determination to rise above one's peers, recording with ambivalent emotion how the fulfillment of personal drive leads to social death.

In *Mildred Pierce* (Michael Curtiz, 1945), for example, what seems to be a woman's innocent ambition to provide for her family ends in a horrendous act of murder. Mildred (Joan Crawford, who played many such ambitious women in the 1940s) is full of energy and hopes for her children, but in fulfilling those hopes she turns into a hardworking but cold and ambitious "bitch," both heroine and villainess together. The same drive for power (represented by both money and control over the men in a woman's life) is shown in *The Strange Love of Martha Ivers* (Lewis Milestone, 1946). Played by Barbara Stanwyck, another actress who was able to seem simultaneously heroically and castratingly strong, Martha is constantly asserting herself; as a child, she kills (with audience sympathy) a vicious, power-hungry aunt and then grows up like that aunt, ruthless in her business dealings, contemptuous and manipulative of her husband. Finally, she even attempts to get her "old love" to kill her husband. Like the gangster, of course, both Mildred and Martha end up badly, the first isolated, and the second dead.

The "weepie," which represents the dark side of domestic life in the way that the crime film represents the dark side of business life, was made primarily in the later 1940s — in the postwar period — representing, perhaps, in a melodramatic dream landscape the fear of what would happen to the economic power assumed by (and thrust upon) women during the war years. As the gangster film of the 1930s can be seen as a pessimistic response to the realities of the Depression, a "nay-saying" on an unconscious popular level to the positive American myth of success, so the "weepie" of the 1940s can be seen as a pessimistic response to social changes initiated by the Second World War, a "nay-saying" on an unconscious popular level to the American myth of domestic bliss and willing female subservience.

★★★ **Genre as Myth**

> The fact is that each generation must create its own myths and its own heroes, or else regenerate those of the past. . . . We desperately need a renewal of faith in ourselves as Americans, as good guys on the world scene, as men and women, as human beings who count, and so we return temporarily to the simpler patterns of the past. The old superheroes rise again — *Wonder Woman* and *Superman* — and we get old-fashioned genre films like *Rocky* and *Star Wars*.
> Andrew Gordon[5]

When we think carefully about genre films, we see that they reveal unconscious fears and desires beneath the surface plots. The makers of most genre films over the past fifty years or so were not, of course, deliberately trying to depict on the screen the repressed fears and desires of their audiences (they were not students of Freud or Jung or even of genre film theory), but surely one can assume that genre films are enormously popular because they fulfill some sort of psychological need. It is too simple to say that these movies are only entertainment, are just sheer fun, are escapist, and don't mean anything. Genre films are popular films, the films most of us grew up with and the films most people go to see. If we can understand their appeal we can learn something important about ourselves as social beings, and about the growth of our culture.

It is no accident that all of the films in each film genre tend to tell the same basic story, with sometimes only the most minor variations. This repetition is less a cause for criticism than for the recognition that each genre deals with a certain basic conflict which, unresolved in real life, is comfortingly resolved on the screen. The genre film can deal, for example, with the conflict between the individual desire to be different from others and the desire to be like others, with the conflict between individual needs and group needs, and with the conflict between material success and spiritual success — and it can deal with such conflicts in ways in which more intellectual and unique films can't.

The filmmaker may have intended only to entertain his audience when he made *The Wolf Man* (1941); he may, in fact, have had no particular conscious reason for choosing his material other than that it allowed Lon Chaney, Jr., to follow in his father's footsteps, put on bizarre makeup, and perhaps make a bundle for the studio. Yet perhaps the choice of material itself and the response of audiences to it was not trivial. Right there, on the screen, is particularized the unnamable beast we may try to keep hidden beneath our civilized skins. That animal emerges on the screen bristling with hair and violence. Temporarily, and within a clearly fantastic and therefore unthreatening context, we may be purged of our asocial, uncontainable desires. We may think we've just seen an inconsequential escapist fantasy, but our personal and unconscious fears may actually have been transformed from personal nightmare into a depersonalized and group myth.

It is not surprising that recent studies of genre films have tended to look at the films' structures as comparable to the structures of myth and fairy tale. Myth and fairy tale transform individual dreams into group dreams in which the problems presented and the solutions effected are valid for all mankind. Thus, one can see strong parallels between the structure of what scholar Joseph Campbell calls the "monomyth" (the underlying similarity in myths) and the structures of all genre films, between the composite heroes of world mythology and their progress and the composite heroes of genre films and their dramatic progress. Recognizing that despite the infinite variation of locale and decoration there is only a limited number of human and socially supportable responses to life problems, Campbell illuminatingly reduces the mythological adventures of a host of heroes from a host of cultures to one great adventure experienced by one composite hero. This "Hero with a Thousand Faces" (to use the title of one of Campbell's books) responds to the call of adventure and separates himself from the society of which he has been a part. He is then confronted with a series of tests and trials in a process of initiation which culminates in his successful completion of crucial tasks. He then returns and reintegrates himself with society and passes on the lessons he has learned, or he is rejected because of the threat to society his experience presents. Always, however, the hero is a person of exceptional gifts.

One can draw parallels not only between the genre film and myth, but also between the genre film and the folktale or fairy tale. The Russian Vladimir Propp's analysis of over a hundred fairy tales revealed not only certain basic plots, but also a certain basic cast of *dramatis personae*, defined by their function; under various guises, the cast is also basic to genre films. Propp names the Hero, of course, and then goes on to identify the Villain, who chases and engages in combat of some sort with the Hero; the Donor or Provider, who gives the Hero some magical device or agent which will aid him in accomplishing the major tasks imposed by his adventure; the Helper, who performs various supportive roles for the Hero and who may aid the Hero in a crisis and who transfigures the Hero by the contrast provided by his lesser gifts; the Princess and her Father (or one of them), who assigns the Hero his task and who rewards him when it is accomplished; the Dispatcher, who sends the Hero off on his adventure and who is often an agent of the Princess and her Father in some fashion; and even the False Hero, who counterpoints the real Hero, aping the latter's search and being found wanting in his abilities and talents.

If, as Campbell suggests, the distinction between the myth and fairy tale is that myth is microcosmic (a miniature representation of the world, analogous to the larger world) and that the hero's resolution of problems carries with it the possibilities of regeneration for his whole society, and that the fairy tale is macrocosmic (the larger world) and the hero's resolution is basically personal and particularized, then the genre film is both myth *and* fairy tale. On the surface, it is a fairy tale, concerned with a particular hero and adventure and with the resolution of a fairly circumscribed problem in the only world there is. Under the surface, however, it is mythic in its presentation of broad conflicts played out by participants who stand for forces in the larger world. In addition, on both levels its impulses are social: the hero returns the world to order.

The genre film can also be seen as a ritual in which the viewer participates, as he would by attendance at other social and religious rituals such as a baseball game or a church service. Ritual activity, as defined by social scientists like Bronislaw Malinowski and Claude Lévi-Strauss, has several requirements and characteristics. It is, of course, repetitive.

It is cumulative, in that action is built serially upon action and that power comes from the accumulation of action rather than from concluding action. (A classic example in the genre film would be the emotional power and weight accumulated by the rebellious female in the "weepie," which far outweighs the "moral" ending of the film which demands her being cast out from the society.) Ritual is symbolic and uses various simple objects and signposts (for example, a cross) to evoke complex associations. Ritual is also nostalgic in that it celebrates the past, what has been done before and will be done again. Ritual is simplistic in that it presents a clearly identifiable and dualistic universe: light is in conflict with darkness, good with evil, male with female. (This dualism is clearly seen in most genre films in the hero-versus-villain plot structure, in the very simple but visually communicative use of light and dark clothing to separate the good guys from the bad guys in the early years of film melodrama, and in the paradoxical dualism of themes which directly oppose notions of success and failure and of individual fulfillment and group satisfaction.) Another characteristic of ritual is that it is predictable; one knows what is going to happen next and what is going to happen at the end, and that knowledge, rather than producing boredom, is comforting and pleasurable. Finally, ritual is functional; it provides its practitioners with something psychologically, emotionally, and socially valuable: the purgation of personal anxiety and fear, a feeling of well-being, and a sense of belonging to a group with homogenous goals. The genre film is similarly functional, temporarily resolving what in the real world remains an irreconcilable or paradoxical conflict. The genre film assuages individual anxiety and, like ritual, does so magically and seemingly without effort, always affirming an established and socially acceptable order of things.

★★★ Genre Films and Society

> ... The crucial factors which distinguished a *genre* are not *only* characteristics inherent to the films themselves; they also depend on the particular culture within which we are operating. And unless there is world consensus on the subject (which is an empirical question) there is no basis for assuming that a "Western" will be conceived in the same way in every culture. The way in which the *genre* term is applied can quite conceivably vary from case to case. *Genre* notions — except the special case of arbitrary definition — are not critic's classifications made for special purposes; they are sets of cultural conventions. *Genre* is what we collectively believe it to be.
>
> Andrew Tudor[6]

Genre films can also function as a cultural barometer. The viewer can look at the evolution of a particular genre, say the western, and see reflected in its shifts in attitude, changes which can be likened to shifts of attitude in the contemporary society which made and attended the films. It cannot be dismissed as mere accident that the western hero has changed from a figure like Bronco Billy Anderson, who bore some strong resemblance to his real-life counterpart, to a white-hatted hero on an intelligent horse, like Roy Rogers or Gene Autry in the 1930s and early 1940s; to the psychologically contemplative or disfigured hero-villains of the 1950s and 1960s; to the corporate hero-villains of the late 1960s and 1970s such as those in *The Wild Bunch* (1969); to those recent films which present the hero as septuagenarian. Those shifts reflect the contemporary concerns of the culture in which the films were made, and while it may not be useful to assign a one-to-one correspondence between occurrences in the social and political and economic life of movie viewers and occurrences on the screen, it can be productive to examine genre films as a response to social history and contemporary concerns. Surely it is reasonable to see, in the changes in the hero of the western, from the single-minded Gene Autry and Roy Rogers to the pragmatic Bill Holden and Lee Marvin, a shift in the way in which America defines its heroes. Seeing genre films as a barometer of popular and often unconscious tensions and moods can help explain why, for example, certain genres suddenly reestablish their popularity after lying dormant for a period of time, or why certain foreign countries adopt and transform as their own a particular American film genre and have little interest in others. Japan, for example, has made many science fiction films, Italy many westerns. Looking at genre films as a reflection of the culture that produced and responded to them can lead to the contemplation of such questions as whether the popularity of the disaster film was a natural response to contemporary ecological concerns — or whether it was popular because it appealed covertly as a fantasy drama in which man was the helpless victim of cataclysmic forces beyond his control and for which he could not possibly be held responsible, a cinematic response of sorts to a world already beset with famine, drought, and Watergate.

★★★ ## Genre Parody and Anti-Genres

In fact, the history of convention in American film has always been the history of successive exhaustions of convention. The exposure and elaboration of certain actors and actions pleases and solaces the audience but then finally leaves it cold. When the genre conventions can no longer

evoke and shape either the emotions or the intelligence of the audience, they must be discarded and new ones tried out. Genre films essentially ask the audience, "Do you still want to believe this?" Popularity is the audience answering, "Yes." Change in genres occurs when the audience says, "That's too infantile a form of what we believe. Show us something more complicated." And genres turn to self-parody to say, "Well, at least if we make fun of it for being infantile, it will show how far we've come."
Leo Braudy[7]

Generally speaking, film genres (at least up until fairly recent times) have been unself-conscious. Their styles have been relatively invisible; the viewer is conscious chiefly of the narrative rather than of the *way* the camera tells the narrative. Genre filmmakers, moreover, were intent on telling a story, and they were not particularly aware of the covert psychological and social content of the subtext of the films they were making. Today, however, both audiences and filmmakers have become more aware of the covert implications of genre films. Audiences are more cinematically sophisticated — and many of today's top film directors are keenly aware of the myth-making accomplished by film genres. This self-consciousness of both audience and filmmaker can best be demonstrated by the work of two contemporary filmmakers who have used genre films for differing purposes: Mel Brooks, calling the viewer's attention to the formal structure of genre films, to the delightful familiarity of generic plots, conventions, and **iconography,** has produced comedy; and Robert Altman, using and abusing audience expectations of familiar genre plots, conventions, and iconography, has subverted the genre from within, shaking the audience from a passive state of dream-viewing into an active state of thought.

Brooks's films pay homage to film genres rather than criticize them. He has parodied the musical in *The Producers* (1968), the western in *Blazing Saddles* (1974), the traditional horror film in *Young Frankenstein* (1975), silent slapstick comedy in *Silent Movie* (1976), and the. Hitchcock suspense thriller in *High Anxiety* (1978). In all his films, he uses genre conventions and iconography to confirm — by the emphasis of exaggeration — the audience's knowledge and familiarity with the kind of movie it is watching. The surprises in Brooks's films are not disturbing, do not call into question the concept of genre or its possibly faulty notions regarding social values; instead, Brooks's surprises celebrate the limited world set forth by the genre. When the gunfighter in *Blazing Saddles* demonstrates the quickness of his draw by not moving his hands at all and then asks the sheriff whether he saw it, the humor stems from the audience's knowledge of westerns and their rules; when the monster marries at the end of *Young Frankenstein* and ends up sedately

★ **4-23** New configurations of genre elements are required periodically to revitalize a genre. Simple repetition of a particular configuration leads to a loss of power. The second Frankenstein film, THE BRIDE OF FRANKENSTEIN (James Whale, 1935), is as effective as the first, but by the 1940s, when ABBOTT AND COSTELLO MEET FRANKENSTEIN (Charles Barton, 1948) appeared, the pity and terror produced by the monster had changed to laughter.

reading the *Wall Street Journal* in domestic bliss, the humor is a product of the viewer's past sympathy for the unloved misfit whose ugliness sent those around him into screaming paroxysms of horror (Figure 4-23). The humor of Brooks's movies is never at the expense of the genres he parodies; rather, it is derived from a loving extension of the familiar, from carrying all the laws and rules of a particular genre to their furthest extreme.

Robert Altman's films, on the other hand, subvert genre films from within. Those films he's made which at first seem to be traditional genre movies end up unsettling the viewer, making the viewer realize how passively he's previously accepted genre conventions and rules. *M*A*S*H* (1969) was Altman's first commercially successful film to play against genre, but its comic thrust somewhat softened the attack on the conventions and social affirmation of the traditional war movie. All the characters in the film are selfish rather than traditionally heroic; the Korean war (a thin disguise for the Vietnam war) is made analogous to a vicious football game in which nobody plays by the rules, and the practice of medicine is seen as a dirty and ridiculous business rather than as a heroic calling. *McCabe and Mrs. Miller* (1970) subverts the western; amidst a meticulously recreated Northwestern town bathed in constantly nostalgic light, a drama is played out between a hero who is stupidly vain (if touching) and a heroine who is a prostitute with business acumen and a more literal than proverbial heart of gold. The classic gunfight at the end of the film fulfills audience expectation in that McCabe actually kills the "bad guys," but it subverts audience expectation by leaving McCabe wounded and finally dead in the snow, the town and his true love withdrawn into their own pursuits. *Thieves Like Us* (1973) and *The Long Goodbye* (1973) both combine violence, serious and stereotypical characterization, and genre plotting with comic or wry elements purposefully used to distance the viewer from an emotional involvement with the film's created world. *Thieves Like Us* is a gangster film which emphasizes the ugliness of place and the plainness of its characters, as if in response to the glossy and gauzy beauty of its cinematic predecessor, *Bonnie and Clyde* (1967). At the end of *The Long Goodbye*, after private eye Philip Marlowe kills the friend who has duped and used him, the detective walks away, kicking up his heels in a long shot while the tune "Hooray for Hollywood" is playing. Unlike Mel Brooks's films, Altman's films refuse to cooperate with the audience; rather than congratulating the viewer for his knowledge of genre convention and movie history as does Brooks, Altman assaults the viewer by using that knowledge against the viewer, who is made particularly vulnerable by his assumptions about what is going to happen next — assumptions that Altman does not share.

The films of Mel Brooks and Robert Altman are, of course, at opposite poles. Brooks perpetuates genre forms and mythology while Altman subverts or demythologizes genre forms. Brooks's films suggest that audience and filmmaker share an affection for the familiar, that they are both party to an unwritten and congenial contract which specifies what the audience expects and what the filmmaker will give it. Altman's films, however, are anti-generic; they deny there is such a contractual agreement with the audience, suggesting that the viewer makes himself a potential victim of the film and its maker by expecting something never promised. Despite their differences of purpose, however, Brooks and Altman are similar in that they both have made audiences aware of genre conventions, aware of their own previously unrecognized expectations. Genres have thus become more self-conscious today and both audiences and filmmakers have become more knowledgeable about genre forms and their ritual function.

NOTES

[1] *Violent America: The Movies 1946–1964* (New York: Museum of Modern Art, 1971), p. 19.

[2] *Underworld USA* (New York: Viking, 1972), pp. 23–24.

[3] *The Immediate Experience* (New York: Atheneum, 1971), pp. 129–130.

[4] *The Immediate Experience*, p. 130.

[5] "Star Wars: A Myth for Our Time," *Literature/Film Quarterly* 6, no. 4 (Fall 1978): 324–325.

[6] *Theories of Film* (New York: Viking, 1973), p. 139.

[7] *The World in a Frame* (Garden City, New York: Doubleday/Anchor, 1977), p. 179.

5
★ *FILM MOVEMENTS*

Contemplating films in groups rather than individually can be both aesthetically and culturally illuminating. Genre films, which are grouped by their clear use of common narrative patterns, conventions, and iconography, offer in their quantity a reflection of our culture. Non-genre films, grouped by the individual filmmakers who made them or by themes or style, can as a group reveal new trends in aesthetics and in philosophical stances. There is yet another sort of grouping of films which may connect both genre and non-genre films. This grouping is based on both common style and theme, on both form and content — a group of films which constitute the product of a **film movement.** The term film movement describes the activity and product of filmmakers in a particular country in a particular historical period who consciously share a common cinematic ideology.

Certainly, each national cinema can be considered as a related group of films with common characteristics (say, Japanese cinema or Indian cinema). One can explore the cultural identity of a nation through its films, or examine the influence of a national culture on a single film-maker and his work. One can ask questions about, say, those national characteristics which make French films French, or Czech films Czech. Film movements, however, are not synonymous with the creation of a national cinema. The term *film movement* is used here to describe cinematic activity among a group of filmmakers who are conscious of themselves as part of an artistic and/or political movement rather than simply as individuals who share a common culture.

Usually the emergence of a film movement can be directly related to a period of national economic, social and political upheaval; it seems a way in which artists — through their art — demonstrate and show themselves to be social and political beings with responsibilities to their fellows. Thus, new film movements occur simultaneously with new movements in other art forms: painting, literature, music, theater. Artists in one medium tend to know and gather with and influence artists in other media. Indeed, one of the defining characteristics of a film movement is that the filmmaker sees himself as part of an artistic community which is self-consciously attempting to do something other than what has been established as traditional. Because of this self-consciousness, film movements often produce — along with the films which are their primary product — a body of critical writings on film aesthetics, manifestos on the social and political responsibilities of filmmakers.

Films which emerge from a film movement are not necessarily stamped from the same mold, but because the filmmakers share some intellectual and artistic assumptions, the films may be linked by clearly identifiable aesthetic and thematic bonds, marking the films as, for example, German expressionist or Italian neorealist.

★★★   German Expressionism

The Expressionist does not see, he has "visions." According to Edschmid, "the chain of facts: factories, houses, illness, prostitutes, screams, hunger" does not exist; only the interior vision they provoke exists. Facts and objects are nothing in themselves; we need to study their essence rather than their momentary and accidental forms. It is the hand of the artist which "through them grasps what is behind them" and allows us to know their real form, freed from the stifling constraint of a "false reality."
Lotte H. Eisner[1]

German expressionism did not suddenly spring into existence in 1919 with the release of Robert Weine's *The Cabinet of Dr. Caligari*, the most widely known and influential German expressionist film and popularly considered the "first" of the expressionist movement. Before and during World War I, expressionist doctrine had first made its presence felt in literature, painting, and drama. Even in the cinema, *Caligari* had forerunners in *The Student of Prague* (Paul Wegener), made in 1913, and in Wegener's first version of *The Golem*, made the following year. In all the arts, Germans had been influenced by the work of Swedish dramatist August Strindberg and his dream plays, of Norwegian artist Edvard Münch, and of their own writer E. T. A. Hoffmann, a Gothic romantic. Freud's writings about the unconscious mind and the dream state, too, became well known to intellectuals and artists. Coupled with this awareness of a hidden psyche, and with this history of artistic preoccupation with occult and demonic themes (as in Goethe's *Faust* and Hoffmann's *Tales of Hoffmann*), was the intellectual's horror at conditions in Germany following the World War. The Weimar Republic (1919–1933), attempting to deal with poverty, unemployment, and the depression of a defeated populace, was at best uncertain — and this uncertainty, this social and political malaise in the face of potential chaos and disorder was reflected in all the arts of the time. Expressionism rejected the external world, which could not provide stability, and, instead, embraced the subjective world, the interior world of human emotion and feeling.

Unable to control the world in which he lived, the German artist controlled his art, mastering technical skills to create his own world from within himself — and literally from within the confines of the film studio in which every element of filmmaking could be carefully manipulated. Thus, through the 1920s, the various elements of the cinema were masterfully and consciously controlled to serve the soul and emotions of the films' protagonists, to convey to the viewer not simply a story, but the characters' feelings. At first this control consisted, as in the expressionist theater, primarily of manipulating and distorting those elements which the eye saw: the performances of actors, costume, décor, and lighting. For example, the walls of a room might be set at crazy angles to convey the character's sense of hysteria. Later, however, as filmmaking became more sophisticated, the camera itself became more subjective; it learned to move and to "see" as if it were a feeling character itself. Thus, as the new decade introduced sound to the cinema, the expressive function of highly stylized performance, costume, and décor was shifted to the expressive function of the subjective camera. Thus, the camera might wobble, to convey instability. With this shift, German films became more psychologically realistic, more subtle and credible, and the traditional expressionist cinema full of vampires and mirror images coming to life, and strangely made-up characters moving within gravity-defying sets, became a thing of the past.

During this entire period, however, whether the films seemed highly stylized and fantastic in their content, like *The Cabinet of Dr. Caligari* and *Nosferatu* (F. W. Murnau, 1922), or whether they seemed more realistic in their surfaces and their psychology, like *The Last Laugh* (F. W. Murnau, 1924) and *Variety* (E. A. Dupont, 1925), their tone was similar. The German artist's reliance on the interior world of emotion, impulse, and instinct in an exterior world full of social and political upheaval, chaos, and uncertainty, led to the creation of films which emphasized the horrors of nightmare rather than the pleasures of dream.

What surfaced on the screen was an unstable world or a world turned upside down, exaggerated and distorted by feelings of fear and isolation which permeated the chosen story, the characterizations, the décor and lighting, and the camera's vision and movements (Figure 5-1). Nearly all of the films made during Germany's "Golden Age" and into its decline — from *The Cabinet of Dr. Caligari* to the films of G. W. Pabst like *Pandora's Box* (1929) — are in some way violent and despairing. Murder, deceit, and the fragility of normal bourgeois life in the face of lurking chaos are major concerns of the films. The violence and shock of murder can be seen in its stylized form in *Caligari*, where a hypnotically controlled somnambulist stalks the night — or it can be seen with some degree of realism in *Variety*, where a crazed and jealous husband kills his wife's lover. Deceit could take the form of a young man's mirror image passing itself off as his "real" counterpart in *The Student of Prague*, a vampire posing as a wealthy aristocrat in *Nosferatu*, a female robot substituted for her human double in *Metropolis* (Fritz Lang, 1927), or the realistic deception of a pretty but heartless woman playing with her lovers in *Pandora's Box*. And the eruption of chaos into the normal routine of middle-class life could manifest itself fantastically with the arrival of a vampire to Bremen or realistically, as in *The Last Laugh*, with a letter announcing to a hotel doorman that he is to be demoted and will lose the splendid uniform which has always defined him to himself and others.

Along with certain consistent thematic emphases, German expressionist cinema is marked by certain readily identifiable formal characteristics. In the early films of the period, particularly in those which reject realism, those characteristics are obvious; in the later films of the period, which are expressive in a more realistic context of setting and character, those stylistic traits are less immediately obvious but are still present. To some degree, then, all the films are linked by the following characteristics:

Manipulation of setting: Whether the film is shot in the studio or "on location," the setting and architecture are chosen for the feeling they convey. The painted sets of *The Cabinet of Dr. Caligari* are gravity-defying physical impossibilities but they convey the crazed mind of the film's narrator and the instability of the bourgeois world. The vampire's rented house in *Nosferatu*, though shot out of the studio, "found" on location, is affecting not for its realism but for its expressive and shudder-evoking bleak, skeletal appearance.

Chiaroscuro lighting: Pools of light and dark ("chiaroscuro" is Italian for "light-dark") within the frame, and the constant use of shadow,

★ **5-1** German expressionism used highly artificial sets — tilted and painted flats — to create a sense of nightmarish unease in THE CABINET OF DR. CALIGARI (Robert Weine, 1919). Other filmmakers of the movement (like F. W. Murnau) preferred more realistic settings but then used strong contrasts between the light and the dark areas of an image to gain their emotional effects as in this scene from THE LAST LAUGH (1924).

create a menacing, uncertain, unstable world which is visually fragmented rather than unified by slow gradations of light.

Animation of the inanimate: The size and proportion, the shrinkage and expansion, of what we see on the screen is determined by its emotional significance, not by the laws of nature. The object seems to possess a life of its own apart from its function. In the crudely stylized films, one can point to Dr. Caligari's strangely fascinating gloves or the obviously metaphoric machinery in *Metropolis*; in the more realistic films, the doorman's huge overcoat in *The Last Laugh* is a good example.

Emotional cinematography: Feelings, rather than logic, are expressed through the use of unnatural camera angles, a high ratio of point-of-view or subjective shots, and a mobile camera used to convey subjective states physically. In the very early films like *The Cabinet of Dr. Caligari* the camera was, of course, immobile — but various devices like the iris or the use of grotesquely angled scenery attempted to convey subjective states, such as those conveyed by the camera's movement in later films. In *Variety*, for example, the camera swings from a trapeze to express the danger and vertigo and chaotic possibility of death.

Stylized acting: Acting in the films is stylized and broad, its intent being to transpose the interior feeling and rhythm of the character's life into direct, emotional gestures. Characters, particularly in the early films like *Caligari* or *Nosferatu*, become through their movements almost visual codes of abstract feeling. In the later films, although performances become less broad and abstract, they still depend on gestures in the performance which, with repetition, come to represent the character; a classic example is Emil Jannings as Professor Rath in *The Blue Angel* (Josef von Sternberg, 1930) taking out his handkerchief and blowing his nose or aligning his schoolbooks precisely in the same manner each time so as to succinctly define his prissy and ordered character.

German cinema declined for many reasons: Hollywood's importation of German talent after the worldwide success of German films, the self-consciousness of filmmakers who became more and more ponderous and pretentious in the light of world attention, and the rise of Hitler, which caused many of those film artists who had not already been seduced by Hollywood promises of artistic power and high salaries to leave their homeland for other parts of Europe and for America. Despite its brief life span as a movement, German expressionist films exerted a permanent influence on world cinema. Certainly, its themes and stylistic traits can be traced in America from the rise of the horror film in the 1930s through the film noir of the 1940s and 1950s. And, surely, the basic belief that cinema should be *expressive* informs most of the feature films made today.

★★★ Soviet Social Realism

> Sergei Eisenstein's *The Battleship Potemkin* appeared at the moment
> when the best among the pre-revolutionary intellectuals were being pro-
> foundly affected by all the great and the new things which were brought
> into life by the victorious working class. In art, the traditions of the past
> were engaged in a merciless struggle with the ideas of people who had
> linked their art with the work of the proletariat — ideas still not fully
> formulated, but directed towards a unique and precise end.
> V. I. Pudovkin[2]

Just as the aftermath of World War I crystallized the social and intellectual climate in Germany, giving rise to the German expressionist cinema, the aftermath of the 1917 Russian Revolution provided the climate
for the emergence of Soviet — rather than Russian — cinema and the
social realist movement. The group of filmmakers who began by theorizing and writing about films because they had little access to raw film
stock with which to make films had been freed socially, politically, and
intellectually by the Revolution. By the mid-twenties, they began making films which put into practice their theoretical ideas, but which were
by no means theoretical or dry. The new Soviet filmmakers' work was
extraordinarily dynamic and exciting in form — and the content was
exuberant in its exploration of the past history of the Revolution and its
documentation of the Soviet spirit.

In some ways it is difficult to justify discussing Soviet Social Realism
as a movement that shaped the narrative or "story" film. Many of the
works of key filmmakers in the movement were non-narrative films,
"documentaries" recorded as the events happened. In this they were
led by Dziga Vertov, who made the first Soviet film — *The Anniversary
of the October Revolution* (1918) — out of a compilation of footage sent
in from all over the Soviet Union. He believed that the factual film
would explain the Russian Revolution and the Soviet Union to the people. In 1922 he began a series of weekly newsreels called "Kino-Pravda"
or "Film Truth," a term which would later be picked up by documentary
filmmakers in the 1960s and translated into cinéma vérité. While Vertov
was not alone in his belief in the primacy of documentary cinema, he
was the only one of the major four Soviet filmmakers (the other three
were Sergei Eisenstein, Vsevolod Pudovkin, and Alexander Dovzhenko)
to emphasize the recording of events as they happened and to argue
against the re-creation or dramatization of history. Despite Vertov's
singularity in the quartet of the key filmmakers of early Soviet cinema,
his belief in the factual film was not far removed from the practice of
his colleagues. And it is here that the line between, on the one hand,

"documentary" and "non-narrative" film and, on the other, the "narrative" and "story" film becomes less clear.

The ideology behind the new Soviet cinema, however, was constant. Whether, as in the films of Vertov, the content was indeed documentary footage recorded as it happened, or whether film content was acted and history was re-created and even dramatically altered as in the films of Eisenstein, Pudovkin, or Dovzhenko, the aim was the same. Each film-maker, in his own style and with his own approach, attempted to communicate to the world what had happened in Russia, how it was that through the courage and heroism of simple people, a new order of life, a new birth of honor and dignity and freedom had come about in the once feudal state of Mother Russia (Figure 5-2). Thus, even in the fictional re-creations, an educative function was being served — and the impulse was, even at its most poetic and symbolic, documentary.

Despite this major impulse to inform the Soviet people (particularly those in the far reaches of the U.S.S.R.) and the rest of the world about the Revolution and to build a sense of national unity and pride, an impulse which could be considered the basis of documentary filmmaking, most Soviet cinema was narrative. Although most of the films treated the historical reality of the Revolution, they were created by the camera, carefully scripted and structured — and in some cases history itself was altered, as in Eisenstein's *Potemkin* (1925), whose critically renowned and dynamically edited massacre on the Odessa Steps never really took place as shown but is the synthesis of two other historical events. The films were meant to be structured as dramatically satisfying works which were emotionally affective.

It is, then, not surprising that the Soviet filmmakers studied D. W. Griffith's epics, for their films did tell stories and did have, in some form, "heroes" and "villains" and dramatic structure. Eisenstein believed in the "mass hero." No individual was singled out for a major portion of cinematic attention; instead, individuals were the details of a larger mass protagonist — in *Potemkin*, for example, the crew of the battleship and the town of Odessa itself. The same was true of the villains — in *Potemkin*, the officers aboard the ship and the Cossacks on shore. The viewer becomes more familiar with objects associated with these antagonists — eyeglasses, a crucifix, boots — than with the specific faces and characters of individual people.

Pudovkin, whose film content, like Eisenstein's, centered on the Revolution and related events, differed from his friend and colleague in both editing theory (see pages 104–105) and in his use of an individualized hero. Like Eisenstein, Pudovkin was interested in conveying the epic sweep of history, but he believed that the story of an individual caught

★ **5-2** The subject of Soviet social realism was generally constant whether the form was fiction or documentary: the Russian Revolution and how it changed the life of the people. The actual history of that revolution was interpreted and sometimes dramatically altered in such films as Sergei Eisenstein's STRIKE (1924, above) and POTEMKIN (1925, Figure 2, pp. 70–71).

up in epic movement was more affecting than a story which lacked specific characterizations. In this respect, Pudovkin takes after D. W. Griffith, who in *The Birth of a Nation* (1915) tells his audience the epic story of the Civil War but personalizes it through the individual story of two families. Similarly, Pudovkin in *Mother* (1926) tells his audience the epic story of the awakening of social consciousness in oppressed factory workers through the personalized story of a mother and son. Whereas Eisenstein's editing of details humanizes and particularizes his predominantly epic scope, Pudovkin's editing of details adds epic scope to what is predominantly a smaller domestic story. In *Mother*, for example, Pudovkin metaphorically enlarges the particulars of a prison escape by cutting to the breaking up of ice during the spring thaw and its increasingly free and buoyant momentum on the river — and this relationship between the specific social act and the huge and inexorable forces of nature is further strengthened with images of that ice crashing against the pilings of a bridge intercut with shots of demonstrators clashing with police.

Dovzhenko's films were also epic but their approach lay somewhere between Eisenstein's and Pudovkin's. Like Eisenstein, this Ukrainian film poet was less interested in a tightly structured story than in epic scope, and he, too, was attracted to the striking formal possibilities of the editing process which could suddenly shock viewers into a new state of awareness. Like Pudovkin, however, he was interested in telling stories with individualized characters. What is unique about Dovzhenko's films is their mixture of realism and fantasy, their sustained and leisurely sequences of visual poetry punctuated by moments of violence or humor. In *Arsenal* (1929), the film's realistic hero becomes a symbolic figure of the revolutionary spirit as he turns out to be impervious to bullets from a firing squad, and in the same film horses sing and speak; in *Earth* (1930), a lyric, beautiful sequence which visualizes twilight in the country is shockingly disrupted by a murder. Dovzhenko's work usually treats revolutionary themes, but he tends to emphasize them in a universal and timeless context and within the larger themes of land and fertility, love, life, and death. In *Earth*, for example, the film's rhythm is slow and its images are filled with sky and clouds and fields and trees; the human characters — though participating in a life-and-death revolutionary struggle to collectivize their farms — become part of a cosmic and eternal landscape, part of the struggle of men everywhere and in every time.

Most of the Soviet films made between 1925 and 1930 still convey to us their sense of discovery about the medium of film, the vital force of their editing, and the historical reality of the vast social changes which transformed Czarist Russia into the Soviet Union. Eisenstein's *Potemkin* and *October* (1928), Pudovkin's *Mother* and *Storm over Asia* (1928), Dovzhenko's *Arsenal* and *Earth*, and Vertov's *The Man with a Movie Camera* (1928) are only a few of the marvelous films produced in this brief span of five years. Though Eisenstein made several brilliant films during the sound period, the change in Soviet regime and the rise of Josef Stalin put an end to the unrestrained, dynamic creativity of those earlier years. Soviet social realism was still the dominant approach to filmmaking; films were to portray realistically the life of the people during and after the revolution. But the creative energies of those very filmmakers who had made Soviet social realism a force in the world cinema were suppressed by charges of "formalism," that is, by charges that they were more interested in form, than in content. The new regime determined that the Soviet viewer could not comprehend the content of a film which used innovative cinematic technique, and so a more conservative style replaced dynamic and poetic creativity.

★★★ **Italian Neorealism**

ITALY, 1944 . . . The project came to me months ago, born from the conviction that only in this moment people have a power of sincerity that they will lose again very soon. Today a destroyed house is a destroyed house; the odor of the dead lingers; from the North we hear the echo of

the last shellings; in other words, our stupor and fear are whole, it's as if we could study them in a test-tube. Our cinema must attempt this documentation, it has the means to move about like this in space and time, to collect within the spectator's pupil the multiple and the diverse, provided it abandons its usual narrative methods and adapts its language to the content.
Cesare Zavattini[3]

Between the years 1935 and 1940, the Italian film industry, which had been under the control of independent producers, came under the governmental control of Benito Mussolini's Fascist regime. Before and during Fascist domination, films in Italy were not either particularly innovative or particularly national in character. Rather, Italy churned out various epics and a whole range of what came to be called "white telephone films," the latter so-named because of the white telephone in the boudoir of this socially irrelevant genre's heroine. Even when the Fascists came to power, financed major studios, and set up the Centro Sperimentale (the state film school), there were few changes in Italian films. Unlike the Germans, who made clearly propagandistic movies, the Italian government seemed content so long as no films attacked Mussolini's regime or dealt with real and contemporary social problems. Thus, during the war years many Italian filmmakers were able to learn and practice their craft in relative peace and obscurity and were creatively ready and technically skilled when the Nazi occupation of Rome ended.

Clearly the war itself and its grim realities, along with the long-enforced irrelevance of the Italian cinema to the life of Italy's people, combined with the financial problems of making movies in a war-torn city to initiate a film movement which would have worldwide impact. As Rome was being liberated in 1944, Roberto Rossellini — a director who had previously made some propagandistic documentaries — began shooting what was to become the key film for the Italian neorealist movement, *Open City* (1945). This stark, violent film depicts the heroism of the anti-Fascist underground during the dark days of occupation — but even more important than its contemporary content was its look and form, the treatment of the content. Although it was a narrative film, it looked and felt like a documentary. Even though professional actors were used in the principal roles, they appeared to be ordinary people, rather like the non-actors in the backgrounds of the film which was shot on location in the streets of Rome and at the sites where real events of the Nazi occupation had taken place. Counter to the tradition of Italian films with handsome actors, glossy photography, and white telephones in the boudoirs of the rich, *Open City* unflinchingly showed the war-devastated streets of Rome, the alleys, the back rooms of dilapidated flats. Because of financial difficulties and because much of the film was made secretly during the occupation itself, the film is technically rough; it uses salvaged film stocks of varying grain and is poorly lit in interior scenes, and (following what became usual Italian practice) the filmmaker dubbed the voices in when the film was edited. But these flaws, caused by expedience as much as by Rossellini's filmmaking aesthetic, became virtues and became characteristic of Italian neorealist cinema and those films which attempted to imitate the films of the movement. The flaws gave the film an immediacy and urgency which seemed dynamic and contemporary and emphasized Rossellini's underlying aim, which was to record life objectively as it was lived in Italy during the occupation. *Open City* was an international success — perhaps because of the charismatic ordinariness of its leading actress, Anna Magnani, and perhaps because the world was ready to address itself to contemporary social issues in its entertainments now that the war was over.

A host of equally impressive films followed *Open City*, made by Rossellini and by his friends and associates and countrymen who had studied at the Centro Sperimentale and had made films in government-controlled film studios. Although the films varied, they nearly all used the same stylistic approach — on-location shooting, natural lighting, nonprofessional actors along with professional performers, dubbing of the sound track, and an overall cinematic style which was objective rather than subjective (Figure 5-3). There were also similarities in content and structure. Stories tended to concentrate on ordinary people, little people on the edge of poverty trying to make do in an impersonal urban environment, trying to live with the awesome problems of postwar life. And often, as in Rossellini's next film, *Paisan* (1946), stories were episodic; short unrelated vignettes, each with different characters, strung together in a chain of cumulative power. Indeed, the objective approach and the desire for realism dictated less traditional narrative structure, less neatly delineated beginnings, middles, and ends; instead, filmmakers attempted to give the viewer "a slice of life," an open-ended narrative which suggests that life continues, whether the camera records it or not.

Along with Roberto Rossellini, two other figures were key to the Italian neorealist movement: Cesare Zavattini and Vittorio De Sica. Zavattini was a screenwriter who worked with Rossellini and went on to collaborate often with De Sica. De Sica was the director of internationally acclaimed neorealist films which concentrated on the heartrending stories of people attempting to maintain their dignity and hope in the face of overwhelming social and economic problems, like the young boys in *Shoeshine* (1946), the father looking for work in *The Bicycle*

★ **5-3** Italian neorealism used fiction to document the bitter realities of post-World War II Italy. OPEN CITY (Roberto Rossellini, 1945) detailed the brutalities of Nazis against the Italian Resistance. BICYCLE THIEF (Vittorio De Sica, 1949) examined the plight of an out-of-work father who must recover his stolen bicycle so that he can take the only job offered to him. Failing to locate his own, he is driven to theft himself. Documentary-like images and nonprofessional actors added to the sense of realism displayed in these films.

Thief (1949), and the elderly gentleman and his dog trying to stay alive on a meager pension in *Umberto D.* (1951). Other key films of the neorealist movement were Alberto Lattuada's *To Live in Peace* (1946) and *Without Pity* (1947) and Luchino Visconti's forerunner of the neorealist movement, *Osessione* (1942), and *La Terra Trema* (1948). Federico Fellini, who was to go on to blend surrealism and fantasy into a film form uniquely his own, was associated with the neorealists first as a script writer and then as codirector. Some of the early films he directed in the 1950s are essentially neorealist even though specific motifs and images foreshadow Fellini's desire to move beyond the confines of realism; *I Vitelloni* (1953) dealt with a group of idle young men in a small Italian town, *La Strada* (1954) revealed a poor and realistically observed Italy despite the allegorical quality of its central characters, *Il Bidone* (1955) dealt directly with social subject matter in its story about a group of swindlers bilking the poor and greedy, and *The Nights of Cabiria* (1956) recorded a real landscape of poverty and meanness.

Like other film movements, Italian neorealism in any pure form was short-lived. As people recovered from the war, as film production became regularized and technical difficulties were not a necessary fact of filmmaking, the films themselves changed. Realism has its limits — and after a while filmmakers like Fellini and Visconti and De Sica found the consistently grim subject matter and literalism of neorealism confining. Italian film began to look in other directions and began a new cinematic renaissance in the early 1960s — but that renaissance comprised individual filmmakers making individual films and was not really a movement as such.

Italian neorealism had a far reaching effect on the cinema. Its look of gritty realism and its socially aware content which dealt with ordinary rather than glamorous people influenced even the Hollywood film in the postwar period and into the 1950s. The popularity of the neorealist films demonstrated that audiences were looking not only for entertainment which took them away from reality or which obscured it in a mythic form, but also for films which made them socially conscious, made them think or made them cry. The look of Hollywood films changed to accommodate this treatment of social reality — and although much of the change could be attributed to the general effects of the war and its aftermath on American society, some of the change was influenced by the Italian films shown in the United States. Any time a fictional film is crafted to give the viewer the look and feel of documentary, of newsreel, any time a filmmaker uses non-actors to present the halting or spontaneous illusion of reality, we are seeing the influence of Italian neorealism. Even today, those Third World countries which are developing national cinemas and attempting to use film in the political and social struggle for a better life are influenced by films made during the neorealist period.

★★★   ## The French New Wave

> I remember we approached Resnais, and asked him if he was interested in participating in our group. On paper, it looked wonderfully simple: Astruc would make a film with Resnais as assistant, Resnais would make a film with Rivette as assistant, Rivette would make a film with myself as assistant, and so on with Bitsch and Chabrol. . . . We then had the further idea of approaching such and such a producer, and saying: "You make a film for £75,000 without knowing whether you'll get your money back or not. We'll make you four films for the same price, and one of them is damn well bound to be a success."
> François Truffaut[4]

The French new wave (*nouvelle vague*) was a film movement arising out of a dissatisfaction with traditional aesthetics rather than with traditional politics or with the structure of society. France had a group of long-practicing "old guard" film directors, such as Julien Duvivier and Rene Clément, who during and after the war made films in what seemed a traditional, respectable and unchanging manner. Their films were technically proficient and often beautifully mounted and performed, but they also tended to be heavily dependent upon literary sources and melodramatic subject matter with characters irrelevant to contemporary French culture. Claude Autant-Lara's *The Red and the Black* (1954) is a classic example of such a film; it adapted a classic Stendahl novel and starred two leading performers, Danielle Darrieux and Gerard Phillipe, who had become associated with such melodramas.

After the war, a group of young men rebelled against what they saw as a repressive tradition. Reaching maturity during the 1950s, these young men had spent the postwar years in the Paris Cinématheque, a film archive which showed movies from all over the world around the clock in their original language and in no programmatic order. Thus unconventionally schooled in cinema, the group became film critics and reviewers, writing most often for *Cahiers du Cinéma*, a magazine founded by the humanist and film theorist André Bazin. Initially, François Truffaut, Jean-Luc Godard, Alain Resnais (the three major and most influential filmmakers of the movement), and others as well wrote articles attacking the "old guard" tradition which had produced what these young men thought to be boringly predictable movies. Film, they thought and wrote, should be created less by the pen than by the camera, less by the scripted material than by the filmed mise-en-scène; thus, came about the term *camera stylo* or camera pen, which was regularly used to define the new aesthetic approach.

In 1954, the French new wave crystallized as the result of an inflammatory and celebrated article on film authorship by François Truffaut in *Cahiers du Cinéma*. In what was to be called the *politique des auteurs*, Truffaut attacked the "tradition of quality" he felt had killed all the dynamism and spontaneity which could be found in the French cinema of the 1920s and 1930s — and in the American genre films made by such directors as Howard Hawks, Otto Preminger, and Alfred Hitchcock. The filmmaker, and not the dictates of a script, Truffaut argued, should shape the film. Truffaut and the other new wave critics held up to the French cinema the models of those American directors they called **auteurs,** directors who infused personal style and cinematic imagination into clichéd material and brought it to distinctive life on the screen. Finally, with limited financing and with a great deal of help from each other, these young, cinematically literate French film critics began to make their own movies — films which astonished the world with their originality, wit, daring, and vitality (Figure 5-4). In 1959, for example,

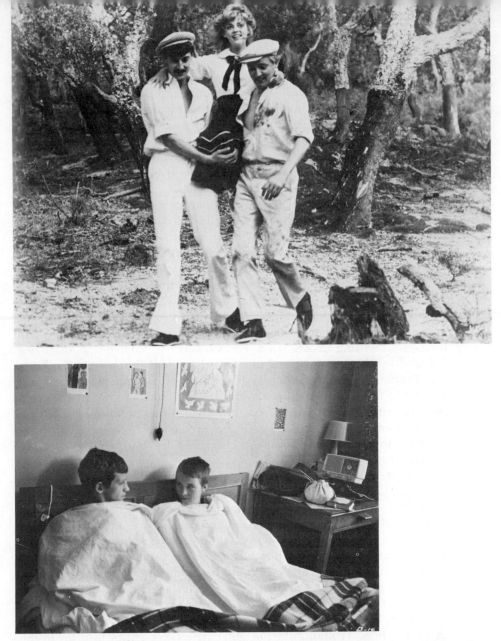

★ **5-4** The French new wave was led by two former critics from *Cahiers du Cinema* who felt that the well-made French film lacked vitality. François Truffaut created a strange story about a *ménage à trois* in JULES AND JIM 1961, above). Jean-Luc Godard's BREATHLESS (1959, below) at first seems to be the badly shot and poorly edited footage of a beginning filmmaker, but its power is undeniable. These two young directors made it possible for a whole group of other young Frenchmen to make innovative movies: Claude Chabrol, Eric Rohmer, and Phillipe de Broca, to name a few.

the top prizes at the world-famed Cannes film festival were awarded to Truffaut for his first feature, *The 400 Blows*, to Alain Resnais for his first feature, *Hiroshima, Mon Amour*, and to Marcel Camus for his second feature, *Black Orpheus*; all three filmmakers were French and all were relatively unknown. In only a few years, a burst of energy and creativity changed the technique, style, and subject matter of French film.

What united these brilliant, individual directors, and what allows us to see them as constituting a film movement, was a belief in cinema as a vital art that owed no allegiance to other arts, specifically literature and drama. The new wave filmmakers, thumbing their noses at their predecessors' "tradition of quality," were often purposely artless and inconsistent in tone and style. Most of the films appeared to be spontaneous efforts made on modest budgets and with a certain playful sloppiness, not quite the same stuff of which Italian neorealism was made. Furthermore, many of the new wave films self-consciously called attention to their own techniques, playing with elements of cinema and quoting cinematic references from various films the young filmmakers had seen in the Cinématheque. For example, in Jean-Luc Godard's *Breathless* (1959), the protagonist, a Parisian hoodlum, consciously imitates Humphrey Bogart's mannerisms, going so far as to stand in front of a revival movie marquee's poster of Bogart, in order to see if he matches up to the image of his idol. The tone of many of the films varied internally so that the audience could not be sure what would happen next, or whether the film they were watching was a comedy or melodrama or something more serious. In Truffaut's *Shoot the Piano Player* (1960), for example, the story, which centers on a former concert pianist and his underworld associations and involvements, constantly shifts from melodrama to comedy to existential tragedy; when one of the characters swears falsely to something on his mother's life, Truffaut inserts a shot of the mother dropping dead.

François Truffaut, originally the chief spokesman of the new wave, has revealed through the passing years a wide-ranging talent marked by a certain nostalgic lyricism often tinged with irony, or, to put it a little differently, by a humanism which focuses objectively yet compassionately on the relationships between men and women, between children and their elders, both parents and teachers, and by a certain refusal to treat political and social themes except indirectly. Yet, despite his lack of overt political involvement, one could hardly call Truffaut's films tame or complacent. They often end with a lack of resolution, an irony, a question mark. For example, his first feature, *The 400 Blows*, a semi-autobiographical film about a young boy on the brink of serious delinquency, ends with a freeze frame of the face of the protagonist as he looks out into a world which provides no pat answers. Truffaut has not stayed with one formula, however. Some of his most critically acclaimed films after *The 400 Blows* and *Shoot the Piano Player* are *Jules and Jim* (1961), which records (in all manner of innovative technique, including an aerial shot, special editing effects from the optical printer, and antique newsreel footage), the story of two male friends and the unpredictable woman they both love; *The Wild Child* (1970), which is an austere, moving account of the relationship established between a scientist/teacher — played by Truffaut himself — and the "wolf-boy" he sets out to civilize; *Day for Night* (1973), which explores the filmmaking process at the same time that it explores human relationships in front of and behind the camera; *The Story of Adele H.* (1975), which explores the nature of romantic obsession in a disturbingly clinical yet visually beautiful way; and *Small Change* (1976), which celebrates childhood, recording both the resilience and fragility of youth.

Alain Resnais, though not quite so incredibly prolific or commercially popular as Truffaut, has also continued to make films. Resnais has had a tremendous influence on the shape and subject matter of contemporary cinema, not just in France but throughout the world. Before the emergence of the new wave as a film movement, Resnais had made several critically acclaimed short documentary films, including *Night and Fog* (1955), which dealt with the horrors of Nazi concentration camps. Even in these early films, Resnais's major thematic focus clearly indicated the approach he would take in his feature films. Resnais is obsessed with exploring the themes of time and memory, particularly their fluidity, their subjectivity, their unreliability, their negation of pragmatic reality. Both his first feature, *Hiroshima, Mon Amour* (1959), and his second, *Last Year at Marienbad* (1961), not only thoroughly dealt with these themes, but also in their very formal structure duplicated the processes being explored. Neither film told a story. Past and present merged with future or with wishful thinking, all causality was emotional and unreliable, and one could hardly speak of the films' structure in such traditional terms as dramatic climax, resolution, conflict. On film, Resnais explored (and is still exploring) what had hitherto seemed the province of literature — and particularly the province of the new French literature exemplified by the *nouveau roman* ("new novel") of Alain Robbe-Grillet and Marguerite Duras, both of whom have collaborated with Resnais. Unlike Truffaut, Resnais has dealt with political and social subject matter — particularly with war and its psychic effect on individuals and on countries. But Resnais is primarily obsessed with the distortions to which time is subject, with memory and the possibility of forgetting even that which seems too horrible to ever forget: the Nazi camps in *Night and Fog,* the death of one's lover in *Hiroshima, Mon Amour,* details of the Algerian war in *Muriel* (1963). The same themes inform all of Resnais's films, and so it is not surprising that he has made *Je T'Aime, Je T'Aime* (1968), a science fiction story of time travel, *Stavisky* (1974), a study of a mysterious swindler who rejects a past which finally catches up with him, and, most recently, *Providence* (1977), a fantasy mixing "real" people and fictional "characters" created by the mind of an aging novelist. Unlike many of the other new wave filmmakers, Resnais always uses a literate script, written in collaboration with leading French authors, and Resnais has given as much weight to the dialogue and narration of his films as to the images, believing they work in concert and in counterpoint.

Of the three major new wave film makers, Jean-Luc Godard was from the start the most political. A Marxist, in his first feature, *Breathless* (1959), he borrowed from Marxist dramatist Berthold Brecht devices that prevent the audience from achieving an emotional and unthinking involvement with the film's characters and situation. For example, to distance the audience from the film, he has used title cards, thus making the film less real. But the early Godard films also reveal a love for American genre movies and star performers. *Breathless* was, in fact, a homage to Humphrey Bogart and the American gangster film; it puzzled and pleased and annoyed its viewers because its central characters — a petty Parisian thief and his casually acquired American girlfriend — seemed to lack comprehensible motivations, its situations seemed to have little to do with causality, and its cinematic style seemed jumpy and frenetic as abrupt cuts disoriented viewers and whisked them from place to place. *Breathless* even jump cut *within* scenes, jolting audiences into an awareness that they were sitting in a theater watching a film — a film that, perhaps, had too many repaired splices in it. Godard continued to make films which were self-reflexive, which interrupted themselves and called attention to their own devices and forms, which used all sorts of Brechtian distancing devices to make more objective the entire process of film viewing. At the same time, Godard's early films had an exuberance and spontaneity and love of movies that was extremely engaging; in *A Woman Is a Woman* (1961) he paid homage to the American musical, in *Alphaville* (1965) he paid homage to the American science fiction film, and in *Pierrot le Fou* (1965) he returned to the surfaces of the American gangster film.

Godard's political films, such as *Masculine-Feminine* (1966), which not only explores sexual roles but also looks at modern perception and communication as it is practiced by the "children of Marx and Coca-

Cola," at first were excitingly bold in their use of print media, like signs, advertisements, titles. He also used assaulting color, for example in *La Chinoise* (1967), which excited the eyes with its use of primary colors — particularly red — as it revealed to us a Maoist "cell" of young people in France. And increasingly Godard interrupted what little narrative his films contained with long interviews of his actors/characters, with titles, and bits of polemic. Eventually, Godard's politics and his vision of himself as a film essayist seemed irreconcilable with any form of narrative film, and in the 1970s he left bourgeois cinema to make political documentaries and other films which have had limited exhibition. His films are now made as part of a group effort and he has disowned the value of all his films before *Le Gai Savoir* (1968), a film reduced much of the time to a black background against which a male and female sit and talk to each other about Marxism and contemporary life.

Godard's influence on contemporary narrative film is enormous. He demonstrated that political concerns could be cinematically treated and that audiences would see such films and understand and enjoy them. His

★ **5-5** Louis Malle, like other French new wave directors, follows his own course in both subject matter and form. In MURMUR OF THE HEART (1971), he tells the story of a young boy who is introduced to physical love by his mother. This Oedipal relationship sounds shocking, but its tasteful, touching, and often funny treatment in the film provoked less controversy than his earlier film about adultery, THE LOVERS (1958). Here the young boy in MURMUR makes his confession before the unpremeditated encounter with his mother.

devices to keep spectators aware that they were watching an artificial process (rather than being caught up in the illusion of reality of the film) are widely used for various purposes in today's films: the interview of a character, or the actor playing the character; the use of titling and other forms of pop culture print media; the disruption or discontinuation of story.

In addition to François Truffaut, Alain Resnais, and Jean-Luc Godard, the French new wave was rich with the further talents of Claude Chabrol, who is noted for his Hitchcock-like psychological thrillers such as *Le Boucher* (1968), with Phillipe DeBroca's witty and gentle comedies such as *The Five Day Lover* (1961), and *The King of Hearts* (1966), and Eric Rohmer's series of "Six Moral Tales," including *My Night at Maud's* (1970) and *Claire's Knee* (1971). And, of course, there were others: Agnès Varda, Louis Malle, Claude Lelouch and Jacques Demy. The French new wave is not new any more — though many of its originators are still directing fascinating and critically acclaimed films (Figure 5-5). These young men, now in middle age, critics and theorists before they became filmmakers, have demonstrated that artistry and entertainment can go hand in hand.

★★★ British Free Cinema

> So we got together and we thought that the thing to do was to put all our films together in a program. . . . And we decided to try to get the National Film Theater to show them. And we thought that to do this we must call the program something. We hit on the title of Free Cinema.
>
> Then we formulated a kind of manifesto, propaganda, which was a sort of declaration of freedom for the film artists, an attack on the British cinema of that particular time — which was completely middle-class-bound. Ealing Studio comedies — for example, *Kind Hearts and Coronets* — and the like. Emotionally quite frozen.
>
> Lindsay Anderson[5]

The British cinema has been chiefly known for its documentary contributions. True, many fine feature films have come from Britain through the years, but it was not until the late 1950s that the British narrative film gained world attention. At that time a film movement called British free cinema emerged, chiefly because of three factors. The first was the already established documentary tradition of filmmaking in Britain, which recorded the everyday life of the country and its working people. The second was a growing dissatisfaction with the British class system and the limitations it set upon the ambitious youth of the working classes. The third was the antiestablishment work of a new and socially

conscious group of young novelists and playwrights like Shelagh De-
laney, Alan Sillitoe, and John Osborne, who, rejecting traditional subject matter and form, were called the Angry Young Men — apparently
regardless of their sex. Their novels, plays, and short stories focused on
frustrated working-class heroes who were on the edge of violence because their social origins rather than their abilities determined their lives
and the degree of success they could possibly achieve.

Lindsay Anderson, Karel Reisz, and Tony Richardson began the British free cinema movement, which was described in a manifesto as a
"belief in freedom, in the importance of the individual and in the significance of the everyday." Originally these men made experimental
documentary films which were less optimistic about British life than
their predecessors, and when they moved into feature filmmaking, this
philosophy went with them. Their belief in the individual and the ordinary was fired into nervous energy by the dramatic and literary work
of the Angry Young Men who had confronted the British establishment
with the gritty reality of working class life. Indeed, many of the films
of the movement were adaptations of literary and dramatic sources.
Room at the Top (Jack Clayton, 1958), the first of the new anti-estab-
lishment narrative films, was adapted from a John Braine novel which
recorded in detail the efforts of a young man from the lower classes to
break into the establishment world of business and upper-middle-class
society. Besides treating subject matter hitherto absent from British
films, *Room at the Top* also brought to the screen the landscape of
industrial England and more explicit sexuality than had been seen before. Another of the earliest films was *Look Back in Anger* (Tony
Richardson, 1959), adapted from a highly successful play by John Osborne and featuring Richard Burton in an electrifying performance.
Other adaptations from literary works were *Saturday Night and Sunday
Morning* (Karel Reisz, 1961), which followed its working-class hero
through his dreary weekly routine to his weekend bash (Figure 5-6);
A Taste of Honey (Tony Richardson, 1962), which told the story of a
young girl, pregnant and alone, and her homosexual friend in a working-
class section of London; and *The Loneliness of the Long Distance Runner* (Tony Richardson, 1962), which with arresting flashbacks told the
story of a track star in a British reformatory (Figure 5-7). Besides numerous adaptations, there were also original films like *This Sporting
Life* (Lindsay Anderson, 1963), which grimly recorded the bruising
physical and emotional life of a rugby player whose sport had provided
an upward social mobility not otherwise open to him.

Despite the fairly large number of films adapted from literary works
of some kind, the British free cinema movement was not at all literary

★ **5-6** The hopelessness of British lower-class life, with its weekly round of dull, routine workdays followed by weekends of idle drunkenness and fistfights was poignantly captured in Karel Reisz's SATURDAY NIGHT AND SUNDAY MORNING (1961) based on Alan Sillitoe's novel. Reisz's background in documentary film gave this fiction film's images the starkness of reality. On-location filming, black-and-white stock, and relatively unknown performers were typical of the serious British film of the 1960s.

★ **5-7** Tony Richardson's THE LONELINESS OF THE LONG DISTANCE RUNNER (1962) is typical of the British free cinema movement. By focusing on the life of the working class, the films of this movement gave vent to frustrations produced by the rigid class system in England.

in the way that some earlier British films had been in their heavy dependence on dialogue or in their novelistic structure. Thematically, the films were often the story of a young hero who rebelled against the role in society for which his lower-class background destined him. This role was usually that of a laborer in a factory, which meant that these films showed a stifling, polluted, drab England where the sun never seemed to shine. The films were also characterized by exceptionally fine performances, both by newcomers like Tom Courtenay and Albert Finney and established actors like Sir Laurence Olivier. Despite the overall pessimism of this "kitchen sink" drama, the visual style of the films was less grim than dynamic: combined with the social realism of the story and cinematography was a certain exuberant editing, for example, a fluid use of flashback.

The anger of the Angry Young Men had diminished by the mid-sixties and British artists, particularly filmmakers, began to move away from the grimness of their previous work and toward a certain comic and ironic stance to the same subject matter. Tony Richardson was extraordinarily inventive in adapting Henry Fielding's eighteenth-century novel *Tom Jones* (1963) to the screen: its hero and his economic and class problems were somewhat analogous to contemporary problems, but the film was clearly not made to protest anything but stodgy and grim cinema. Director Richard Lester and the Beatles also radically altered the face and shape of British film. Adopting a style to suit the youth, dynamism, humor, and exuberance of his pop subjects, Lester made *A Hard Day's Night* (1964), which not only showed the Beatles singing, but had them cavorting in playgrounds, moving about in fast motion — all in a film which at the time seemed almost incomprehensibly fast in its editing and still is spontaneous, fresh, and happy. With the Beatles' success, the British free cinema movement in its pure form died — perhaps in acknowledgment that at least on the screen the British working class had finally made it. Films which followed still treated lower-class characters in urban settings, but they were seen differently — and certainly were filmed differently. Those key filmmakers who started the movement continue to make films, but their styles have changed to accommodate not only the change in Britain but the evolution of their personal aesthetics as well.

★★★ **Brazilian Cinema Novo and El Nuevo Cine**

> Our time is one of hypothesis rather than of thesis, a time of works in process — unfinished, unordered, violent works made with the camera in one hand and a rock in the other. Such works cannot be assessed ac-

cording to the traditional theoretical canon. The ideas for *our* film theory
and criticism will come to life through inhibition-removing practice and
experimentation.

Fernando Solanas and Octavio Getino[6]

Most of the film movements so far discussed have revealed a connection
between politics and art. Successful revolution, the problems of a postwar society, even the gulf between prospective young filmmakers and a
monolithic or tradition-bound film industry may be the cultural catalyst
which helps to create an artistic movement. But not since the early
Soviet cinema has there been a movement so politically oriented and
militant as the now defunct cinema novo in Brazil and the currently
proclaimed **el nuevo cine,** as New Latin American cinema has called itself.

The new Brazilian cinema — cinema novo — gained world attention
in the early 1960s with *Barren Lives* (1963), a film made by Nelson
Pereira dos Santos, who is considered the father of the movement. The
film, set in the 1940s, dramatizes the plight of peasants and cowhands
in Brazil's northeast ·sertao, an area long drought-ridden and dominated
by landowners. Usually cited as the founding film of cinema novo,
Barren Lives was on one level extremely realistic in its detailed depiction
of social conditions, and in its visual style; on another level, however,
the sparseness and harshness of its imagery moves the film from realism
to symbolism or allegory. Another filmmaker, Glauber Rocha — who,
like Pereira, was a journalist and film critic before becoming a filmmaker
— was to become the most dominant force behind cinema novo. His
film *Black God, White Devil* (1964) also dealt with social conditions, but
Rocha was interested in finding a cinematic language rooted in his own
culture which would speak of the plight of his people, both the peasant
and the intellectual. Rocha's films, such as *Antonio das Mortes* (1969),
in telling their stories draw on the folklore, religions, mysticism, witch-
craft, music, and dance of Brazil. These stories are generally violent,
filled with physical conflict, and characterized by dislocating editing.

The cinema novo films were innovative in their blend of social realism and fantasy, of narrative and song, of realistic and allegorical figures. Such a strange blend of cinematic elements in a feature film initially
took the government censors off guard; social and political criticism got
by as musical and fairy tale. Thus, the cinema novo artist retold, in a
form that appealed to the illiterate as well as to the educated, the stories
of the *Cangaciros,* the Robin Hood–like bandits who helped free the
country from aristocratic, feudal land barons in the nineteenth century.
In telling these popular tales, the films conveyed the message that the
present government is similar to the land barons of old, and that a

revolution of the people was called for to rid the country of its contemporary capitalist rulers. Out of this leftist political message wedded to the ancient tales have come violent, beautiful, stylized and expressionistic films in which allegorical figures move back and forth in time and space, often with no thought for the ordinary relationship of cause and effect. The cinema novo films are sometimes so loaded with references to Brazilian culture that they are incomprehensible to outsiders, but films like those of Rocha have a rare power and beauty that overcomes cultural barriers.

Other national film movements in Latin America (including Cuba) are covered by the rubric el nuevo cine, also identified as "guerilla cinema" and "militant cinema." Except for the Cuban cinema, which has produced a large body of impressive and innovative work, the state of other Latin cinema varies from what seems day to day. Brazil's ruling government finally exiled, jailed, or killed many cinema novo filmmakers; Glauber Rocha, for example, now lives in self-imposed exile and makes films elsewhere in the Third World. Indeed, in all of Latin America (with the exception of Cuba), el nuevo cine is threatened daily. Andres Racz, a Chilean filmmaker and former critic, has said that "the government hates the artist as much as it hates the revolutionary, because it realizes they are the same."

Most films emerging from Latin America have been documentaries, but many are features in the neorealist tradition, depicting social reality to achieve social and political change. The stylized, allegorical cinema of a filmmaker like Rocha has, on occasion, come under fire; the criticism suggests that extensive use of "native" mythology and folklore tends to create a nostalgia for the past at the expense of the present .

★★★ **The New German Cinema**

> When we started making films there was no audience. There was nobody in Germany who cared to see German films. It was only after recognition of these films in France, England, and America that people started being curious about them in Germany. It took us five years to get an audience back to seeing German films. There was a hole of forty years which was very hard to fill.
> Wim Wenders[7]

The new German cinema (*das neue Kino*) is the most recent film movement to influence the shape of contemporary narrative. Although it can be traced back to the early 1960s, it wasn't until the 1970s that international film festivals began showing the works of Alexander Kluge,

Wim Wenders, Rainer Fassbinder, and Werner Herzog to a wide audience. Critically acclaimed, the films of these directors often seem to have little in common, but all of them, in fact, subvert traditional narrative forms to attack the limited perspective and complacency of Germany's bourgeois middle class. Led by Alexander Kluge in reaction to what they called "Papa's cinema" (the commercial and traditional film industry which emerged in West Germany after World War II), in 1962 a group of young and politically leftist filmmakers announced that they could make better movies than the established industry — and for half the cost. Their unified efforts led to the founding of a national film school and to government subsidy of their work in both film and television.

The films of Alexander Kluge and Wim Wenders are perhaps the least widely seen of those by the major directors in the new German cinema. Combining documentary footage and techniques with traditional narrative fiction, contrasting fantasy sequences with starkly realistic scenes, using distancing devices such as printed messages to the audience, Kluge's films are funny and satiric explorations of contemporary society. *Occasional Work of a Female Slave* (1974), for example, presents a heroine who, as a housewife unable to manage on a scanty budget, becomes an abortionist, and then — as the result of her experiences — a one-woman socialist crusader against social injustice. Wenders's films, in contrast, are less flamboyant in style, their satire less obvious. His low-key and stark imagery, sparse dialogue, dependence on popular music, and narrative focus on alienated characters who travel meaninglessly across a contemporary landscape combine elements of existentialist drama and social criticism. Often, as in *The Goalie's Anxiety at the Penalty Kick* (1971) or *The American Friend* (1977), Wenders uses the form of the suspense thriller to explore his characters and the world through which they pass.

Better known than Kluge and Wenders are Rainer Fassbinder and Werner Herzog. Fassbinder, the most prolific of the new German filmmakers, uses a repertory company of performers, and makes his films quickly for both television and theatrical release. Films like *Ali, or Fear Eats the Soul* (1974) or *Mother Kusters Goes to Heaven* (1975) appear to be highly traditional narratives photographed in a rather undistinguished style; indeed, in their domestic subject matter and melodramatic treatment, they are reminiscent of those "women's" films made in Hollywood in the 1940s and 1950s. But Fassbinder bends the conventions of melodrama so that they become social commentary. His flat images heighten the viewer's awareness of the flatness and banality of his character's lives and transform their most violent and passionate acts

★ **5-8** Brilliant color, inventive camera work, creative editing patterns, and fascinating music, made a simple "boy meets girl" love story complex and beautiful in Claude Lelouch's A MAN AND A WOMAN (1966). Though Lelouch's story is trite, his fascinating treatment of it shows the liberating influence the French new wave had on mainstream cinema.

into sad, squalid, and ineffectual protests against the limitations of bourgeois life. Werner Herzog's films are the least conventional of all the new German filmmakers'. Their subject matter is often bizarre and displaced from contemporary and ordinary life. *Even Dwarfs Started Small* (1969), for example, is about a rebellion of dwarfs in an institution; *The Mystery of Kasper Hauser* (1975) is about a man who had been kept in isolation since childhood and was suddenly released into civilized Nuremberg society in 1828; and *Heart of Glass* (1977) concerns a medieval town which, at the death of one of the townspeople, loses the secret formula for the red glass which it has manufactured and, as a result, goes mad. Despite their strange subject matter, Herzog's films are quite modern and critical in their exploration of different modes of perception; his main characters often see life differently from those characters in the film who share a vision of life more familiar to the viewer, and tragedy results from that limited vision imposed by tradition and society in collision with the protagonist's new way of seeing.

Because it is still an active movement, it is hard to assess the influence of new German cinema on traditional narrative films. As the films are seen, however, it is certain that their common attempts to reject or subvert conventional dramatic development and subject matter will have some impact on contemporary filmmakers around the world. Indeed, film movements have greatly influenced the narrative film. Although they are usually short-lived, their unified reaction against traditional cinema has had strong impact on films made long after the movements themselves have dissipated. Their new forms and significant content have broadened the possibilities of cinematic storytelling in mainstream cinema (Figure 5-8). The films of modern Hollywood, for example, would not have their present range of technique and subject matter were it not for the Italian neorealism and the French new wave.

NOTES

1 *The Haunted Screen* (Berkeley: University of California Press, 1973), pp. 10–11.

2 In Luda and Jean Scnitzer and Marcel Martin, eds., *Cinema and Revolution* (New York: Hill and Wang, 1973), p. 128.

3 *Zavattini: Sequences from a Cinematic Life* (Englewood Cliffs, New Jersey: Prentice-Hall, 1970), pp. 9–10.

4 In Peter Graham, ed., *The New Wave* (Garden City, New York: Doubleday, 1968), p. 10.

5 In Joseph Gelmis, ed., *The Film Director as Superstar* (Garden City, New York: Doubleday, 1970), p. 98.

6 "Toward a Third Cinema," in Bill Nichols, ed., *Movies and Methods* (Berkeley: University of California Press, 1976), p. 57.

7 In Lony Ruhmann and Ivan Solotaroff, "No Wave," *Cinegram Magazine* 3, no. 1 (Summer 1978): 27.

6
★ *NON-GENRE*
NARRATIVE AND
ITS MAKERS

★★★ **Non-Genre Narrative**

Countless story films employ conventional, easily recognizable characters in familiar plots which take place in familiar settings and which
use traditional sorts of cinematic techniques to achieve traditional dramatic momentum and resolution. The most familiar and recognizable of
these films, the most patterned and repeated, we call genre films. The
western, for example, is one genre, and the horror film another. But
there is no recognized name for the other sort of story film, the film that
presents unfamiliar characters and situations or that is always ready
to surprise us (to either our delight or dismay). Because these films are
the creations of people who are deeply concerned with film as a serious
art, they have often been referred to as "art films." Unfortunately, however, the term *art film* has also come to suggest only those films made
by foreign directors for an elite audience. Since there are many American
directors who make works of film art and because many artistic films
appeal to large audiences, the term *art film* is problematic. For want of
a better term, we use the term *non-genre films* for these films that usually are regarded as individal works rather than as part of a group of
films.

Non-genre films attempt either to render human beings as unique,
idiosyncratic, surprising, and finally indecipherable, or else they will use
archetypal or allegorical figures which make little pretense at presenting
credible characters. Such films, extremely surprising and novel in their
content and/or their form, are usually valued for their originality, their

new way of *seeing*, for the unique vision of their creators. Whether **realistic** or expressionistic, these films often address themselves to philosophical issues, social dilemmas, politics, the human heart and soul, and usually — even when they are politically or philosophically committed — the films find no ready or absolute answers to the questions they pose. Such films may be serious or comic or may alternate between modes. Serious examples include *The Seventh Seal* (Ingmar Bergman, 1956), *Last Tango in Paris* (Bernardo Bertolucci, 1972), and *The Conversation* (Francis Ford Coppola, 1974). Comic examples, that is, films that although roughly called "comic" nevertheless go beyond the traditional formulas of comedy, include Charles Chaplin's *Modern Times* (1936), *Playtime* (Jacques Tati, 1967), and *Annie Hall* (Woody Allen, 1977). And those films which are both serious and comic non-genre films can be illustrated by Stanley Kubrick's *Dr. Strangelove; or, How I Learned to Stop Worrying and Love the Bomb* (1964), *The Discreet Charm of the Bourgeoisie* (Luis Buñuel, 1972), and Lina Wertmüller's *Seven Beauties* (1976). Whether the non-genre film is serious, comic, or a mixture of modes, its major characteristic is that it does not follow conventional story patterns.

Although all non-genre films achieve a kind of personal identity, they can be grouped into three general categories: realism, expressionism, and comedy.

CHARACTERISTICS OF NON-GENRE FILM REALISM

> You have to strike a mean between naturalism and a certain thing which is artistic, which is selective, you see. If you get the right balance, then you have this strange feeling of being life-like, everything looking very life-like and natural. . . . I think the cinema is the only medium that challenges you to be naturalistic, be realistic and yet be artistic at the same time.
> Satyajit Ray[1]

The realistic non-genre film has a plausible plot — that is, events and actions are comparable to the viewer's experience in the world outside the theater. Usually this kind of film is set in contemporary times; the viewer's own experience brings an immediacy to the film. If, however, the film is set in the past, is historical, the filmmaker does not revel in the charm and romance and nostalgia evoked by "the good old days"; rather, he usually demystifies, or demythologizes, the past. The re-creations of a past time in such realistically textured films as *The Seven Samurai* (Akira Kurosawa, 1955) and *The Last Picture Show* (Peter Bogdanovich, 1971) bear little resemblance to the re-creations of a

★ **6-1** The drab, hopeless quality of life in a small Texas town in the 1950s was evoked in Peter Bogdanovich's THE LAST PICTURE SHOW (1971) through the use of black-and-white film stock at a time when most feature films were shot in color.

somewhat sentimentalized past time in more traditional film genres such as the western and the musical (Figure 6-1). The Western adaptation of Kurosawa's film, *The Magnificent Seven* (John Sturges, 1960), presents its Western gunfighters much more heroically than does *The Seven Samurai*, and the re-creation of an earlier era in Vincente Minnelli's *Meet Me in St. Louis* (1944) is patently nostalgic.

The characters in the realistic non-genre film usually act and speak in strict accordance with the rules of psychological probability. They also tend to be more complex and therefore less completely comprehensible to the viewer than the characters in genre films. Much as we respond to a real human being, never completely knowing or understanding all facets of another person, so we usually respond to the realistic non-genre film's characters. Those cinematic characters often surprise us, not so much by speaking or acting out of character, but by little pieces of random, spontaneous idiosyncratic behavior which do not advance the story but which make the character credible and unique. Such characters also speak more naturally — and often, therefore, speak less communicatively than characters in genre films. The very inarticulateness of a character, however, the very choice of vocabulary or of silence reveals something about that character.

The stories and plots, too, of realistic non-genre films tend to be complex, untidy, open-ended. The happy ending in which the protagonist neatly triumphs over his problems is rare; such a pleasant "wrapping-up" of the story is generally reserved for comedies and genre melodramas. Tidy sad or near-tragic endings are also avoided. While the central character may come to some self-realization or solve some problems, the viewer is led to believe that the lives (and problems and triumphs) of the characters go on after the film has ended. Since life is continuous, the film, in a sense, is also continuous, even though the viewer has been privileged to see only a part of it.

Stylistically, the realistic non-genre film tends to reinforce this notion of the film frame as a window on the real world. Thus, space and time in the film closely approximate the viewer's personal experience of space and time. There is an emphasis, therefore, on invisible editing, on long takes (duration) and camera movements which preserve spatial unity and occur in units of real time. Settings tend to be ordinary and recognizable, and locations are nearly always real. Performers may be unknown or well known, but the realistic mode usually works better when the actors are not star personalities — or if they are stars, they are able to submerge themselves in the role (Figure 6-2). There is a great deal of

★ **6-2** The realistic film assumes that the frame is a window on the world. Thus, actors who are not "star" personalities frequently work better in this mode. Gene Hackman, who played the wiretap expert in THE CONVERSATION (Francis Ford Coppola, 1974), is one of those well-known actors with an undistinctive face who always merge with their roles.

difference, for instance, between such stars as Robert Redford and Dustin Hoffman playing Bob Woodward and Carl Bernstein in *All the President's Men* (Alan Pakula, 1976) and Gene Hackman playing a professional wiretapper in *The Conversation*. Redford and Hoffman are fine actors, but their faces are too well known and uncommon to allow the viewer to believe fully in the characters' existence as real. They bring their own personae to the screen and tend to negate the realistic texture of the film, turning it from a potentially surprising and real film into a genre movie with two stars playing investigative reporters. Gene Hackman, on the other hand, may be a star, but his face is somewhat anonymous in its ordinary features, and the viewer is able to believe in the real existence of the tortured character who lives in a real world where every human act may be under surveillance.

CHARACTERISTICS OF NON-GENRE FILM EXPRESSIONISM

A lie is always more interesting than the truth. Lies are the soul of showmanship and I adore shows. Fiction may have a greater truth than everyday, obvious reality. The things one shows need not be authentic. As a rule, they are better if they aren't. What must be authentic is the feeling one is trying to see and to express.
Federico Fellini[2]

As Griffith is the great early creator of the realistic non-genre narrative film, so Sergei Eisenstein is the great early creator of the expressionistic non-genre narrative film. Although George Méliès first exploited the unreal qualities of film to tell stories and is the progenitor of those films which are patently unrealistic, Eisenstein nevertheless can be considered the spiritual father of formalism, that style of filmmaking which takes advantage of the form or properties of cinema that make it different from real life. On pages 104–105 we saw that in his writings about the editing process, and in his films, Eisenstein demonstrated that meaning could be created by the filmmaker, that feeling or thought could be generated by the way in which the filmmaker juxtaposed images. Events could be created — in the mind of the audience — which were never really shown on the screen but which the audience invariably inferred; geography could be created, metaphors could be communicated by concrete images of objects, time and space were totally malleable, and film owed no particular allegiance to reality.

The expressionistic non-genre narrative film may or may not have a plausible plot (Figure 6-3); events within the film may or may not conform to the viewer's experience of the world outside the theater. Thus, Fritz Lang's *M* (1932), which tells of a city's search for a pathetic,

★ **6-3**   Federico Fellini, shown here checking the setup on a crane shot, has created films which are expressionistic; through color, costume, decor, and strange characters he reveals both his own and his characters' personal visions. If the plots and the sequences frequently appear illogical, no matter. Fellini insists: "What must be authentic is the feeling one is trying to express."

yet horrible, psychotic child murderer (Figure 6-4), has a plausible plot, but other films have not so much a plot as a pattern of events which seem to occur and recur as in a dream. Examples include Luis Buñuel's *The Discreet Charm of the Bourgoisie* or Pier Paolo Pasolini's *Teorema* (1968) or Alain Resnais's *Last Year at Marienbad* (1961). Or the film may have a plot which is patently unrealistic yet tells a story which is at least narratively coherent, like *The Man Who Fell to Earth* (Nicholas Roeg, 1976), Carl Dreyer's *The Passion of Joan of Arc* (1928), or *The Seventh Seal*. And, finally, the expressionistic non-genre film may have no plot at all to speak of, no usual story development or narrative movement to propel it forward in the ways most viewers have come to expect. Such films tell stories less through plot than through characterization and through the presence of the filmmaker (in his cinematography), exploring an idea or creating a mood. Michelangelo Antonioni's *L'Avventura* (1959) and *Red Desert* (1964), for example, tell stories about contemporary human beings lost in a cold, empty modern world to which man has not yet adapted himself and his emotional needs. The viewer who expects a traditional plot in *L'Avventura* will be disappointed, possibly even enraged, that the filmmaker never answers the question seemingly posed by the events which begin the film: Where has the film's established heroine, Anna, disappeared on the desolate volcanic island? A conventional story film would answer this question, but Antonioni never answers it because the answer has little to do with the story of his film. His story is not a conventional romance or mystery; rather, the girl's disappearance and her easy replacement in the lives of the other characters and in the film itself is what is important in conveying to the viewer the superficial relationships of modern man with even those he is supposed to love.

The American filmmaker Robert Altman also tends to reject traditional notions of plot, although the American cinema is the most plot-

★ **6-4** Expressionistic films often use objects to suggest actions rather than show them directly. Fritz Lang indicated the death of a little girl in M (1931) by first showing us her little ball rolling on the ground by itself and then her balloon rising freely in the air only to be caught by the utility wires. The balloon's drawn-on face and the fact that it looks like a doll further associates it with the child, trapped and finally murdered by the psychopathic killer.

oriented in the world; in *Nashville* (1975), Altman has the thinnest of plots and a minimum of complex characterization, and yet the film is able to engage the viewer and to say something about the American experience, the discrepancy between our ideals and the reality of our lives. *Welcome to L.A.* (Alan Rudolph, 1977), which Altman produced, is constructed almost like a piece of jazz. As modern jazz has no melodic line, *Welcome to L.A.* has no plot — and yet, like modern jazz, which *implies* a melody through counterpoint and harmony, the film implies a plot and central conflicts. Plot of a traditional nature is also missing from many politically oriented films which must disguise their political content — either for an audience which would not sit still for polemic or for a government which might suppress the film or jail the filmmakers. Entertaining political films are made by Lina Wertmüller, who surprises and delights her audiences by her bold and exuberant inconsistency and lack of traditional story in films like *Let's Talk about Men* (1965) and *All Screwed Up* (1974). A number of Latin American filmmakers (particularly from Brazil) have used folk music, dancing, allegorical figures from folktales and religion and popular culture to make political films which have no story but which have strong impact visually and intellectually.

Other sorts of films which depart from the traditional methods of narrative are those which purposely distance the viewer from the film, preventing identification with characters or emotional involvement with what is happening on the screen. This kind of distancing, by reminding the viewer that he is watching a movie, that he is being manipulated by someone outside the film frame, usually causes the viewer to respond intellectually rather than emotionally. Such distancing can be achieved by films whose surfaces and random construction and interruptions make them seem almost like cinéma vérité documentaries; the effect is not one of verite or truth, but of artificiality. Such is the case with a good number of Jean-Luc Godard's films, among them *Masculin-Feminin* (1965) and *La Chinoise* (1967), which use long, rambling interviews, interruptions of the action to bring attention to a particular issue, and the insertion of material which seems to have no connection with the narrative.

Even if the characters in an expressionistic non-genre film are psychologically comprehensible, the ways of depicting them will be quite different from those in the realistic non-genre film. Take, for example, films which look at madness. An example of a non-genre film in the realistic mode is *A Woman Under the Influence* (John Cassavetes, 1974). We see Mabel Longhetti in the realistic context of home and family, in an almost tediously catalogued environment. Mabel's illness is never shown subjectively; we watch her being ill, reacting to the pressures around her — her husband, children, family, neighbors. The realistic mode of the film dictates Cassavetes's style, which depends on long shots as much as on close-ups and which relies heavily on long takes. The audience is worn down emotionally not by vicarious subjective experience but by the duration of long scenes in which real space and real time are preserved, often interminably.

On the other hand, a filmmaker working in the expressionistic mode conveys the madness of his characters in more subjective or interior ways, depending less on observing the madness than on conveying the *experience* of it to the audience. In the expressionist *Juliet of the Spirits* (Federico Fellini, 1964), for example, the central character's madness is visually expressed via scenes which convey daydreams, hallucinations, and distorted memories. The very substance and visual content of such scenes conveys her state of mind unrealistically but effectively; sitting on the beach with friends, in one instance, Juliet closes her eyes and sees a group of dark figures pulling to shore a raft upon which is a dead horse, its stiff legs pointed skyward. *Repulsion* (Roman Polanski, 1965) also conveys the central character's madness through sharing her hallucinatory experiences directly with the viewer. Visually surreal, but psychologically valid, the hallucinations communicate a state of mind not observed, but felt; the sexually repressed and psychotic Carol hallucinates cracking walls in her apartment, their plaster turning into clutching, rapacious hands.

Characters in expressionistic non-genre films differ from characters in realistic non-genre films in other ways too, not only in the way their interior states of being are expressed. Characters in these expressionistic films need not be at all like people in the real world. Death is a character (both chilling and comic) in *The Seventh Seal*; he wears black, plays chess, and literally chops men down in their prime. And Jean Cocteau's

Orpheus (1949), although set in the contemporary world, reenacts the legend of Orpheus in an unrealistic way. The messengers of Death ride motorcycles and wear black leather, but they are not meant to be interpreted realistically.

Because it need not present a credible world or probable characters, the expressionistic non-genre film can also manipulate dialogue and plot. Whereas the viewer of the realistic non-genre film expects characters to speak like people in the real world, characters in expressionistic films can speak unrealistically. Ordinarily inarticulate character-types, for example, may utter profound statements, characters may sing instead of talk, may speak in verse or in impeccable grammar. They may tell us about themselves with an awareness which really is the filmmaker's and not the character's. They may even step forward and tell us about what is going to happen next. For instance, *Days of Heaven* (Terence Malick, 1978) employs a narrator whose persona is that of an uneducated child. Nevertheless, she provides sophisticated commentary about the characters and action which not only belie her background, but also clash unrealistically with her usually limited vocabulary.

Similarly, whereas the realistic non-genre film is expected to be somewhat open-ended and untidy in its structure, the expressionistic film can hold an experience so highly structured it could not possibly exist in the real world. Films like *The Scarlet Empress* (Josef von Sternberg, 1934), *Tom Jones* (Tony Richardson, 1963), and *Valentino* (Ken Russell, 1977) take place in a highly artificial world — and not merely because of settings or costumes. The balanced structure of the plotting and the formal developments within the film tell the viewer he is watching a world on film controlled by the filmmaker (Figure 6-5).

★ **6-5** One of the great auteurs of the 1930s, Joseph von Sternberg (with megaphone) is noted for his fluid moving camera, artistic lighting effects, and sumptuous settings and costumes. His story lines seem no more than excuses around which to pattern a dazzling visual display. In films like BLONDE VENUS (1932), SHANGHAI EXPRESS (1932), and THE SCARLET EMPRESS (1934), Marlene Dietrich serves as the focal point for von Sternberg's expressionistic techniques.

★ **6-6** The expressionist film makes great use of shadows. As the authorities wait in a dimly lit square for the appearance of Harry Lime, a wanted criminal in THE THIRD MAN (Carol Reed, 1950), a shadow of a man coming down a side street is thrown upon a wall. The suspense mounts as the shadow gets bigger and bigger. At last the man is visible, but it's not Harry Lime, only a balloon seller. The suspense is broken, at least for the moment.

Stylistically, the expressionistic non-genre film tends to emphasize its created nature. Time and space are more often broken down into separate units (shots) and reassembled than maintained in some prolonged and whole state (mise-en-scène). Thus, in the expressionistic film there tend to be more shots, and often cutting is highly visible, flamboyant, or disjunctive, flagrantly defying normal or real chronological time. Montage, rather than mise-en-scène, is the predominant editing pattern. Images are frequently filmed with distorting lenses or filters and color is used expressively rather than realistically (Figure 6-6).

Generally speaking, the expressionistic non-genre film is associated with European filmmakers; the realistic non-genre film is associated with American filmmakers, partly because the predominant Hollywood tradition of invisible filmmaking for all kinds of films tends to mask style in favor of action and story, and this tendency, in turn, has influenced non-genre film style. Today, however, even American film has broken its allegiance to any particular mode. Because the highly structured Hollywood studio system of the late 1920s through the early 1960s is no more, filmmakers working on independent productions can make a non-genre film which need not have a studio "look." Our recognition that realism has its limitations (as does technology) perhaps has brought about a change in attitude. We no longer demand that the art of film, the *artifice* of film, be invisible to the viewer.

The chief quality of the expressionistic mode is its artificiality and its chief effect is that the viewer is constantly reminded — by the visible technique, the created structure, the manipulated characters — that what he is watching is a movie created by an artist. An expressionistic film demands that we look *at* the frame rather than *through* it to a real world, that what we see contained in the frame is a world set apart from the real world. Obviously, few commercial expressionistic films are completely so. Just as the general ticket-buying public (both in the United States and abroad) does not usually patronize the most extreme examples of cinematic realism — the **uncontrolled documentary** — so too the public does not patronize the most extreme examples of cinematic expressionism — the independent **avant-garde** film. Although we have thus far separated realistic and expressionistic films in terms of their chief characteristics, it must be remembered that most films use *both* expressionistic and realistic techniques (Figure 6-7). There are no set rules that say a film *must* be one thing or the other. Sometimes, in fact, a blatant mixture may result in a movie which is for that very reason innovative. *Bonnie and Clyde* (Arthur Penn, 1967), for instance, mixing realism and expressionism in its construction, use of music, cinematography, and characterizations, becomes a film which surprises the viewer by creating an unsettling disequilibrium; thus, what might have been a generic and formulaic and familiar movie experience of a film gangster and his moll becomes something quite different and novel.

CHARACTERISTICS OF NON-GENRE FILM COMEDY

> I not only plan for surprise in the general incidents of a picture, but I also try to vary my individual actions so that they, too, will come as a surprise. I always try to do the unexpected in a novel way. If I think an audience expects me to walk along the street while in a picture, I will suddenly jump on a car. . . . Figuring out what the audience expects, and then doing something different, is great fun to me.
> Charles Chaplin[3]

Most comic films repeat conventional comic plots (say, the early films of Laurel and Hardy, or musical comedies), but there are comic films which organize their material in such a way as to exhibit characteristics similar to those found in non-genre films. They are seriously concerned with important human issues, their humor intends to instruct as much as entertain, and their moral centers will frequently be critical of the status quo. Renoir's *Rules of the Game* (1939), Chaplin's *Monsieur Verdoux* (1947), Nichols's *The Graduate* (1967), and Allen's *Annie Hall* are notable examples of comic non-genre films.

Many of the most recognizable comic non-genre films are satiric, but even films without **satire** can be funny without conforming to any traditional formula or structure. François Truffaut's *Small Change* (1976), for

★ **6-7** Describing a film as "realistic" or "expressionistic" is often difficult and sometimes beside the point. Ingmar Bergman's THE SEVENTH SEAL (1956) combines the two seemingly opposed modes of storytelling with ease. On the one hand, Death is personified as a character with magical powers (expressionistic), while on the other hand, the recreation of the life of the Middle Ages is documentary-like (realistic). The march of the penitents seems frighteningly real, what it might have looked like in those times.

example, depicts the odd and amusing behavior of children and their parents, but never condemns either group or holds them up to ridicule. The structure of the film is episodic — we see incidents in the lives of a group of children, some from this family, some from that — and the unpredictability of the events arouses surprise and amusement.

Most comic non-genre films, however, are satires. Even though one might be able to recognize certain conventional patterns of exposition in some of these films, the fact that they satirize a particular element in man's nature or some specific aspect of society tends to make them unique. Jacques Tati's *Monsieur Hulot's Holiday* (1953) derives its structure from the picaresque tradition — following one person as he moves from one absurd encounter to another — but the picture of life at a French seaside resort is so specific that the film is one of a kind.

The fathers of silent comedy, Max Linder in France and Mack Sennett in the United States, never concentrated primarily on satire and social commentary, yet both inevitably used comedy to comment upon society and its foibles. In the comic world rich people are stuffy, cops are clumsy, merchants are stingy, and so these early makers of formula comedies can still be seen as the progenitors of cinematic satire, the comic form most found in non-genre films. By its very nature (think, for example, of the political cartoon in a newspaper making us laugh at the absurdity of inflation or the arms race), satire is seriously concerned with important human issues. Its structure and its targets are complex. Indeed, criticism of social and political institutions has traditionally been refracted through satiric comedy.

Thus satire always has some connection with the real world, the world inhabited by the viewer, though that connection can be weak or strong. Woody Allen's *Bananas* (1971) and *Sleeper* (1973), for instance, are satires which have referents to the real world in which we live but which are finally so grotesquely exaggerated in incident and character that the films strongly resemble fantasy. On the other hand, although Allen's *Annie Hall* uses unrealistic devices and incidents which arise out of fantasy, the film's connections with real characters and real human problems make it more clearly satiric. Whether satiric plots are realistic or probable as in *Annie Hall* or Tati's *Playtime*, or whether they are unrealistic and improbable as in *Dr. Strangelove* or *The Ruling Class* (Peter Medak, 1972), they share a serious underlying purpose, which is to reveal the audience and the society to itself.

Whether the comic films are satiric or not, whether they are superficially realistic or blatantly grotesque, almost all will end in a happy resolution. In the few that don't, for example, *Dr. Strangelove*, in which the world is blown up at the film's end, the distancing techniques of the film (chiefly exaggeration) will keep the viewer from feeling distressed. Because the usual comic film ends happily, its structure will be much more tidy and balanced than the structure of a realistic non-genre film.

Characters in the comedies are also likely to be exaggerated in some fashion. Even when they are relatively realistic, they can be drawn rather broadly, without the complexity of real people. The bourgeois couple who run away together at the end of *Cousin, Cousine* (Jean-Charles Tachella, 1975) are quite realistic, but their behavior (for example, their flamboyant displays of affection in front of children and family) is out of the realm of fairy tales; we are pleased at their "happy ending," but we are also aware that such "happy endings" are unreal.

Stylistically, the comic non-genre film borrows from the realistic mode and the expressionistic mode. However, because satire is so large a part of the comic non-genre mode, exaggerated lighting, acting, dialogue, compositions, and camera technique are commonly used. Thus, one can point to three rather different sorts of satire — *Dr. Strangelove*, *Zero for Conduct* (Jean Vigo, 1933) and *À Nous la Liberté* (René Clair, 1931) and find exaggerations in characterization, lighting, decor, and costuming in all three. The furthest extension of this kind of stylization and exaggeration is, of course, the animated **cartoon** — the film which is all stylization

★ **6-8** Animated cartoons often follow genre patterns of comedy (mouse chases cat, cat chases mouse, and so on), but some modern animators have broken with the formulas to create satiric comedies with animated figures. Ralph Bakshi uses drawn animals to explore contemporary society's attitudes towards sex, violence, drugs, and politics in FRITZ THE CAT (1972), a feature-length cartoon.

and exaggeration (Figure 6-8). In animated films and their closest representational counterparts, adherence to common laws of time and space are as unnecessary as is adherence to normal human behavior. Characters may be flattened by cars, but a moment later they pop up and resume the chase. Although the typical cartoon tends to fall into various generic forms (one Roadrunner cartoon is much like another in plot and characterization and incident), some animated films, such as those made by the Zagreb Studios in Yugoslavia, are quite innovative in concept and structure.

THEMES AND AESTHETICS OF THE NON-GENRE FILM

The classics in any art form have a particular quality of transcendence through which they outlive the fashions and tastes of the times in which they were made. A play by Shakespeare, a painting by Renoir, an opera by Mozart all deliver rich aesthetic satisfactions to generation after generation. In each instance, the artist's work is marked by a complexity of organization (whether it appears simple or not) coupled with meaning which speaks to mankind's basic and recurrent problems directly. (Genre films may address these same problems, but they do so indirectly.) Individual or non-genre films, insofar as they use the cinema to directly explore important human questions, must be considered "serious" art, even if they are comedies. Serious art need not be viewed grimly, but it is always taken seriously (this is not the same as solemnly) by both the artist and his audience.

Many non-genre films are not popular; they are considered "difficult," "slow-moving," "not entertaining." Of course, even the most difficult and esoteric of films must appeal to some relatively large group of people

★ **6-9**   John Ford's STAGECOACH (1939) is an example of a popular film which not only meets the requirements of the western genre but also exists on the level of high art. Critics who ordinarily dismiss genre films have lavish praise for its complex treatment of moral issues and its superior handling of visual material.

to earn back the large investment made in film production, but in comparison with the millions of people who go to more generic films for their entertainment, the number of people interested in viewing innovative films is relatively small. These films, though usually not distributed widely across the country in commercial theaters, nevertheless are often considered the most important films of any year. They are the films talked about by influential critics and reviewers and scholars and students. They are the films which win awards at film festivals around the world and which, though they may not be big box-office hits in the year of their release, will continue to be shown long after their more financially remunerative counterparts have been forgotten. These non-genre films are usually considered intellectual fare parallel to modern poetry, opera, serious painting, fiction, and drama. Yet lest one imagine a vast dichotomy between non-genre films and genre films, it is important to remember that some exceptional genre films such as *Stagecoach* (John Ford, 1939) may, by virtue of their freshness or imaginative power, be high art as well as popular art (Figure 6-9). Conversely, some excellent non-genre films have been made in Hollywood and have achieved great popular success, winning praise from both the movie critic and scholar and the average filmgoer. Films like *The Birth of a Nation* (D. W. Griffith, 1915) and *2001: A Space Odyssey* (Stanley Kubrick, 1968), and *Annie Hall* were commercial as well as artistic successes.

★ **6-10** Always the serious and committed film artist, Ingmar Bergman in his early career probed the relationship between man and God in the twentieth century. His characters are realistic: they wrestle with problems of faith and despair. Like the parson in WINTER LIGHT (1962), they often fail to make sense out of the world they live in, struggling against great odds to find a reason for living.

The great themes found in these sorts of films are very general when stated outright: what is man's relationship to his fellow man? his environment? his God? his mortality? In fact, abstracting these themes from the work in which they are embedded and elaborated upon often reveals clichés: "Art is long, life is short." "Man must suffer to win redemption." "Heroes are made, not born." "Man is always alone in an empty universe." But in the working out of these themes, in the specific ways in which a particular film visualizes and gives dramatic statement to these themes, they resonate beyond clichés and catchphrases. Since narrative films examine human beings in specific situations and since humanity has always been concerned with these general issues and finding answers to them, all non-genre films will attempt a new working out of the same old themes (Figure 6-10). Working them out in a new context makes them not the "same old" themes at all.

It is not, however, simply a matter of a film addressing itself to great themes which deserves our attention; it is also a matter of the ways the artist who created the work has used the materials at his disposal, the way his techniques and structures have rephrased those old and answerless questions. Sheer technical brilliance alone is not enough. The perennial questions must lie at the heart of a film that moves and touches its viewers in rich and meaningful and renewable ways. In general, stories and narratives can encompass only a limited amount of variety in their basic plotting and construction, but each new treatment of it through the materials and techniques of the cinematic medium may be excitingly different.

★★★ **Personal Visions**

> I know that I have the ability to articulate images that sit deeply inside
> us, that I can make them visible. It is an athletic endeavor, like life itself.
> Things work inside of me for a long time, images become clearer, and at
> a certain point I just sit down and write the script in three days. There
> is always a key image; everything emerges from that, physically, not by
> analysis.
> Werner Herzog[4]

One characteristic of the non-genre narrative film is that it tends to make
the viewer sense that it is the work of a unique artistic consciousness.
This is true even when we know that filmmaking is a collaborative art
and that films, like great cathedrals, are the work of many hands. In
literature, painting, or music, the artist who created the work is usually
easily identifiable. In drama or music, there are two kinds of artists: the
writers or composers and the performers. The film artist, however, is
more elusive. Not only does a film have a writer (perhaps several), and
a director and performers, but it also has a producer, a cinematographer,
an **art director,** and an editor (perhaps several). A film which is unified
by an overall conception and execution may be attributed to the strong
personal force of any one of these figures as much as it is the actual result of their combined efforts. The elaborate business of developing a
movie from its inception to its release makes it extremely difficult to
know who contributed what to a particular film, whose personal imprint
on the film was the strongest. Screen **credits** are dictated more by tradition (and by union regulations) than by accuracy; they reflect only those
people who last worked on the film before its release. Thus, although
many writers may have contributed to the finished **script** at various
points in its development, although directors may have been changed in
mid-movie — as was true, for example, with *Gone with the Wind* (1939),
attributed to Victor Fleming — usually only the last person associated
with a particular function gets the credit.

Attempting to unravel the intricate fabric of the collaborative effort
which goes into the making of any film is an interesting, if sometimes
hopeless, activity. Though most people tend to talk about *Citizen Kane*
(1941) in terms of Orson Welles, its director and star, it is also possible
to discuss the film's artistry in terms of Gregg Toland's cinematography,
Robert Wise's editing, and Herman J. Mankiewicz's **screenplay;** all of
these film artists have shown their artistry and the strength of their personalities in other fine films, and they all played important roles in the
realization of *Citizen Kane*. On the other hand, there are directors like
Federico Fellini and Ingmar Bergman who write their own scripts, super-

★ **6-11** Robert Bresson is one of France's most significant and original film-makers. Never a part of the new wave or any other movement, Bresson over the years has perfected an extremely austere personal style. He has simplified the visual surface of his films so that the viewer, having so little to watch, might penetrate into the very soul of his characters. In PICKPOCKET (1958), Bresson focuses on a directionless man who becomes a professional thief. Through his original techniques he invites the audience to look into the guilt-ridden heart of the pickpocket.

vise the camera work closely, oversee the editing, and so dominate the making of their films that they may be easily and clearly identified as the primary creative forces behind their works.

Contemporary discussions of film tend to focus on the director as the key person in control of the creation of the finished work (Figure 6-11). But one could almost as easily focus on a performer, a cinematographer, a writer, or an editor whose presence is the dominant factor in the film's artistic success. To illustrate these difficulties, we will discuss the director here. This does not mean, however, that the other members of the film production unit are less important — merely that they are usually less visible.

Film directors can be separated into three major categories: first, **film craftsmen,** who, though they make highly acclaimed and well-wrought films and thus must be considered good directors, never develop an individual and consistent body of work either stylistically or thematically; second, **film auteurs,** directors who, even though the script, the performers, and the production crew are imposed on them, establish their authority and stamp their films with a recognizable style or vision; and third, **film artists,** who are in nearly total control of every aspect and phase of the filmmaking process and the film itself.

THE FILM CRAFTSMAN

> I don't *seek* to interpret, to put my own stamp on the material. I try
> to be as faithful to the original material as I can. This applies equally to
> Melville as it applies to the Bible, for example. In fact, it's the fascination
> that I feel for the original that makes me want to make it into a film.
> John Huston[5]

The first group of directors (e.g., Michael Curtiz, Henry Hathaway,
Clarence Brown) might be considered fine craftsmen rather than artists;
chameleonlike, they thoroughly match their style to the given material.
In the past, these directors almost always worked for a studio. They were
given scripts by the producers, which they were to transform into a completed film using a certain number of dollars and a certain amount of
time. Almost all of these directors were committed not to personal visions but to bringing out the values of the script in the most effective
and economical way possible. Camera work and editing were usually
left to subordinate or equally powerful collaborators who had the same
commitment to the story. These directors would film a gothic tale of horror with the appropriate music, the proper number of creaking doors, dark
shadows, and odd camera angles. They would film a detective story with
an appropriate sense of pace and an eye on the denouement, a biblical
epic with a cast of thousands and the right number of spectacular scenes.
Such director-craftsmen seemed most at home filming genre films, films
whose very conventions are the familiar mainstays of commercial cinema.

A case in point is John Huston, who, over the years, has handled every
genre of film there is and done them all well. His suspense films include
The Maltese Falcon (1941) and *The List of Adrian Messenger* (1963). He
has done adaptations of such literary works as *The Red Badge of Courage* (1951) and *Moby Dick* (1956), *Fat City* (1972) and *The Man Who
Would Be King* (1976). He has made "period" films such as *Moulin
Rouge* (1953) and *The Barbarian and the Geisha* (1958), and adventure
films such as *The Treasure of the Sierra Madre* (1948) and *The African
Queen* (1952). Despite this large body of work, including films which
have become classics of American cinema and which, like *Treasure* and
African Queen, have attributes of both genre and non-genre films, no
one of Huston's films bears a distinct relationship to the others (Figure
6-12). Without his name on the credits, no one of Huston's films can be
recognized immediately as such from its style or form. The films have in
common only their emphasis on narrative and their efficiency and com-
petence; even moments of artistry in the individual films, moments of
extreme brilliance, do not add up to communicate a sense of the director's personality, his stamp or imprint or personal seal.

★ **6-12** John Huston is a master craftsman among American film directors. He
has worked in a wide variety of genres and has adapted his style to the requirements of his stories. TREASURE OF THE SIERRA MADRE (1948) is
an adventure genre film, telling the classic tale of "three men and the gold."
To tell the story of a down-and-out fighter and his protégé in FAT CITY (1972),
Huston shot on location, used toned-down color, and cast less well-known
performers.

THE FILM AUTEUR

> Certain scripts you get, of course, you just feel hopeless. So you must
> try to do something with lighting, acting, décor, pace . . . all those elements.
> Or else the material is too usual, so you try to find an element of strange-
> ness.
> Douglas Sirk[6]

Directors of the second group — those who worked for Hollywood studios, but who transcended their routine assignments to create a body of
work stamped with a distinctive style or vision — have been labeled *auteurs* by French critics. Although there has been a good deal of discussion
of such directors as Howard Hawks, Alfred Hitchcock, and John Ford,
until very recently they were virtually unknown to the general moviegoer. Only Hitchcock, because of his appearances on television, could be
said to be a household word (Figure 6-13). The director's imprint in
American films has never been as obvious as in many European films.
The work of such directors as Fellini, Truffaut, and Bergman is, in fact,
so distinctive that one can recognize their films without benefit of the
director's credit at the beginning of the film.

6-13 Alfred Hitchcock is one of the
few film auteurs whose name is familiar enough to mass audiences that
people speak of going to see a "Hitchcock picture." Here he is shown in
distinctive profile working with Janet
Leigh on the set of PSYCHO (1960).

Most American directors' films, however, seem not to be so clearly
identifiable as those films made by European film artists. At first glance,
most American films from the late 1920s to the present seem to be made
from the same cloth; they all look like Hollywood films. They came from
studios like M-G-M, Paramount, and Warner Brothers and they featured
performers who were familiar stars. The actual physical look of the films
seemed determined less by a single individual artistic consciousness than
by the studio; Warner Brothers movies looked contemporary, were rapidly edited and scripted around social problems; M-G-M films looked
rich and glossy, with high production values. These films were usually
advertised with the star's name above the title; Warner Brothers gave
us Bette Davis movies or Humphrey Bogart movies, and M-G-M gave us
Greta Garbo and Elizabeth Taylor. Until quite recently, the names of
American directors were seldom featured in advertising copy or on movie
marquees; D. W. Griffith, Frank Capra, and Alfred Hitchcock were the
chief exceptions.

Aside from the presence of stars in the American film, the most important part of an American film was its story, the good tale that seemed
to slip effortlessly through the projector as if from the lips of some expert and omniscient narrator. And these good movie tales tended to fall
into identifiable groups dealing with similar subject matter. There were
westerns, romances, mysteries, war movies. Not until the French film
critics of the 1950s began to look closely in admiration at American films
was it remarked that beneath the homogenized surface appearance of the
Hollywood film there were works of distinction and quality and that often these works were those of the same directors.

The names of such American directors as John Ford, Samuel Fuller,
William Wellman, William Wyler, and Douglas Sirk were added to the
more familiar list of American film artists: Chaplin, Keaton, Capra, and

★ **6-14** Now revered by students and scholars of film, film auteurs like John Ford usually thought of themselves as people who made motion pictures in the entertainment business. They rarely discussed the theme or style of their work. It was not until the French critics from *Cahiers du Cinema* "discovered" our American directors that we deemed them worthy of study.

Hitchcock. Still, it was apparent that these directors were not like the European film artists who had relatively complete control over their work and who could explore their personal aesthetic and thematic preoccupations with relative freedom. Rather, these Hollywood directors worked under studio rule, presumably as journeymen employees involved in the mass production of popular entertainment. They were assigned a script rather than choosing one. They were given a cast of performers and told by a producer to shoot the film in so many days. They did not have the right of **final cut** and so the studio and the producer could reedit and sometimes reshoot scenes and alter the film to their liking and their notion of what the public would like and pay money to see. Yet despite all these restrictions and enforced collaborations, somehow these directors, over the years, managed to make films which were stamped with their particular vision. Certain stylistic touches — like John Ford's use of the horizon line — or certain recurrent themes — like Douglas Sirk's exploration of the traditional roles of women — were consistently evident in nearly all the films of each of these directors. To be sure, they frequently worked, over the years, with one or two particular screenwriters or with a particular cinematographer or film editor — or they were able to specialize in a certain film genre, hence some of the consistency in their work. These directors were critically discovered by a group of young French film critics in the 1950s, who hailed them as film auteurs (Figure 6-14).

Although the literal translation of *auteur* implies that the director is the author of the film in much the same way that a writer is the author of a book, the term is traditionally reserved for those directors who have *not* had complete control over their work, yet who have left a personal mark on their films. Alfred Hitchcock is just such a director — although since the mid-fifties he has had relatively complete control over both the choice of script and the final version of the film by virtue of his enormous financial as well as critical successes. Hitchcock's films are all linked together by certain thematic and stylistic qualities. For the most part, he has made suspense thrillers. In most of his films, an innocent bystander, an upstanding and law-abiding citizen, becomes involved in an extraordinary and often nightmarish adventure because his identity is mistaken (*The Wrong Man*, 1956 or *North by Northwest*, 1959); or he or she is in a certain place at the wrong time (*The Lady Vanishes*, 1938 or *The Man Who Knew Too Much*, 1935 and 1956); or he is falsely accused of a crime because of circumstantial evidence (*The Thirty-nine Steps*, 1935 or *Frenzy*, 1972). Suspense is created to a certain extent simply by the nature of the plot, but through the years Hitchcock has developed a style of editing and camera movement which always creates a high degree of suspense and viewer identification purely through visual means. The parallel editing in *Strangers on a Train* (1951), for example, which alternates the tennis match in which the innocent hero plays and the movements of the real killer who is attempting to frame him, builds an amazing tension solely in the alternation and rhythm of the shots.

As well as the auteur directors like Hitchcock or John Ford, there are some directors like Anthony Mann who, although they have made many studio-inspired films which are hardly distinguishable from any other director's, have made a smaller group of films within their total body of work which does have a distinct and personal identity. Though Mann directed *The Glenn Miller Story* (1954), *God's Little Acre* (1958), *El Cid* (1961), and *The Fall of the Roman Empire* (1964), a varied and impersonal bunch, he has also made a group of westerns including *Winchester 73* (1950), *Bend of the River* (1952), *The Naked Spur* (1953), *The Far Country* (1955), and *The Tin Star* (1957). These latter films, although generically westerns, are also specifically Mann-made movies, exhibiting certain themes which link them together as the work of one individual. All are studies of civilized men who go beyond the law and ordinary conventions of behavior in order to exact revenge for some past hurt, and yet who end up reliving the traumatic events which led to their initial separation from society. Mann's heroes travel through time, place, and experience, but the travel is cyclical, for they ultimately return to confront and accept their place in a social world.

A few auteur directors are valued less for their thematic consistency from picture to picture than for their cinematic style, their use of technique, which has remained visible and personal throughout their careers. Certain camera movements, particular kinds of visual compositions, what the camera "likes" to look at, can to the trained eye be seen as the distinctive elements in a Josef von Sternberg or Max Ophuls or Nicholas

Ray or Joseph Losey film. Though Joseph Losey's films, for example, have frequently focused on disturbed human relationships (*The Servant*, 1964; *Accident*, 1967; *Secret Ceremony*, 1968; *The Go-Between*, 1971), there seems to be no personal thematic vision; Losey also directed *The Boy with the Green Hair* (1948), *These Are the Damned* (1965), and *Modesty Blaise* (1966). And yet, despite a lack of thematic clarity and unity, each Losey film seems marked by certain visual elements which are recurrent in film after film. Losey is fascinated with furniture and furnishings. His camera frequently moves obsessively around the interior of rooms, usually grand rooms, and it examines the details of the decor as if their texture and shape were more revealing of some reality and truth than the texture and shape of the room's inhabitants. In keeping with this desire to reveal the animate through the inanimate, Losey often focuses on mirrors, silver, and other polished surfaces which reflect and distort the images of his characters (most effectively used and related to the film's theme in *The Servant*).

The typical auteur director, unlike film artists such as Fellini, Truffaut, and Bergman, seldom seems comfortable taking credit for those personal thematic and stylistic elements which critics have found in the films. The auteurs, tending to see themselves as craftsmen and storytellers, are somewhat embarrassed by the attention of critics. Unlike the film artists, these auteur directors do not see themselves as "artists" with a personal vision of the world, but rather as entertainers. Nevertheless, much like Shakespeare, who wrote his plays for a living, the film auteurs may be men for all seasons, men whose work appeals not only to the popular audience of its own time, but also to audiences and scholars and critics of later generations. The auteur director, usually because he worked for a studio producing popular entertainment, often was handed familiar and generic material from which to make his films: westerns, mysteries, adventure films. His work, therefore, is an odd combination of genre film and non-genre film. Occasionally, however, the auteur director has made a completely innovative film such as John Ford's *The Informer* (1935) or *The Quiet Man* (1952).

Young American directors whose work has been received with great critical and financial enthusiasm are peculiarly difficult to classify. Are they film artists or film auteurs? Most of their movies, appearing after the demise of the strong studio system, are the products of independent production companies. In this new kind of production, each film is treated individually rather than as part of a total studio output made by studio personnel and geared to a studio "look" or reputation. Some contemporary filmmakers, of course, started within the studio system. Stanley Kubrick, for example, began making films in the early 1950s, working

★ **6-15**   Stanley Kubrick's A CLOCKWORK ORANGE (1972) is an example of a non-genre narrative film that uses expressionistic rather than realistic elements to create a vision of the near future. Bizarre sets and costumes, ritualized violence, ironic music, distortion lenses, and rapid montage are some of the means used by this director who went from auteur to film artist.

with such studios as Universal, M-G-M, and Columbia. Although he has always been intimately involved with the selection of his scripts, he did not form his own production company until after *2001: A Space Odyssey* (1968), when he went on to make *A Clockwork Orange* (1971) and *Barry Lyndon* (1975). Thus, Kubrick went from being a film auteur to being a film artist who originates his own projects and keeps total control over them (Figure 6-15). Francis Ford Coppola makes big budget studio-type movies like *The Godfather* (1972) and *The Godfather, Part II* (1974) which are as personal as the smaller films he's made supposedly for himself, like *The Conversation* (1974) (Figure 6-16). *Apocalypse Now* (1979), Coppola's vision of the Viet Nam war, is a hybrid: a big-budget film (reportedly over $30 million), but very unlike a studio film. It was made, rather, to express a private view, an interpretation of history and human nature. Sam Peckinpah (another transitional director), Robert Altman, Martin Scorsese, and Roman Polanski are only some of those contemporary directors who seem committed to making films which are personal statements, and which even if they have generic elements at times are non-genre films. Whether we identify these directors as film artists or film auteurs is, of course, open to discussion. In fact, the terms film artist and film auteur have recently been used interchangeably, auteur now generally meaning anyone (director, performer, cinematographer, screenwriter, or the like) who has stamped a film with his personality — whether or not he worked within or without a studio system. In any case, artist or auteur, these filmmakers are currently making films

★ **6-16** Francis Ford Coppola makes big-budget movies like THE GODFATHER, part I (1972) and part II (1974) for a studio (i.e., he is a film auteur) and then uses the money he makes from those films to finance more personal films like THE CONVERSATION (1974) (i.e., he functions as a film artist).

whose narratives share much of the novelty and artistic excitement formerly generated only by foreign directors.

THE FILM ARTIST

> Freedom is the absolute necessity. From the beginning, I've had total control over my films. . . . I can be very free even if I am surrounded by ten gorillas or one producer. And if I cannot feel free enough, then I will simply leave without making the film.
> Bernardo Bertolucci[7]

Though everyone who works on an aesthetically successful film may be considered an artist of sorts (including the cinematographer, composer, editor, and so on), the term film artist here refers only to directors who make a film to communicate their personal vision of the world. These directors belong to the third category of directors, artists in total control of the films they make. They are father, mother, and midwife to their films. They take themselves seriously, frequently writing aesthetic manifestos, granting interviews, arguing theories, and supplying interpretations of their work. These directors do not see themselves merely as craftsmen, doing a job for an employer, but rather as individual artists uncompromised by financial exigencies and marketplace demands. Among these directors are Federico Fellini (Italy), François Truffaut (France), Andrei Tarkovsky (Russia), Akira Kurosawa (Japan), Satyajit Ray (India), Werner Herzog (Germany), and John Cassavetes (U.S.A.). It is notable that relatively few of these film artists are American. In foreign countries, film production is heavily subsidized through taxes on individual admissions, and in any case foreign films can often be produced for less money than can American films. Foreign film production, moreover, has always been at some remove from the American studio system,

★ **6-17** Many of America's most exciting new directors grew up watching retrospectives of traditional Hollywood films. Martin Scorsese made NEW YORK, NEW YORK (1977) as homage to the big-band musicals of the 1940s; Brian de Palma honors Hitchcock's VERTIGO (1958) in his OBSESSION (1976). Peter Bogdanovich, shown here talking to Boris Karloff on the set of his film TARGETS (1968), was first a film critic and then a director, and he frequently makes cinematic allusions to his favorite directors and films in his own work. The use of Howard Hawks's RED RIVER as the final movie playing in the broken-down theater in THE LAST PICTURE SHOW (1971) is calculated to remind us of both the heroic ideal of the cowboy and the great age of Hollywood moviemakers.

which was run by strong-willed producers such as Jack Warner, Sam Goldwyn, and Daryl Zanuck, whose primary criterion for filmmaking was financial success rather than artistic success. Finally, however, foreign attitudes about film probably have helped foreign directors to consider themselves film artists. Americans initially considered film lowbrow entertainment, but Europeans have long considered film as serious art.

Especially since World War II, European directors have often originated an idea for a film, have gotten financial backing from banks, independent sources, or even government subsidy, and then have followed the film through production to completion and release. This arrangement usually allows the director to include in his contract the right to the final cut, the final decision as to how the actual release print of the film will look. These directors most often work with a handpicked production crew who stay together for picture after picture, forming what amounts to a repertory production company, one knowledgeable about and sympathetic to the director's style and vision. Thus, a Rainer Fassbinder or an Ingmar Bergman repeatedly works with the same crews and often with the same performers. It is only recently that one can point to an American equivalent in the production habits and films of such contemporary directors as Robert Altman, Martin Scorsese, Francis Ford Coppola, and Peter Bogdanovich (Figure 6-17).

The work of these film directors often embodies such distinct personal characteristics that we often refer to the artist's "vision" — a term familiar from literary criticism but especially appropriate here. This vision

★ **6-18** Ingmar Bergman (shown working with Liv Ulmann on FACE TO FACE, 1976) is typical of the film artist. He has total control of his films from the writing of the script through to the final print released for distribution. He has certain philosophical, religious, and psychological concerns about which he cares and which dictate the themes of his films.

★ **6-19** Michelangelo Antonioni is one of Italy's foremost film artists. His primary concerns have been the boredom and ennui affecting the middle and upper classes of the post–World War II world. His characters in such films as L'AVVENTURA (1961), BLOW-UP (1967), and THE PASSENGER (1975) drift through life, unable to make a commitment, without hope or direction.

can be either thematic or stylistic, but usually it combines both. Bergman's films from his first internationally acclaimed hit, *The Seventh Seal* (1956), to *Autumn Sonata* (1978) all deal with such profound questions as these: Is there a God? What is reality? What hope is there for man in an unresponsive world? How can one exorcise demons of the mind and soul? Although these questions are chiefly embodied in Bergman's dialogue which the characters speak, they are also embodied in the lighting and the color, the cinematography and the editing, and the acting, all of which Bergman supervises. All of these elements are distinctively Bergmanesque — in other words, recognizable from film to film — and are distinctively used to underscore and amplify the philosophical themes (Figure 6-18). Sound, or the lack of it in *The Silence* (1963), embodies ideas that Bergman wishes to express about communication; lighting in *The Magician* (1958) serves the thematic questioning of the difference between illusion and reality; color in *Cries and Whispers* (1972) weakens or strengthens in sympathy with the characters' emotional involvement in the events of the film.

The roll call of the names of such film artists is long; these directors come from all countries and appear throughout the historical development of the art. D. W. Griffith, Sergei Eisenstein, F. W. Murnau, René Clair, Orson Welles, François Truffaut, Akira Kurosawa, Satyajit Ray, Lina Wertmüller, Rainer Fassbinder — these are a few of the artists who have used film as their medium. These film artists can be obtuse, vague, argumentative, shocking, self-indulgent, ascetic, sublime. They can present philosophic conundrums, they can ambush and attack the very audience that they are addressing — and yet, because of their individuality and their mastery of the medium, they are respected and loved by their relatively small but loyal audiences. Film artists such as Michelangelo Antonioni (Figure 6-19), Jean-Luc Godard, Luis Buñuel, Bernardo Bertolucci, Robert Altman, Stanley Kubrick, and Terence Malick see themselves creating art which has something important to say, which may potentially exist on a level with the works of da Vinci, Beethoven, Dostoevski. This attitude toward the medium and its capacity for expression rests not so much on an inflated ego as on a personal obsession objectified and translated into the finished work of film art.

★★★ **Acting: Actors and Stars**

> You can be trained to hell and gone, but if you don't have the imagination to conceive a performance, you'll be technically trained to achieve mediocrity. You have to tell the truth, with as much attention to detail as you can. I usually have a visual, visceral image of the character — I see what he looks like and how he walks and talks immediately on the first reading of a script; then I try to achieve that visual image. . . . My preparation seems to be much more subconscious than conscious.
> Richard Dreyfuss[8]

The story film gave rise to the now faded "star system," in which the charismatic screen personalities of certain people were often used in certain familiar roles. Douglas Fairbanks as the swashbuckling hero, Joan Crawford the forceful, independent woman, Jimmy Stewart as the naive and sincere righter of society's ills, drew people into the theater to see them reenact familiar personae.

Although audiences attended the first films to see movement of any kind captured on the screen, and then next went to see narratives dramatized, from the year 1910 — when the uncredited "Biograph girl," Florence Lawrence, joined the Independent Motion Picture Company and was made a "star" and given screen credit — to the present, most people

★ 6-20 Many actors in films are neither recognized actors like Sir Laurence Olivier nor personalities like Jimmy Stewart. Their names are relatively unknown though their faces are familiar. Charles Durning played a harassed police detective in DOG DAY AFTERNOON (Sidney Lumet, 1975).

have gone to films to see both a story and a star. It is only in recent years that American audiences have been drawn into the theater to see films of specific directors like Stanley Kubrick, Francis Ford Coppola, or Steven Spielberg. Most often audiences still go to a movie specifically to see a star like Robert Redford in *The Candidate* (1972) or Barbra Streisand in *On a Clear Day You Can See Forever* (1970), and not because the former film was directed by Michael Ritchie or the latter by Vincente Minnelli. Because stars drew people into the movie theaters and because sometimes they had a major part in shaping the films in which they appeared, they bear consideration — both as phenomena and as artists.

As the star system developed in the United States, a peculiar division arose between **film actors** and **film stars.** Some performers could play any part in any film and play it well; yet no matter how often these actors appeared on the screen, audiences seemed not to remember their names or their faces. These actors didn't have that charismatic quality or personality which somehow transcended the roles they played; since every role was different, the audience could never locate what seemed to be the person behind the mask, that consistent quality, that noticeable "something," which for some performers was there, movie after movie. They were actors, not stars.

These actors usually fill the backgrounds, playing the lesser characters in films whose feature roles are played by stars. Sometimes their faces are recognizable after we've seen them perform often enough, but usually they so subordinate themselves to the narrative that they do not stand out apart from their roles; we tend to remember the movie character rather than the performer (Figure 6-20). In general, though there are exceptions, these actors are not likely to play leading roles in "big" movies, especially in America. American audiences — until recently — have for the most part paid their admissions to see stars, not simply actors. Foreign directors, on the other hand, have frequently used actors rather than stars for leading roles in their films — and they have, on occasion, even used non-actors, people off the streets, as in the Italian neorealist narrative films made towards the end of World War II.

Screen actors and actresses such as John Mills, Rod Steiger, Dame Edith Evans, Gena Rowlands, and, more recently, Dustin Hoffman, Gene Hackman, and Shelley Duvall, occupy a middle ground between film actor and film star. They are not those nameless performers who are regularly **typecast** in specific roles (the sleazy landlord, the female barfly), nor are they — no matter how skillful, no matter how prominently advertised — personalities who dominate or transcend their characters, appearing on the screen as both the character they are playing and as themselves. Instead, they *become* any character the role demands, and we learn to know the character and to forget the actor (Figure 6-21). Dame Edith Evans becomes Lady Western in *Tom Jones* (1963) and she also *becomes* the old, peevish, and slightly senile protagonist of the gritty English film *The Whisperers* (Bryan Forbes, 1967). Gene Hackman, despite his featured status and the resultant familiarity of his face, becomes Buck Barrow in *Bonnie and Clyde* (1967) and later becomes the quite different character of Harry Caul in *The Conversation* (1974). And Shelley Duvall has completely changed character from the hot-rodding opportunist of *Brewster McCloud* (Robert Altman, 1970) to the homely and shy Keechie, a young and pathetic gangster's moll in *Thieves Like Us* (Altman, 1973), to the attractive if vapid young lady who has stepped from the pages of the *Ladies' Home Journal* in *Three Women* (Altman, 1977).

Film stars, however, are a different breed. These screen performers do not act in the customary theatrical sense of the word, and they should not be judged by theatrical standards. Although their names, costumes, and makeup change from picture to picture and though to an extent they do portray different characters, yet from film to film their own personalities are so strong that they can always be identified. They are always — to differing degrees — separate from the roles they play. From film to film the likes of Bette Davis, Joan Crawford, Barbara Stanwyck, Katherine Hepburn, Gary Cooper, James Stewart, Clark Gable, Gregory Peck, Humphrey Bogart, Cary Grant, John Wayne, Charles Bronson, Barbra Streisand, and Robert Redford remain the same. They do not act to the point of submerging themselves in their parts; they are themselves as well as their parts. They do not *become* the characters; rather, to put it a bit strongly, the characters become *them*, for the actors' personalities inform and dominate the characters they play. Sometimes this imposition of the personality onto the role is the result of typecasting. That is, an actor is chosen to play a role because he physically fits the part or the part has been written for him, and if he proves successful in the

★ **6-21** Some actors and actresses occupy a middle ground between typecast character actors and stars. They are instantly recognizable, in voice and gesture, but they still make the audience forget the actor and remember the character. Dustin Hoffman performs that trick in STRAIGHT TIME (Ulu Grosbard, 1977); Shelley Duvall does it in THREE WOMEN (Robert Altman, 1977).

role, that role with variations will be given to him again and again. John Wayne was, of course, the classic example of this kind of typecasting; he was so successful in embodying the western hero that he was never readily accepted by audiences in other roles (except as the hero in World War II movies, which he played with some frequency).

More often than not, however, big stars will be given a variety of roles to play in their careers, yet still they convince us, in film after film, that the surface distinctions in character are just that — surface; the stars are still the men or women we paid our admission to see *pretend* to be someone else. True, Humphrey Bogart was always best when he

★ **6-22** Humphrey Bogart is a good example of a film star, one of those screen personalities who, year in and year out, in picture after picture, always seemed somehow to be the same. His own inimitable personality is never completely submerged, whether he is playing Sam Spade in THE MALTESE FALCON (John Huston, 1941) or Rick in CASABLANCA (Michael Curtiz, 1942), or Charlie Allnut in THE AFRICAN QUEEN (John Huston, 1952). In fact, his personal qualities and screen presence made him the popular figure he was (and still is), rather than his ability to completely submerge himself in a fictional character.

was playing the cynical tough guy (perhaps because those roles brought him stardom), and yet in such markedly different roles as Charlie Allnut in *The African Queen* (1951) and Captain Queeg in *The Caine Mutiny* (Edward Dmytryk, 1954), he was still unmistakably himself — Humphrey Bogart. In a comedy like *Beat the Devil* (John Huston, 1954) or in a light romance like *Sabrina* (Billy Wilder, 1954), Bogart was still the "Bogey" we knew and loved (Figure 6-22) in *The Maltese Falcon* (1941), where he made the character of Sam Spade forever his own, or in *Casablanca* (Michael Curtiz, 1942), where he made the cynical and

★ **6-23** Sometimes the distinctive quality of a star can dominate a film. Such an influence can be great enough to determine the performer as the true auteur of the film. No matter who the director, the Marx Brothers' films seem to reflect their particular comic vision. They combined physical slapstick humor with verbal wit as they attacked middle-class values in their Paramount films, like HORSEFEATHERS (Norman Z. McLeod, 1932).

world-weary Rick one of the most memorable screen characters of all time.

In a way, what we appreciate about stars such as Bogart is that they cannot act — or do not act. They return to us picture after picture, incompletely submerging their own selves in a characterization, and so they become familiar friends; we feel that if we met them in the street, we would have a fairly good idea of what to say to them, what they would say to us, how they would say it. Bogart's craggy face, his immobile upper lip, the way he spoke his lines, the mannerisms which so marked his appearances on the screen, could never be taught in acting school, though they are the stuff of which impressionists' acts are made. Bogart was what he was. He was himself in all of his pictures and, fortunately, he — not the character — was what the audience came to see. This star quality has, in a sense, the same appeal and interest that the genre film has. There is the consistent, recognizable actor who varies only slightly from movie to movie. In one film, Bogart is called Sam

Spade, the detective; in another, he is Duke Mantee, a fugitive; in yet another, he is Rick Blaine, an expatriate who owns a bar in Casablanca during World War II: what we see is the constant persona only thinly disguised by the particular character he is playing.

This peculiar or distinctive quality which a star exhibits can be so pervasive that it may dominate a film, subduing the cinematography, the direction, and the editing (Figure 6-23). In this sense, the star may create the film, and if such great influence is exerted over a body of films, the star can be considered a true film auteur. After seeing several movies in which such a particular star appears — perhaps Bette Davis, Cary Grant, or Marilyn Monroe — we can identify some unique element which firmly links these films; there is a special and constant tone to the films, the indelible imprint of a personality. Although viewers probably remember specific films and specific plots in which these stars appeared, they remember more vividly the star's physical imprint on the films: a particular face, a way of moving, a look, and an idiosyncratic and memorable voice.

Film actors and film stars function in different but equally necessary ways — and it is important to remember that one group is not necessarily better or more inherently valuable than the other. Indeed, both kinds of screen presence are crucial to the story film and carry the burdens of characterization.

★★★   **The Source**

> My movie is born first in my head, dies on paper; is resuscitated by the living persons and real objects I use, which are killed on film but, placed in a certain order and projected onto a screen, come to life again like flowers in water.
> Robert Bresson[9]

Both genre and non-genre film must have a beginning, some point of origin, some moment in time when the idea for the film arises in someone's mind. That someone can be a producer, a director, a **screenwriter,** an actor — or even someone who is not professionally involved in the filmmaking process.

Because of the astronomical cost of filmmaking (Steven Spielberg's *Close Encounters of the Third Kind,* 1977, cost 25 million dollars to make), the kinds of stories which finally become released films, and the sorts of aesthetic devices used to relate those stories, will be determined in great part by businessmen and by the ticket-buying public. This means, of course, that many worthwhile and potentially entertaining ideas will never become films because their appeal is judged to be too narrow. On the other hand, some original stories or adaptations, even though they may seem trite and banal, are turned into realized movies because similar ideas have already demonstrated box-office success. Which stories will be made into films is as much a financial decision as it is an intellectual and aesthetic one. And this fact is less an indictment of the commercial filmmaking process than a response to an economic reality that viewers, critics, and scholars too often dismiss or forget.

The movie musical is an example. From the 1930s through the mid-1950s, most screen musicals were made from original ideas conceived specifically for film. Examples include *Love Me Tonight* (Rouben Mamoulian, 1932), *Singin' in the Rain* (Stanley Donen and Gene Kelly, 1952), and *Seven Brides for Seven Brothers* (Stanley Donen, 1954). During the late 1950s, however, the costs of movie production and star salaries rose so much that such musicals — usually the most costly films to produce because of costumes, sets, rehearsal time, performers, and so on — became unable to guarantee a profitable return on the investment in them. Studios turned to already demonstrated successes — and that meant the Broadway stage. One thinks of *West Side Story* (Jerome Robbins and Robert Wise, 1961), *My Fair Lady* (George Cukor, 1964), and *Cabaret* (Bob Fosse, 1972). The musical genre is so expensive to produce that what might be a brilliant *original* idea for a screen musical may never have a chance at being realized as a film.

ORIGINAL STORIES

The characters and plot of a story may be the inventions of a writer or other person who would like to see his ideas transformed into a film. In some ways this path of origin has much to recommend it: the eventual audience will not be able to make comparisons with a source, and the story idea will be conceived in terms which are the most compatible with the elements of film. In other words, an original idea, originally conceived in the mind *as* a film, will likely take full advantage of the artistic potential of the medium. Starting with an original story written expressly for the screen does not, of course, automatically guarantee that the final film will be either an artistic or commercial success, but it does mean that the filmmakers need not attempt the often difficult job of translating and transforming a story idea conceived in another medium into the quite different film medium.

All kinds of narrative patterns can be worked up into original film story ideas: boy meets girl, pursuit and rescue, the quest, man in conflict with himself or others or his environment. All these patterns may be treated as tragedy, comedy, or melodrama. The film is able to dramatize

★ **6-24** In a famous essay, Sergei Eisenstein suggested the influence of Charles Dickens's narrative techniques on D. W. Griffith. It is no wonder, then, that Dickens has always been a popular choice as a source for film adaptation. David Lean, the noted English director, used rich shading and texture to depict the hard life of a poor boy in Victorian England in his version of OLIVER TWIST (1948).

biography, historical epic, the picaresque tale, the psychological drama; it can show and tell stories about war, marital conflict, vampires, and social problems. In short, any conceivable human action in any conceivable situation can become the subject of a story film.

ADAPTATIONS

Far more story films have been made from literary and dramatic sources than have been made from stories originally conceived for films. The economics of filmmaking and its reliance on mass taste makes its presence strongly felt in the choice of a story for a film. A novel or play or Broadway musical which has done well financially or is an established classic has a presold audience and advance publicity (Figure 6-24). Everyone who has been exposed to the original work or who has even heard about it will naturally be curious to see what the film version is like. Some may come to scoff at the way Hollywood simplifies a reputable literary classic — for example, the two versions of *The Great Gatsby*, one made in 1949 by Elliott Nugent and the other in 1974 by Jack Clayton. Others may come to applaud the flesh-and-blood creation of characters and events hitherto only described on a printed page and imagined in the mind — as with *Gone with the Wind* (1939) (Figure 6-25) and *The Godfather* (1972). For many, the opportunity to see quality performers in great plays and musicals outside the major metropolitan areas provides the impetus; one can point to the superb performance of Sir Laurence Olivier in his self-directed *Richard III* (1956) or to Barbra Streisand repeating on film her Broadway performance in *Funny Girl* (William Wyler, 1968).

★ **6-25** Though it is undoubtedly easier to make a good film from a book which has not been widely read, GONE WITH THE WIND (Victor Fleming, 1939) is an example of a film which captured the spirit of the novel in such exciting images that the many readers of Margaret Mitchell's best-seller were not disappointed. Indeed, modern readers of the novel generally think of Rhett Butler as embodied in Clark Gable and Scarlett O'Hara as Vivien Leigh.

Granted that **adaptations** from previously successful sources are economically sound (and perhaps a great deal easier to script, for the characters are already drawn, named, and personalized, the setting chosen, the plot worked out), many serious aesthetic problems arise in translating a story effectively from one medium to another. Sometimes what works wonderfully well on the stage or on the page disappoints on the screen.

The main problem, of course, is that film is primarily visual communication; literature and drama are primarily verbal communication. Although literature and drama printed in a book use "images" or figures of speech, those images are constructed from language rather than from concrete objects. The language supplies information from which the reader then constructs his own specific mental image. Film, on the other hand, by recording physical objects, gives every viewer the same set of images — and although each viewer may presumably interpret the meaning of those objects, the physical specificity of those objects is never in question. Therefore, it is not unusual that a film version of a favorite book or short story will not satisfy the viewer because the specific images chosen by the filmmaker — for example, the actor who plays Gatsby — will never be exactly the same as the images the reader conjured up from the printed word.

Dramatic Adaptation: Shakespeare As an Example

Even performed drama — theater — relies heavily on word pictures to create many of its effects. Since stage space is limited, other "real" and "imaginative" spaces must be conjured up through the magic of verbal metaphor and description spoken by the actors. In *Macbeth*, for example, King Duncan sets the scene for us when he says, "This castle hath a pleasant seat; the air/Nimbly and sweetly recommends itself/Unto our gentle senses." But when a filmmaker *shows* us a castle, it may jar with our impressions of what Macbeth's castle should be (Figure 6-26). Then, too, since the audience at a theatrical performance sits in a fixed position, usually a far greater distance from the performer than in the equivalent of the film's close-up, language is more often weighted to carry emotion and nuance than is the stage actor's physical presence. This is not to say that the actor's physical presence is not crucial to drama or that the various movements of the performer do not create emotion and meaning, but that language becomes extremely important when you are not able to see the speaker's eyes or watch the expression on his mouth from a close vantage point. Film, having both unlimited space and unlimited vantage points, is far less dependent upon dialogue than is theater. Adapting a drama from the stage to the screen may be more difficult than it first appears, for the filmmaker must find an appropriate cinematic space to match the imagined space in a particular play (and that does not always simply mean "opening up" the play so that scenes take place in a number of different locations). And he must find some way so as to neither merely duplicate nor unwittingly contradict the mental images created by the play's language.

Sir Laurence Olivier's film version of Shakespeare's *Henry V* (1945) provides examples of the various choices open to the filmmaker seeking spatial equivalents of the imaginative space created by the drama itself. In the beginning of the film we watch a production of *Henry V* taking place on the stage of the Globe Theater in London circa 1600. Since we are watching something which has the cinematic aura of a "documentary reenactment" — a re-created performance in Shakespearean England — we accept the fact that the camera has placed us in the subjective position of a spectator in the pit of the theater. We are there — the camera, our eyes — watching Shakespeare's play or looking up at the nobles and wealthy merchants in the boxes or at the orange sellers and then back

★ **6-26** When dramas are translated into films, stage space is often exchanged for "on location" cinematic space in order to heighten the sense of reality. Roman Polanski's version of MACBETH (1971) was filmed in an authentic old castle. Sometimes a director's choice of physical details may jar with our impressions of what such details should look like.

to the play. This time and space in the film take on an existence which is undeniable: the construction of the Globe Theater and the weathered look of its texture; the costumes of the audience; the contrast between the audience and the players, the former moving randomly and the latter striking poses; and, most particularly, the rain which begins to fall and slightly distracts the players from the scenes they are playing.

Our interest is focused less on the play itself than on the re-creation of a performance in a historical period and in a particular geographical bit of space. To draw our attention to the play — Shakespeare's play, which is Olivier's true subject — Olivier breaks completely away from the performance in Shakespeare's England to cross the Channel to Henry V's fields of France and the battle of Agincourt. The documentary re-creation of an Elizabethan production is dropped in favor of re-creating the narrative, acting out not only the play but the story of Henry V as well. All the things that Shakespeare could only refer to briefly in words ("alarums and excursions") the camera gives us in full movement and color, in physical representation: hundreds of men in armor, banners fluttering in the breeze, the attack of the mounted knights, the hordes of English longbowmen with their showers of arrows. The film is doing what the movies do best — putting the viewer both imaginatively and visually right there in the actual place and in a time become present. In later sections of the film, however, the illusion of both the reality of the story as it is lived and of the "documentary" stage performance is deliberately broken; Henry woos Katherine of France in a patently cardboard castle and we find that Shakespeare's language is more dynamic and alive than the set within which it is spoken. Our own mental images created by the love play and poetry of the couple take precedence over the filmed images; the verbal metaphors are stronger than the visual accompaniments.

This effect can be reversed. In Olivier's *Richard III*, for instance, after Richard has been killed, his crown is kicked about in the dust by battling horsemen. The viewer sees it for a while, first rolling about like so much trash, ignored beneath the horses' hooves, and then rolling free and toward the camera, finally coming to a stop which is then translated into the film's final image and credits. The viewer cannot quarrel with the literal reality of the crown and the appropriateness of its appearance in the scene; it fits the facts of the situation. And yet, because of the preceding events, and because the camera has kept it focused in the frame, and because the viewer has so much time to contemplate it on the screen, the crown takes on a metaphoric value as well as its literal one. Another example, among many, is in Akira Kurosawa's version of *Macbeth*, entitled *Throne of Blood* (1957). The Japanese director, taking up Shakespeare's references to Birnam Wood (never shown on the stage, of course), on the screen gives us Birnam Wood as a dark, mysterious labyrinth in which Washizu (Macbeth) is lost. This visible, actual forest becomes a metaphor for the state of Macbeth's mind; not only is he physically lost in the woods, but he is morally lost. He cannot find the way out of the complex and conflicting desires he has for human power. This same kind of visible metaphor occurs in the Russian version of *Hamlet* (Grigori Kozintsev, 1964). Elsinore is a fortress-prison built on rocks; its drawbridge and portcullis are massive and forbidding, and we see them close on Hamlet as he rides from the freedom of the countryside back into a prison whose massive bulk literally blackens the screen and closes out the daylight. Hamlet is imprisoned in Elsinore just as he is imprisoned by his state of mind. Early on, after he has returned home for his father's funeral and his mother's wedding, he walks amid a crowded court and we hear a Shakespearean soliloquy as Hamlet thinks to himself. But the film's images do not merely duplicate the verbal metaphors; rather, we might say that the images match the metaphors, for we see the courtiers moving slowly in a clockwise circle, while the tragic hero, mentally isolated from them, moves more quickly, in sharper focus, counterclockwise.

In each of these examples, the geography becomes an integral part of

★ **6-27** The setting selected by a filmmaker for an adaptation of a literary work can affect the meaning of the film greatly. This is especially true of drama, in which physical space is usually described only briefly, if at all. Sir Laurence Olivier set his HAMLET (1948) in an undefined, labyrinthine space, full of pools of light and heavy shadows. This Elsinore is elusive, inconcrete. The ill-defined setting creates a sense that Olivier's HAMLET is taking place as much in the nightmare world of Hamlet's mind as it is in physical space.

the film's structure. In a movie, whether or not it is based on Shake-speare, the background is not just "where" the action takes place. The detective's tacky office or the sandy beach or the saloon is an intimate part of that action, sometimes even the cause of the action. And that background need not be highly conspicuous. Shakespeare set *Hamlet* in Elsinore, but what should Elsinore look like on a screen?

A comparison of the setting in three different film versions of *Hamlet* illuminates how much the background can affect the meaning and move-ment of the play. Olivier's version (1948) takes place in an undefined, labyrinthine space that is further removed from a connection with every-day reality because the lighting of that space creates separate areas of light and dark and we cannot see the backgrounds against which the characters play. This Elsinore, then, is elusive; we can't quite form a picture of it. Combined of course with the other elements of this particular version of *Hamlet* (the performers' interpretation of the dialogue, the director's decision to cut or rearrange certain scenes, and the Oedipal imagery of Hamlet's mother's bed), the space that we see, the backgrounds against which the action figures, makes Olivier's *Hamlet* take place as much in the nightmare world of Hamlet's mind as it does in concrete space (Figure 6-27).

In Kozintsev's *Hamlet*, as already mentioned, light is shut off by the massive and dark bulk of doors closing, of rock walls blotting out the sky and vertical barlike aspects of the background. Unlike the space in Olivier's version, however, the space in this Russian *Hamlet* is clearly seen and coherently connected, and we do not, therefore, feel we are being taken into Hamlet's mind.

Tony Richardson's version of *Hamlet* (1969) takes place in yet another setting, one which combines strategies of the previous two and yet creates its own meanings and sends its own messages. It is played indoors except for one scene, and that indoors is a claustrophobic, damp stone setting which seems to contain all the characters in such close proximity that it makes a viewer feel that (to quote from Jean-Paul Sartre's *No Exit*) "hell is other people." The backgrounds are seen clearly and so closely that the stone walls seem to sweat — as do the central characters. The background may sometimes be indistinguishable because we are watching the characters in such extreme close-ups, but when we see it, it is never unclear. The stones suggest the wetness and coldness of the place, and yet the flames and tapers which flicker through the film suggest a humid, sticky warmth; the disturbing contradiction parallels the similarly disturbing contradiction in Nicol Williamson's performance of the central character, a performance which emphasizes Hamlet's frenzied passion one moment and his cold and intellectual calculation the next. Because the camera stays quite close to the characters, the background at times complements Shakespeare's poetic imagery. While in the two other versions of *Hamlet*, Ophelia's death is shown to the viewer, Richardson, like Shakespeare, chooses to let us imagine it. But Richardson uses the background to help us *feel* Ophelia's death more strongly. As Queen Gertrude relates the description of how Ophelia died, she stands against a tapestry. Her shoulders are quite bare and her hair soft; the background of the tapestry is dull gold, against which we see the threads of dark green leaves growing from the branches of an artificial and woven tree. The contrast between the bare human skin and soft hair of the living Queen and the stiff gold and green of the false, dead tree is heightened by — and itself illuminates — Shakespeare's description of Ophelia's death by drowning. During the Queen's monologue we are forced to view an image which, though appropriate, does not weakly duplicate the language; rather, the image comments upon the words.

Adaptations of Prose Fiction

As sources for films, novels and short stories seem in some ways to offer more flexibility to the filmmaker than do plays. For one thing, filmmakers are not usually expected to preserve all the dialogue in a novel; rather they can alter it, abridge it, or omit parts of it without the controversy which such modifications cause if a drama is similarly adapted for the screen. An audience regards a play as chiefly dialogue, and it expects to hear that dialogue, whereas it recognizes that a novel is not solely nor even primarily what the characters say. Narrative fiction abounds with descriptions of people, places, and things which often can be easily translated into their concrete and representational cinematic equivalents. A description of a character's actions in a novel or short story often tells us more about him than do his words, and these actions can also be easily captured on film. Many characters in fiction, after all, are revealed as they go about their business alone, walking down streets, doing chores, peering into shop windows, looking at other people, puttering about the house — all without necessarily stopping once to have a conversation with any other character, something almost impossible to achieve in a play. Because a novel usually includes many characters and incidents (both major and minor) and because the novel is not normally read at a single sitting, it seems natural for the filmmaker to make a selection of what to keep and what to omit. This freedom creates problems as well. Omission of certain scenes or certain characters, or of secondary plots, is bound to disappoint readers who found those things important (Figure 6-28). And although some novels take very well to the screen, others depend for their power and development on their lengthiness, and they seem thin or abrupt on the screen.

The filmmaker is more likely to have success in adapting a lesser-known novel to the screen than a widely read one. Two films of Mike Nichols, a director who has adapted both dramas and novels for the screen, may be revealing. Nichols adapted a fairly unknown novel by Charles Webb, *The Graduate.* The book has very little physical or psychological description and its prose is unimpressive; in fact, the novel reads much like a movie script of dialogue without any of the camera angles indicated, thus allowing the director freedom to choose his own method of representation. In a way, it is a non-novel, lacking the flesh which usually covers the basic skeletal structure of a single plot and few characters; it also lacks the longer form's rich language, which a writer normally uses to create various points of view, moods, tones, am-

★ 6-28 John Ford's version (1940) of the Steinbeck novel THE GRAPES OF
WRATH changes the emphasis of the original. Instead of making a film
attacking the social and economic ills that led to the displacement of thousands of Dust Bowl farmers, Ford shows us the enduring quality of the family
and the way it can survive the worst of hardships. Ford deleted the inter-
chapters which Steinbeck used to explore the political climate of the 1930s
and instead concentrated on relationships within the Joad family.

biguities. Nichols in *The Graduate* (1967) was able to provide the viewer
with more than the novel provided: more details rather than fewer, more
characterization rather than less, and more ambiguity and contrasting
humor and pathos than did the book. In short, the film is better than the
book from which it was adapted.

Nichols's adaptation of Joseph Heller's *Catch-22* (1970) was another
matter. Heller's well-known novel is rich in word play, its best tools the
absurdities of language. The theme of the book is not simply that war is
stupid and crazy — something which does come across in Nichols's film
— but that man lives in a quicksand of unintelligible meanings, symbolized by confused, inadequate, and unreliable words. Time and space
are not presented chronologically; characterization is bizarre and stereotypical rather than realistic. The war and all its crazy participants are a

★ **6-29** In an attempt to transfer Franz Kafka's peculiarly claustrophobic vision of life to the screen, Orson Welles elected to use a variety of expressionistic techniques including *chiaroscuro* lighting, fog and shadow effects, and (as here) subjective close-ups filmed with a wide-angle lens to produce distorted perspective in THE TRIAL (1962).

complex literary metaphor, carefully worked out, word by word, pun by pun, paradox by paradox. Thus, a highly intellectual construct gives meaning to the comic-strip characters.

The film, however, must complete the subtle transformation of humor into horror not through the incremental accumulation and repetition of language devices, but through action shown on the screen. In Nichols's *Catch-22* we get real flesh-and-blood actors, we see real airplanes and have a real Orson Welles inhabit the fictional General Dreedle. These physical presences — people and things — detract from the power of the novel's central metaphor, which sets off a chain reaction of images in the mind. In the novel, for instance, the "soldier in white," a soldier wrapped completely in bandages so that the men in the ward are not convinced there's anyone inside, works simultaneously as a comic device and as a powerful symbol. In the film, however, he is merely a plaster cast, an object which we see and recognize and know. He is a great deal less haunting and disturbing in the flesh (or, rather, in the cast) than he is in the novel. He becomes merely a funny bit on the screen. In the novel, the bombardier Snowden and his wound achieve mythic proportions as Yossarian recalls more and more details of an event we might really rather not find out about; in the film, the final revelation stops with the shocking picture of Snowden's entrails spilling out of the unzipped flak suit. The effect is certainly visceral, but it does not cause a great movement of the mind towards meaning. As it happens, the filmic treatment of Snowden is one of the best things in the adaptation. Because its images are bleached and cold and because its accumulation of small revelations as the scene recurs horrify and tease, it does create some of the suspense and mystical quality of its equivalent in the novel. But even so, the experience of Snowden in the film is too concrete and literal to create the cosmic horror of the novel's revelation of Snowden's "secret" — mortality.

Film and Literary Symbolism

Film literalizes what may function symbolically in literature; it robs the symbol of its mystery. Unless the filmmaker is able to recharge the image with some cinematically communicated richness (Figure 6-29) — in effect, to recharge the literal with its own mystery and symbolism — that literary symbol will not function successfully on the screen. In Melville's novel *Moby Dick*, the great white whale symbolizes the mysterious power of the universe, but in John Huston's movie version (1956), what we see is just a big mechanical fish. And the malevolent great white shark of *Jaws* (1976) is much more menacing when we see through its eyes than when we look *at* it, more threatening as a symbol of mindless rapaciousness when we see its presence marked by two yellow floats which bob up and down in the ocean than when we actually see it present. Because film is necessarily representational, it is extremely difficult for objects to accumulate symbolic meanings; rather, they usually become increasingly ordinary and only physically meaningful. But because it is difficult does not mean that it can't or hasn't been done.

Erich von Stroheim's masterwork *Greed* (1924) demonstrates how a filmmaker can transplant symbols and motifs from a novel to a film in a way which will not decrease their power. Although less than a fourth of the original (and unreleased) forty-two reels remain of *Greed*, this adaptation of Frank Norris's naturalistic novel *McTeague* succeeds in building a symbolic structure in the midst of incredibly realistic detail. For example, von Stroheim takes the novel's use of the characters' hands and transfers it to the screen in a way that adds force to the motif (Figure 6-30). From the first moment when we see the film's central female character — Trina — we are made aware of her constantly fluttering hands and her long white fingers. Von Stroheim emphasizes them by dressing Trina in dark clothing so that the movement of her white hands is constantly, but naturally, highlighted against a dark background as she touches the buttons on her dress nervously, or adjusts her dark hair. Our first awareness of those hands is their whiteness and their constant fluttering movement, which visually connects them to another motif in the film — the pair of caged birds which, later in the film, are McTeague's wedding present to his new wife — Trina. Although the

★ **6-30** Erich von Stroheim's GREED (1924) demonstrates how a filmmaker can successfully transplant symbols and motifs from a novel to film. Trina in the novel is characterized by her hands — the hands that make children's toys and also count hoarded money. Von Stroheim emphasizes Trina's hands by highlighting their pale, fluttery movement against the darkness of her clothes.

birds are not introduced until long after we have met Trina, von Stroheim has carefully prepared us to connect them with her, so that what happens to the birds will serve as a symbolic parallel to what befalls Trina and McTeague. After Trina marries McTeague, we see her growing obsession for money, as her miserly actions of counting money are connected to a sequence which ends with Trina sitting on her bed rubbing her hands with night cream. Again the context is realistic, but her actions make her look like a gloating miser rather than a woman preparing to go to sleep. Her hands are thus linked with her greed. After McTeague can no longer practice as a dentist, we see Trina whittling toys to sell and flexing her fingers in pain; her obsession is revealed not just by her actions as she counts and polishes and murmurs to the gold coins she is hoarding, but by images which show the gold in her hands; the coins lie across her palm in close-up or her long fingers hold a coin toward the light to see it sparkle. In the scene in which McTeague attempts to get Trina to give him some money by grabbing her hand and biting the fingers, the sadism of his actions is enhanced by all the earlier associations which the viewer has had, the accumulation of emotion and experience which makes Trina's hands more than physical appendages. The night that McTeague decides to leave Trina, they stand at the door of their hovel and Trina asks McTeague if he still loves her. Although Trina and her question are pathetic, we have seen Trina's sickening and unsympathetic stinginess and manipulation of her husband. It is therefore particularly horrifying when we watch Trina's long white fingers, now wrapped in scraps of bandage, slide insinuatingly and slowly up McTeague's dark jacket to embrace him around the neck. The image is ambiguous but powerful and carefully controlled: the hands have taken on an almost independent life of their own and yet they also belong to a simultaneously pathetic and repugnant Trina. Von Stroheim took the motif directly from the novel, but in visually representing the hands as hands he also was careful, by using techniques which add mystery and evocative power to the merely physical, to compensate for the photographic image's reductive concreteness.

The success of an adaptation from book or stage to screen will not depend on whether or not it is a line-for-line transfer from one medium to another, or on whether or not its metaphors or symbols or motifs are the same in both media. A successful adaptation depends on how imaginatively the filmmaker is able to use his medium to convey what was conveyed in another medium. A film adaptation of a play or novel is simultaneously an individual *reading* of that play or novel and the actualization of that reading in moving images. The filmmaker must decide what the play or novel says, what it is about (a matter not only of plot and character but of tone and imagery), and then he must find cinematic equivalents. Many film adaptations have accomplished this difficult job, sometimes even surpassing their source material. (Some others, of course, have simply used the source as the basis for an entirely new and individual work.) As one does not criticize Shakespeare for not giving his audience a line-for-line adaptation of Holinshed's *Chronicles* or for not seeing that the "essence" of the *Chronicles* was historical rather than poetic, one should not automatically criticize a filmmaker who is fired into originality by the drama, short story, poem, or novel he is supposedly adapting for the screen.

★★★   **The Script**

What is written down or drawn on paper, so as to communicate the idea for a film to those people who will undertake the production of the film or who will finance it, is virtually invisible to most film viewers. Unlike the text of the play, which can be easily separated from the play's performance by the theatergoer who can read the play the week after he's seen it performed or who can see various performances of the play throughout his lifetime performed by different actors in different settings, the written idea for a film is not readily separable from the film itself — the performance of that idea on the screen. A play has a *text* before it is performed, even if it is never performed. But a film has only a *pre-text* that is written and that can be read. A performance of a play is a *reading* of a preexistent text, but a film *is the text itself;* what existed on paper, before the film was made, is the barest hint of those elements which make a film a film. It is a mere skeleton of the film it may become. The following is an excerpt from the **shooting script** of *Citizen Kane* (1941), written by Herman J. Mankiewicz and Orson Welles:

21 EXT. MRS. KANE'S BOARDINGHOUSE — DAY — 1870
The white of a great field of snow. In the same position as the last word in above insert, appears the tiny figure of Charles Foster Kane, aged five. He throws a snowball at the camera. It sails toward us and out of scene.

22 REVERSE ANGLE — ON THE HOUSE, FEATURING A LARGE SIGN READING:

MRS. KANE'S BOARDINGHOUSE

HIGH CLASS MEALS AND LODGING

INQUIRE WITHIN

Charles Kane's snowball hits the sign.

23 INT. PARLOR — MRS. KANE'S BOARDINGHOUSE — DAY — 1870
Camera is angling through the window, but the window frame is not cut
into scene. We see only the field of snow again. Charles is manufacturing
another snowball. Now —

Camera pulls back, the frame of the window, appearing, and we are
inside the parlor of the boardinghouse. Mrs. Kane, aged about twenty-
eight, is looking out towards her son.

MRS. KANE
(Calling out) Be careful, Charles!

THATCHER'S VOICE
Mrs. Kane —

MRS. KANE
(Calling out the window) Pull your muffler around your neck, Charles —

*But Charles runs away. Mrs. Kane turns into camera and we see her face
— a strong face, worn and kind*

THATCHER'S VOICE
I think we'll have to tell him now — [10]

Before there was a film there was a written idea, a sort of scaffold
from which the film was constructed and which was then dismantled
when the structure (the film) could stand alone. Except for some free-
wheeling and usually unsuccessful experiments in improvisational narrative cinema, such as Norman Mailer's *Beyond the Law* (1968), *Maid-
stone* (1971), and *Wild 90* (1972), no matter how spontaneous and
improvised a film seems, almost every story film has had a detailed written
script during its preproduction, shooting, and editing stages. Certainly,
improvisation may occur during shooting — a script is not written down
merely to be slavishly followed no matter what happens — but making
films is so expensive that planning and structuring are absolutely necessary. Unless there is a detailed script, financial backing will be hard to
come by. And it cannot be forgotten that film is a collaborative art form.
No matter how well thought out the idea is in the mind of its originator
or its director, that idea cannot be fulfilled on the screen unless it has
been communicated clearly to those people who will undertake its production. Even if a film crew is relatively small, perhaps three (cameraman, sound man, and editor) for a low-budget production, the idea for
the film and how it is to be realized must be clearly communicated to a
number of people who do not all visualize things the same way. Therefore, a written or drawn script is necessary if the crew is to achieve some
unity of vision.

On occasion, some variations of film scripts have been published for
both the general public and for film scholars and buffs, but unlike plays,

most film scripts are not available in published form; some can be read only in special library archives or through direct access to motion picture studio files. The reason is fairly obvious: because film scripts are not even an approximate substitute for the film itself, they are of little interest to most people. Film scripts can be useful, however, to the person seriously interested in the film medium. First, reading a film script can refresh the memory and allow accurate citation of the dialogue (if the reader is sure that the script he is citing is, indeed, the same as the film that was finally made). Second, an actual shooting script can reveal much about the process of how a film becomes transformed from the words on paper into the visual and aural complex that is the final work. And, finally, although it is true of only a handful of screenplays, some film scripts have literary value of their own which exists independently of the film itself.

A film's pre-text or script can take several forms, and some films go through all the forms before they get made (although this is not always true): the **treatment,** the **storyboard,** the **writer's script,** the **director's script** (shooting script), and the **viewer's script.**

TREATMENT

The simplest written form of a film, meant to communicate the idea of the film to people other than the filmmaker, is called a treatment. Of course, before doing a treatment, the writer or filmmaker may have jotted down a statement of the film's purpose so that he can clarify for himself why he is making the film. This statement of purpose, although useful for filmmaker or writer, is not useful in evoking the film for those people who will have to decide whether or not to finance and produce it. Again, for his own purposes, the filmmaker may decide to write a brief synopsis, a short chronological outline of the events important to the story. But again, this synopsis is really for the writer or filmmaker, acting as a private guide to writing the much more communicative and detailed treatment.

The treatment is usually a sort of combination of short story and report. Because it must effectively communicate to other people the writer's or filmmaker's vision of the completed film, the treatment generally does not use screenwriting terminology; it will not deal with camera movements or editing or sound effects. Chiefly it tells the story and gives the reader a clear idea of both the content and emotional appeal of the finished film. The treatment may be almost any length, from a few pages to perhaps thirty pages, so long as it manages to put the film on paper so that others may evaluate it, discuss it, decide whether it merits production. The interests of the people who look at the treatment will be less in the techniques of filmmaking than in the characters, plot, and settings. Thus, the treatment will describe these elements of the story and their relationship in readable prose.

STORYBOARD

The storyboard is a pictorial equivalent to the prose treatment — and, like the treatment, it may be brief or lengthy so long as it conveys a clear and coherent vision of what the finished film will be like. The storyboard consists of individual drawings which together, rather like a comic book, give a sense of the finished film's **continuity,** major action, and characters. As well, brief written statements clarifying the film's movement may accompany the individual drawings.

Generally, storyboards are not used for narrative films which are live-action, that is, which use real bodies, objects, and locations. The storyboard is most effective in conveying the gist of **animated films,** those films which tell stories through drawings. Occasionally, however, even the maker of a live-action narrative may storyboard his projected film. One director who does so is Alfred Hitchcock — and it is interesting to note that before he became a director he was trained as a commercial artist and actually drew title designs for silent films. Hitchcock's preference for drawing his film idea rather than writing it down suggests that he is perhaps more visual than literary. Similarly, Satyajit Ray, the great Indian filmmaker, formerly a graphic artist, uses pen-and-ink and wash drawings to lay out the sequences of his films before he goes behind the camera.

FORMS OF THE SCRIPT

The primary purpose of writing a script or drawing a detailed storyboard is to communicate the *same* film to a number of different people. Although all of these people will be involved in the film, they will be doing very different things, sometimes separately. The script, then, is chiefly a handbook or blueprint. But the script exists also in several different forms and for several different secondary functions. The script that the screenwriter puts down on paper does not take the same form as the shooting script which the director will use on the set. And the script which may be published for the reader/viewer to enjoy will be quite different from either the writer's or director's script and will, in fact, be more closely related to the finished film than to the film in its preproduction and production stages.

The Writer's Script

The script that a screenwriter puts down on paper might well be called a dialogue script. It is an expansion of the treatment, and although it can take several written forms, its chief purpose is to provide, in dialogue and key description, the elements of the dramatic scenes which will appear in the finished film. The writer's script, setting forth the dialogue, coveys the characterization and the plot. It includes, of necessity, some descriptive prose — most detailed when it introduces characters or settings for the first time and least detailed when it indicates time and place and peripheral action or camera movement or angle. Thus, the screenwriter's script includes a curt description of the place, time, and situation of the characters (e.g., "Barn, Interior; Night; the Vet inspects the horse while Johnny and Susan watch"). This will be followed by the dialogue to be spoken by the actors, and prose descriptions of characters' actions will be included at appropriate points in the dialogue (e.g., He lights a cigarette; She collapses in his arms, sobbing). The screenwriter will not indicate camera setups, particular lighting effects, or other cinematic elements which are the director's responsibility when the scene is actually shot. The only usual exception to this is when a specific camera movement or cinematic element is necessary to forward the plot, or create suspense, or build character (e.g., "The camera moves back so that the viewer sees there is a body in the room").

The screenwriter, especially of the Hollywood film, can be credited with conceiving the characters, the plot, and the dialogue. In Hollywood's most successful and prolific years, scripts were produced almost by a production line. Each studio had its "stable" of writers, and many writers worked on a single script — one at a time or together — or many writers worked on various versions of the same script independently of each other. Today, now that the structure of Hollywood filmmaking has appreciably changed, the writer's script is usually his and his alone, and he must sell it or get a specific assignment through his agent. Because the agent generally sells the script to actors, directors, and people who finance filmmaking, the screenwriter's script is geared to these readers — and they are interested in dialogue, characterization, and plot, rather than in camera angle, camera movement, and editing. Thus, the writer's script is not the script in the form in which it will be actually filmed. The exception to this, of course, is when the scriptwriter and the director are the same person; then, the writer's script and the director's or shooting script will often also be the same.

The Director's Script (Shooting Script)

Once a director gets a film script, whether it has been assigned to him or whether he has chosen it from among those his agent has submitted to him, that script must be changed into a shooting script. The writer's script usually comes to the director in one of two formats: the dialogue and visual descriptions of the scene alternate down the page, or the dialogue and visual description are divided, the former running down the left side of the page and the latter down the right. In both formats, however, the shots and scenes are numbered in chronological order as they shift their locales and content. It is the director's task — before the actual shooting — to break down the writer's script into specific shots (also numbered in some way to correspond with the script). All the camera movements must be entered, camera angles and distance, lighting instructions, subject movement and **special effects.** It is at this time that a storyboard may be particularly helpful in clearly pictorializing the desired shot.

At this time, too, the director begins to put his personal imprint upon the film idea, specifying shots and actions to indicate his interpretation of the writer's vision. If the screenwriter and the director have the same general imaginative view of the finished film, then both of them will be in agreement at this point. In fact, an imaginative sympathy between a director and screenwriter may lead to repeated partnership between the two, for example, screenwriter Dudley Nichols and director John Ford, or screenwriter Harold Pinter and director Joseph Losey. The creative and collaborative relationship between some screenwriters and directors has been so constant that it is difficult to single out the dominant personality behind the finished film; one such team is I. A. L. Diamond and director Billy Wilder.

However, if the director and the screenwriter have different visions, and both are present on the set during shooting, the going will be somewhat difficult, particularly if changes in the script are necessary. The conflict between screenwriter and director is satirically presented in Federico Fellini's 8½ (1963), an exploration of a film director's search for creative spirit. The director has nothing in common with the screenwriter, who has been hired by the producer. They talk *at* each other constantly without ever getting together on what the film is about; they do not even have a common vocabulary. Eventually the project is canceled, the huge set is dismantled, and the movie originally planned is never made. This kind of confrontation between director and screenwriter seldom occurs in Hollywood, however, because the screenwriter is not usually present on the set. When the screenwriter's script is bought, his job on the film ends. Changes made on the set are made by the director or by others participating in the production process. During the 1920s and 1930s in Hollywood, for example, the producer was also frequently a key figure in the scriptwriting process.

★ **6-31** Susan Alexander works on one of her puzzles in Xanadu in CITIZEN KANE (Orson Welles, 1941). Did the idea of the puzzle — "What is Rosebud?" — come from the director or from the screenwriter? The shooting script of the film was published in *The Citizen Kane Book*, which also contains an essay by Pauline Kael that discusses the issue of film authorship.

The writer's script is transformed by the director/producer as he plans the production and then shoots and edits the film. The director's script, the shooting script, is for the use not of readers but of filmmakers; it is the guide the director uses to aid him in making the film, and he shares parts of it with those of the crew who will handle the lighting and cinematography and performing. A shooting script is rarely published complete with the director's marginal notations about lighting, set details, performance, or camera movements. These shooting scripts are usually available for study in film archives or special collections. Shooting scripts without the director's marginal comments are published, however, along with various editorial devices which indicate to the reader differences between the shooting script and the way in which the film actually appeared on the screen. For example, the shooting script of *Citizen Kane*, an excerpt of which appears on pages 328–329, was published in *The Citizen Kane Book*, along with the cutting continuity of the completed film. In this controversial book, film critic Pauline Kael attributed the brilliance of *Citizen Kane* to the screenwriter, Herman J. Mankiewicz, and, correspondingly, minimized the contribution of the coscenarist and director, Orson Welles (Figure 6-31). But film is a collaborative art, and both men are responsible for the movie. What is useful about *The Citizen Kane Book*, however, is that it allows the general reader to examine a shooting script and to compare it to the continuity script, which is a record of the released film.

The Viewer's Script
Published scripts of many films are available for viewers to read. These scripts, however, differ from both the writer's script and the director's shooting script. They differ because the reader's chief interest is in the film itself. The writer's script, we have mentioned, does not contain individual shot descriptions of any complexity, which means that it gives too little "feel" of the released film to satisfy the reader who is interested in recreating a past film experience. On the other hand, the director's shooting script usually contains an abundance of detail which, for most readers, obscures the narrative thrust of the finished film.

The interested nonprofessional filmgoer is most interested in reading a script which approximates the finished film, which describes all of the action and gives all of the dialogue, but which does not contain much technical language about shooting. In other words, the viewer's script is most usually the cutting continuity script, a recording and notation of what occurs and what is said in the film that is finally released. It may even interpret the action for the reader, as the following excerpt from the continuity script of *Bonnie and Clyde* (1967) demonstrates:

EXTERIOR MAIN STREET
They are now on a small-town street of barber shops, cafés, groceries, etc. At the moment, it is deserted. They continue walking down the empty street, talking. *CLYDE looks the place over.*

CLYDE: Hey, what do y'all do for a good time around here? Listen to the grass grow?
BONNIE: I guess you had a lot more fun up at State Prison. *CLYDE laughs, enjoying her repartee. They continue walking. At a hydrant, CLYDE stops.*
CLYDE showing off, but serious: I tell you, see my right foot. *He points at his right foot.*
BONNIE: Yeah.
CLYDE: I chopped two toes off that foot. With an axe.
BONNIE shocked: What? Why?
CLYDE: To get off work detail. You wanna see it? *CLYDE goes and rests his foot on the fire hydrant.*
BONNIE a lady of some sensitivity: No! . . . *She bends down: then turning cute:* I . . . I surely don't intend to stand here in the middle of Main Street and look at your dirty feet. *They continue walking in silence past a few stores, each planning what next to say.*
BONNIE: Boy, did you really do that? [11]

Most published scripts are continuity scripts, written *after* the film has been made. A similar publishing enterprise has been the publication of actual frame enlargements from a particular film, the **stills** (including notation for dissolves and other **optical effects**) accompanied by printed dialogue. Because illustrations are much more expensive than printed words, this kind of visual rendition of a film is still relatively uncommon and the written continuity script remains the major source of scripts available to the general reader.

Although the continuity script is the most popular form of viewer's script because it re-creates a film already seen by the reader, the public's interest occasionally has been captured not only by the film but also by the film's director. The director's *original* script may be published even if it is at variance with parts of the released film. Both Ingmar Bergman and Federico Fellini, for example, are writer-directors whose films interest the public. Thus, publishers may issue the director's script without the technical directions and sometimes even without the changes made during shooting; essentially they are releasing a kind of writer's script but because the director is also the writer he has recorded more visual details.

In addition to these various kinds of scripts published for the viewer/reader, there are other published versions of films which are hardly scripts. For example, a film that has become tremendously popular may later be turned into a novel, reversing the usual adaptation process. The process may even work both ways for a single film. *2001: A Space Odyssey* (1968) was originally inspired by a short story written by Arthur C. Clarke called "The Sentinel." Working with the film's director, Clarke expanded and changed the original story and wrote a screenplay: the writer's script. Kubrick changed the screenplay into a director's shooting script, putting his own distinctive imprint on it and the finished film. Then, because of the film's tremendous popularity, and because of the confusion about several narrative issues in the film, Clarke expanded his original short story by combining it with the material in the released film, thus creating a novel adapted from the film. Usually, however, "novelizing" a film takes place after the film has been released, and it is generally the work of a writer who has had no connection with the production of the film and who most likely has not ever seen the film's scripts. Such film-into-novel adaptations, although interesting as cultural and aesthetic phenomena, tell us little about either medium and need not concern the student of film.

Any published script available to the filmgoer is an invaluable aid. Unlike a favorite book, a favorite film cannot be picked up and referred to on a moment's notice for ready reference. Even when scripts are unidentified — that is, when the publisher gives no indication whether the script is a writer's or a continuity script — they still provide a handy way of calling back to memory the experience of the film.

NOTES

1 Interviewed by James Blue, *Film Comment* 4:4 (Summer 1968), p. 6.

2 *Fellini on Fellini* (Boston/New York: Seymour Lawrence/Delacorte Press, 1976), p. 100.

3 "What People Laugh At," in Donald W. McCaffrey, ed., *Focus on Chaplin* (Englewood Cliffs, New Jersey: Prentice-Hall, 1971), p. 52.

4 In Gideon Bachmann, "The Man on the Volcano: A Portrait of Werner Herzog," *Film Quarterly* 31, no. 1 (Fall 1977): 7–8.

5 In Andrew Sarris, ed., *Interviews with Film Directors* (New York: Avon Books, 1969), p. 257.

6 In James Harvey, "Sirkumstantial," *Film Comment* 14, no. 4 (July–August 1978): 55.

7 In Joseph Gelmis, ed., *The Film Director as Superstar* (Garden City, New York: Doubleday, 1970), p. 118.

8 In Michael Goodwin, "Close Encounters with a Rising Star," *The New York Times Magazine* (January 15, 1978): 14.

9 *Notes on Cinematography* (New York: Urizen Books, 1977), p. 7.

10 In Pauline Kael, ed., *The Citizen Kane Book* (Boston: Little, Brown, 1971), pp. 136–137.

11 *The Bonnie and Clyde Book* (New York: Simon and Schuster, 1972), pp. 42–43.

NOTES

PART III
CINEMATIC
CONTENT:
THE
NONFICTION
FILM

★★★ **Knowing and Understanding the Nonfiction Film**

The average moviegoer thinks of film as narrative, that is, he thinks of the fictional stories he sees in commercial theaters and on television. Yet, in fact, the vast majority of films produced, shot, and distributed around the world are nonfiction films. Although some of these films are created solely for aesthetic reasons, most nonfiction films are produced for educational and promotional uses. Such films range from films for training insurance salesmen and films urging viewers to go to Disneyland to films which explain a complicated scientific principle. Some of these nonfiction films are complex and aesthetically pleasing, yet compared to the fiction film, the nonfiction film has hardly captured the critical imagination as an object of study.

Because most nonfiction films have been made and distributed for specialized audiences, they are shown primarily in classrooms, in factories, at sales meetings and conventions, to civic groups, or on instructional television channels, and they are seen by people who are generally more interested in film content than in film *as* film. In recent years, the audience has become larger because many of these films have been produced for more general viewing on television — along with another form of nonstory film, the television commercial, but even here the audience is chiefly interested in content, not form.

Whether seen on television or in a movie theater, the largest body of nonfiction films viewed by the general public is the **documentary,** a film that explores or documents the world of fact. Documentaries may, of course, differ widely in their philosophic, aesthetic, and technical approach to their subject matter. *The Incredible Machine* (PBS, 1977), a documentary recording the processes of the human body, aims to convey specific information objectively and entertainingly; such a film will simplify, perhaps, but it will attempt to be as clear and comprehensible as possible. A film like Robert Flaherty's *Man of Aran* (1934) is a documentary too, but its aim is less to convey the specific details of a process than to record a life of struggle as man confronts a beautiful but hostile environment. *The Incredible Machine* attempts to communicate information, and *Man of Aran* attempts to communicate a theme, but both films attempt to use the tools of cinema artistically. *The Incredible Machine* avails itself of the spectacular imagery which can be obtained through **microcinematography** and color. *Man of Aran* uses the moving camera, natural lighting, composition in the frame, and sound to create visual and aural beauty and, hence, to move its audience to appreciate the film's human subjects and their struggle. Yet another kind of documentary, like *Hunger in America* (CBS News, 1968), is equally interested in affecting its audience, but its emphasis on artistic devices is negligible. A documentary can be as primitive as a home movie (indeed, those first films taken by the Lumière brothers *were* home movies) or as complexly constructed as the Nazi propaganda film *Triumph of the Will* (Leni Riefenstahl, 1935) or the American antiwar film *Hearts and Minds* (Peter Davis, 1974).

There is another body of nonstory films which is as diverse as it is generally unheralded. These films have been called (inadequately) **experimental films, avant-garde films, independent films,** noncommercial films, abstract films, and art films. Whatever the name, most of these films are chiefly concerned with film form. Most are made by filmmakers who wish to create a cinematic art object, who use the camera and film stock and light source as substitutes for the paints and canvases, chisels and stones of fine artists. Sometimes the films are representational, showing the viewer human beings who speak and move in comprehensible or incomprehensible situations. At other times, the films can be totally abstract, using color and light and motion to create random or structured patterns. Some of the films are just to be looked at for their aesthetic appeal, while others make statements or explore the meaning and function of art and the cinema through their assault on the audience and its expectations. Nearly all use the medium in a nontraditional manner.

Chapter 7 will examine the major forms of the documentary film and Chapter 8 will look at the experimental cinema.

Historical Overview:
The Development of the
Documentary Film

FROM SILENT TO SOUND

Influenced by the Industrial Revolution's emphasis on science and technology, Louis and Auguste Lumière made their first films in 1895 not from an urge to tell stories but to reproduce reality, to record and document life around them. These filmed scenes from real life (workers leaving the factory, a train arriving), however, could not indefinitely hold the imagination and attention of the viewing public. Although from 1895 to 1907 most films were documentary films — or, perhaps more appropriately, film documents — after 1907 such films were on the decline. Audience interest in film's ability to capture reality was undercut by the growing production of fake documentaries, which were often much more exciting to watch than the film record of the "real thing." The narrative film in which the emergent art of film editing *altered* reality and created drama as it manipulated time and space appealed to audiences more than films of unstructured reality. Although **newsreels** became a regular part of the movie program in 1910 when both Pathé and Gaumont in France released the first sets of composite documentary "news" footage, the public's chief interest in the movies had permanently shifted to the narrative film. As a result, although many documentary films throughout the century functioned as theatrical entertainment, the history of the form has generally been allied to noncommercial enterprise and has been developed by those filmmakers, governments, and social institutions who saw in the cinema a medium which had the power to move people to social and political action.

After the Revolution of 1917, for instance, Lenin, seeing the need to educate people in remote areas of Russia to the purposes of the Revolution, asserted the alliance between film and the newly formed Soviet government. This educative function, along with the pressing political need to establish a sense of national unity and pride, became the basic motive for nonfiction filmmaking in the Soviet Union. Thus, the Soviet newsreel *Kino-Nedelia (Film Weekly)* was not only taken across the country on trains which screened films aboard for rural patrons but the films were also changed en route, as chief editor Dziga Vertov filmed additional material and, in a kind of ongoing process of documenting reality, incorporated it into subsequent screenings.

Vertov, a seminal figure in Soviet filmmaking and in documentary aesthetics, called for cinema to reject the artificiality of scripts, constructed sets, and actors in favor of its true subject: real life. Despite this call for cinema to avoid manipulating its subject matter before the camera, Vertov also believed it necessary that the cinematographer and the film editor illuminate unmanipulated and spontaneous reality through full use of the camera's unique properties and through editing. Thus, in his own weekly newsreel, *Kino-Pravda,* which ran from 1922 until 1925, and in his later and highly influential *The Man with a Movie Camera* (1928), Vertov uses slow, fast, and reverse motion, animation, microcinematography, and **multiple exposure** as cinematic devices which revealed life as it was lived in ways physiologically unavailable to the viewer but "real" nonetheless (Figure 1). Vertov's writings and films — though themselves limited to the period between two wars — have continued to influence both those filmmakers who wish to record life as it is lived with a minimum of mediation between that life and the camera, and also those filmmakers who wish to shape reality by participating in it during shooting and editing.

In America, after World War I, the documentary impulse manifested itself in the emergence of the feature-length **travelogue.** Americans were interested in seeing life as it was lived — but as it was lived elsewhere. Beginning with travelogue records of their explorations made as early as 1912, Martin and Osa Johnson pleased commercial audiences with exotic films from darkest Africa in which great white filmmakers unself-consciously patronized their native subjects. Although the Johnsons' films proved immensely popular, it was the success of Robert Flaherty's *Nanook of the North* (1922), a film about Eskimo life, which really initiated a concerted effort to film other cultures in other lands. Because of its artistry and its exoticism, *Nanook* excited a twofold interest: in what has come to be called the **ethnographic film,** and also in the documentary's commercial potential for dealing with real life in a dramatically satisfying cinematic structure. Flaherty dramatized as he recorded, using varying camera angles and distances which best showed the heroic qualities of a man using simple tools and great skill to survive in a beautiful but hostile landscape. The film gave

★ **1**   The trolley cars in Dziga Vertov's THE MAN WITH A MOVIE
CAMERA (1928) are a good example of the difficulty of categorizing this
film. Frequently (as here) the trolley cars are simply a mode of transportation
recorded in normal time, with a normal lens. The image is documentary. At
other times, however, the speed of the trolleys is increased, mirror images are
used, and the trolleys turn into abstract forms, hurtling across the opaque frame.

rise to the term "documentary," and because of its application of cinematic
technique to real subject matter deserves to be cited as the first true
documentary feature film.

   Nanook began a trend in dramatic ethnography exemplified by the efforts
of explorer-filmmakers Merian C. Cooper and Ernest Schoedsack in *Grass*
(1925), which followed a mass migration of herdsmen through mountains
in Turkey and Persia and in *Chang* (1927), a follow-up which moved toward
fiction in its dramatization of a Siamese family. These film explorers seemed
bent on discovering spectacle (and finally created their own in a total fiction
enlivened by documentary technique, *King Kong,* 1933). Flaherty himself was
sent to Samoa by Paramount to make "another *Nanook,*" but returned
instead with *Moana* (1926), a gentle film with little of the natural conflict
between man and his environment found in *Nanook*. In commercial despera-
tion, Paramount misguidedly advertised the film as "the love life of a
South Sea siren" and the film, not delivering what was promised, proved a
box-office flop. Flaherty's short association with Hollywood was terminated,
but he continued making his documentaries under various nontheatrical
auspices; his first sound film, *Man of Aran* (1934), was made in England,
for example, and his *Louisiana Story* (1948) was sponsored by an oil company.

SOUND AND SOCIAL REFORM

Despite the relative success of exotic documentaries in the 1920s, it was not until the introduction of sound to the cinema in 1927 that the documentary form could begin to realize its potential as an educative, social, and political force. In America, Fox Movietone News in May of 1927 began releasing newsreels using the first optical sound system; such newsreels became part of nearly every theatrical exhibitor's programming. But, newsreel production aside, there was little interest in developing feature-length documentaries in the United States, where film was regarded as show business and movies were a commercial product.

The situation in England, however, was different. When the Depression hit Great Britain in 1929, a brash, inexperienced, self-taught student of media named John Grierson went to a governmental unit called the Empire Marketing Board and convincingly argued that film production should be one of the board's ways of informing the public about Britain's food supply. Thus, Grierson became the director of the board's Film Unit and in 1929 released the first of the only two films he ever actually made. *Drifters,* a classic example of the kind of film that was to exemplify British documentary's golden age, makes exciting and socially relevant the everyday dangers faced by herring fishermen in the North Sea. Filmmakers who joined Grierson's unit were instructed to make ordinary reality and peacetime as exciting and provocative on the screen as were extraordinary events like war. Grierson was intent on showing the British workingman to himself and educating him to the social realities around him.

These British documentaries at first were relatively straightforward in their glorification of the British workingman, but as time went on the productions became more complex and drew on the talents of such leading artists as poet W. H. Auden and composer Benjamin Britten to explore the dynamic possibilities of sound. *Night Mail* (Basil Wright and Harry Watt, 1936), for example, is intended on a factual level to show the process of mail delivery by train. Aesthetically, however, the film is an aural and visual poem to man, machine, and the work they perform. Montage editing combined with Britten's score and Auden's chanted narration demonstrates the complexity and formal beauty of the British documentary of the 1930s at the same time that it demonstrates its basis in the everyday activities of British life. Although the Film Unit was terminated as part of the Empire Marketing Board in 1932, production did not cease; the unit was taken over by the General Post Office with Grierson still at its head.

The British documentary strongly influenced the emergent genre in Depression America. So, too, did a handful of documentaries made in various European countries, films that took social and political stands like *Borinage*

(Henri Storck and Joris Ivens, 1933), which pled the cause of Belgian coal miners, or *Land Without Bread* (Luis Buñuel, 1932), which savagely and shockingly recorded poverty in Spain. By the early 1930s an organization named the Film and Photo League had been founded in New York City, and its various branches devoted themselves to the creation of socially significant documentaries addressed to the problems of Depression America. But it wasn't until 1936, when the Roosevelt Administration through its various work programs gave financial backing to filmmaking, that American social documentary had any real impact.

Pare Lorentz, a rebel film critic with no filmmaking experience, was to symbolize the documentary filmmaker of Depression America. Backed by the Resettlement Administration, he made a film depicting the conditions leading to the creation of the Dust Bowl, *The Plow That Broke the Plains* (1936). With the aid of talent culled from the ranks of the Film and Photo League, Lorentz implicated the whole United States in what might have been seen by some as merely a localized agricultural problem. Lorentz's second film, *The River* (1937), made for the Department of Agriculture, traced Mississippi River floodwaters from their beginnings in land depletion to their harnessing by the Tennessee Valley Authority. It so impressed President Roosevelt that he established the United States Film Service through presidential order, a service which was unfortunately short-lived because of criticism of its funding and the distracting conditions leading toward the Second World War.

PERSUASION AND PROPAGANDA

The production of documentaries in America during the Depression and prewar period was not, however, limited to governmental agencies. Thirties America, increasingly conscious of social and economic forces, was caught up by a documentary impulse. In 1935, an emotional, controversial, and blatantly editorial newsreel emerged — *The March of Time*. Practicing "fakery in allegiance to truth," it was so successful in theatrical release that it didn't halt production until 1951, when television began absorbing the visual news function that had been performed by the movies. Supported by American partisans and intellectuals, *This Spanish Earth* (Joris Ivens, 1937) attempted to inform and influence American opinion against the anti-Fascist cause in Spain. At the 1939 World's Fair in New York City, Willard Van Dyke and Ralph Steiner showcased *The City*; using various experimental techniques, it represented those kinds of films which dealt with problems on the home front like housing conditions, racism, unionization, urban blight. And an offshoot of the Film and Photo League, Frontier Films, moved from national to international concerns as the world — and the United States — stood on the brink of war.

During this prewar period the word **propaganda** came into popular use. The "white" propaganda of social reform became the "black" propaganda of Nazi distortion. Hitler, long aware of the potential persuasive power of the cinema, named Joseph Goebbels as Minister of Popular Enlightenment and Propaganda in 1933, the year he came to power. Hitler also assigned Leni Riefenstahl, an actress turned filmmaker, to record the Nazi Party rally in Nuremberg in 1934. The result was *Triumph of the Will,* a film which mobilized all the effects of the medium to cover an event staged as much for the cameras as for the Nazi Party members in attendance. Using simple content (clouds, church spires, flags, crowds, speeches, marching parades), Riefenstahl so skillfully shot and edited her images and sounds that seen today — even with hindsight — *Triumph of the Will* attests to the awesome and frightening power the cinema can wield. Although Riefenstahl went on to make the epic *Olympiad* (1938) about the 1936 Olympic Games held in Berlin, she will be chiefly remembered for *Triumph of the Will.*

In England, the General Post Office Film Unit was renamed the Crown Film Unit. The efforts of the Grierson Golden Age came to fruition in the war films of Alberto Cavalcanti, Harry Watt, and Paul Rotha. In addition, new filmmakers appeared, most notably Humphrey Jennings, who became the leading filmmaker of the war period with *Listen to Britain* (1942), *Fires Were Started* (1943), and *A Diary for Timothy* (1945), films filled with human details which personalized the war effort and lifted morale. In the United States, films were needed for training military personnel and for explaining the United States to her allies abroad. Impressed and chilled by familiarity with brilliant German film propaganda, former Hollywood director Frank Capra borrowed enemy propaganda techniques to produce the *Why We Fight* series for the Signal Corps, the United States Army's filmmaking unit. Originally meant for distribution only to members of the armed services, the series was publicly released and shown in theaters around the United States. Other American-made films which portrayed the dreadful costs in human life caused by the war were victims of suppression; John Huston's *The Battle of San Pietro* (1944) and *Let There Be Light* (1945), for instance, were thought to be too pacifist or depressing in their implications to be shown even to their intended audiences, the men who were doing the fighting.

Although documentary production flourished during the war, it declined in the postwar period. The government's urgent need for propaganda and national mobilization had abated. Industry support also was not widespread. Perhaps, too, a nonfictional presentation of pressing social ills was not what a public weary of wartime deprivation wanted. Two other factors were also largely responsible for the decline of documentary. The first was the emergence of a new medium: television. In the early 1950s, newsreels began to fade from theater screens as television sets began to become part of the furniture of the American home. The new medium immediately proved itself more responsive than weekly newsreels in documenting current events while they were still current. The second factor contributing to the decline of documentary was cinematic technology, the heavy, bulky camera and sound equipment which, as much as any aesthetic or moral philosophy, dictated the structure of documentary film. The lack of portable equipment meant that the documentary form had reached an impasse in its development. This did not mean, of course, that film documentaries were no longer being made. Several classics appeared, among them *The Quiet One* (Sidney Meyers, 1948), which, though scripted, documented a young boy's turmoil in the real context of Harlem, and *Night and Fog* (Alain Resnais, 1955), which explored time and memory in relation to the Nazi death camps (Figure 2). In addition, with John Grierson initially its head, the National Film Board of Canada was busy with documentary production given impetus by the need to define a national character.

DOCUMENTARY AND TELEVISION: NEW TECHNOLOGY AND NEW FORMS

It was television, however, which solved those technological problems and revitalized the film documentary. Initially, television documentary borrowed its social impetus from the tradition of the 1930s and 1940s. Its major form, perfected by the veteran newsman Edward R. Murrow at CBS in the mid-1950s and still predominant today, combined a panoramic view of an American problem interspersed with humanizing interviews with people involved in the problem. Murrow's documentaries on such problems as the plight of migrant workers and hunger in America were emotionally affecting, and seemed hard-hitting at the time, exposing social ills and bringing them into the American living room. But despite some few exceptions, Murrow's belief that television documentary could become the conscience of its time was vitiated by the fact that it was also the conscience of its sponsor and its network; as the form evolved, it tended to take safe positions (e.g., everyone is against hunger) and to ignore or avoid controversial ones. Nonetheless, early television contributed greatly to the changing form of nonfiction filmmaking. The interview was redeemed as a source of visual and aural interest, and this fascination with people revealing themselves led to the development of more improved, portable equipment which would be able to follow people about as they talked and lived their lives. During the 1950s portable 16mm cameras began to replace the bulky

★ **2** In NIGHT AND FOG (1955), Alain Resnais intercuts long color tracking shots of the abandoned concentration camps, as they are over twenty years after the Holocaust, with black-and-white documentary still photos and captured films taken in the camps during the war. Music and poetic narration disturb the viewer's attitude towards the action and places shown in the images, asking him to be aware of the tricks that time and memory play on the human mind.

35mm equipment; shoulders replaced tripods and often the old steady gaze of the camera was sacrificed for hand-held immediacy. But the revolution in documentary filmmaking could not occur without wireless microphones and recording units, a technological breakthrough accomplished by a film unit of Time-Life under the leadership of Robert Drew.

Organized in 1958, the Drew Unit consisted of filmmakers who were to become key figures in the modern documentary movement. There was D. A. Pennebaker, who caught the contemporary and youthful moviegoer's attention with his musically oriented documentaries like *Don't Look Back* (made with Richard Leacock, 1966) and *Monterey Pop* (1968) (Figure 3) and began what was to become a genre of theatrically released and commercially successful rock documentaries, culminating in *Woodstock* (Michael Wadleigh, 1970). There was Albert Maysles, who was to go on to make (with his brother David) one of the enduring classics of modern **direct cinema**, *Salesman* (1969), which followed four Bible salesmen on their rounds and into their motel rooms. And the Drew Unit nurtured Richard

★ 3   D. A. Pennebaker, a key figure in America's modern documentary movement, captured the musically-oriented youthful moviegoer's attention with films like MONTEREY POP (1968). Janis Joplin performs.

Leacock, a filmmaker who had served an apprenticeship with Robert Flaherty and who had come to hate documentary narration that told him what to think instead of letting him think for himself. The unit was finally successful in liberating the camera and microphone and recorder in 1961. But the key film which conveys the excitement of that liberation and which changed the look and sound of the documentary film actually was made a year earlier — before all the "bugs" had been completely ironed out. Made by Robert Drew and Richard Leacock, *Primary* was an on-the-spot record of a campaign for a presidential nomination in a primary election; no narrator acted as mediator between the events and the viewer, and the drama was found through camera movement rather than through emphasis on editing juxtapositions. This film marked the beginning of what was to be properly termed direct cinema — a form which seemed uncontrolled and minimally manipulated by the filmmaker/observer.

Although it was common practice at the time for television networks to commission and broadcast only their own documentaries, the innovative work of the Drew Unit caused ABC to contract for a series of films, making the Drew Unit virtually part of the network. As a result, television viewers became accustomed to a new documentary form which was as ambiguous and immediate as life itself. Public television has also supported the new documentary, commissioning yearly films from one of the direct cinema's leading practitioners, Frederick Wiseman. Once a lawyer, this prolific observer has let his camera record the complexities of public institutions like hospitals, high schools, juvenile courts, and basic training camps.

The American development of direct cinema was not the only documentary response to the new technology which allowed filmmakers to film and record sound with maximum mobility and minimal intervention. In France, the release of *Chronicle of a Summer* (Jean Rouch, 1961) heralded the birth of cinema verité — a form of documentary indiscriminately confused with direct cinema at first because of its similar rejection of traditional narration and manipulative editing and its use of the interview and the long take. Unlike direct cinema films, *Chronicle of a Summer* allows the filmmaker and his camera to play a part in the film, acknowledging their ability to alter and yet reveal reality by their presence, letting them act as catalysts and provocateurs of action. Indeed, the term *cinema verité* — derived from *cinéma vérité*, the French translation of *Kino-Pravda* (literally film-truth) in homage to Dziga Vertov — is meant to describe the film truth generated and created by the filmmaker as well as by the subject matter itself. Practiced chiefly by European documentarists, the form has produced such classics as *Le Joli Mai* (Chris Marker, 1963), and it has strongly influenced such **epic documentaries** as *Phantom India* (Louis Malle, 1968) and *The Memory of Justice* (Marcel Ophuls, 1976).

Today, documentary film has a number of traditions from which it can draw both its philosophical and aesthetic approaches. Most nonfiction films, of course, are created and absorbed by television, but the form still manages to survive independent of television as well. In addition to the popularity of the "rock" documentaries of the 1960s, there have been such relative successes as *The Endless Summer* (Bruce Brown, 1966) and *The Great American Cowboy* (Keith Merril, 1976). The socially conscious documentary also has been popularly represented by *Hearts and Minds* (Peter Davis, 1974) which explores U.S. involvement in Vietnam, and *Harlan County, U.S.A.* (Barbara Kopple, 1976), which combines direct cinema with some cinema verité techniques in a film about striking coal miners. Currently, documentary's strongest impact has been in Latin America, where politically dissident filmmakers have used cinema as a weapon with which to fight political illiteracy and governmental oppression.

7

★ THE DOCUMENTARY FILM

★★★ **The Image of the Real**

> What I think they do is provide something that fiction films cannot pro-
> vide, which is actuality, which is a sense that this is really happening.
> This woman is really having this baby. She is not an actress. She could
> die, right before your eyes. Or perhaps a cretin could be born, or perhaps
> her husband will kiss her and they'll be happy; but whatever is going
> to happen, it will really happen. Fiction films just can't do that.
> Arthur Barron[1]

Documentary film, the representation of real events and people on the
screen, places its major emphasis on educating and persuading the viewer.
The fiction film places major emphasis on entertaining the viewer (though
it may also enlighten him). Because of these seemingly obvious differences, we all tend to know — or think we know — when we are watching
a fiction film and when we are watching a documentary. On what do we
base this assumption? After all, both documentary and fictional image and
sound end up on the screen as only a *representation* of reality. What
distinguishes them is their *presentation* of that representation. It is *why*
the filmmaker approaches the reality before his camera and then *how* he
presents it to the viewer which signal our response to the representation.
The basic premise on which the documentary film is based is that it is
nonfiction — that what is seen and heard on the screen and sound track
was not created expressly for the purposes of making a film — and that
it bears a strong resemblance to what you or I would have seen and
heard had we been at the scene of the filmed event.

Perhaps the most useful way to organize a discussion of the various kinds of documentary film is to look at the relationship the film assumes between its subject matter and the viewer. Does it primarily observe its subject matter? analyze it? shape it to promote or persuade? poeticize or dramatize it? In the process of looking at the films' primary functions we will, of course, also discuss their forms — for certain functions have an affinity for certain structures. But, given the prevalent connection that most viewers make between documentary film and some abstract notion of reality, it is first necessary to examine some of the techniques and choices available to the documentary filmmakers which shape the relationship they create between the original subject matter and the finished film.

★★★ ## Form and Technique

Raw footage is the basic building block of documentary film. This footage is a document, a record of an event which has been minimally influenced by either the process of filming or the process of editing. All film, of course, is subjective (even gun-camera or bank surveillance films show us only selected images of reality), but raw footage is the least subjective, the least influenced by the manipulations of the filmmaker. Thus, even though we occasionally regard the one-shot Lumière films of 1895 Paris as documentaries, they — like raw footage — are better considered documents, primary material which exists as an unconsidered, unevaluated, unordered record. Indeed, therein lies their fascination and beauty; they bring the viewer as close to the primary, real experience they record as is humanly possible. And the presence and sensibility of the filmmaker who made the record is virtually invisible.

But the documentary film that is exhibited is no longer raw footage. Indeed, the term documentary includes, in addition to its associations with reality, the notion of filmic structure unified by a philosophy, ideology, and aesthetic, an *ordering* of that reality from a chosen human perspective. Thus, by ordering the raw footage, the filmmaker acts as a mediator between the viewer and the real event represented by the raw footage. That mediation may be highly visible or it may seem invisible because certain characteristics which indicate the filmmaker's intervention between the subject and the viewer, such as narration, music, and montage editing, have become so conventional through frequent use that they have become invisible to the viewer. In some mediated documentaries, the filmmaker's role as manipulator is obviously revealed to the audience in an attempt at truthfulness which includes the act of making the film as part of the event being filmed.

Whether or not a viewer is consciously aware of the filmmaker's intervention between the subject and himself, certain documentary techniques have evolved through the form's history and are available to the filmmaker who wishes to use them. Thus, the filmmaker can choose to make a film based on long takes which preserve space and time and seem unmediated, or he can choose to stress montage editing with its imposed juxtapositions. He may use only synchronous sound, letting the subject speak for itself, or he may use narration and commentary in voice-over explanations. He may use music for uniting disparate images and for building drama; he may keep the sound track the way it was recorded on the spot, or he may "clean it up" through mixing. He may film only events as they occur (from a suitable distance), or he may interview people confronted by the camera. He may create an entire film from material shot by others, archival footage which, when edited together, makes what has been called the compilation film. Or he may straddle the line between reality and fiction by restaging and re-creating events or by combining actual events with fictional events. A few or many of these devices may be used, depending upon the filmmaker's philosophy of documentary and his film's ultimate function. And these techniques will be embodied in a film structure which is also responsive to the filmmaker's belief and goals. A documentary's structure may be dramatic, based on events which have a built-in or created crisis or culmination like an election or a big rock concert, or they may be organic and cyclical, based on the natural (and not necessarily dramatic) sequences dictated by the subject matter, such as the passing of seasons or the cyclical routine of an institution. They may be shaped so that events are revealed chronologically as they happen or have happened. Or the filmmaker may choose to use sound and images, together and separately, to evoke not only the present but also the past (and often both simultaneously). The filmmaker may even ignore time completely as an ordering device, so that we are not aware when the images we are watching happened.

Which techniques and which structures a filmmaker chooses for a given film tell us something about the filmmaker's relationship to the reality of the raw footage and about his relationship to the viewer and the film's intended function.

★★★ **Documentary Functions**

OBSERVATION

I've been trying to make a series of films on contemporary American institutions, but each time I go out, it's a kind of voyage of discovery. I think if you knew what the film was going to look like before you

started, then you'd simply be imposing a stereotype on a situation, and you wouldn't be learning anything or thinking about what you'd experienced.
Frederick Wiseman[2]

The maker of a documentary chooses to be a certain kind of observer. The decision not to interfere in the event happening before the camera and not to impose more than a minimal structure in the editing process is not inevitable; rather, it reflects a specific documentary philosophy. This philosophy is based on three beliefs: (1) that the integrity of the reality being filmed must be maintained, (2) that there is an inherent meaning in the event, and (3) that the camera cannot only record but also reveal this meaning to the viewer without explanatory mediation by the filmmaker. Two major forms of documentary adopt this philosophy of intervening as little as possible: the **ethnographic film** and **direct cinema.**

Ethnography, a branch of anthropology, attempts to describe the specific cultures of the various peoples of the world. Because ethnographers emphasize description over analysis, and because their major arenas of study usually have been exotically located, those who have used the film medium for ethnographic purposes have also been able to create films that the general public finds fascinating. Thus, *Dead Birds* (Robert Gardner, 1963), made to observe the war-based culture of the Dani tribe of New Guinea, is more than scientifically gripping; its exoticism and pictorial beauty hold us, and our cultural collision with another system of war raises certain philosophical issues (Figure 7-1). The film, of course, is not sheer raw footage. It combines long takes and a moving camera, which preserve the integrity of time and space with some lyrical and suggestive montage, and it uses narration to tell us what the people we are watching are doing — and occasionally what they are feeling. However, the film maintains a generally cool, scientifically observant position and is thus both good science and good film.

The same basic problems face today's ethnographic filmmakers that faced Robert Flaherty long ago when he made the first ethnographic feature, *Nanook of the North* (1922). Certainly, the technology has changed to allow today's ethnographer to follow his subject and preserve that spatial and temporal continuity which authenticates his observation and allows the viewer freedom to draw his own conclusions from the filmed material — and, of course, there is sound. But the ethnographer must still find the structure which best represents his material. Flaherty chose a chronological one, showing the life and inherent drama of an Eskimo as he moves through the seasons of the year (Figure 7-2). The ethnographer must also consider and avoid or recognize and incor-

★ 7-1 Ethnographic film attempts to capture a native culture as a record for anthropologists with as little interference as possible by the camera crew — either during the filming or afterwards in the editing process. Robert Gardner, however, in DEAD BIRDS (1963), though describing aspects of the daily life and customs of the Dani tribe in New Guinea, focused on their peculiar formalized warfare system in order to make an implicit comparison with contemporary civilized man's more brutal, spontaneous, irrational forms of warfare.

porate his own cultural bias and the way it influences what he looks at and from what vantage point. *Nanook* occasionally falls victim to cultural bias, as when a title equates an Eskimo baby with a Husky puppy, but it redeems itself by the fact that Flaherty enlisted the Eskimo's help in determining the events in the film. Indeed, some current practice harks back to Flaherty; today, ethnographers often teach the group to be filmed to use the camera and thus to make the film, so that the cultural bias exhibited is that of the culture under study.

Stylistically, ethnographic film is marked by plentiful use of long takes, the zoom lens, and a moving, often hand-held, camera — all of which serve to maintain temporal and spatial continuity and thus preserve the integrity of the individual shots. Both synchronous source sound and asynchronous voice-over narration are used, the first to authenticate the reality of the image and the second to explain what would otherwise be incomprehensible to the Western viewer. Perhaps because ethnographic films so frequently record primitive and agrarian cultures, their editing is often based on seasonal cycles or on ritual events.

In some ways direct cinema is very similar to ethnographic film. The aim of the filmmaker is to observe and record an uncontrolled situation — one neither controlled by the dictates of the camera or by the filmmaker's initial conception of the material nor influenced and changed by the act of filming itself. But whereas scientific observation motivates the ethnographer who films an alien culture, the direct cinema filmmaker generally looks at some aspect of his own and the viewer's culture and has no specifically defined or socially approved motive for his act of observation. What is considered respectable scientific observation in a film like *Dead Birds* may often seem like unethical voyeurism in a direct

★ 7-2   Many of the same problems face ethnographic filmmakers today that faced Robert Flaherty when he made NANOOK OF THE NORTH (1922). The filmmaker must try to eliminate his own cultural biases, and at the same time find a structure which best represents the material. Flaherty chose a chronological structure for NANOOK based on seasons of the year.

cinema film or series of films like *An American Family* (Alan and Susan Raymond, 1973), a series which raised extremely controversial questions about the presence of camera and crew as intruders and catalysts in the lives of a California family. Thus, in direct cinema the very choice of subject matter often raises ethical and moral issues, issues dealing with distinctions between observation and voyeurism, with violations of privacy, and with the insidious or unconscious manipulation of events so as to create drama where there was none. And all these issues seem to be heightened by the complex ambiguity of direct cinema, which, unlike the ethnographic film, uses no narration to explain itself or to distance the viewer (through the mediation of an intervening human voice) from the event being filmed.

   One of direct cinema's leading practitioners, Frederick Wiseman, has to some degree circumvented some of these issues by choosing to observe and explore well-defined American social institutions supported by public taxes and therefore legitimately open to examination. In films like *High School* (1968), *Law and Order* (1969), *Hospital* (1970), *Basic Training* (1971), *Juvenile Court* (1973) and *Welfare* (1975), Wiseman's aim — like the ethnographer's — is to present the everyday life of institutions rather than to compile a string of dramatic but exceptional moments. Like the ethnographer, he is interested in the ordinary process of the institution he records, and his films, therefore, take their shape from the recurrent and cyclical functions of institutional life. Wiseman sees his function as recording with as little polemic, rhetoric, or ego as possible the thing itself — so that the viewers are finally responsible for what they make of what they see on the screen. It is evidence of his success that many of his films have excited controversy and have produced opposing interpretations of their meaning; *Law and Order*, for example, has been viewed as presenting a very fair and somewhat positive portrait of the Kansas City police department — but it has also been praised (by groups unsympathetic to increasing police power) as an antipolice documentary which emphasizes police brutality and ineffectiveness.

The ambiguity of another type of direct cinema is more problematic, raising those moral and ethical issues previously cited. Albert and David Maysles have been perhaps the foremost practitioners of films whose subject matter tends to bring both the filmmaker and the viewer into uncomfortable confrontation with the nature of their curiosity and with the purposes and implications of the act of filmmaking and the act of viewing. Although Wiseman seems socially justified in turning his cameras on public institutions, it is less clear what justifies the choice of a group of door-to-door Bible salesmen or two bizarre and eccentric relatives of Jacqueline Bouvier Kennedy Onassis as subject matter, choices made by the Maysles brothers in their landmark film *Salesman* (1969) and in *Grey Gardens* (1976). They initially avoided such issues by focusing their cameras on people who were already public figures: politicians in *Primary* (1960), performers in *Meet Marlon Brando* (1965) and *Gimme Shelter* (1970). Indeed, these public subjects not only helped the filmmakers sidestep the issue of an exploitative invasion of privacy, but they also helped to give the filmmaker a dramatic structure for the films: a political contest accelerating toward a climactic election, a performer moving toward the moment of performance. Unlike the ethnographer and unlike Wiseman, the Maysles brothers look for the extraordinary and exceptional moments in ordinary life and for subjects which offer a built-in dramatic structure as they show crises, contests, and conflicts. Thus, their films avoid cyclic editing and tend to be shaped dramatically, emphasizing through camera movement and editing what has been called the "privileged moment" in which another human being reveals himself to the camera and the viewer.

Stylistically, direct cinema is much like ethnographic film in its use of the long take, zoom lens, and moving, hand-held camera. It does not, however, use narration, relying only on synchronous sound. Often the images and sound in early films were characterized by their technical crudity; unsteady, out-of-focus images, poor lighting, and flawed sound tracks were the result of inadequate technology in uncontrolled and spontaneous filming circumstances. Paradoxically, these flaws have come to suggest both immediacy and authenticity to the film viewer and even with today's technological advances, many contemporary filmmakers deliberately choose a crude style as proof of their film's unmanipulated and uncontrolled nature.

Direct cinema is an excitingly controversial documentary form. Often its unvoiced but omnipresent moral tensions are what make it so fascinating, compelling, and illuminating, and it has been praised as nonreductive in its approach, respecting rather than explaining life as it is lived. But such tensions have also led to criticism that the form is exploitative and voyeuristic. It has been charged with being overeager to catch people in private moments, with appealing to a suspect curiosity, and with pretending — through the effacement of the filmmaker's presence behind the camera — to offer an objectivity neither really felt nor practiced. In the final analysis, direct cinema is a film form and methodology only as ethical as the filmmaker behind the camera.

ANALYSIS

> I try to get all the facts from both sides, but I always accept the challenge to take sides. I don't even believe in the word "objectivity." I try to express my political views in my films. . . . But my views come out by means of irony and contrast and methods like that, not by editorializing or distorting the facts.
> Marcel Ophuls[3]

Documentary filmmakers who choose to analyze their subject matter rather than simply record it have also chosen to acknowledge their own mediation in the filmmaking process. Like ethnographers and the practitioners of direct cinema, documentary analysts believe both in maintaining the integrity of the reality being filmed and in the ability of the camera to uncover meaning in the doings of people. But unlike those documentarians, the analysts wish to explain and illuminate reality by finding and creating relationships between people and events rather than solely by observing them. Thus, the **analytic documentary** is rarely as detached from its subject matter as the ethnographic film or as ambiguous in its presentation as the direct cinema film. While the analytic filmmaker admits his own presence as mediator, he depends on the integrity of the film record and the very scope and breadth of his presentation to give the viewer the feeling that the film is fair-minded even while it is not objective. Thus, analytic documentaries tend to use a broad canvas and to cover the same subject matter from a variety of sources and techniques. There are three major forms of the analytic documentary: the compilation film, cinema verité, and what might be called the epic documentary.

The compilation film is a documentary made solely from already existing footage. The filmmaker may never use a camera himself; rather, he functions primarily as an editor, presenting and analyzing raw footage (made by others for other purposes) through juxtaposition and ordering of the material in the editing process. The most obvious kind of compilation film, and once the most plentiful, is the newsreel — although, strictly speaking, a great deal of its compiled footage was shot for inclusion in such a news magazine format. Key news events of national and international importance, incorporating footage often shot for other purposes (for example, battle footage), would begin the newsreel. This was followed by lighter material which almost always included some footage about women (such as a fashion show or bathing beauty contest) and finally sports. The selection of material was determined as much by its ability to remain interesting and "news," despite the weekly intervals between issues, as by its actual importance. Analysis was supplied primarily by voice-over narration and secondarily by "headline" titles between segments. Much more significant is the feature-length compilation film which, through the juxtaposition of archival footage, attempts to analyze history through film records of events and people. Indeed, the compilation film generally makes history its subject matter, availing itself of raw footage found in national archives, newsreels contemporaneous with the historical events under scrutiny, and even "home movies" (Eva Braun and Hitler's have found their way into many compilation films about the Third Reich). The resultant films tend to be panoramic, and thus are often shown as a series of films as well as separate works; one can point to a twenty-six-episode series like *Victory at Sea* (NBC, 1952–1953), which analyzed U.S. naval action in World War II or to the feature-length *To Die in Madrid* (Frédéric Rossif, 1962), which analyzed General Franco's rise to power.

Stylistically, the compilation film is fairly easy to identify. It is composed of relatively short pieces of footage which are linked, most commonly, by voice-over narration, occasional music, and by the editorial relationships imposed on the images by the filmmaker. Compared to other kinds of analytic documentary, the compilation film tends to mask the presence of the filmmaker-analyst; because the authentic raw footage often overwhelms the viewer, interpretive narration and editing seem almost invisible or simply true. Indeed, one contemporary practitioner of compilation film — Emile de Antonio — has done away with external narration completely in some of his films like *Point of Order!* (1964), which analyzes McCarthyism, and *Millhouse: A White Comedy* (1971), which presents a scathing and often funny analysis of Richard Nixon's political career. De Antonio depends on the juxtaposition of sound as much as he does on the juxtaposition of imagery; *Point of Order!* is austere in its use of synchronous source sound, but *Millhouse* goes so far as to use asynchronous music to shape our responses to the imagery. At one point, for example, the image shows us a head being reverently lifted into position atop a wax-museum statue of Nixon while the sound track plays "Pomp and Circumstance." Whether the compilation film seeks to analyze history through panoramic means or through a selective use of primary film and television documents, it remains the most seemingly unmediated by the filmmaker.

The second major form of analytic documentary, cinema verité, is a form unfortunately often confused with direct cinema because of many stylistic similarities between the two types of films. Both forms tend toward technical crudeness: **high-grain** images produced by fast film which can record under poor lighting conditions, frequent use of the hand-held camera, haphazard composition, flawed sound tracks. Both forms also depend primarily on a cinema of duration, on the long take and the moving camera (which preserve the temporal and spatial continuity of the event being filmed), on minimal manipulation through editing, and on a synchronous sound track. Indeed, there is very little stylistic difference between direct cinema and cinema verité — except for the fact that cinema verité makes extensive use of the interview and therefore contains many images in which "talking heads" address the camera. Philosophically and functionally, however, cinema verité is quite opposite from direct cinema. The verité filmmaker sees himself not as an observer but as catalyst and participant. Recognizing that the act of filming changes the event being filmed, the verité filmmaker becomes an active part of the film; one can hear him asking his subjects questions and engaging in dialogue with them, and one can occasionally see him and his camera reflected in mirrors or even in the action itself. Indeed, this notion of the filmmaker as participant rather than mere observer harkens back to Dziga Vertov, the Soviet theorist and filmmaker responsible for the newsreel *Kino-Pravda* (for which cinema verité is the French translation) and *The Man with a Movie Camera* (1928), in which the cinematographer is an integral part of the action. This participatory function of the filmmaker explains the presence of the interview in so many verité films. The practitioner of direct cinema, dedicated to non-interference, can only observe an interview if it should happen before his camera; the verité filmmaker can cause it to happen and can be either the interviewer or the interviewed.

The function of cinema verité is analytic — to explore relationships among people and events and to understand them. Thus, as a way of countering its subjectivity, it tends to focus panoramically on its subject matter. The titles of the films often indicate their attempt at breadth: *Chronicle of a Summer* (Jean Rouch, 1961), *Le Joli Mai* (Chris Marker, 1963). *Chronicle of a Summer* — made by the father of the verité movement and coiner of the term in homage to Vertov — asks Parisians on the street if they're happy, follows several of them about as they live their lives, interviews them on camera and also leaves them to their own devices in front of it, resulting at times in confession and moments of extreme emotion. In addition, Rouch screened the raw footage for the film's featured participants, provoking a discussion of the footage which also became part of the film. And, in a final attempt at film "truth," he and his collaborator Edgar Morin discuss — in the film — what they have learned from their experience making the film. This is far removed from direct cinema.

The compilation film and cinema verité come together in the third major form of analytic documentary, which because of its relatively recent appearance has no "official" designation. However, the form might well be called the **epic documentary** because it is characterized by its broad scope and its great length. Its combination of compilation film techniques (the juxtaposition of archival footage) with cinema verité techniques (primarily the interview) results in a unique structure; both past and present become temporal realities in the film when a piece of archival footage is juxtaposed with a contemporary interview of someone who had been present in that past event, or — even more complexly — when a piece of archival footage might be simultaneously accompanied by a past participant speaking in the present and with hindsight. The foremost practitioner of epic documentary has thus far been Marcel Ophuls. His *The Sorrow and the Pity* (1970) attempts through four and a half hours of archival footage and contemporary interviews to understand occupied France under the Nazis (Figure 7-3). Indeed, it is through its very breadth and duration that the complexity of the event is recorded with all its contradictory evidence. In another epic film, *The Memory of Justice* (1976), Ophuls similarly explores and analyzes the

★ **7-3** Marcel Ophuls, the foremost practitioner of epic documentary, attempts through over four hours of archival footage and interviews in THE SORROW AND THE PITY (1970) to understand occupied France under the Nazis.

issues of individual and collective responsibility, focusing primarily on the Nuremberg war crimes trials of 1946–1947 but also making visual, aural, and thematic reference to France's relationship to Algeria and America's to Vietnam. The film runs more than four and a half hours in its careful accumulation of human and historical documentation — and again the filmmaker is an intimate and obvious part of the film.

PERSUASION

I sat alone and pondered. How could I mount a counterattack against *Triumph of the Will;* keep alive *our* will to resist the master race? I was alone; no studio, no equipment, no personnel. Commandeering a Hollywood studio for this effort seemed out of the question. Could I plan idea films and turn them over to the Signal Corps for production? Did they have the creative brains to cope with such propaganda blockbusters as *Triumph of the Will?* No. . . . The struggle for men's minds was too new, too highbrow, too screwball for old-line colonels who still referred to soldiers as "bodies."

Frank Capra[4]

★ **7-4** Though documentaries can be made about any aspect of human life, the documentary impulse frequently is allied with a social conscience. The documentary filmmaker turns his camera on problems within the society. In THE EXILES (Kent Mackenzie, 1959–1961) the life of Native Americans in Los Angeles is presented, showing the hardships and difficulties faced by Indians living in an alien culture.

There are many kinds of **persuasive documentary** films, films which attempt to make a pitch, sell or promote an idea, change a point of view, make an appeal for some cause, incite the viewer to economic, social, or political action (Figure 7-4). Some of the films excite little controversy despite their manipulative techniques because the viewer already agrees with the position of the film, or because the film attempts to persuade by selectively emphasizing known characteristics of a given subject matter, or because the filmmaker or some spokesman openly and unthreateningly proclaims his position. Some films on controversial topics are so insidious or so effective, however, that they are usually termed *propaganda*. These films are seen as dangerous because the viewer disagrees with the film's position, or because the film distorts its subject matter, or because its method of persuasion is hidden or particularly meant to appeal to emotion at the expense of reason. Whether used for good or ill, the persuasive documentary can be extraordinarily powerful because it manipulates all the elements of film to make its point — a fact recognized by Adolf Hitler and Franklin Delano Roosevelt, by Leni Riefenstahl and Frank Capra.

Stylistically, persuasive films tend to be eclectic, using whatever means will accomplish their ends, whatever technique will best convey their messages. Thus, persuasive films may include archival footage, film shot contemporaneously, animation, reconstruction and dramatization, music, narration, synchronous and asynchronous sound, interviews, and so forth. Despite their variety, however, persuasive films have one element in common: they are all highly dependent upon the editing process for their power, and therefore they generally have a greater number of separate shots in them than do other documentaries. Whereas the analytic documentary attempts to be panoramic and inclusive, the persuasive documentary's focus is narrow and selective. There are two major forms of persuasive documentary: the **exposé** and the propaganda film.

The documentary exposé owes its popularity to television and the particular efforts of Edward R. Murrow, who pioneered the form for CBS and created a documentary series in 1951 called *See It Now*. The form uses analysis toward a persuasive end that is openly stated, usually by an on-camera narrator or reporter. The strategy is to lay bare what are assumed to be hitherto unknown facts to the viewer and, then, to appeal to the viewer as a reasoning and responsible person who, now aware of previously unknown or unavailable information, cannot do otherwise than take a position toward the subject matter similar to the filmmaker's. Once the evidence is exposed, the filmmaker's position seems rational and hardly controversial. But, on occasion, the subject under scrutiny may be extremely controversial. For example, Murrow's *Report on Senator McCarthy* (1954) not only exposed the Red Scare and the man who exploited it, but also called for America to censure his activities; and the more recent *The Selling of the Pentagon* (Peter Davis, 1971) both exposed the ways in which the United States Department of Defense promoted militarism with propaganda and also called for an end to such bureaucratic and dishonest manipulation of both the press and the American people. At other times, the exposé may shock or surprise viewers into awareness but the subject itself — and the position taken — is not controversial. Both *Harvest of Shame* (David Lowe, 1960) and *Hunger in America* (CBS, 1968) treat issues — the abominable living and working conditions of migrant workers and the widespread incidence of starvation and malnutrition in the United States — which, once presented, can only evoke the unanimous response that such conditions are socially undesirable. Thus, the exposé s primary method is to educate viewers and then explicitly or implicitly exhort them to action. The filmmaker usually plays an overt role, acknowledging his mediation between reality and the viewers by presenting himself or a surrogate figure — the narrator or an onscreen investigative reporter — within the film. Although the selection of raw footage and the juxtaposition of shots in editing (commonly to shock the viewer), are made to seem relatively invisible, the purpose of the film (to reveal inequities) and the presence of the filmmaker (an informed and indignant guide) are made internally clear.

Since all films examining reality are in some way social and political utterances which intend to influence the viewer, they all share elements of the most manipulative documentary form, propaganda. In *Mein Kampf* (1924), Adolf Hitler defined propaganda as an art that by using "appropriate psychological form" can "awaken the imagination of the public through an appeal to their feelings." This definition of propaganda describes all persuasive film which moves us emotionally — from the social propaganda films of the golden age of British documentary in the 1930s (made to instill pride in the viewer by celebrating the English workingman through driving editorial rhythms and emotionally stirring music and rhetoric) to the exposé documentary like *Harvest of Shame*, which shocked the viewer as it educated. (This film was shrewdly broadcast on Thanksgiving Day, so that Americans stuffing themselves with turkey might feel guilty as they realized the food they were eating came from the backbreaking and poorly rewarded labor of exploited migrant farm workers.) Although none of us likes to feel that our feelings have been manipulated through the use of an "appropriate psychological form," nearly all persuasive films fit Hitler's definition of propaganda.

Propaganda is not inherently evil. It can, however, be evil in its function if it persuades its consumers to perform unjust actions. Because the Nazis extensively used propaganda, certain Nazi assumptions have come to seem permanently linked to the notion of propaganda. Hitler assumed that people were fairly stupid and their memories short-lived. Based on these assumptions, Nazi propaganda found the appropriate psychological format in the reduction of reality to simple, easily remembered symbols and stereotypes and in outright distortion, so that it presented, as Hitler wrote, "only that aspect of the truth which is favorable to its own side."

Such was the method of two propaganda works (one German, one American) which are today considered classics of the form: Leni Riefenstahl's *Triumph of the Will* (1935) and Frank Capra's *Why We Fight* series (1942–1945). Although there are many differences between them, there are also many similarities, notably editing that stimulates the audience to sympathize with the cause being espoused. Thus, while it may seem shocking to link a film that promotes Nazi ideology with a film that promotes a democratic ideology, stylistically they have a great deal in common.

Both Riefenstahl and Capra (who studied Riefenstahl's films to combat them) juxtaposed relatively simple imagery to create emotional con-

★ **7-5** Leni Riefenstahl created in TRIUMPH OF THE WILL (1935) one of the most talked-about examples of propaganda film ever made. This film depicts Hitler and his cause favorably, and the word *propaganda* has become associated with evil ends. During World War II, however, the Allies also relied upon propaganda films to motivate their populations.

nections. The opening sequences of *Triumph of the Will* connect low-angle shots of Hitler with recurrent images of clouds and church and building spires, linking the man visually with stereotypical images connoting spirituality, loftiness, the deity; later sequences repeat images of marching parades, boots in step, flags flying in the wind — all edited together to amplify a feeling of exuberance and rhythm and joyful unity (Figure 7-5). In Capra's series, the editing arouses emotion more through contrast than accumulation and repetition. *War Comes to America* (1945), for example, juxtaposes shots of American children playing innocuous games with shots (which were staged) of Japanese children and German children playing war games. Neither Riefenstahl nor Capra was reluctant to create and stage the content of images that were presented in the film as reality. Riefenstahl's job was easier than Capra's because the Nuremberg rally of 1934 was itself staged as much for her cameras as it was for the Nazis in attendance; Hitler had planned on a film being made to glorify the event and to rally the German people to his cause. Capra went even further, since his film was primarily a compilation film; not only did he stage certain sequences but he also intercut raw footage with fiction footage (never identified as fiction) gathered from many sources. Capra also used animation which was geared to evoke a simple, almost visceral, response from the viewer: the Axis powers' march through Europe is reduced to an almost primally frightening black ooze which threatens to engulf a map of the world in darkness, or like an octopus, the march is represented by tentacles which stretch to grasp anything within reach in a stranglehold.

Finally, both filmmakers use music and sound to sway the viewer's emotions. The sound track of *Triumph of the Will* is pervasively insidious. There is no spoken commentary; rather, the sound track consists of martial parade music mixed with the sounds of marching feet, cheering crowds, and the speeches made by Hitler and his associates at the rally. Again, as with the imagery, the effect is cumulative: Hitler becomes associated with constant cheering and the viewer, rhythmically caught up in the drumbeats and marching footsteps, becomes united with those at the rally. Although *Why We Fight* is word-dominated, music and sound effects are still extremely important. For instance, Capra shows images of Hitler touring a captured Paris juxtaposed with a sound track on which Judy Garland sings "The Last Time I Saw Paris." The narration is authoritative and exhortative; the language (for example, words like "free" and "slave"), strong in emotional associations; the individual sentences relatively short and phrased like slogans (easy to remember): the narrator, speaking over a triumvirate shot of Hirohito, Mussolini, and Hitler, orders the viewer to "take a good look at this trio. Remember their faces. If you ever meet them, don't hesitate." Elsewhere in the film the narrator assures the viewer that despite Axis aggression "free men are like rubber balls. The harder they fall, the higher they bounce."

Clearly, the methods used by both Riefenstahl and Capra are similar: there are few differences, if any, between the techniques of "good" and "evil" propaganda films. Techniques are themselves neither good nor evil. It is the cause they wish to persuade us to which is open to moral judgement.

AESTHETIC EXPRESSION: POETRY AND DRAMA

> From Flaherty I really learned almost feeling things instead of looking at things with a camera . . . ; he conveyed to me what it's like to discover something visually with a camera. They're very, very subtle things, extremely hard to talk about meaningfully. Flaherty had a little line he was fond of: How in the world do you teach somebody to smell a rose?
> Richard Leacock[5]

John Grierson, founder of the British documentary movement of the 1930s, once said that documentary was the "creative treatment of ac-

★ 7-6 NIGHT MAIL (Basil Wright and Harry Watt, 1936) used poetic devices
(including a narrated poem on the sound track) and a highly aesthetic
visual style to communicate the energy and excitement inherent in what
might be considered the commonplace delivery of mail from England to
Scotland.

tuality." Though he believed that film should always be used in the
service of socially relevant subject matter, he recognized that applying
the techniques of poetry and drama to documentary material could educate and illuminate the viewer in ways that a straightforward approach
might not. The Grierson-produced *Night Mail* (Basil Wright and Harry
Watt, 1936), for example, uses poetic devices (including a narrative
poem on the sound track) and a highly aesthetic visual style to communicate the energy and excitement inherent in what might be considered the commonplace train delivery of mail from England to Scotland (Figure 7-6). Although style and poetry are used to reveal the
subject, the film's subject is still the mail delivery, not its own style.

Robert Flaherty, too, although he has been criticized for forsaking
social concerns, always subordinated his visual poetry to the reality of
his subject. Generally considered the foremost, as well as the first, practitioner of the poetic documentary, Flaherty had a sense of beauty that
was an integral part of his vision. Flaherty has produced monumentally
beautiful images on the screen, but his subject matter, the "noble savage" who struggles and wins against the forces of nature, is always
primary. Nature is simultaneously recorded as a harsh reality and as a
metaphor for man's life. The Arctic wastes and drifting snows of *Nanook of the North* awe us with their visual beauty. For example, the
image of a sleeping sled dog, its coat covered with falling snow as it

sleeps outside an igloo, transcends the literalness of its content to function as a metaphor for human sleep, rest, and death. In *Man of Aran* (1934), Flaherty used natural sound to heighten the thrilling images of giant waves crashing against the rock shelves of an island during a storm; the waves are photographed and the film constructed so that the sea becomes personified, seeming in its anger to climb the rock face as if to pursue and destroy the vulnerable family which dares to struggle against its might (Figure 7-7). Whatever the environment, Flaherty found beauty and preserved it in his images: the gentle curves of South Sea palms and beaches in *Moana* (1926), even the majestic carriage of an oil derrick in the Louisiana bayous moving through a natural environment more like a stately dinosaur than a mechanical invader in *Louisiana Story* (1948).

Along with lyric devices, the documentary will often use dramatic devices to engage its audience with the reality recorded in the individual shots. Indeed, almost all documentary films, from the least mediated forms of direct cinema to the most mediated, use drama to varying degrees and from varying sources. Drama may be "found" in front of the camera as part of the reality being recorded, or it may be created, constructed by the editing process.

Perhaps the most widely seen documentary dramas photograph the natural world. Footage of animals and exotic landscapes becomes the raw material of films which tell stories. These films create characters from their animal subjects, and the script and editing create dramatic action. Walt Disney Studios has long been the foremost producer of such films, generally geared for family audiences. Sometimes the footage of unstaged material is combined with staged scenes in which actors perform — and these films really do not fit comfortably into the documentary category. But in many other films, drama is imposed on raw footage; while nothing is staged, the film is created, constructed through editing, to entertain in the manner of fiction. Thus, in *Charlie, the Lonesome Cougar* (Disney, 1967), the two central figures are a cougar named Goodtime Charlie and a terrier named Chainsaw and the funny and dramatic action takes place in a lumber camp in the Cascade Mountains of the Pacific Northwest. The very fact that the animals are characterized by names indicates the tone and the attitude taken toward reality, and an amiable narrator further anthropomorphizes the creatures through his choice of words and his ascribing human feelings and motives to the animals. The film that does not anthropomorphize nature and that still uses it for dramatic purpose is relatively rare, but it does exist. *The Hellstrom Chronicle* (Walon Green, 1971), for example, imposes a science fiction narrative structure on a feature length documentary film

★ 7-7 Many documentaries seem little interested in detailing the facts about a place, a happening, or a culture. Instead they attempt to give the viewer an emotional experience related to the subject. Robert Flaherty, for instance, used natural sound to heighten the thrilling images of giant waves beating against the shore as frail humans attempt to live in an inhospitable landscape in MAN OF ARAN (1934).

about insects; the movie posited an ultimate battle between man and the insect world while it observed its subjects in scientific fashion.

Dramatic documentary uses dramatic structures (such as suspense) and devices (such as parallel editing and the compression and extension of time) to vitalize its content. Sometimes, the drama is "found" in the event being filmed and it does not have to be imposed through editorial structuring. This was true, for example, in *An American Family*, when during the course of the filming, Pat and Bill Loud began to reveal marital problems and decided, on camera, to get a divorce. Indeed, direct-cinema filmmakers who wish to minimize an imposed editorial structure will often choose a subject which is inherently dramatic, which is self-structured toward climactic resolution, which has a built-in crisis. *The Chair* (Drew Associates, 1963), for instance, asks and answers the question: Will a condemned man be executed or will the governor commute the sentence at the last minute? The film uses direct-cinema technique but with multiple cameras so that it can dramatically use parallel editing and cutaway shots showing the electric chair being readied, the defense lawyer hard at work, famed attorney Louis Nizer arriving to help. Indeed, the film opens with an introductory line of narration — "Somewhere in the city of Chicago there is a chair" — which parallels the fictive "Once upon a time." It has even been argued that the film exploits the real events and people in a stereotypically fictional manner: the "hero" is not the condemned man but his attorney, who, relatively untried, is working for nothing; and the prosecutor, made into the "heavy," has the odds on his side. This kind of crisis structure informs many documentaries, from a highly mediated film like *Assault on Mount Everest* (Mike Hoover, 1977), which asks whether the assault by the climbers will end in success, to a minimally structured film like *Waiting for Fidel* (Michael Rubbo, 1976), which amusingly anchors its otherwise self-exploratory nature on the question whether Fidel Castro will show up for a promised interview with three Canadian filmmakers in Cuba to see him.

★★★ Re-Creation: The Ethics of Documentary

When Albert E. Smith returned to New York from Cuba with his San Juan Hill footage, he was worried: in spite of the Roosevelt posturing, it looked like a dull uphill walk, in no way fitting the "charge up San Juan Hill" trumpeted by newspapers. Meanwhile theaters clamored for the Cuban material, already publicized. So Vitagraph held off its distribution until Smith and his partner J. Stuart Blackton had shot a table-top "battle of Santiago Bay" complete with profuse cigarette and cigar smoke, explosions, and cardboard ships going down in inch-deep water. Combined with the shots brought from Cuba, it became the hit of the war coverage.
Erik Barnouw[6]

The basic assumption most viewers make about documentary film is that it is about reality rather than an imaginatively created fictional world, that it in fact documents, records, and preserves with a degree of integrity the real world as it is commonly experienced. However, as this chapter has shown, it is possible to take images of reality and manipulate them, for example, to turn Hitler into a man-god moving against a staged background. The "creative treatment of actuality" can turn truth into a lie, reality into fiction. As viewers, we have come to expect that the film which looks and feels like a documentary will show its subject matter "like it is." In fact, however, it may show it as it isn't. Because viewers expect truth, the documentary filmmaker must face ethical issues concerning the nature of truth and reality which are irrelevant to fiction film. And the boundaries between "creative treatment" and distortion, between fact and fiction, truth and lies, are frequently difficult to see clearly.

How should the filmmaker and the viewer regard the act of re-creation and reconstruction, for example? Flaherty's *Nanook of the North* and *Man of Aran* ignore many contemporary practices of the Eskimo and the Aran islanders. Moreover, old and no longer practiced methods of hunting and fishing were staged for Flaherty's cameras; that these episodes were re-creations was not announced to the viewer. The capture and killing of the huge basking shark in *Man of Aran*, for example, is accomplished by harpooners hunting from a small open boat, seeking to obtain the shark's fat for lamp oil. The method and purpose were facts for an older generation of islanders, but for most of the men we see in the boat it was the first time they'd hunted that way; indeed, oil lamps were no longer in general use. Have we been deceived? And if we have, is the deception in the act of re-creation and staging — or is it not telling the viewer that he is watching a re-creation? Some viewers might feel deceived, but others might feel Flaherty was justified in practicing what has been called "salvage ethnography" and that the islanders and their heritage were being served by the film. In *Nanook*, Flaherty wanted to record life inside the Eskimo's igloo, but both room and light were insufficient to allow his camera to function properly. To solve the problem, the Eskimo built a larger igloo than would have been normal and then cut away part of it to allow for more light. How do we regard this kind of staging for the cameras? Is it less or more deceptive than the Aran islanders' shark hunt? Today, if such films were being made to be screened on television, they would have to carry a message, either at their beginning or end, such as "Some of the events depicted are re-creations. But all are accepted as factual occurrences by naturalists." This explanatory line now appears on almost all of the nature documentary series on television, from *Wild Kingdom* to the remarkable documentary explorations of Jacques Cousteau.

Sometimes, in order for the viewer to decide what constitutes a film "lie," it becomes useful to attempt to determine the filmmaker's intent. But evidence of his good or bad faith may be hard to come by. We know that Flaherty, despite his re-creation or staging, was scrupulous in his attempts to show Eskimo truth because we have written records by and about him, and also because he related his reliance on Eskimo suggestions concerning footage. On the other hand, bad faith and the desire to make a commercial enterprise out of deceiving the viewer is evident in the many staged re-creations which passed as newsreels in the early days of film. Sometimes they combined the real and the fake. Indeed, sometimes an entire news film was faked from totally irrelevant and already existent footage. In 1899, Frances Doublier (once a Lumière cameraman) reconstructed the famed Dreyfus case for audiences around the world, identifying shots of an anonymous French captain as Dreyfus, a Parisian building as the scene of his court-martial, and even a long shot of the Nile delta as "Devil's Island" (really off South America), where Dreyfus was imprisoned; the irony of all this was that Dreyfus was court-martialed in 1894, a full year before the cinématographe and the first films were shown in Paris. Although considered good business by its practitioners, this kind of reconstruction was clearly deceitful.

Some films, however, are honest about their acts of staging and reconstruction, announcing through various conventional means like film credits or disclaimers that they are not true. Paradoxically, the best of these films are made in such good faith and are informed by such an honest desire to illuminate reality through the act of staging that often the viewer sees them as documentaries and remembers them as documentaries, despite the various disclaimers. Such is the case, for example, with *The Quiet One* (Sidney Meyers, 1948). With a script written by James Agee, and using subjective as well as objective cinematography, the film follows a fictional character, a young black boy named Donald, in his turbulent and moving emotional odyssey from sickness to the beginnings of mental health as he moves from the isolated ghetto of Harlem to the Wiltwyck School for disturbed children. Donald's problem was real and the film was shot against real backgrounds and in the real school, but Donald himself was an actor, and the credits admitted the fiction. Still the film, perhaps because of the sincerity and low-key tone of its dramatization, remains permanently associated with documentary film.

This same kind of association occurs with a quite different kind of recreation and staging, one which has had far-reaching political implications. Adopting the techniques and style, the very look and sound and feel of newsreels, direct cinema, and cinema verité, *The Battle of Algiers* (Gillo Pontecorvo, 1966) might, by analogy with analytic documentary, be called analytic fiction. The film makes no pretense at deceit. After its initial credits, which indicate the presence of a story and screenplay, the following caption appears alone on the screen: "Not one foot of newsreel has been used in this reenactment of the battle of Algiers." The film which follows then appears to "document" the Arab uprising against the French in Algiers during the 1950s. The film, despite its disclaimer, is so much like a documentary in style and structure that it convinces like

truth. Stylistically, it uses hand-held camera, high-speed film which results in grainy and often overexposed images, and an imperfect sound
track. Structurally, it seems to have the randomness of real life, beginning in the middle of an unexplained action which becomes comprehensible only as the viewer accumulates more data. It uses no heroes and
it avoids the notion of characterization; what we know about the people
in the film is what we see and hear. That such an announced fiction can
convince us we are watching documentary should make us aware of the
degree to which documentary film is a *style* which we have learned to
recognize and not a truth in itself. *The Battle of Algiers* has had tremendous impact, particularly on Third World filmmaking, which has
found it politically effective to combine elements of documentary and
fiction in one film. An interesting variant on Pontecorvo's film exists in
the powerful Bolivian film *The Courage of the People* (Jorge Sanjines,
1971); the film re-creates and stages an army massacre of striking miners
which occurred in 1967. Smoothly shot and in color, the film lies somewhere between fiction and documentary not only because of its historic
specificity, but also because many of its actors were actual participants
in and survivors of the real massacre and were called upon as advisers
and collaborators in the filming.

What, then, are the boundaries of documentary? At times, they are
flexible, bending to accommodate Flaherty's "salvage ethnography," allowing the polemic reconstructions and total distortion of the Nazis so
long as they are labeled propaganda, accepting the association with the
kind of fictional document represented by *The Quiet One*. There is only
one certainty about documentary and film truth. And that is that documentary film — like fiction film — is composed of two-dimensional images and thus presents an illusion of substance and reality. Whether
what we see on the screen reflects or distorts a particular truth, whether
we are watching an eyewitness account of uncontrolled situations or a
staged re-creation, cannot be ascertained from the film itself (Figure
7-8). Its truthfulness, its reality, must be corroborated by other sources,
a corroboration which is sometimes difficult to obtain.

Ultimately, if we seek truth and reality in the documentary film, we
are dependent upon the good faith of the filmmaker and our own con-
structive skepticism. Although it is perhaps the moral responsibility of
the documentary filmmaker to remember that the film form within which
he has chosen to operate has become inextricably connected with truth
and reality, it is also the responsibility of viewers to remember that they
are, after all, watching a film. Every documentary is merely an interpretation of reality, an interpretation of events mediated by filmmakers,
whether individual, industrial, institutional, or governmental. It is finally

★ **7-8** Viewers generally believe they can distinguish between documentary and fiction films. In a fascinating exploration of viewer expectations, Mitchel Block's short film NO LIES (1973) appears to be a cinema verité interview in which a film student films and talks to a friend who reveals that she had only a few days before been attacked and raped. The setting, the young woman, the hand-held camera, the poor sound quality, the out-of-focus shots all combine to give the impression of a real, unrehearsed moment of intensity which accidentally was captured on film. At the end of the film however, credits indicate that the woman was a professional actress and that the whole film had been scripted. Viewers are forced to rethink their attitudes toward the woman's plight, since now they realize that the rape didn't "really" happen — and yet they may feel cheated because they didn't know that they were in fact being lied to by the filmmaker.

the option and the responsibility of the individual viewer to question and test the validity of that interpretation of reality through whatever means are possible for him.

NOTES

[1] Quoted in G. Roy Levin, *Documentary Explorations* (Garden City, N.Y.: Doubleday, 1971), p. 308.

[2] Thomas R. Atkins, ed., *Frederick Wiseman* (New York: Monarch Press, 1976), p. 34.

[3] "Why Should I Give You Political Solutions?" *Film Critic* 1, no. 2 (November–December 1972): 56.

[4] *The Name Above the Title* (New York: Macmillan, 1971), p. 329.

[5] Quoted in G. Roy Levin, *Documentary Explorations*, p. 210.

[6] *Documentary* (New York: Oxford University Press, 1976), p. 24.

Historical Overview:
The Development of
Experimental, Independent, and
Animated Filmmaking

BEGINNINGS: THE BREAK WITH REALISM

One can distinguish between, on the one hand, the recording function of cinema and, on the other hand, its creative or expressive function even at its earliest stages of development. The Lumière brothers were interested in reality, pointing their cameras at relatively uncontrolled subjects in natural surroundings without any thought of altering that reality through the cinematic apparatus itself. Georges Méliès, however, immediately recognized the cinema's ability to create illusions, to present images which defied the physical laws of the real world. Thus, while the Lumières simply pointed their camera and turned it on, Méliès painted elaborate backdrops and created artificial sets and then further manipulated his staged fantasies in the camera itself, running the film backward and forward, stopping and starting it up again to create magical appearances and disappearances. Although his films depended chiefly on narrative, and so led the way to the creation of the popular and commercially successful fiction film, Méliès can also be regarded as the father of the avant-garde and experimental cinema, for he was the first to stress film's dissociation from reality rather than its connection to it. His films were the first to demonstrate the aesthetic autonomy of which the medium is capable. It has been to this possibility of film that artists from other art forms have been drawn, and thus the history of the avant-garde, experimental, independent, and animated film has been peopled with filmmakers who were also fine artists, sculptors, architects, and musicians.

The first attempts to create motion pictures antedated photography, and resulted in mechanisms like the Zoëtrope which "animated" drawings on paper frames; it is not surprising, then, that the animation of drawn figures was one of the first kinds of fanciful film art. Indeed, the earliest creators of the film cartoon delighted in the magic of the medium and its power to confer reality upon the absolutely impossible. Although the animated cartoon appeared as early as 1900, Emile Cohl, a French cartoonist who found in the new medium an outlet for his fertile imagination, was the first filmmaker to adopt the form wholeheartedly. Between 1908 and 1918, Cohl specialized in cartoons which transformed drawn objects from one thing to another in a surreal world in which nothing was stable; a man turns into a window and the window then turns into something else, defying logic and physical law and delighting the viewer with the unexpected. In the United States, Winsor McCay, already a noted cartoonist, made his first animated film in 1909; its protagonist was his famed comic-strip character "Little Nemo," and his cartoons were extraordinary in the complexity of their drawings and their use of perspective. Other animated films were being made, too, expanding the possibilities of the form. In Russia, Ladislaus Starevitch began a long career in model and **puppet animation.** The fact that he used three-dimensional figures in no way made his work less imaginative and more realistic than drawn animation; his *The Revenge of the Kinematograph Cameraman* (1912), for example, animates insect models to tell a story of a love triangle. And, in the United States during the 1920s, Max and Dave Fleischer combined animated drawings with live action in their popular *Out of the Inkwell* series, the cartoon figures materializing literally out of the inkwell of the "live" cartoonists and wreaking havoc until they were returned to the ink bottle. In all of these animated works, what is seen on the screen owes more to the artist's imagination, of course, than it does to the laws of physical reality. The world shown in the frame is an independent world, governed by its own laws. To be sure, these early cartoons were not considered seriously as art by the audiences who saw them: they were entertainments and hardly to be linked to such weighty art movements as expressionism or surrealism. Yet, in fact, in its creation of worlds in which logic and cause and effect do not operate as they do in the real world, the cartoon is the first avant-garde film form — and perhaps the only avant-garde film form readily appreciated by mass audiences.

While imaginative film artists in the United States submerged and popularized their expressionist and surrealist impulses in the animated cartoon, more overt experiments with the medium went on in Europe, a Europe which was caught up in artistic ferment in the 1920s. Movements such as German expressionism, **dada,** and surrealism were all radical artistic responses to modern life. These movements rejected traditional notions of reality and representationalism, and this rejection found its way into literature, painting, theater, and film. Thus, the seminal film of the German expressionist movement, *The Cabinet of Dr. Caligari* (Robert Wiene, 1919), used painted sets, deliberately distorted into perspectives that imitate not what the eye sees but what the tormented soul experiences. The sets were designed by Hermann Warm, who declared that "films should be living paintings." This important notion of film as a canvas also underlies the work of the German abstract painter Hans Richter and his Swedish collaborator, Viking Eggeling. Interested in adding the dimension of time to abstract painting, they turned to film. In *Rhythmus 21* (1921) and *Symphonie Diagonale* (1921), they experimented with abstract forms and gradations of black and white to explore geometric shapes. These were the first consciously artistic abstract and avant-garde films; their creators were not concerned with presenting reality or telling stories, but rather with making film works analogous to paintings and music of the day. Richter continued using both drawn and photographed forms to create what he called "absolute" or "pure" films with no actors, no plots, and no allegiance to the external world, films bent only on creating abstract patterns out of the plasticity of the medium. But he also was later influenced by the French avant-garde filmmakers and went on to make anarchic dada films.

SURREALISM AND THE AVANT-GARDE

The most dynamic contributions to the history of avant-garde film came from the French. It was to Paris in the 1920s that artists from around the world went to join with other artists in that explosion of aesthetic sensibility called "modern art." Expressionists, **constructivists,** cubists, **futurists,** dadaists, and surrealists argued and practiced their aesthetic philosophies, each in its own way a response to the complexity and ambiguous nature of reality in the modern world. They wrote manifestos and outraged the conservative "bourgeois" public with their unconventional art, in a reaction against the excesses of World War I. They were also inspired by the daring and controversial work of Sigmund Freud, which dealt with such taboo subjects as sex and power, the fantasy and nightmare worlds of the unconscious. Because of its ability to realize the impossible in images and to add the dynamic elements of time and transformation in and through space, film seemed a highly appropriate medium through which to explore and represent the human unconscious as well as the configurations of abstract patterns. And, above all, it seemed to offer the opportunity to shock viewers into a new awareness of their relationship to reality.

Both the dadaists and the surrealists used film to attack and upset bourgeois notions of art and reality. Indeed, the dadaists based their creative efforts in acts of destruction meant to emancipate the visual imagination from any dependence on bourgeois tradition — and that even meant a rejection of Freudianism because the new psychology was inextricably linked with a bourgeois unconscious. The dadist films thus rejected any kind of logic, dream logic included. Man Ray, an expatriate American photographer, for example, "destroyed" notions of traditional filmmaking in *Retour à la Raison* (1923) by sprinkling salt and pepper and tacks and various other objects on unexposed film and developing the resultant images as a film made to insult his fellow dadaists. And René Clair, who went on to become one of France's greatest directors, made a short film to serve as an intermission for a ballet, entitled appropriately enough *Entr'acte* (1924). It is full of the anarchic, absurd, and illogical images and occurrences so loved by the dada movement: a ballerina turns into a bearded gentleman with a pince-nez, a game of chess is played on the rooftops of Paris, a man is shot and carried about in a coffin which becomes the object of a wild funeral and a chase led by a camel, and when the coffin is finally recovered, the dead man jumps out unharmed. Performing these zany antics were artists whose work soon became world famous: Darius Milhaud, Marcel Duchamp, Erik Satie, Man Ray, and Francis Picabia. This film movement, however, came at the end of the dadaist movement in general, which by 1925 consumed itself in its most extreme manifestations and was finally absorbed by the surrealists.

The surrealists, like the dadaists, believed in the liberating qualities of illogic and shock. But the surrealists adopted Freud's view of the illogic of dream and of the aspects of human consciousness. Thus, the surrealists valued psychic automatism, the free, shocking associations made by an unconscious liberated from the control of reason, morality, and a planned aesthetic. These associations, according to the surrealists, were a reality superior to the reality apprehended by a reasoning, socialized, and constrained consciousness — thus the term "surrealism." One of the first clearly surrealist films was *The Seashell and the Clergyman* (1928); made by a French woman filmmaker, Germaine Dulac, it linked Freudian imagery with sex and religion. It was shortly followed by the film that has since come to be regarded as the classic of surrealist cinema, *Un Chien Andalou* (1928). A collaborative work of painter Salvador Dali and filmmaker Luis Buñuel, and titled meaninglessly (translated, the title is *An Andalusian Dog*), the film is loosely structured along the free-associational paths taken by a Freudian dream. In its images of a cloud passing across the moon, an eyeball slit by a razor, a hand from which insects emerge, priests pulling a piano which serves as a coffin for a dead donkey, rational connections and cause and effect are inoperative. The film turned many stomachs and became a cause célèbre. Buñuel's next film, *L'Age d'Or* (1930), used shocking imagery to attack both capitalism and Catholicism and was received even more violently; rioting broke out in the theaters when it was shown.

Not all experimental and avant-garde films were quite so aggressively threatening. French cubist painter Fernand Léger, for example, used ordinary objects like pots and pans to construct a rhythmic ballet in his *Ballet Mécanique* (1924), believing that a new drama could be created which would allow man "to be free and yet not . . . lose touch with reality." Oskar Fischinger in Germany continued in the tradition of Richter's "absolute" film, beginning in 1925 his series of film studies which were based on mathematics. Also in the 1920s a group of relatively popular avant-garde films known as **city symphonies** emerged, so called because of their urban subject matter and their attempts at a musical structure. As early as 1921, Paul Strand (chiefly a photographer) and Charles Sheeler (chiefly a painter) in their *Manhatta* impressionistically recorded New York City, but the city symphony reached maturity in films like *Rien que les Heures* (Alberto Cavalcanti, 1926), *Berlin: Symphony of a Great City* (Walter Ruttmann, 1927), *Rain* (Joris Ivens, 1929), *The Man with a Movie Camera* (Dziga Vertov, 1928), and *On the Subect of Nice* (Jean Vigo, 1930), films which all used fragments of real life as the basis upon which to construct abstract film poetry.

Most avant-garde and experimental filmmaking was centered in Europe, but there was some avant-garde filmmaking in the United States, although the American films tended to be more aesthetically conservative than their European counterparts. Three films appeared in 1928 representing the range of these efforts: *The Fall of the House of Usher* (Melville Webber and James Watson), which used expressionistic techniques to adapt Poe's story; *The Life and Death of a Hollywood Extra* (Robert Florey), which used expressionist techniques to spoof *The Cabinet of Dr. Caligari* in its tale of a Hollywood extra whose dreams of fame and fortune are frustrated; and *Steamboat Willie* (Walt Disney and Ub Iwerks), which introduced Mickey Mouse and sound to the animated cartoon in a totally surreal evocation of barnyard life. Although there were a few other experimental films, like Ralph Steiner's H_2O (1929), which abstracted images of light on water into patterns, it was primarily the animated cartoon that kept experimentation alive and well in the United States until the 1940s.

DECLINE: SOUND AND THE WAR YEARS

With the introduction of sound to the cinema in the late 1920s — a technological advance which coincided with the economic step backwards of worldwide depression — avant-garde and experimental filmmaking fell into decline. Part of the problem was caused by the difficulties the new technology presented; the independent filmmaker could not afford to use sound, and the artist working within commercial production systems had to undergo the difficult and frustrating process of rethinking and readapting his art. In addition, the same kind of political and social commitment that drove the European avant-garde to make shocking, untraditional, and abstract films in the 1920s provided the impetus for their acceptance of a style more relevant to the social, economic, and political ills facing Europe in the 1930s. Although there were rare instances of personal films like poet Jean Cocteau's *The Blood of a Poet* (1930) (Figure 1) or Len Lye's experiments with drawing and painting directly onto the film stock as in *Colour Box* (1935), most filmmakers were in some way committed to the effort to end the Depression, and subsequently to help win the war.

Although avant-garde and experimental filmmaking declined during the war years, those years stimulated the development and widespread use of 16mm cameras and projectors both abroad and in America. This equipment became readily available and was relatively inexpensive (much of it was war surplus), allowing for the growth both of independent filmmaking and of an audience (chiefly organized in small film societies) for the independent, personal, avant-garde film. During the mid-1940s, then, the conditions supported a resurgence of independent film production in America.

RENAISSANCE: THE RISE OF THE INDEPENDENT FILMMAKER

Maya Deren, a modern dancer, almost single-handedly originated the new American avant-garde. In *Meshes of the Afternoon* (1943), a film made with her husband, Alexander Hammid, she created a world in which reality and dream merged into a stream of consciousness communicated by imaginative cinematic techniques and personal symbolism. Deren was important not only as an artist and as a filmmaker, but also as the creator of an audience for avant-garde films. In 1945, she toured university campuses across the country with *Meshes of the Afternoon* and two of her other films, *At Land* (1944) and *Choreography for the Camera* (1945). The tour successfully tapped a hitherto unidentified audience, and film societies began to spring up in urban and educational centers to offer showcases for this new form of personal cinema. The Museum of Modern Art in New York expanded its circulating film library, making experimental and avant-garde films more available. In 1946 the San Francisco Museum of Art began its "Art in Cinema" series, stimulating avant-garde film production in the Bay area. And in 1947, Amos Vogel founded the Cinema 16 group in New York with the express purpose of exhibiting unusual films, whether modern or classic, documentary or experimental.

From that time to the present, the output of experimental films has continued unabated. Indeed, as filmmaking equipment has become less expensive and more portable (Super 8mm and videotape are now practical

★ **1**   Jean Cocteau uses representational images — houses, humans, animals, automobiles — in his films, but as in BLOOD OF A POET (1930) the way in which he uses them is surreal. People become poetic symbols through their stylized acting, dialogue, and costumes.

alternatives to 16mm) and filmmakers have experimented with distributional film cooperatives to rent their works for exhibition, independent filmmaking has increased. Every type and kind of film has been made, the only common characteristic uniting them being their independent mode of production and the idiosyncratic vision of their creators. Still, the influence of their predecessors can be discerned.

★ **2**   Norman McLaren's BEGONE DULL CARE (1949) is representative of the abstract, nonrepresentational film. This frame enlargement shows the scratches and globs of paint that have been applied directly to the film stock.

The "absolute" and "pure" cinema of early artists like Richter can be found in the work of Norman McLaren, one of the great contemporary animators, who also paints directly on film, as demonstrated by *Begone Dull Care* (1949) (Figure 2). Pure cinema can also be found in the works of the avant-garde "structuralists," who believe that a film's shape is determined by the mechanics of the cinematic apparatus. Michael Snow's *Wavelength* (1966–1967), for example, is a forty-five-minute slow zoom through a room into a photograph on a wall; whatever occurs in front of the camera lens is recorded with equal lack of emphasis: a possible death, the changing of filters and focus, empty space, the occasional presence of people. The desire to make of film a nonrepresentational art is reflected in such contemporary works as *Permutations* (John Whitney, 1968), which uses computers to create abstract forms, and *Corridor* (Standish Lawder, 1968–1970), which combines stroboscopic light patterns so as to simulate brain waves.

The influences of the dadaist and surrealist movement continue in an active **underground cinema,** geared to shock the viewer into examining his culture and his notions of art. Both Kenneth Anger and Andy Warhol have been key figures: Anger with his series of films, culminating in *Scorpio Rising* (1963), *Lucifer Rising* (1966–1967), and *Invocation of My Demon Brother* (1969), which explored machismo and homosexuality and was charged with obscenity, and Warhol with his experiments in minimal cinema like *Empire* (1964), which focused a static camera for an eight-hour look at the Empire State Building and which outraged audiences accustomed to drama and "things happening" in film. In a more humorous vein, Bruce Connor has used old movie footage to satirize an audience's dramatic expectations in films such as *A Movie* (1958).

Personal cinema has flourished in the work of Stan Brakhage, Ed Emshwiller, James Broughton, Bruce Baillie, Jonas Mekas, and Shirley Clarke. Brakhage, particularly, has been a key figure with his epic avant-garde work *Dog Star Man* (1961), combining representational images with painting and scratchings on the film stock.

ANIMATION

Finally, of course, the animated film has remained the most popular and widely seen form of experimental cinema. In America, during the golden age of animation in the 1930s and 1940s, Disney Studios, Warner Brothers, and MGM created enduring cartoon characters like Mickey Mouse, Bugs Bunny, Roadrunner, and Popeye. Seeing the world with surreal vision, animators like Bob Clampett, Tex Avery, Chuck Jones, and Max and Dave Fleischer made the American cartoon an art which explored the collision between matter and space at the same time it entertained and delighted a large public. In Europe, contemporary animation has been greatly influenced by the work of Jiří Trnka's sophisticated puppet films in Czechoslovakia and the formation of the Zagreb Studio in Yugoslavia (1956); animated films were made for adult audiences and were often intellectual and satiric in their treatment of thematic material like war and modern society. Since the golden age, American animation has found new voices in the work of Ralph Bakshi and Robert Crumb, whose *Fritz the Cat* (1972), using animated characters in a feature-length film far removed from Disney, dealt with contemporary issues like sex, violence, and drugs. Further, many experimental filmmakers like Robert Breer use animation to give a liberated form to their exploration of cinematic time and space.

Many of the techniques of experimental and avant-garde cinema have been absorbed and popularized by filmmakers of mainstream theatrical films. Indeed, some experimental filmmakers have gone on to become theatrical filmmakers. But many prefer the total control the individual artist has over a single small work, independently produced for noncommercial purposes. These independent filmmakers, working in isolation or in groups, are creating what they believe is true film art, an art which has little to do with the narrative film as we know it in theatrical release or on television. They view their films not as commodities meant to appeal to a mass audience or as the results of collaborative effort. The camera and film stock are their equivalent of paint and canvas, of pen and paper, a medium of individual expression.

8

★ *EXPERIMENTAL,*
INDEPENDENT, AND
ANIMATED FILMS

★★★ **Film as Film**

> You must set aside the existence of the commercial films. You must forget
> the arts in general. But what is left, you may ask? My reply is simple.
> What is left is film as film. Film which contains as much of metaphor,
> simile, and allusion as any of the basic poets which you have studied.
> Gregory Markopoulos[1]

The films grouped in this chapter do not share easily identifiable characteristics. Indeed, the very fact that the films are called by a variety of
terms is a sign of their diversity. "Experimental," "independent,"
"avant-garde," and **underground** have been used synonymously, but
each term also carries its own distinct meaning and emphasis. "Experimental film," for example, suggests a film made for the purposes of trying out some new technique, some new aesthetic, some new structure, or
some new apparatus. "Independent film" suggests a film made outside
the traditional system of commercial theatrical production; generally,
such filmmaking is characterized by its extremely low budget, its small
crew, and its lack of access to widespread distribution, promotion, and
exhibition. The term *avant-garde film* (literally "advance-guard") implies
that the film is ahead of its time, in the forefront of an aesthetic movement, that it is a film not concerned with traditional means of communicating traditional content. And the term *underground film* seems
given to films which are potentially shocking to traditional moral and
aesthetic values, films which are subversive in their intent and effect.

Some of the films considered in this section merit all these names, while others are best described by only one of the terms.

Even the animated film, despite its relatively clear distinguishing characteristics, needs some qualifying terminology. Animation can be applied to live action, three-dimensional models, and two-dimensional drawings, or it can be accomplished through computer graphics. And the animated film may be a traditional narrative feature, a surreal but commercially made cartoon, or an experimental, independent, avant-garde, or underground film.

Still, we can see some resemblances. With the exception of the animated film produced for theatrical release within the traditional collaborative Hollywood production system, most of the films discussed in this section do share some general characteristics. First, the films are usually made by a single artist or a small group, aiming not at commercial success but solely at artistic expression. Second, these films tend to be short, generally running anywhere from a minute to half an hour. Although a few films run an hour or more (feature length), both financial and structural considerations tend to curtail the length of the films. Third, financing for the films generally comes from institutional grants and from patrons, friends, and relatives of the filmmaker. Fourth, and last, almost all production is 16mm, although recently Super 8mm and videotape have become popular.

The filmmaker who engages in this sort of cinematic enterprise is a singular artist who, with a few friends, a few dollars' worth of raw film stock, and a haphazard collection of equipment, attempts to create a personal piece of cinematic art determined more by his own vision than by the demands of a prospective audience. These filmmakers, of course, make their movies for an audience, but they envision this audience as a small, specialized group of viewers who might appreciate the ingenuity, the invention, and the creativity of the artist working with limited resources to make a personal statement. The audiences for such films are generally college and university film societies, museum members, student and professional filmmakers, and the intellectual avant-garde usually found in urban centers. For the most part, the viewer who wishes to see these films must seek them out. Although major metropolitan areas like New York and San Francisco frequently have relatively well-publicized showcase and retrospective screenings at museums and little theaters, screenings elsewhere are generally scarce and are likely to occur not in auditoriums regularly used for films but anywhere a screen and projector can be set up. The films must be rented from filmmakers' cooperatives and 16mm rental companies. Finally, whether the films are shown in large cities or small towns, because of their brevity and because audiences are accustomed to buying tickets for film programs running at least an hour, the films are exhibited in "packages." Thus, although each was conceived individually, the films are almost always shown (not always to their advantage) in groups.

Because these films are diverse, and because terms like experimental, independent, avant-garde, and underground film are fuzzy, it is best to discuss the films according to their basic aesthetic approaches.

★★★ The Representational Film

Many independent films use images which closely resemble the real world outside the film frame: human beings, animals, objects, landscapes. Real things represented on the screen are the stuff of which the film is made. In some films they are cinematically treated without distortion and tell short narratives in a fairly traditional, realistic mode. Indeed, sometimes only the film's brevity keeps the film outside of the mainstream of commercial theatrical cinema. One example is *An Occurrence at Owl Creek Bridge* (Robert Enrico, 1961), a film which imaginatively tells a story about recognizable characters but which, because its running time is less than an hour, is too short for normal theatrical distribution. In other films, however, although human figures appear, they are treated less traditionally — as allegorical figures, perhaps, or as visual objects which reveal some quality of beauty or grotesqueness we might not notice as we go about our daily lives. And because these highly personal representational films are short, they might be considered comparable to short stories, poems, essays, diaries, and journals in their concerns and structures.

The most traditional short representational films are narratives comparable to short stories. There are many such films and they vary tremendously both in subject matter and in style, but they are united by their attempt to tell a complete story, marked by a fairly identifiable beginning, middle, and end, and by their introduction of and final resolution of a dramatic conflict. Some are simply shortened versions of the kind and variety of narrative films one might expect to see in regular theatrical release. Thus, highly imaginative and personal films like *The Red Balloon* (Albert Lamorisse, 1956) and *An Occurrence at Owl Creek Bridge* are understood and appreciated by the mass audiences which have had a chance to see them. The story of a young boy and his magical and anthropomorphized friend, a red balloon, and the story of a man mentally living a split-second of wish fulfillment which takes the form of an exciting escape from his soldier captors are completely com-

★ **8-1** Sometimes it is only a film's brevity that keeps it out of the mainstream of commercial cinema. Originally intended as one of three Ambrose Bierce short stories that Robert Enrico would film and release as a feature, AN OCCURRENCE AT OWL CREEK BRIDGE (1961) is usually screened as a short. Its half-hour running time makes it difficult to program in a commercial theater. The same is true of THE RED BALLOON (Albert Lamorisse, 1956). Though both films are fantasies and are somewhat innovative in their treatment of their stories, they appeal to mass audiences; they are not the difficult, hard-to-understand personal visions that one often finds in other short, independent, more experimental films.

prehensible and quite traditional in their structure and drama (Figure 8-1).

Other short narrative films, however, are less traditional in either their structure or their cinematic treatment of representational subject matter. It is not their length alone which separates them from the mainstream of commercial narrative cinema. Roman Polanski, for example, made several such short story films during his student and apprentice days in Poland and France before he emigrated to Hollywood and turned to theatrical filmmaking. Although his cinematic techniques were fairly straightforward (his characters were filmed representationally, with little distortion, against real landscapes), his stories themselves were unconventional in subject, structure and theme — strange parable-like tales reminiscent of absurdist drama in the mode of Eugene Ionesco and Samuel Beckett. In *Two Men and a Wardrobe* (1958), for instance, the camera rather straightforwardly follows two men who appear from out of the ocean carrying a wooden wardrobe on a strange odyssey through a town whose inhabitants seem oblivious to either the charm or oddness of their strange burden. After several misadventures and many rejections, they finally return to the sea, carefully maneuvering their way across a beach covered with regimented sand castles made by a little boy, and they march into the ocean with their wonderful and evocative burden to disappear in the waves. This kind of film is hardly a traditional narrative; its human characters enact a combination of realistic and fantastic actions in order to make a philosophical point.

A short film narrative also may make relative sense, that is, its characters are recognizably human on an emotional as well as a physical level and its actions are generally determined by comprehensible causes. What may be untraditional is the film's form, the way it is narratively and visually constructed. For example, one of the key films of experimental American cinema is Maya Deren's *Meshes of the Afternoon* (1943), a film about a girl who, returning home in the afternoon, falls asleep and *dreams* about her return home, her feelings of isolation and unhappiness, and in the dream finally commits suicide. Deren does not see her film as divorced from connection with reality: "This first film is concerned with the relationship between the imaginative and the objective reality. . . . It is a whole creation out of the elements of reality — people, places and objects — but these are so combined as to form a new reality, a new context which defines them according to their function within it." [2] A different kind of short narrative film which makes sense, that is, tells a traditionally comprehensible story, is Chris Marker's *La Jetée* (1962). A short science fiction film, it creates images of a post–World War III France from which the film's hero is sent into the past and future. What is completely untraditional about this science-fiction exploration of time travel, however, is that the film, except for one brief moment, is entirely composed of still photographs which freeze motion and destroy the distinction between past and present as we usually perceive it in the ongoing immediacy of the *motion* picture. Thus, the entire film, a complex study of time and its relationship to human memory, goes far beyond the traditional concerns of its basic narrative story.

Even more removed from the narrative tradition to which mass audiences respond are those films which use a combination of cinematic tricks and bizarre occurrences to turn recognizable people and objects and places into a work of cinema which bears only the slightest resemblance to reality as it is normally experienced. One of the classic surrealist films — *Un Chien Andalou* (Salvador Dali and Luis Buñuel, 1929) — is not abstract in its images. Indeed, the shock the film elicits is derived from its very representational quality: a real eyeball is slit by a razor for no comprehensible reason, real ants crawl out of a wound in a real hand, a real donkey is wedged into a real piano which is being towed by two real human beings in real space. Thus, the film uses the material of reality as we normally perceive it but puts it to incomprehensible, shocking, and funny use. And in addition to the bizarre relationships established between real things, places, and people, as well as a structure which lacks an allegiance to cause-and-effect narrative, *Un Chien Andalou* uses cinematic "magic" in images which give the illusion of being strictly representational: hair in a woman's armpit is suddenly transformed by a dissolve into a man's beard, a face lacks a mouth, a book turns into a gun. The film has less a story than a purpose. Using representational images, it subverts reality and obvious causal logic; indeed, inserted titles mock traditional narrative expectations, beginning as they do with "Once upon a Time" and moving to a sporadic and unrelated "Eight Years Later," "Towards Three in the Morning," "Sixteen Years Before" and, finally, "In the Spring." In the surrealist tradition, the film embraces the illogical logic of dreams. It uses reality as the base from which to liberate the human spirit to a better and higher reality, a surreality. Thus, almost all of the dadaist and surrealist films are representational, aiming to shock audiences into new perceptions of reality, to criticize repression and the lack of imagination, and to give a stale and civilized society a kick in the pants. As Buñuel himself puts it:

> The sources from which the film draws inspiration are those of poetry, freed from the ballast of reason and tradition. . . . This film has no intention of attracting nor pleasing the spectator; indeed, on the contrary, it attacks him, to the degree that he belongs to a society with which surrealism is at war. . . . The motivation of the images was, or [was] meant to be, purely irrational! They are as mysterious and inexplicable to the two collaborators as to the spectator. NOTHING, in the film, SYMBOLIZES ANYTHING.[3]

With similar aims, some contemporary filmmakers have made films using the images of real life. The most representational and the most aggressive in his attack on traditional perceptions of art has been, perhaps, Andy Warhol, a painter turned filmmaker. Much as he gave the bourgeois art world a jolt with his painting of Campbell's soup cans, he has enraged audiences with his minimal films: movies taken of real events from a fixed vantage point, of an often interminable length dictated by the event being filmed, and minimally edited — if at all. *Eat* (1963), for example, is forty-five minutes of a man eating mushrooms, *Sleep* (1963–1964) is six hours of a sleeping subject who occasionally moves or turns in the bed, and *Empire* is an eight-hour record of the Empire State Building seen from one location. Crucially dependent upon their representational qualities, Warhol's films are aimed less at documenting reality than at mounting an assault on the viewer's complacent perception of and relationship to reality and art.

Sometimes that assault can be funny as well as shocking. Filmmakers such as Bruce Connor and Robert Nelson use humor and satire to criticize the real and social world external to the film. Again, there is an intimate connection between representational images and the world in which the viewer lives. In his important short film appropriately entitled *A Movie* (1958), Bruce Connor uses "found" footage from old narrative movies, newsreels, and educational films. This footage is representational in content, and at first we laugh at Connor's odd juxtapositions of tanks, submarines firing torpedoes, cowboys, and starlets in various states of undress, but soon we realize, with the insertion of increasingly violent imagery, that Connor is saying something about our easy acceptance of violence because it's only "a movie." In a similar tradition but using his own footage, Robert Nelson attacks our culture's racial stereotypes with a watermelon as his protagonist in *Oh Dem Watermelons* (1965), a film which plays with the cliché connecting blacks and watermelons. After an initial static shot of lengthy duration showing a watermelon which, isolated on the screen with no function, becomes an increasingly funny object, the first moving footage of the film shows a group of black males pushing and rolling a watermelon down a steep incline in a park. Intercut with this material are images of watermelons being squashed, kicked, exploded, rubbed over a woman's breasts, animated into a rocket, and found to have intestines. Over all this outrageous, funny visual material, a chorus of voices sings the phrase "Oh, dem watermelons" again and again and in such a rhythm as to evoke primitive tribal drumming. Finally, the initial footage of the watermelon being rolled downhill in front of the boys is run in reverse at high speed, the watermelon now chasing the boys, who are scuttling uphill backwards. The entire film is ridiculous, ebullient, and funny, but in its way it is also serious, for anyone seeing it would have great difficulty in ever again taking seriously clichés about blacks and watermelon.

The major difference between the films of Connor and Nelson and those of Polanski and Warhol is that Connor and Nelson have used highly manipulative editing and optical trickery. Thus, Connor's editing imposes relationships between representational images (tanks, cowboys, starlets) which were never filmed for such a purpose, and Nelson's close-ups of watermelons, combinations of animation and representationalism, and use of reverse and fast motion are cinematic techniques that change the meanings implied in the straightforward representational cinematography of individual shots. Polanski's and Warhol's films, on the other hand, maintain a recognizable space-time continuum; they visually achieve their special quality through the distortion of narrative tradition. Polanski's men carrying a wardrobe move inexplicably through a series of actions which make little realistic sense and which must be interpreted symbolically, and Warhol's films of the Empire State Building or a sleeper have neither characters nor dramatic action.

These two approaches to the representational image may be combined in a single film that often lies somewhere between a documentary and an abstract film. In Norman McLaren's *Ballet Adagio* (1971), the major impulse seems documentary, for the camera records as an observer the difficult pas de deux performed by two dancers; there is no editing of the dance, and the film is shot in slow motion, which reveals the dancers' craft and artistry. On the one hand, the film seems to duplicate — but much more pleasantly — the minimal cinema of Warhol, with its preservation of space and time. On the other hand, the fact that the film is in slow motion places *Ballet Adagio* closer to films which optically or through editing distort the space-time continuum. Another of McLaren's films, *Pas de Deux* (1967), is more spectacular in its effects and seems more the result of an aesthetic than of a documentary impulse (Figure 8-2). *Pas de Deux* uses multiple exposures to record two dancers, so that their movements are seen broken down into tiny movements of normally imperceptible time. On the one hand, the representational images of the dancers are transformed into black-and-white patterns of light and movement. And yet, on the other hand, the dancers performing the dance are also represented. *Pas de Deux* is generally regarded as an experimental or avant-garde film; it is less obvious, however, how one categorizes *Ballet Adagio*.

Dance films, nature films, and sports films often combine a documentary (or, we might say, realistic) preservation of space and time with abstracting techniques, creating a form which, through optical effects and editing, imposes rhythm on representational images. Such films often use slow motion, superimpositions and dissolves and multiple imagery, graceful camera movements, kinetic and rhythmic editing to document and to convey a sense of beauty. Indeed, they often create events which never occurred. A sport film called *Solo* (Mike Hoover, 1971), for example, seems to document a particular climb up a mountain; departure from reality seems confined to the use of sun flare off the lens and certain extremely lyrical camera movements. Actually, however, the climb we see never took place — for it is a combination of many different climbs in twenty-one separate locations. *Solo* is not a document of a mountain climb; it is a celebration of mountain climbing, a personal evocation of feeling rather than an objective recording of an activity.

★ **8-2**   Norman McLaren used an optical printer to show each increment of movement of two dancers in PAS DE DEUX (1969). Using a dark background and vivid side lighting on the figures, McLaren created abstract patterns within the two-dimensional frame.

Along with dance and athletics, objects and particular geographical locations have lent themselves to this rhythmic transformation from representational image to abstract image. At one end of the continuum, a filmmaker using images from real life makes documentaries. At the other end, a filmmaker may use the images of the real world chiefly as abstract patterns of light and motion. Somewhere in the middle are those filmmakers who create lyrical celebrations of events, of experiences, of places with representational images (Figure 8-3). Sometimes it is difficult to categorize those films in the middle range. *Rien que les Heures* (Alberto Cavalcanti, 1926) and *The Man with a Movie Camera* (Dziga Vertov, 1928), for example, are more socially oriented and thus closer to the documentary pole of the continuum than either *Berlin: The Symphony of a Great City* (Walter Ruttmann, 1927) or *Rain* (Joris Ivens, 1929), whose documentary images are primarily used for their form and as a base for a musical editing structure. Ruttmann, for example, inspired by Vertov's writings on editing, got "the idea of making something out of life, of creating a symphonic film out of the millions of energies that comprise the life of a big city." [4]

Despite the difficulties of attempting to categorize noncommercial representational films, the process of categorizing can be illuminating. We can learn about the nature of film by asking questions, even if the questions have no definite answers. Is, for example, *Night and Fog* (Alain Resnais, 1955) a documentary about the Nazi holocaust or is it a per-

★ **8-3** Trick effects can be created when two different images are printed separately on the same frame. In this image from THE MAN WITH A MOVIE CAMERA (Dziga Vertov, 1928), it appears as though the cameraman has mounted his tripod atop a giant camera. This film uses a host of editing techniques to reveal the rhythm of life in post-Revolutionary Russia. Thus it might be called a "city symphony."

sonal and emotional film essay? Is Fernand Léger's *Ballet Mécanique* (1924) a celebration of everyday objects rhythmically edited — or is it really abstract and nonrepresentational in approach, because it takes those objects out of their connection with a three-dimensional reality and makes them seem two-dimensional?

What unifies the films discussed in this section is a cinematic attitude on the part of their creators. Despite the variety of their techniques, whether subtle or brazen, a certain respect for three-dimensionality is observed, a respect which acknowledges the film frame as a window rather than as a canvas. The images *represent* things in an acknowledgment of a world which exists outside the film frame, a world which has dimension and substance (Figure 8-4). Thus, the representational film, no matter how experimental, is not totally self-contained or independent, for its reference point is the ordinary world — outside the frame — in which all of us live.

★★★   **The Abstract Film**

Imagine an eye unruled by man-made laws of perspective, an eye unprejudiced by compositional logic, an eye which does not respond to the name of everything but which must know each object encountered in life

★ **8-4** Robert Wood deftly plays with the sound track in ETUDE (1972). A young man in an overcoat carrying a small case trudges through the woods until he comes to a roaring creek. There he sets up a music stand and begins to conduct an imaginary orchestra. The sound track, which up to this point had included only natural sounds, abruptly shifts to the music being conducted. The audience hears what is in the mind of the young man. From then on both the natural sound track and the music sound track are intercut with the images of the conductor and the falling water to create a beautiful interplay between image and sound.

> through an adventure of perception. How many colors are there in a field of grass to the crawling baby unaware of "Green"?
> Stan Brakhage[5]

The second category of experimental, avant-garde, or independent films refuses an alliance with the real world outside the film frame. The film frame is not used to represent the three-dimensional world in which we move. Rather, it is regarded as a sort of canvas that can be adorned with various combinations of shapes and forms and colors and movements to create independent, autonomous works of art. Rather than functioning as a transparent window *through* which the viewer looks into a third dimension, the frame and the film become opaque. No longer do we look through the frame to the real world outside — we look *at* it. In such an opaque film, the film artist assumes that his images express meaning in themselves, that the form of the film is similarly meaningful, and that both form and content are not used to *represent* something else. Even when real objects are photographed, they lose their reference to an external world, becoming pure forms and colors and movement. Thus, real objects and places and beings are removed — abstracted — from a connection with reality, and they become as autonomous in their function as a design composed by a computer.

These films are often meant to stir the viewer intellectually, and to stimulate the eye, but not usually to rouse emotions. Indeed, in many abstract films the viewer becomes a participant in an intellectual and perceptual drama whose theme is aesthetics. We may, for example, begin by looking through the frame and end by looking at the frame — the entire film thus serving as a lesson in perception. Such is true of Michael Snow's *Wavelength* (1966–1967), a forty-five-minute film structured around a single zoom shot taken from a stationary camera position in a large loft-type room. The viewer is first exposed to the room in a long shot: it is bare except for some shelves along the sides and a desk, chair, and telephone at the far end; there are three long windows, also at the far end of the room, through which light from the street enters. For the entire duration of the film, the camera zooms slowly and constantly toward the far wall, taking forty-five minutes to transform the long shot of the room into an extreme close-up of a portion of a photograph of waves tacked up on the wall. The film thus explores, by demonstration, the structure of the zoom — and it also explores and plays with the viewer's perception and expectation. At the beginning of *Wavelength* the audience sees the representational image of a room — but as time passes, no one enters and nothing seems to happen. When some people at last do come into the room (they move a bookcase and then leave), the audience is teased into having certain dramatic expectations. Such teasing occurs again late in the film when a man walks into the frame and then collapses out of it, presumably dead, and when a woman, discovering the body (an act we don't see), makes a telephone call. A tension is thus created between the viewer's perception of the film as transparent, as a window through which one looks at something real, and the perception of the film as opaque, as a canvas which explores its own created space. Although nothing happens if one regards the frame as a window, a great deal happens if it is seen as a canvas: throughout the film, the light changes as the daylight comes in the window, and as the filmmaker adds artificial light and uses filters; exposure settings are changed as well, sometimes allowing the viewer to see clearly out the windows and at other times confining his vision indoors. *Wavelength* is frustrating, boring, tantalizing, and intellectually exciting in its exploration of cinema, aesthetics, and perception. It is also — like many other abstract films — a teaching film, for it teaches the viewer to look at the frame instead of through it.

Another example of this kind of abstract film which explores its own devices, its own construction, and which engages the viewer in active intellectual participation, is *Zorn's Lemma* (Hollis Frampton, 1970). The hour-long movie is divided into three sections: the first shows the viewer a black screen while a voice reads couplets from an eighteenth-century alphabet primer, the second introduces a series of one-second shots of alphabetically organized street signs, which are replaced "letter" by "letter" with more random imagery as the pattern is continually repeated, and the third is one long, static shot of a snow-covered landscape against which a medieval text on light and form is read by various voices in a repetitive rhythm. Basically, *Zorn's Lemma* is a film about learning, about reading (letters and images). Its first section presents us with the abstraction of words and letters heard from a reading primer. The second and most engaging section is a reading lesson, for the viewer attempts to learn the visual alphabet being set forth in place of the more familiar but equally arbitrary system of characters of the written alphabet. The viewer is quick to recognize that Frampton's choice of street signs is presented sequentially and each begins with a corresponding letter from the familiar alphabet (although there are some "letters" missing, among them most appropriately "I" and "U"). Thus, when random images of animals, objects, and places begin replacing the lettered signs, the viewer begins to equate them with alphabetical characters and tries to remember their signification as they are repeated. The entire section demonstrates the arbitrariness of language and the conventional demands of learning to read; it is also, perhaps, the most entertaining part of the film, for it gives the viewer "something to do," engaging him in active participation. The third section of the film seems frustrating and boring by comparison — and perhaps its very difficulty is the point. The viewer is confronted by a static long shot; if it is to be "read," then rote learning and alphabetical or visual signification will have to be abandoned and a new means of reading applied. Thus, *Zorn's Lemma* explores an intellectual and perceptual problem by demonstration and it is, in its own way, as rigorous and admittedly difficult as a written essay on a similar subject.

Not all abstract films are difficult in the manner of *Wavelength* and *Zorn's Lemma*. Films like these two, concerned with structure and perception, tend to be the most frustrating and hard to understand for an untutored audience. Many abstract films, however, like such works of art as paintings, sculpture, music, are meant to give aesthetic pleasure or to produce a physical sensation. Such films are conceived less to be understood than to be felt, sensed, experienced. These abstract films do not play with audience expectations or create shifts of perception of the film frame from transparent to opaque. They simply begin as opaque films — exploiting all the tools of cinematic technology to create art objects made from two-dimensional images which move on the canvas of the screen. Design and color become dominant elements in such works, much as in painting, but of course movement is an additional and unique element.

This sort of abstract film was one of the first forms of avant-garde and independent cinema. Indeed, some of its practitioners were artists in another medium. In the early 1920s, for example, Hans Richter and Viking Eggeling were painters who turned to film because the new medium offered opportunities to explore plastic expression and to add time to the kind of abstract works they were doing on canvas. Thus, in their *Rhythmus 21* (1921) they explore the form of the square, and in *Symphonie Diagonale* (1921–1924) they experiment with diagonal lines over a period of time. Similarly, Oskar Fischinger explored geometric forms and created abstract patterns based on musical structures and forms; he used shapes in time the way a composer uses notes in time. Usually quite short, this kind of absolute and abstract film has been made from film's early history to the present, and it has been particularly popular when combined with music. Fischinger, for example, was delighted when sound film made music an integral part of cinema, and further removed his "absolute" film studies from a connection with everyday reality: "Under the guidance of music . . . there came the speedy discovery of new laws — the application of acoustical laws to optical expression was possible. As in the dance, new motions and rhythms sprang out of the music — and the rhythms became more and more important." [6] The influence of Oskar Fischinger's work can be seen in the Bach "Toccata and Fugue in D minor" section of Walt Disney's *Fantasia* (1940), and many of Norman McLaren's films — paint directly applied to the film stock in rhythm to appealing music — have delighted audiences who might not enjoy other experimental films. McLaren's *Begone Dull Care* (1949), for example, uses bright colors and has a fluidity which gaily expresses a piece of jazz played by the Oscar Peterson Trio.

During the 1960s and 1970s other kinds of abstract cinema came into being, aided by advances in contemporary technology. In some films the images are quite beautiful and the film is a pleasurable experience; in other films the images are abrasive and assaultive, experimenting with the viewer's physiological responses to light and color and duration and sound. Jordon Belson's *Allures* (1961) uses subtle superimpositions to transform a pulsating globe of color and light into beautiful variations, in what he has called "cosmic" cinema. John Whitney's work depends upon computer graphics; the designs of a film like *Permutations* (1968) demonstrate Whitney's contention that the computer's ability to detail and repeat precisely with the minutest incremental variations a particular image, allows individual film images to function like musical notes. And many of the abstract films of Standish Lawder, dependent on stroboscopic lighting and a knowledge of human physiology (particularly brainwave patterns), are literally physical assaults on the viewer; *Corridor* (1968–1970) and *Raindance* (1974) are difficult to watch.

Finally we come to the nonrepresentational and abstract film which also, paradoxically, attempts to make a personal statement. What occurs on the screen insists on the opaqueness of the image. Yet what emerges is a personal vision rather than an abstract design. The greatest practitioner of what we can call humanist abstract film is surely Stan Brakhage, an independent filmmaker who has been making films which combine representational and nonrepresentational techniques for over twenty-five years. His first masterwork, *Dog Star Man* (1961) attempts to convey the idea of the creation of the universe, through personal and subjective images. As in many of his subsequent films, Brakhage uses color filters, hand-draws images, paints on top of photographs, makes holes in the film, and uses distorting lenses, hand-held camera, and multiple exposures. He is fascinated by the act of seeing, and in his films he attempts to capture the subjective, physiological, and social nature of vision. He wants the viewer's vision unfettered by the conventions of seeing; he wants to make us see freshly, rather than as we are *supposed* to as dictated by conventions of painting and optics. In a collection of his writings called *Metaphors on Vision*, Brakhage explains the philosophy behind his work: "I suggest that there is a pursuit of knowledge foreign to language and founded upon visual communication, demanding a development of the optical mind, and dependent upon perception in the original and deepest sense of the word." [7] Brakhage's recent works such as *The Act of Seeing with One's Own Eyes* (1971) and *Text of Light* (1974) continue his personal exploration of vision and perception.

Though its subject matter, structures, and techniques are so various as to make even broad classifications extremely difficult, all abstract, nonrepresentational cinema explores the film medium as a plastic expressive device. Film and the cinematic apparatus function like the canvas, paints, and brushes of the modern painter, like the score and instruments of the modern composer. The abstract film is a self-contained experience and expression. It is referential chiefly to itself. Its form is its content; its content is revealed through its form.

★★★   **The Animated Film**

> Animation is an animated film.
> A protest against the stationary condition.
> Animation transporting movement of nature directly cannot be creative animation.
> Animation is a technical process in which the final result must always be creative.
> To animate: to give life and soul to a design, not through the copying but through the transformation of reality.
> Life is warmness.
> Warmness is movement.
> Movement is life.
> Animation is giving life; it means giving warmth.
> . . .
> Take one kilo of ideas (not too confused if possible), five dkg of talent, ten dkg of hard work and a few thousand designs. Shake it all together and if you are lucky you will not get the right answer to the question.
> Collective statement of cartoonists of the Zagreb studio[8]

Although most animated films are generally associated with mainstream commercial cinema and thus seem far removed from difficult and shocking experimental, underground, and avant-garde films, it is appropriate to discuss animation in the same chapter as these other, less accessible, works of film art. On the one hand, many avant-garde, abstract films are animated — from the work of early abstract filmmakers like Eggeling and Fischinger to contemporary film artists like Norman McLaren and Robert Breer. On the other hand, even commercial narrative animation is removed from reality, since the figures are drawn and not photographed. Couple this with animation's penchant for the fantastic transformation of space and matter, and you have a form which is closer to the abstract film than to the documentary.

All animated films — whether using pictures, models, or live actors — are based on **single-frame cinematography.** During the shooting process, instead of the continuous and automatic movement of the film stock through the camera at the rate of twenty-four frames per second, the film moves through the camera at a rate controlled by the filmmaker. Because the filmmaker can photograph three frames of a subject or twelve frames or twenty-four, he controls how long a particular image will be seen on the screen. Controlling the time an image occupies the screen also controls the speed of its movement in space. A cartoon rabbit can be made to appear as if its movement were human and natural; a human being can be made to appear as jerky in movement as a doll or puppet. How smooth or how disconnected the animation will seem is determined by how many single frames are shot of the movement in question or how many are eliminated.

Imagine, for example, that it takes one second for a person in real life to raise his hand above his head. In a non-animated film, that action would be recorded through the course of twenty-four frames as they move automatically through the camera; one increment of movement of the arm would be contained in each of those twenty-four frames — a second of film time. If a filmmaker wanted a drawn animal or a model puppet to seem lifelike in its movement, ideally he would make twenty-four different drawings corresponding in their increments to human movements or move the puppet twenty-four different times — each change recorded on one frame of film photographed singly (Figure 8-5). When that film was ready for projection, it would be moved automatically through the projector, like any other film, at the rate of twenty-four frames per second and the action on the screen would appear lifelike, smooth and unbroken. Because of the monumental labor involved, no human animator attempts this ideal — although computer-created animation can achieve it. It has been generally recognized that relatively smooth and lifelike animation can be accomplished if that one second of real action is translated into eighteen increments of movement, single-framed, and then projected at twenty-four frames per second. Less smooth but still acceptable as lifelike are nine increments of movement, each photographed two times and comprising two frames (double-framing). And often student filmmakers whose time and resources are limited may settle for six increments of movement, each photographed three times and comprising three frames (triple-framing). How many separate drawings or movements a filmmaker uses finally depends, however, on how lifelike he wishes the movement to be, how representational of real movement. While some animators wish their drawn characters or puppets to move like humans, other animators may wish their subjects to move like drawn characters or puppets. Just as with any other kind of filmmaking, the art of animation may be shaped by an urge to realism or, on the other hand, by an urge to fantasy. Indeed, the history of animation leads in two directions — the one taken by Walt Disney in the 1940s and after, in which the drawn figures become more and more lifelike, and the other taken by abstract artists like Robert Breer, a contemporary animator whose work makes no attempt at realism. Yet, despite these two divergent impulses, all animated film is to a fairly great degree unrealistic, for it uses the screen as a world disconnected from the one in which the viewer moves continuously and smoothly through time and three dimensions.

★ **8-5** Directing animator Ollie Johnston makes faces in a mirror to help him capture subtleties of expressions for drawing characters for Walt Disney's ROBIN HOOD (1973).

What unites all animated film is its basis in single-frame rather than continuous cinematography. What separates different kinds of animated film is the material to be animated and how that material must be manipulated before the camera to achieve movement. There are basically two sorts of material: two-dimensional and three-dimensional. Two-dimensional animation can consist of drawings or paper shapes and cutouts or pictures, photographs, and paintings. Three-dimensional animation uses as its material such diverse subjects as clay, puppets, miscellaneous objects like a pack of cards or pieces of fruit, and human beings. Each kind of animation, although based on single-frame cinematography, has its own requirements determined by the material.

TWO-DIMENSIONAL ANIMATION

Animation is a chorus of drawings working in tandem, each contributing a part to the whole of a time/space idea. If a single drawing, as a drawing, dominates the action it is probably bad animation, even though it may be good drawing.
Chuck Jones[9]

The most popular and oldest form of two-dimensional animation is made with drawings. Drawn animation requires that many separate drawings be made of an object or character's consecutive movements. In simple animation (a single stick figure, for example, against a blank background), the drawings may be done on paper and the changes made (for example, an arm is drawn a trifle higher, and in the next drawing, still higher) after the basic shape has been generally traced. Then two or three frames of each drawing are photographed; when the film is run continuously, movement is achieved. More complexly drawn animation requires another method, for if there are several drawn figures who will move against a drawn background which will also change to correspond to their movements, the task of making entirely separate sketches would be prohibitive in time and therefore in cost. Instead, an efficient method of complex animation has been devised called **cel animation.** An individual scene in the script is broken down into its background, middle ground, and foreground components, each of which is painted on an individual sheet of transparent celluloid. Together — one on top of the other — they form a "sandwich." Without having to draw the same background again and again, the animator may simply move his middle-ground cel containing cartoon figures across it, single-framing as they move. Those figures may be complete but for a few crucial omissions of feet and hands. Those parts of their anatomy which indicate movements of walking or pointing and so forth will be drawn on the foreground cel so that they contain all the tiny variables of movement to be seen in the finished film. Thus, for some portions of his film, the animator may be able to use the same drawing of a background and the same drawings of his characters and will only have to alter the top layer of his sandwich. Although cel animation is efficient compared to the process of making individual drawings, it is still complex, time-consuming, and expensive, and thus the range and aesthetic complexity of cel-animated film varies widely, dependent upon how many layers exist in a given sandwich and how many drawn items move simultaneously. Cartoons made in the 1930s and 1940s, the classic Walt Disney features and short cartoons of artists like Max and Dave Fleischer, Walter Lantz, Paul Terry, Bob Clampett, Tex Avery, and Chuck Jones, for example, used many more individual drawings with a great deal more movement than the current animated cartoons made expressly for Saturday morning television viewing.

From film's beginnings, the animated drawing has been associated with the cartoon; it is the moving version of a comic-strip narrative. Drawn human or anthropomorphic animal characters enact a short and simple tale, in the process usually violating physical laws which govern the external and undrawn world. For example, a mouse may flatten a cat with a hammer and a moment later the cat resumes its usual shape. These cartoon stories are almost always fantasy creations, their humor derived from the visual articulation of the impossible: animals talking and moving like human beings (Figure 8-6), the subversion of natural laws of gravity and cause and effect, the fluid transformation of the physical from one object to another, and the removal of pain and mor-

★ 8-6 Through the years Mickey Mouse became less animal-like and more
human, a general trend to greater realism taken by the Disney Studio until
they moved into making live-action films. Above left, STEAMBOAT WILLIE
(1928); above right, THE DOGNAPPER (1934); below left, FANTASIA
(1940); below right, MICKEY'S BIRTHDAY PARTY (1942).

tality from physical violence. Animal protagonists from the earliest
Gertie the Dinosaur, who made her screen debut in Winsor McCay's
1910 cartoon, through Felix the Cat, Mickey Mouse, Bugs Bunny, and
Roadrunner live in a world in which violence and mutilation are carried
to extremes but never lead to permanent disfigurement and death. In
Chuck Jones's *Rabbit Punch* (1947), for example, Bugs Bunny is a boxer.
Confronted in the ring by a huge opponent who literally is transformed
into a speeding locomotive as he charges Bugs, the resourceful and self-
conscious rabbit disintegrates the film space and destroys the cartoon by
"cutting" the film and facing the audience in triumph. Like live slapstick comedy, though carried much further, such cartoons let us laugh
with delight at an impossible world liberated from mortality. We almost
never feel sorry for the victims in a cartoon. Thus, it is extremely surprising and unsettling when an animator introduces death into his film,
whether it be in a Disney film like *Bambi* (1942) or a modern animated
feature like Ralph Bakshi and Robert Crumb's *Fritz the Cat* (1972) (Figure 8-7). Although the social milieu in which the animated animal protagonist moves during much of this film is realistic, treating as it does
sex, drugs, greed, and opportunism, its violence is still cartoon violence
and characters are quickly resurrected to act again. At one point in the
film, however, one of Fritz's friends and advisers — a crow — is killed.

★ 8-7 It usually is a given of the cartoon in which animals act like human beings that sex and death usually do not exist. But Ralph Bakshi's FRITZ THE CAT (1972) is an example of a cartoon feature made for adults in which both sex and death are an accepted part of his creatures' world, just as they are of ours.

In intense and surreal images, drops of its blood turn into billiard balls and are sunk into pockets on a pool table which fills the screen. Once they are gone, we find that the crow has died and there is no resurrection to meet our cartoon expectations. The result is disturbingly effective, for the viewer is thrown back into a real world, one in which violence and murder lead to expected ends.

Putting aside such an unusual introduction of the laws of the real world, cartoon animation is basically surrealistic, following not the causal logic of human experience but, instead, creating its own logic (Figure 8-8). There is, however, another major impulse in the animated cartoon, particularly evident in its feature form which sustains its length by depending on a more highly structured narrative. Begun by Disney and his studio in *Snow White and the Seven Dwarfs* (1937), a range of animated narratives has pretended to a certain kind of representationalism and verisimilitude in the midst of fantasy stories and drawn worlds. Along with animals who have been anthropomorphized, the films begin to feature human characters who are meant to seem real and who, thus, seem to function in a less imaginative sphere and according to more comprehensible physical logic than the liberated animal characters of the cartoon short. Despite this urge toward greater realism, however, the animated cartoon — no matter how narratively logical or how anthropomorphic — is drawn, and so it is patently unreal. Indeed, part of the wonder and pleasure the viewer feels toward such attempts at verisimilitude is the skill of its execution, the wonder derived from how lifelike an obviously drawn figure seems.

Drawn animation goes beyond the short or feature cartoon geared to youngsters and theatrical entertainment. A great deal of drawn animation is used for social, political, educative, and aesthetic ends. Often,

★ **8-8** Greater and greater realism in animation both in story and in drawing has not meant the end of fantasy. THE YELLOW SUBMARINE (George Dunning, 1968) is full of outlandish sequences where queer creatures spring to life from the pens and the creative imaginations of the animators.

political satire and social commentary can find an outlet in the animated film where it would be suppressed in a potentially "too real" live-action film. The rise of a full-scale animation movement in Eastern Europe in the mid-1950s probably stemmed in part from this fact. Zagreb, Yugoslavia — the home of the Zagreb Studio, founded in 1956 — has become the center of that movement and the site of an international animation festival held every year to screen and honor short animated films from countries all over the world. Like many of their independent live-action counterparts, these animated films are politically and socially conscious. In their brief, humorous and witty, and occasionally grim stories, they frequently satirize the conventions and traditions of modern society, attack not only capitalism but complacent Communism, promote ecology, and warn against the perils of automation, dehumanization, pollution, and overpopulation.

Serious animation can be used, too, by the avant-garde or experimental filmmaker to explore film structure, perception, the nature of film and its ability to create illusions. Robert Breer, for example, a leading American avant-garde animator, combines representational photographs with exact drawn duplications which then change to something else, which move and then stop. In a relatively accessible cartoon like *A Man and His Dog Out for Air* (1957), Breer has drawn lines which romp across the screen to the accompaniment of natural sounds, and

407

only at the end of the film's three minutes do the lines coalesce to form the subjects of the film's title. Breer uses animation quite differently, however, in *Fuji* (1974), which bases an animated exploration of color and line on Mt. Fuji's initial representational presence in a piece of raw footage Breer took from a train window when he was traveling through Japan. The former painter was instrumental in pioneering rapid and assaultive **collage films** in which single-frame animation techniques are used to capture a different image in each frame; the effect when such images are projected is dizzying, and certainly visually stimulating. Breer is chiefly interested in the artistic possibilities of animation: "Animation implies making something inanimate appear to be animate; though single-frame filmmaking can include that, it isn't necessarily confined to that. A lot of my films don't involve the illusion of motion at all but are constructed out of time intervals and space changes." [10]

In addition to drawn animation, there are other kinds of two-dimensional animation. Many animated films regard the screen as a flat canvas upon which paper shapes and cutouts may be made to move. The results may be simple, or they may be extraordinarily complex. In the 1950s Stan Vanderbeek began making animated collage films using cutouts from magazines, line drawings, and photographs; other filmmakers, influenced by his work, expanded the possibilities of the form. In an amazing work called *Frank Film* (Carolyn and Frank Mouris, 1973), the filmmaker animates, through single-frame cinematography, cutouts from advertisements of consumer goods, pinups, magazine pictures of all sorts, and presents them to the viewer as an autobiographical accumulation of images stored in his consciousness (Figure 8-9). Frank Mouris sees the materials he uses in his films as "found objects, found images, which I rework into my own kind of universe which they make completely from scratch through drawings." [11] Combined with multiple and overlapping sound track, the images overwhelm the viewer with their rapid movement and patterning so that the sensory overload of stimuli the filmmaker speaks of is actually experienced by the person watching the film. A similar technique has been applied to photographs and paintings in the work of Charles Braverman, who has used single-frame cinematography to make visual collages like his *An American Time Capsule*. Originally released in 1968 as a three-minute film, it has since been brought more up to date — to 1975 — and another minute added. In the film, Braverman creates an accelerating collage of secondary source materials — the face of an American President on a piece of currency; a painting by Frederic Remington, the great painter of cowboys; magazine and newspaper photos — to relate the history of the United States visually. The technique of animation not only allows him to show a

★ **8-9** Frank Mouris created a visual and aural biography in his FRANK FILM (1973). With the use of multiple sound tracks and a dazzling collage of images (11,592 in nine minutes), the film depicts the complex continuity of a mind recalling the past and free-associating in the present.

great deal of material in a very short time, but also allows him a very tight control over the rhythms of the editing so that he can simulate in film form the increasing tempo of American life as it becomes more compressed and complex. Finally, a trend in two-dimensional animation is now being created by advances in computer technology. The computer is able to "draw" two-dimensional figures as well as to help animators work out their increments of motion more exactly and efficiently. In addition a number of computer animations have been filmed that resemble the most absolute and abstract avant-garde and independent films.

THREE-DIMENSIONAL ANIMATION

When George Méliès first realized that stopping the camera, changing the position of a single object within the frame while leaving the other elements in the frame constant, and then starting the camera up again would result in the magical illusion of that object popping out of one spot and reappearing in another, he laid the groundwork for live-action and three-dimensional animation. Any inanimate object could be given the appearance of motion simply by manipulating it and photographing it exactly in the manner of two-dimensional animation. Projected, the object would appear to move. In 1910, the great French animator Emile Cohl delighted audiences with *La Chambre Ensorcelée* (*The Automatic Moving Company*), in which the entire furnishings of a house pack themselves away without any assistance. Spoons disappear into drawers, knives march themselves into racks, beds make themselves up. This same technique is used today — sometimes to amuse, sometimes to perturb. A noted Polish animator, Walerian Borowczyk, animates objects to create surreal visions which sometimes evoke the illogic and terror of nightmares. In *Dom* (*House*), made in 1958, for example, a wig inexorably and sinisterly climbs a table and consumes everything on it.

While there is a particular fascination attached to seeing common objects take on an animated existence of their own, three-dimensional animation is also a form for animating what are essentially sculptures. Modeling clay is therefore a particularly attractive medium in which the animator can work and many films use it in humorous and interesting ways. There has been, for example, a children's series of clay-model animation featuring a clay figure named Gumby and his clay horse Pokey. Little pieces of modeling clay join themselves together and turn into fantastic monsters who eventually metamorphose into Man in *Clay: Origin of the Species* (Eliot Noyes, Jr., 1964). Dolls also provide a popular material with which the three-dimensional animator can work. There was, for example, a whole commercial series of doll animation films, called "Puppetoons," made by George Pal beginning in the 1940s. And the foremost pioneer of doll animation, Jiří Trnka, began making his unique films in Czechoslovakia in 1946. He used his figures to explore space, to mimic or create elaborate operatic effects, ballets. And, as well, Trnka used his animated dolls for satire and allegory; in *The Hand* (1956) his combination of cutouts and little animated dolls produces an absorbing allegory of repression in a totalitarian state.

Three-dimensional animation can also take the form of live-action animated film. Again, based on the principles of pixilation which Méliès discovered (stopping and starting the camera after every few frames), animating a live-action subject differs in its aesthetic implications from other forms of animation. Consider that all animated film, whether two- or three-dimensional, confers movement on a normally inanimate subject — a drawing, a doll, a wig. It brings to life — to motion in space and/or time — that which has no life. When the animated subject is already a living creature, however, the process seems to work in reverse.

Instead of adding motion, the live-action animator takes it away — literally cutting time (and increments of motion) away through the process of single-framing, so the resultant motion of the live subject will seem jerky and artificial. Basically, this technique makes live people and animals abstract, unreal, and they are able to function not as credible characters but as cartoon figures.

Animated films range from serious to comic, from simple to complex, from witty and irreverent to subtly beautiful or surrealistically disturbing. They can range from the wonderful and anarchic characters dreamed up by the great Hollywood animators for a mass market to those personal visions which are seen and appreciated by a small, elite audience. No matter which, the animated film will always be with us — for it is a form through which the artist with an interest in color, mass, and movement, with the belief that a film is a canvas, can express himself.

And perhaps this urge to personal expression allows us to sum up the entire group of films surveyed in this section: experimental, independent, and animated films. For the most part these films are made by individual artists, even when made in collaboration with others. Certainly, we have seen that Hollywood studio cartoons bear the stamp of their creators. And non-studio-produced films are even more usually singular works by singular artists. Creating this kind of cinema, the filmmaker closely resembles the traditional artist practicing in a more private medium: the painter, the sculptor, the composer. He can say exactly what he wants to say in moving pictures whether he photographs people or objects, animates drawings or clay, uses a script to tell a story, cracks a joke, or shares a cosmic vision.

NOTES

[1] "What Are You Ready For?" *December* 7, no. 1 (1965): 150.

[2] *Art in Cinema* (San Francisco: San Francisco Museum of Art, 1947), p. 58.

[3] *Art in Cinema*, pp. 29–30.

[4] Georges Sadoul, *Dictionary of Films* (Berkeley: University of California Press, 1972), p. 31.

[5] Interviewed by P. Adams Sitney, "Metaphors on Vision," *Film Culture* 30 (Fall 1963), unpaged.

[6] *Art in Cinema*, p. 38.

[7] Interviewed by P. Adams Sitney, "Metaphors on Vision."

[8] Ronald Holloway, *Z Is for Zagreb* (London: Tantivy Press, 1972), p. 9.

[9] "Animation Is a Gift Word," *AFI Report* (Summer 1974), p. 29.

[10] "Animation Is a Gift Word," p. 35.

[11] "Animation Is a Gift Word," p. 36.

PART IV
A GUIDE TO
FILM
ANALYSIS
AND
CRITICISM

★★★   **Reading and Writing About Film**

We all like to talk about the movies we've seen. Sometimes the talk is simple, an evaluation or a recommendation: "I hated that movie. Don't waste your money." Sometimes, however, the talk is more complex, an attempt to increase understanding of a cinematic experience and to share perceptions: "What do you think all those shots of water are supposed to mean in Robert Altman's *Three Women*?" "Maybe the water imagery has something to do with birth since the one character is pregnant. Water's supposed to be the source of all life." Whether simple or complex, these conversations take place almost anywhere — in dorm rooms, at cocktail parties, over a lunch, while riding a bus to school or work, or, as Woody Allen humorously demonstrated in *Annie Hall* (1977), in lines outside movie theaters. These conversations about films, though often chiefly social, usually become more organized and specific in a classroom. And, of course, at their most structured, these expressions of ideas about film become written discourse taking the various forms of student papers, published critical articles, film reviews, and books on film theory and criticism.

Basically, writing about film can be divided into three kinds: film reviewing, film criticism, and film theory. Each kind presupposes a specific audience and a specific aim. A film review, for example, is written typically for someone who has not yet seen the film in question, and it aims at offering a recommendation to see or avoid the film. A piece of film criticism on the same movie, however, usually assumes that the reader will be familiar with the film, and it aims at analyzing the film. In the review, description of the film will often be quite general; it will say what the film is about, who is in it, what kind of movie it is. The critical article, however, examining a film familiar to both writer and reader, will be more specific and will tend to concentrate on a particular aesthetic, historical, cultural, or ideological issue. Indeed, in the third kind of film writing — film theory — aesthetic, cultural, historical, and ideological issues themselves become the focus, and specific films may not even be mentioned. The aim or function of film theory is to explore the nature of the film medium rather than the particulars of specific films, and such writing assumes a cinematically literate and sophisticated reader.

Though conversation about films can be stimulating and rewarding, reading and writing about films can provide a more coherent and contemplative pleasure. A thoughtful, well-argued book or article can open up the reader's experience and understanding of particular films, film history, film's relationship with other arts, film form and aesthetics, film and its relationship to social, economic, and political realities. Such writing can bring little-known films to the public's attention, resurrect interest in a director or performer or a period of film history, generate new ideas about form.

Students sometimes express irritation at having to read about films they have or have not seen. They may feel that simply watching and talking about the work is enough. Yet for a more than casual understanding of the art and history and mechanisms of cinema, it is necessary to read and write about film. Perhaps especially because the film experience is so transient — we watch the images pass quickly before our eyes and we can't say, "Stop, I want to see that part over again" — the act of reading and writing, which is slow, deliberate, and contemplative, adds a proper balance to the study of film. This section of the book will provide an introduction to the many ways film has been and can be written about. The Historical Overview will treat professional writing about film. Chapter 9 will focus on student writing about film and offer suggestions about the planning and writing of a college paper on film.

Historical Overview:
The Development of Film Reviewing, Criticism, and Theory

THE FIRST REVIEWS

The first English-language article printed about a projected film screening appeared in the New York *Times* on April 24, 1896, the day after the first "Projecting Kinetoscope" exhibition at Koster & Bial's Music Hall. For the next decade, professional film writing did little more than announce a new program of film releases and synopsize their plots. There was no attempt at evaluation or critical analysis, no recognition of film as a new art form. In fact, the first extensive writing about film which appeared on a regular basis recognized it as a money-making business. As the motion picture industry grew, trade journals and papers devoted exclusively to film were founded: *Views and Film Index* in 1906, the *Moving Picture World* and *Moving Picture News* in 1907.

Individual films (nearly all one-reelers, lasting about ten minutes) at first received hardly more than a plot summary in the trade journals. Yet, surprisingly, it was in the trade journals rather than in daily newspapers that longer, more thoughtful articles began to appear. On September 19, 1908, for example, the *Moving Picture World* carried an article which compared acting styles for the moving picture drama with the acting styles used in theatrical live drama. And the piece began this comparison of the two acting styles with a recognition of the film as art: "That the moving picture drama is an art, is a proposition as yet not well recognized by the public at large."

Thus, writers within and without the trade began to see and note the artistic potential of film, addressing themselves to discussions of aesthetic, moral, and social values in the new medium. Between 1908 and 1912

416

Frank E. Woods, for example, wrote a weekly film column under the by-line of "The Spectator" for the New York *Dramatic Mirror*. His thoughtful commentary, going beyond mere plot description to offer his readers evaluative responses, earned him a place in film history as the first major American film critic. He influenced to some degree the viewing habits of his readers, foreshadowing the kind of popular influence enjoyed today by a number of widely read (or seen and heard) film reviewers like Pauline Kael, Rex Reed, and Gene Shalit. Daily newspapers, however, saw no need for specialized film reviewers or critics. Instead, they assigned their regular drama critics or other staff reporters to cover those few films thought to be noteworthy.

D. W. Griffith's *The Birth of a Nation* (1915) was one such newsworthy film. By establishing the possibilities of cinema as a form of highbrow art as well as lowbrow entertainment, Griffith's epic created a subject for serious critical concern. With the release of *The Birth of a Nation,* the movies began to be worth discussion. After their initial discussions of *The Birth of a Nation,* journals like the *Nation* and the *New Republic,* which had hitherto seen the movies as mass entertainment for an uneducated populace, and therefore of no interest to their highly literate readership, began to review films on a regular basis. And from 1915 to the present day, regular film columns and reviews of current releases have been an integral part of daily newspapers and general magazines. Specialized film reviewers have gradually replaced the drama critic gone slumming or the available reporter who, at the moment, had nothing better to do than review a movie for his newspaper.

With the exception of *Photoplay,* founded in 1912 and an extremely literate fan magazine, it wasn't until the 1920s that specialized magazines treating film subjects seriously and aimed at the general public appeared. The National Board of Review (established in 1908 as a regulatory film censorship organization) founded the first such publication in 1920 with *Exceptional Photoplays.* This magazine provided reviews and analyses of current films and aimed at informing the general public of worthy and exceptional entertainments.

The end of the silent era of film began a new era in film writing. It was as if viewers, having lost the great art of the silent film to the crude and noisy stumbling of the early sound film, felt the need to write and to read about the passing of something they suddenly realized was important. Two periodicals chiefly concerned with the theory and the artistry of films, *Close-up* and *Experimental Cinema,* began publishing in 1929. Since then, both in the United States and abroad, journals devoted solely to film subjects and directed toward a readership of non-trade people have enjoyed considerable success.

THE EMERGENCE OF FILM THEORY: AMERICA AND EUROPE

Appropriately, coincidental with the year in which *The Birth of a Nation* was released, 1915, the first book-length study of film was published, *The Art of the Moving Picture,* by the American poet Vachel Lindsay. This book, the first major work of film theory, attempted both to distinguish the properties of film from those of other arts and to synthesize the properties of other arts within the one art of cinema. The second major book about film, Hugo Münsterberg's *The Photoplay: A Psychological Study,* appeared in the following year, 1916, the year which also saw the release of Griffith's second masterwork, *Intolerance.* In this book Münsterberg, an eminent German psychologist on the faculty of Harvard University, explored the psychological relationship between the film viewer and the screen image. Both of these theoretical books argue that cinema deserves a place alongside of the time-honored arts. Both Lindsay and Münsterberg had to deal with the supposedly unartistic mechanical quality of film: its ability to record a representation of reality. Thus, both theorists stressed the ways in which the film medium changed and restructured the normal and lived flow of reality into something new and artificial, that is, artful. They viewed and praised film as artifice, as formal construction, as material shaped by an individual artist's mind and hand.

Similar theoretical arguments appeared in essays all during the 1920s as intellectuals sought to validate as art what appeared to most people to be simply a highly profitable form of show business, and later as appalled critics saw the highly developed art of the silent cinema abandoned for the merely representational qualities of the infant sound movie. Not surprisingly, most of this serious theoretical writing about film thrived in Europe, where intellectuals had been attracted to filmmaking from the birth of the medium. (France, for example, had initiated the extensive filming of classic stage plays and famous novels well before World War I.) It was also in Europe during the 1920s that intellectuals and artists devoted to all the arts gathered and talked and put their aesthetic ideas into position papers and manifestos. In America, however, in the 1920s and early 1930s intellectuals scarcely took part in theorizing about film. There were, of course, some thoughtful reviews of specific films in the major periodicals of the time by critics like Edmund Wilson, Aldous Huxley, and Robert E. Sherwood, but no native major theorists or theories developed between the two world wars. After Hugo Münsterberg's book of 1916, the development of film theory and criticism became chiefly a European activity.

Although two theoretical works by Frenchman Louis Delluc appeared in 1919 and 1920 (*Cinéma et Cie* and *Photogénie*), the first major European work of theoretical importance was a book called *The Visible Man, or Film Culture.* This important book, published in German in 1924, was written by Béla Bálázs, an expatriate Hungarian filmmaker and theorist, and is said to have greatly influenced the ideas and work of the Soviet filmmaker and theorist V. I. Pudovkin. It is one of the few pieces of theoretical writing before the Second World War which sees no contradiction between the representational properties of film and its existence as an art, thus making it essentially a realist theory. It was, moreover, the first of a number of important theoretical works written by Bálázs which are now available in English translation, foremost among them *Theory of Film: Character and Growth of a New Art,* written in 1945 and translated in 1952. Bálázs's views on the medium of film seem remarkably modern, particularly his discussions of the potential of asynchronous sound and the power of the close-up.

Perhaps the most prolific and influential Europeans writing film theory during the 1920s were the Russians. Limited by their lack of access to the photographic materials needed to make films of their own, the early Soviet filmmakers argued, theorized, and wrote in various journals and newspapers about the particular qualities and properties of the cinema, paying special theoretical attention to the editing process. V. I. Pudovkin in 1926 published *Film Technique,* first issued as a series of pamphlets in a group of technical handbooks on film. These essays developed the "linkage" theory of film editing and montage. In a later work, *Film Acting* (1935), Pudovkin examined film performance in one of the few major works exploring the subject. Although Pudovkin insisted on the primacy of the emotional content of the film narrative, he was essentially a formalist in theory, for he emphasized the artistic control of cinematic devices and technique, that is, he employed cinema not as representational or realistic, but as a reshaping of material into an artistic form. Sergei Eisenstein also began publishing during this period, many of his essays provoked by friendly if vehement argument with Pudovkin's editing theories. Eisenstein outlined his theory of montage editing (discussed on pp. 104–105), based on conflict and dialectic, in a series of essays which appeared after his installation as a faculty member in the State Cinema Technicum in 1928. These were later collected, translated into English, and published as the two major theoretical works, *The Film Sense* (1942) and *Film Form: Essays in Film Theory* (1949). Pudovkin's work also eventually was translated into English and collected into one volume, *Film Technique and Film Acting* (1958). The theoretical writings of these important Soviet filmmakers, though long unavailable in English, were widely circulated and discussed throughout Europe and strongly influenced formal and manipulative approaches to the film medium.

TECHNOLOGY AND THEORY: FROM FORMALISM TO REALISM

The transition to sound at the beginning of the 1930s seemed to emphasize the literal, representational, and mechanical potentials of film at the expense of its abilities to communicate figuratively and artistically. Sound, both because it made greater realism possible and, at the same time, seemed crude, implied that the art of the cinema was based less on creativity than recording. For many critics and theorists sound appeared to be the enemy of art; for them, the art of cinema was the art of *silent* cinema, an art found not in film's ability to take representational photographs of real life which happened to move, but in film's *inability* to reproduce and represent real life. This inability to represent real life meant that the film artist had to create an imaginative alternative. The critics of sound felt that it had destroyed a *visual* art form and that filmmakers now merely engaged in the representational filming of verbal dramas.

Although several of the great Soviet filmmakers and theorists like Eisenstein and Dziga Vertov wrote of the possibilities of expressive sound montage, and Bálázs in Germany argued in *The Spirit of the Film* (1930) for the use of asynchronous sound as a counteractive to the literal quality of early sound film, Rudolf Arnheim, a German aesthetician, was thoroughly pessimistic. In a small book called *Film as Art,* published in 1933, Arnheim argued that film was a visual art in which the representation of reality was a minor element. Like other formalist theoreticians before him, he argued that film is art if the artist manipulates the plastic materials of film. The artist, not reality, determines the making of a film, for the artist, by editing and by selecting focal lengths and shot compositions, creates the rhythm and the visual patterns. Indeed, nearly all experimental and non-story films owe their aesthetics to Arnheim's position, as do many narrative films. *Film as Art,* which codifies the formalist theoretical position, has been until recently the most widely read book of film theory ever written.

Less rigid film writing continued on its own course through the 1930s and 1940s, acknowledging and embracing sound and color and other technical advancements which allowed the medium to achieve greater visual and aural fidelity to reality. After World War II, the emphasis on the formal qualities of film lessened and the emphasis on humanistic and contemporary subject matter that had been "caught" on the screen, rather than manipulated onto it, increased. Indeed, following the war, major works of theory and criticism attempted to justify this new realism by asserting that it took full advantage of the unique properties of the cinema. The ability of film to be socially relevant in ways denied to the other arts was much praised and discussed. Critical writing published in Great Britain arose out of the strong documentary movement of the 1930s and the influence of John Grierson, whose work — both practical and theoretical — was concerned with the primacy of the "raw material" of life from which films were made. In the United States, film critics like Harry Alan Potamkin, Otis Ferguson, Robert Warshow, and James Agee discussed film from political and sociological perspectives; although their work tended to discuss specific films rather than the theory of cinema, they suggested paths that today's theoreticians are only now treading. And, finally, in postwar Italy, **scriptwriters** like Cesare Zavattini and film directors like Roberto Rossellini — identified worldwide as Italian neo-realists — in their films, theoretical writings, and manifestos promoted a "new realism" in films.

This shift in theoretical emphasis from **formalism** to **realism** was fully realized with the founding, in 1951, of the *Cahiers du Cinéma,* the noted French film journal. The major force behind the magazine and a constant contributor to its pages was André Bazin, a film critic who has since been recognized as the first of the significant realist theoreticians. Ironically, Bazin, who wrote essays rather than books, really did not develop a codified theory of film like Eisenstein or Arnheim. Bazin's essays, however, were theoretical in their arguments about the nature of the film medium, and he clearly identified those properties of cinema which have since been linked with realist film practice: deep-focus cinematography and the opposition between montage editing and mise-en-scène editing. Bazin's essays were eventually collected and translated into English in a two-volume work called *What Is Cinema?* (1967–1971). By then, however, his work had long since influenced the French new wave films and filmmaker-critics like Jean-Luc Godard and François Truffaut. Indeed, as early as 1956, Godard reacted to realist film theory with an essay prefiguring current theoretical practice, which sees the division between formalist and realist aesthetics, between montage and mise-en-scène, as arbitrary and possibly irrelevant to the viewing experience.

Despite Godard's article, the major emphasis through the 1950s and most of the 1960s was on realist aesthetics. The second most influential work of realist theory was published in 1960 by Sigfried Kracauer, a German who had emigrated to America before the Second World War. His *Theory of Film: The Redemption of Physical Reality* argues that film is a photographic art which, by capturing and organizing images of reality, allows the viewer to see more of that reality than he could merely with his eyes in his ordinary life. The film frame to Kracauer is a window on the world, and the camera eye is able to see not only what we see under usual circumstances but also what is overlooked or imperceptible to the human eye.

CONTEMPORARY THEORY AND CRITICISM

By the late 1960s, the distinctions between formalism and realism, between Eisenstein and Arnheim and Bazin and Kracauer, seemed less illuminating than they had been. In actual practice, films used both formal and realist technique, and little theoretical writing seemed to deal with this contradictory fact. Emphasis in theoretical discourse moved elsewhere. In the United States, attention was directed at first toward the auteur theory, formulated in France and transformed into something slightly different by its American proponent, Andrew Sarris. Less a theory than a methodology, the auteur theory and practice, as set forth in Sarris's *The American Cinema: Directors and Directions, 1929–1968,* initiated a huge number of studies of directors, and it resurrected previously unknown films. It was also responsible for perhaps the only major publicized theoretical debate between two American film critics. Pauline Kael dismissed the auteur theory, and Sarris countered in what proved to be a series of fascinating essays. Eventually, the attention to film directors also extended the auteur theory to consideration of screenwriters, cinematographers, and performers. Critics in the United States and elsewhere also turned their attention to film genres; this inquiry into defining groups of popular films has been largely non-theoretical, but that is currently changing.

Perhaps the greatest shift in theoretical emphasis occurred in 1968 with the publication in France of Christian Metz's *Film Language: A Semiotics of the Cinema.* The work was immediately controversial. Although it has since been amended and argued about and rejected for various reasons, it must be considered an important work of contemporary film theory. Metz's book, initiating an entirely new approach to the study of film, suggested that the theoretician study the viewer's understanding of specific cinematic devices in an attempt to find out if and how film comprises a language (analogous to verbal language) through its structures and codes. This work introduced the application of linguistic sign theory to the study of film. It argued, too, for the study of film as a science, and it promoted close textual analysis of specific works. Metz's position angered and threatened those critics, scholars, and theoreticians who felt that film study was not a science, that the interpretation of visual images could not be codified, and that **semiotics,** lacking a comprehensible terminology and methodology, was a dead end.

After the initial furor over Metz's approach had subsided, his work was attacked for other reasons. His attempts to understand signification in film were criticized by Marxist film critics, who pointed to the contradiction between Metz's theory and his unwillingness to recognize that sign systems are culturally and ideologically based. Since 1975, then, semiological theory has moved into more culturally and politically defined discourse and has, as well, attempted to incorporate psychoanalytic principles into its study of the relationship between film and viewer. Other theoretical positions, too, are currently popular in the United States and abroad: phenomenological, structural, anthropological, perceptual, and even physiological. Indeed, the explosion of interest in the study of film as an art and a scholarly discipline during the 1960s and 1970s has led to a boom in the publication of journals and books which treat film from an extraordinarily wide variety of theoretical positions.

Today many magazines and journals devoted to film provide a platform for critical discourse on any aspect of film one might imagine. There are journals devoted to popular film, to silent cinema, to national cinemas, to interdisciplinary aspects of the medium. And, of course, daily newspapers and magazines for a general audience continue to feature the work of practicing film critics and reviewers. Films are seen, examined, dissected, analyzed, studied, and written about by buffs, collectors, archivists, historians, teachers, scholars, journalists, critics, and theoreticians. At its best, such writing can help the viewer and student of film to understand the medium, its art, and its artists more fully.

A selected list of reading materials designed to help students and viewers expand their general knowledge of film history, theory, and criticism appears immediately following Chapter 9. It is important to recognize that all the ideas about film explored in *An Introduction to Film* are part of the tradition of film writing produced in the past (and in the present) by historians, theoreticians, and critics. In turn, every student asked to write a paper about a film subject becomes a part of this tradition, and adds to the continuing discourse on film. Thus an investment of time reading some of the works suggested will not only help you complete a current assignment, but will also serve as an introduction to the ongoing tradition of film analysis and criticism.

9

★ *WRITING COLLEGE PAPERS ABOUT FILM*

Classes in film study frequently require essays. The reasons are both obvious and significant. Although factual and technical knowledge about film can be tested in short-answer exams, films arouse feelings and opinions, and these, as well as facts, should be open to discussion. Only in a paper can a student demonstrate his ability to analyze his responses.

Writing a paper helps a student to think. Papers force the student to confront the vagueness of unarticulated ideas and therefore to clarify unconscious assumptions. Of course, this kind of confrontation and clarification is hardly ever easy. Writing is not easy — even for those people who do it well. Putting the self on paper is putting the self on the spot, putting the self in possible peril. Even so, getting an idea actually articulated — *said* — so that one understands one's own feelings and communicates them to someone else, can be exhilarating. It's one thing simply to like or dislike a film and leave it at that, but to find out *why* one likes or dislikes it, to puzzle it out logically, is to deepen one's understanding and is a source, finally, of satisfaction.

Papers also serve as a dialogue between student and teacher. Because film study is a relatively new discipline, every student should feel encouraged by the possibility that he may be able to come up with an insight that has never been expressed before. The good film paper may very well instruct the instructor, helping him to see a film in a new way. But to say that students should approach the writing of a paper seriously is not to say that papers should be dull, solemn, or unimaginative. Rather, papers should reflect the way in which the student has interacted with the film in a lively, human, and vital manner. After all, along with close textual analysis and careful research, there is also a place for liveliness in film criticism. Here are two highly readable passages taken from student papers:

One of the best episodes in the whole film [Citizen Kane] is the breakfast table sequence in which Welles details (in miniature) the demise of Kane's first marriage — from endearment to estrangement — in a hundred and twenty seconds.

In My Man Godfrey, William Powell makes as good a disguised prince as any character from the Brothers Grimm. The film loses nothing for beginning in an East River dump rather than in an enchanted castle in Far Far Away. The inhabitants of this dump are kindly, intelligent, and decent, but they have been put under a spell by the evil witch Depression. Fortunately for all, the almost divine being Godfrey is living in their midst having descended from Boston and his wealthy family.

When one goes to see a film, one is carried away by romance, brought to tears or laughter, made tense through suspense, or moved to a recognition of the joy and despair of the human condition. One makes judgments too — consciously and unconsciously — about how well the film did what it seemed to set out to do. Writing papers about film extends this natural human critical act. Transforming one's initial reaction into an organized written commentary can lead to a greater awareness of both the self and the medium. Indeed, at times it is only after writing about a film that one really gets to know exactly what that particular film experience has meant personally. The significance of that first impression — rapid and immediate — only becomes clear in the quiet of the study afterwards.

★★★   ## The Critical Act: How to Start

Whenever we share our experience of art, whether in conversation or on paper, we are engaging in a critical act. Even so simple a phrase as "I liked the movie" or "That film was a waste of money" implies that the speaker has transformed earlier raw and unarticulated emotional response into a critical judgment. Such simple expressions of like or dislike, however, usually fail to communicate satisfactorily the total mass of undifferentiated feelings and ideas provoked by the experience of viewing a particular film. One really means, "It was a waste of money — except for that funny scene when . . ." or "I liked the movie because . . ." and so forth. Writing about the film, on the other hand, forces the writer to think *specifically* — to recall specific scenes, specific pieces of **dialogue,** specific camera movements or editorial techniques. Writing about a film lets the writer relive it, feel it again, "see" it again — but all at a distance from the original experience. Borrowing from the English poet William Wordsworth, one might say that criticism is "emotion recollected in tranquillity." The recalled experience of the film allows one to reflect on the film's structure, **tone** and meaning, and the *reasons* for one's reactions to a film.

Writing about film, like writing about any subject, is not as easy as talking about it. The opinions quickly and enthusiastically offered in casual conversation often are pitifully weak on paper. They are unsupported, inconsistent, vulnerable to attack; they reveal that the writer has not thought enough about the subject, has jumped to conclusions which have no visible means of support. Writing, in fact, is not the most difficult part of creating a paper. What is difficult and demanding is the act of thinking and defining, much of which should occur before one word is put on the page. But writing is also an aid to thinking; as you put down words in your first draft, you will see where you must do some further thinking.

Writing about film is especially difficult because, unlike a novel, a poem, a reproduction of a painting or a recording of a musical performance, a film is not readily available for extensive study. Usually one cannot see a film again and again and again. Even during the screenings one does have a chance to see, it is usually not possible to stop the continuous movement of images on the screen to study one image thoroughly as we might stop our reading of a poem to study a written image. Taking notes in a darkened theater is, unhappily, not the answer. If at all possible, a student should see a film at least twice. The first viewing of a movie should be experienced the way it was intended to be experienced — straight through from beginning to end with the viewer's attention on the screen. Scribbling in the dark alters and undermines the cinematic experience; one cannot give a film full attention while taking notes. (*After* the initial screening, impressions, details, and key scenes should be written down.) During the second viewing, some note-taking might, of course, occur during the screening itself. One might also read through critical articles and reviews and go to star and **genre** picture-books on film, for these often contain plot synopses and production information. Remembering a movie is difficult and requires practice, but the ability to remember generally increases in proportion to the number of films one sees.

Another problem which confronts the beginning film student and writer is, paradoxically, the liveliness of the flat screen. With many films, one doesn't seem as much to *see* them as to *live* or *dream* them. How, some students ask, can one begin to encompass in words that emotional and physical experience of a movie. How can one translate the simultaneous bombardment of the senses of sight and hearing into words that are strung, one after another, along the page? Although it may be difficult, and certainly it does not duplicate the experience itself, the attempt to find the right words and put them into order is the only way the fleeting moments of the film experience can possibly be captured. If the experience is valuable, then preserving that experience is also valuable. Though words may fail to record the exact shape and sound and feel of the film experience, they come a great deal closer to that end than a grunt of approval or disdain.

★★★ ## What to Write About: The Individual Film

The first step in writing is not taking a pen to paper or hauling out the typewriter. The writer first must mentally pre-edit his raw material (that jumble of feeling and thought connected with the film) much as the filmmaker mentally pre-edits the material he will photograph by first selecting the subject matter. Thus, the writer must first select a topic, a focus, an emphasis. Just as it is impossible to make a film about everything and anything, so it is impossible in a short paper to discuss usefully all elements of a film. Just as a filmmaker chooses his subject matter, decides where to place his camera and what will eventually be caught in the **frame** and what will be left out, so must the writer choose a specific subject and position himself before his material. He, too, must limit his focus, decide what should be contained in his paper and what should be left out of it. He must decide whether to write about a particular film's content — its **themes, characterizations,** moods — or whether to focus on the film's form — its cinematography, sound, editing. He may choose to combine the two in a particular way for a particular critical purpose. For example, one might write about the ways in which editing expresses the theme, or the ways in which sound supports characterization.

An individual's encounter with a movie, of course, is a total experience and not chopped up into potential topics. And, of course, the distinction between form and content is arbitrary. It is difficult to talk about one without also discussing the other; form creates meaning just as meaning dictates the form by which it is expressed. Orson Welles's *Citizen Kane* (1941), for example, might be no more than a pedestrian semibiographical fiction if its form were merely a chronological narrative of the events in magnate Charles Foster Kane's life. It might have drama but it would not have the same meaning it does if the camera viewed its subject objectively and omnisciently. It is just because Welles reveals the character nonchronologically — Kane dies at the *beginning* of the film — and nonobjectively — through a newsreel, through the reminiscences of several people with vested interest, that the viewer is intrigued beyond the mere facts of Kane's life. The form, in fact, creates the meaning. A fine paper could be written on the subject of how narrative structure contributes to the film's theme.

Conversely, meaning creates form. The theme of Alain Resnais's *Last Year at Marienbad* (1961) suggests that time and objective reality are nonexistent and that subjective memory and desire create reality and time. The form of the film reflects its meaning; the editing dislocates the viewer so he doesn't know if what he is watching has already happened (and is a **flashback**), is happening, or will happen (and is a **flash-for-ward**) — or, in fact, if it has happened at all, for it may be occurring only in the narrator's mind. The form of the **sound track** also reinforces the meaning; the narrator repeats words in countless variations, the **dialogue** seen in a play within the film is repeated by the film's characters in normal conversation, characters repeat other characters' conversations until the viewer is not sure who said what to whom at what time or in what place. The theme or meaning of Resnais's film creates — almost out of necessity — the form the film takes. A fine paper might be written about how the theme or message a filmmaker wishes to convey may create the form of the film.

Since the split between form and content is arbitrary, since the two combine to create the films on the screen and to affect the viewer, the writer must in some degree deal with both, but he can *emphasize* an aspect of one or the other. As the examples cited indicate, an essay on a film's theme (what the film says and means), will have to include some explanation of *how* the writer knows what the theme is — in other words, how it is revealed through all the film's elements, a great many of which are formal. To emphasize theme, he may need to describe how the camera moves, how the images are illuminated, how the film is edited. Similarly, if the writer wishes to discuss a formal element like editing in a particular film, in order to explain why the editor made the artistic choices he did, he may have to briefly discuss the plot, the characterizations, and what the film is trying to say. All the parts of a film work together to create a total effect. The best papers, however, select one specific element to emphasize, examine that element in detail, and use other cinematic elements of the film only as supportive material. If a topic is assigned, stick to it. If a topic is not assigned, try to write about something that genuinely interests you. Your interest will help you be more specific in details and elaboration of your points.

Below, isolated under the headings of *Content* and *Form,* are specific filmic elements which might be the focus of a paper on a given film. In addition, some questions are presented to stimulate the writer's intellectual responses to the particular film he may wish to deal with. If the questions seem irrelevant to the film in question or simply uninteresting, look for another area of emphasis — or better, generate your own questions, for one of the best ways of getting ideas is to ask yourself questions.

CONTENT

Plot

One can distinguish between the **plot** and the story of a film. The story is *what happens* in a film — the sum of the events in which the characters are involved, the situations in which they find themselves or from which they try to extricate themselves. The plot is not only the events but the *order* of those events as presented on the screen. Thus, two films may tell exactly the same story — say Little Red Riding Hood — but if one uses flashbacks or flash-forwards the plots are different because the order of the episodes differs. Plot is usually associated with fiction films, with stories, but one can also say that some **documentaries** have events which are structured and dramatic enough to be considered plotted. Generally, however, plot is not discussed in relation to documentaries, informational films, **newsreels,** and **avant-garde** and **abstract films** solely dependent upon form.

Summarizing the plot of a single film does not make a critical paper. A summary of what happens in a movie does not require much thought; at best, it requires a good memory. It is no substitute for a discussion of *how* the plot reveals the story. A discussion of *how* the plot occurs (through the use of flashbacks, **jump cuts,** etc.) focuses on the film's narrative techniques, its form. A discussion of *what* the plot reveals or says focuses on the film's theme.

Statement of the plot of a film, then, is usually subordinate to a topic (such as a film's narrative structure or theme) which allows the writer to exercise his critical faculties. Therefore, events of the plot should be used selectively in nearly all papers to *illustrate* and *support* the critical thesis of the paper and to remind the reader of specific events relative to the discussion. The following excerpt from a student paper on *Citizen Kane* demonstrates how plot details in the film are used selectively to support a critical statement:

This feeling of distance from Kane is enriched by the photographic techniques. The long shot comes into play many times:
Kane sits down miles away from Susan in his castle, he is a
small figure in the street shot from his newspaper building,
Xanadu is often dark and in the distance, and Kane's nurse in
the beginning comes out of a very distant door. Even when he is
shot from relatively close up (out of dramatic necessity), he
seems to be distant. We see a portion of his leg as we watch
the drunk Leland after the lost election, Kane looks like
Frankenstein as he wrecks Susan's room in the castle, and a
hundred empty Kane shells appear in the mirrors in the hall as
he walks by.

Theme

The theme of a film is what the film is about, what the *whole* film communicates to the viewer. It is the statement the film makes or the ques-
tion(s) it raises. Unlike the plot, it cannot be seen because it does not
happen. The theme of a film is abstract — an idea. It is extremely important for the writer to understand this distinction between plot and
theme so the two are not used interchangeably. In Ingmar Bergman's
The Seventh Seal (1956), for example, the plot consists of the wander-
ings of a knight and his squire recently returned to their plague-ridden
native land after a Crusade. They meet various people in various places
and the knight asks them a question to which he can find no answer:
Is there a God? The theme of *The Seventh Seal*, on the other hand, is
man's search for certainty, for knowledge concerning the meaning of his
existence, for faith.

The theme of a film, then, is an idea, an abstraction. It cannot be
photographed. François Truffaut, for example, identifies the theme of
Day for Night (1973) in abstract terms: "*Day for Night* revolves around
one central question: 'Are films superior to life?' It gives no definite answer. For there can be none." [1] The abstractness of Truffaut's statement
cannot be photographed, but it can be expressed through the seen moving
images of the film and through the heard sound. It is through selection
of images and sounds, their arrangement and their internal rhythms that
the filmmaker communicates a theme. Since words, unlike images, can
express abstract ideas, sometimes themes are actually stated; the dialogue
of a film may forthrightly say (through narrator or character) what the
film is about. But finding an overt expression of the theme in a film's
dialogue is not often as easy as it sounds. The viewer must select what
he thinks is the film's emphasis from all the verbal evidence given and
must support that selection. And sometimes a speech that seems crucial
to the identification of a film's theme may nevertheless be cryptic.

In Dennis Hopper's *Easy Rider* (1969), the single most important line of dialogue seems to be Wyatt's remark to Billy: "We blew it." But what does that mean? And, of course, a character might make a statement that seems to reveal the theme, but the character may be unreliable, or such direct statements may be thoroughly contradicted and subverted by other, nonverbal, cinematic elements. In effect, discovering a film's theme (or themes) is like doing a piece of detective work. Clues may be everywhere — in the images, in the dialogue, in the juxtaposition between the two. The clues may be obvious, they may be hidden; they may even be red herrings which lead the viewer down a blind alley.

The theme or statement of a film can be large and universal: man's inhumanity to man, in Kon Ichikawa's *Fires on the Plain* (1960); the individual naif as a force for good against the corrupt and cynical, in Frank Capra's *Mr. Smith Goes to Washington* (1939); the exploration of reality and illusion, in Bergman's *The Magician* (1958). The theme can also be narrow and specific: that the Russian Revolution of 1917 was good for the country and the people, in Sergei Eisenstein's *October/Ten Days That Shook the World* (1928); that the American people will elect anyone to higher office if he is properly packaged and sold, in Michael Ritchie's *The Candidate* (1972). Sometimes the theme of a film may be so simple and obvious that it does not bear much consideration. In *Star Wars* (George Lucas, 1976), for example, the theme is that goodness will triumph over evil. This is so simple a theme that it is hardly worth writing a paper about. *Star Wars* itself is an interesting film, but this interest is derived from elements other than its theme.

These three thesis statements from student papers identify the themes of several films:

Bertolucci's The Conformist is a complex analysis of the causes and effects of Fascism, postulating sexual insecurity and guilt as the cause, and debauchery and mindless conformity as the ultimate end.

The final closing shot of Anarene in The Last Picture Show draws together the theme of the movie into a single, grainy, black-and-white photographic expression of emptiness, nothingness, and paralysis.

In Deliverance, a film based on the novel by James Dickey, three basic themes are continually expressed through the actions of the four main characters: Man's struggle against Nature, Man's confrontation with other men, and Man's constant battle with himself.

When a viewer studies the theme, he may be able to piece the theme together using all the film's elements as evidence, but he may then reject the theme because of personal bias; he may even refuse to recognize the theme when he sees it. This is particularly true when a viewer sees a film whose theme is personally painful or distasteful. Two of the major themes of Luis Buñuel's *Viridiana* (1961), for example, are that too much piety is neurotic and corrupting, and that Christianity depends upon human suffering and poverty to keep itself valid and alive. The images of the film are as strong and controversial as the film's themes. One key scene shows us a group of beggars seated around a table in a parody of Da Vinci's painting of *The Last Supper*; their conversation and actions are gross and sacrilegious. A devout viewer who disagrees with the film's thematic statements might dismiss the film as blasphemous and reject any further critical interaction with it. However, because the film reveals its theme masterfully, one should be willing to recognize the artistry of the work even if one doesn't agree with its message. Acknowledging the effective artistic realization of a disagreeable theme does not mean that one has betrayed one's principles or compromised one's moral standards. It is possible to appreciate the artistry of Leni Riefenstahl's *Triumph of the Will* (1936) without being a Nazi, just as it is possible to appreciate Stanley Kubrick's *A Clockwork Orange* (1971) without condoning violence.

There are a few simple questions the viewer can ask himself after he sees a puzzling film. These questions should, in fact, be asked even if the film is not puzzling, for their answers will help clarify the film's theme. They are a part of the thinking process that occurs before the act of writing begins.

1. Is there any clue to the film's emphasis in its title?
2. Does the dialogue offer any obvious expressions of what the film is about?
3. Do the characters themselves suggest the theme — through their names, their personalities, their clothing, their occupations, their situations?
4. If the characters are inarticulate, do their actions indicate the theme?
5. Are there any discrepancies between what the characters say and what they actually do?
6. Are there any discrepancies between what the dialogue indicates the theme is and what the form and structure of the film indicate the theme is?
7. Do the characters' relationships with their surroundings have any meaning?
8. Does the form of the film (the **lighting, composition,** the abruptness or lyricism of the editing, the sound other than the dialogue) reveal the theme?

Characterization

Characterization in a film is effective if a character's actions and dialogue convince the viewer of their appropriateness, so that the character as a whole is seen as credible. In other words, the character must be — no matter how fantastic his actions — a believable person *within the context of the film* for as long as it lasts.

A character, of course, is a created person; he does not really exist. The actor who plays the character, on the other hand, is real and does exist. The difficulty in dealing with characterization in a film is that too often viewers confuse the actor with the character or see the two as interchangeable. When a student sees a film starring well known actors (Paul Newman, Barbra Streisand, Dustin Hoffman, Jane Fonda, John Wayne), he may get confused when he starts writing a paper about the characters in a film. He may say, "John Wayne is a salty-tongued, gone-to-fat sheriff." But John Wayne isn't a sheriff; he is an actor. The writer has confused the actor with the character, Rooster Cogburn (Figure 9-1). What the writer *should* say is "John Wayne plays a man who . . . ." Even though the public persona of some actors appears to be identical to that of the characters they play, the student writing about a character in a single film should recognize the distinction between actor and character.

When the writer hasn't made the distinction between actor and character, he may start to write a paper about characterization but end up writing about acting. If he writes about acting, however, he may find he has absolutely nothing specific to say and has to grope to find even the most banal of observations: "John Wayne rubbed his jaw very expressively." The reason the writer has little to say about acting is simple: it is almost impossible to write about the acting in one film. To write about acting, even to recognize whether a person up there on the screen *is* acting rather than just being, the viewer has to have seen the actor in more than one performance, in more than one film, or in real life as himself. The topic of acting can be dealt with effectively if one is writing about several films in which the same performer appears, but it is usually useless to write about a performance in a single film. What is discussable in a single film is the characterization — the created person. Occasionally, students find themselves writing: "Dustin Hoffman was really great in *The Graduate* (Mike Nichols, 1967)." What they really mean is that they liked the character of Benjamin, which Dustin Hoffman portrayed. Once they realize that it is Benjamin who interests and engages them, they can easily go on to discover *why* they like Benjamin (Benjamin sees the shallowness and hypocrisy of a "plastic" society; Benjamin is caught up in deciding what to do with his life and this is a very real problem facing all young people). The writer knows Benjamin through evidence in the film — and that is the stuff of which good papers are made. It is from

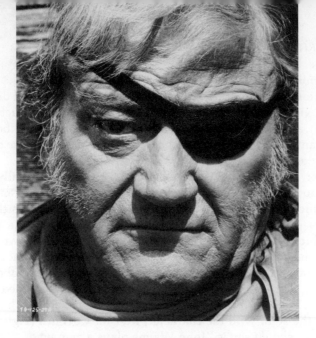

★ 9-1   Some students find it difficult to distinguish the character from the actor in a film. They may say, "John Wayne is a salty-tongued, gone-to-fat sheriff." But in TRUE GRIT (Henry Hathaway, 1969), Wayne plays Rooster Cogburn, "a salty-tongued, gone-to-fat sheriff." The distinction between actor and character should be made clear in a film paper.

the film and from the film alone that we find out who the character is and what he represents. The primary source of this evidence is not Dustin Hoffman's acting ability, but what the character Benjamin says and does in this one film.

This excerpt from a student paper clearly treats the characters and not the actors:

In <u>Jules and Jim</u> we find the imprisonment of both sexes. Each creates the other. Catherine is so idolized as the ulti- mate symbol of woman that she can do no wrong. It is because Jules and Jim define her as an "ideal" woman that they put up with her. She is expected to act the way she does. Hence, Jules and Jim are prisoners of Catherine's whims, while Catherine is bound to their desires.

Before writing about a character in a given film, the viewer should ask the following questions.

1. Is it clear that I am interested in the character rather than in the actor?
2. What is the character's function in the film? Is he the main character or is he a secondary or minor character? Is the film *about* the character or is the character a device through which the filmmaker can make a statement?
3. Is my interest in the character based on what he represents? If so, what is it precisely that he represents?
4. Does the character stay the same or change and develop through the film? What is the significance of his lack of change or of his development?
5. Where is the evidence *in* the film to support my interpretation of the character and his significance? Is it in his dialogue, his actions, his relationships with other characters, his relationship to his environment?

Tone

The tone of a film is its prevailing atmosphere, such as joyousness or horror. This atmosphere can be created by many things, for example the setting, the lighting, the color, the sound, the rhythms of the editing. Tone is not necessarily dependent upon a film's subject matter. There have been horror films in which the established tone is essentially light-hearted, as in Roman Polanski's *The Fearless Vampire Killers* (1967). There have been comedies in which the tone has been quite grim, as in Billy Wilder's *The Apartment* (1960). The tone of a film is never created by just one filmic element; all the elements together give the viewer the "feel" of the film which may, or may not, be supportive of its subject matter.

Not all films have a constant or consistent one. The tone of Orson Welles's *The Magnificent Ambersons* (1942), for example, is at first lighthearted and affectionate, but then it becomes grim, dark, claustrophobic, and withdrawn. The tone in the film parallels the movement of the Amberson family from wealth and solidarity to economic decline and fragmentation. It is created by the lighting, the sets, the camera angles, and the editing. For instance, at the beginning of the film, the interior of the Amberson mansion is brightly lit, it seems large and gracious, characters and the camera move gradually down wide stairways, glide smoothly across the rooms. As the film progresses, the lights seem less bright, shadows encroach on the screen so that, eventually, the interior of the house becomes dark and forbidding; the shadows press in on the characters until it seems that space disappears. The camera seems confined rather than mobile, and the viewer feels that the house has diminished. In *The Magnificent Ambersons,* Welles gradually shifts the tone to support and emphasize the thematic content of the film. More recently, however, modern filmmakers have used abrupt shifts in tone — to startle the audience or to subvert their expectations. Because Arthur Penn's *Bonnie and Clyde* (1967) does everything possible to establish a gay, campy, and lighthearted tone at its beginning, the sudden eruption of violence seems twice as horrific as it would be if it were set against a grimmer background of light, space, and music. And almost all the films of Italian filmmaker Lina Wertmüller keep the audience attentive and in a state of disequilibrium. She uses shifts in tone to subvert the customary passivity of the viewer who normally relies on the tone of a film to let him know in advance what sort of experience to expect.

An inconsistent tone, however, can also mar an otherwise fine movie. It may throw the viewer off base, making him uncertain as to how he is to respond to the film. When a filmmaker deliberately changes the tone, the change is usually functional, but it can also seem confusing or inappropriate. In Hal Ashby's *Coming Home* (1978), for example, one of the characters seems to belong in another movie. His behavior is operatic and so is his treatment by the camera, whereas all the other characters in the film (who are no less troubled but, perhaps, more in tune with their feelings) behave in more low-key fashion. The character, a returned Vietnam war hero, is not able to deal with his feelings about his war experiences and his wife's infidelity. Although perhaps thematically justified, the tone shift which occurs during the sequences in which this character appears is disturbing because it is so jarringly at odds with the principally quiet tone of the film.

Some elements which contribute to the tone of a film are discussed in this excerpt from a student paper:

Despite the hard times of the 1930s in which it is set, The Sting's tone is lighthearted. The flippant acting combination of Paul Newman and Robert Redford and the jovial musical score contribute greatly to this mood. The insertion of storybook-type graphics to separate each portion of the film adds to its unreal quality. Because of the clever script, serious incidents such as gambling, corruption, and murder are subordinated to the process of the "con" and its amusing ingenuity. The result is a joyous film, devoid of any hint of the problems of the Depression.

Tone, then, is the atmosphere of a film, created by the sum of several cinematic elements. To deal effectively with tone in a paper the writer must be prepared to deal with *how* that atmosphere and mood is created. Some questions the viewer might ask follow.

1. What is the tone of the film? (Romantic? Lyric? Claustrophobic?)
2. Does the film's tone change or is it consistent?
3. If the tone shifts, where does the shift occur? Is it gradual or abrupt? Why does it shift, for what purpose?
4. How is the tone revealed? (Through the lighting? the editing? the cinematography? the music?)
5. What relationship does the tone have to the theme of the film? Is it supportive or contradictory? What are its implications for interpreting the film?

FORM

The Image

The images of a film are what the viewer's eye perceives on the screen. The basic components creating an image are the **film stock,** composition, camera angle, lighting, and camera and subject movement. Because so many elements contribute to the film image, the writer probably will not wish to discuss all of them in relation to a given film. Instead, he will select those elements which most interest him and those which seem most relevant to the given film. Probably he will discuss no more than two or three in one paper; in fact, often the best paper deals thoroughly with only one element.

The two basic properties of the film stock which might be discussed in a paper are **grain** and color. Silent and early sound films were, of course, greatly limited by relatively primitive technology, and all were shot in black-and-white. Contemporary filmmakers, however, can choose whether they wish their film to appear grainy or smooth, in color or in black-and-white. Ideally, those choices will be relevant to both the subject and theme of the film.

High-speed film can capture an image with the least amount of available illumination, but the image is (or at least used to be) grainy. Because such film was used by newspaper and newsreel photographers, grainy images are most often associated with journalistic and documentary filmmaking and photography. As a result, such images evoke on-the-spot immediacy, a sense of urgency and gritty realism. In the political thriller *Z* (1969), for example, director Costa-Gavras uses high-speed color film, and the resultant grainy image confers an immediacy on the film that is consistent with its contemporary theme and narrative action. Most musicals, however, tend to be shot with slower-speed film, so that the images are closely textured, smooth, and controlled — in short, prettier.

Although most contemporary films are shot in color, black-and-white is still sometimes used to support both the mood and theme of a given

★ **9-2** Black-and-white film can often emphasize details of texture. If this scene from Bergman's WILD STRAWBERRIES (1957) were in color, part of the viewer's attention would be occupied with the color itself, but without color the texture of fabrics — the woman's lace shawl, the man's evening clothes, the rumpled bedspread — stands out.

film (Figure 9-2). For example, Peter Bogdanovich's *The Last Picture Show* (1972) looks like a low-budget 1950s movie and thus imitates the film style of the period it is about. Sometimes a filmmaker will alternate color with black-and-white in a film, using the shift to signal a change of mode; one can point to *The Wizard of Oz* (Victor Fleming, 1939) and, more recently, to *Jonah Who Will Be 25 in the Year 2000* (Alain Tanner, 1976), both of which use color and black-and-white to differentiate between reality and fantasy.

Since almost all contemporary films are in color, the viewer tends to take the color for granted, as something real which the photographic image duplicates. Color, however, can be used expressively as well as mimetically, and there are now available all tones of color stock so that color images from film to film vary greatly. Color can be controlled — muted or exaggerated — either in the shooting process or in the laboratory so that it, too, supports or contradicts the subject and theme of a film. Jean-Luc Godard, for instance, has used primary and garishly flat colors to create a film image that resembles the comic strip or poster in

★ **9-3** Composition is the arrangements of objects in the frame. Antonioni indicates the distance that separates his characters emotionally by separating them on the screen physically, as he does here in RED DESERT (1964).

its two-dimensional quality; his use of color is consistent with the structure and themes of his films, which explore media impact. The color in Robert Altman's *McCabe and Mrs. Miller* (1971), on the other hand, is muted and generally monochromatic in its scheme; it evokes both bleakness and nostalgia, the latter arising from the resemblance of the image to the brown tones associated with old photographs.

Composition is the arrangement of people and objects within the film frame (Figure 9-3). Even if the frame (the camera's vision) does not move, the rectangular space can be filled up in many ways. It can present pleasing and harmonious images or harsh and unharmonious ones. Those relationships may be achieved by the position of the subject and of the camera (camera angle), and they are also affected by the actual size of the screen itself (Figure 9-4). Composition, one of the most important elements of the image, often provides a large enough topic for an entire paper.

★ **9-4** Composition of objects within the frame can also develop the notion of "offscreen" space when only part of an object is visible within the frame. The viewer presumes that the object continues, whether it be a wall or a forest or a person. In the case of a person like Dustin Hoffman in THE GRADUATE (Mike Nichols, 1967), one can be sure that the lower part of his body does indeed exist below the frame, but without further information, say, shots from different angles, one cannot be sure that the glass upon which his hand rests continues beyond the frame as part of a real wall or whether it is simply a prop.

Again, composition of the film frame — the use of film space — generally tells the viewer something about the nature of the film and its theme. Nobody in an Antonioni movie ever announces his or her state of alienation from other people, but the way the characters stand in relationship to other characters and in relationship to their environment dramatizes their alienation in visual terms. In his westerns, John Ford creates large vistas of open space where the human characters seem dwarfed by the vastness of nature, yet heroic in their attempts to civilize so vast and inhospitable an area. Carl Dreyer chiefly uses **close-ups** of faces to create the intensity in his *The Passion of Joan of Arc* (1928). Sergio Leone creates tension and suspense in the ways he uses both the close-up and the entrances and exits of characters on the wide screen of *Once upon a Time in the West* (1969). And the tilted angles of an entire **genre** of horror films complement the crazed and horrific action that generally occurs within them (Figure 9-5).

Lighting is another crucial element of the image. It is obviously important in creating the depth and quality of the black-and-white film, but

★ **9-5** Decor — the walls, the fabrics, the furnishings, the physical settings created for the film — can add an extra dimension to the image. In THE CABINET OF DR. CALIGARI (Robert Weine, 1919), part of the response to the film is created by the tilted sets, the macabre lampposts, and the twisted cardboard trees.

it is also important to the color film where it may seem less obvious in its uses.

To capture an image there must, of course, be sufficient light. Illumination, however, is not just a technical necessity; it is a component of mood, of drama, of an audience's emotional response to the image. A film heavy with shadows, a film in which there are dark corners, is likely to be somber, ominous, claustrophobic, frightening (Figure 9-6). Light comedy does not usually take place in shadow. Horror films do not usually take place in brightly lit settings. There are exceptions, of course, but artistic departures from the norm only prove the point that light or its absence creates certain definite expectations in the viewer. Alfred Hitchcock often lulls his viewers into complacency by shooting bright daylight scenes in which it appears unlikely that anything nasty will happen, but he tricks the audience by subverting its expectations; in his movies nasty things do happen in daylight and are doubly shocking for their unexpectedness. Light, and the way it is used, can also make objects and people and environments look beautiful or ugly, soft or harsh, artificial or real. Indeed, illumination is perhaps the central element of the film image. All the other components of the image — film stock, composition, decor, camera and subject movement — can only be meaning-

441

★ 9-6 Lighting was used expressively and not realistically by Fritz Lang in M (1930). Peter Lorre's shadow appears against a "Wanted" poster at the exact moment he is luring his next victim, just offscreen. It is the first moment the viewer firmly knows that this unknown man is the child killer.

fully employed when there is light. Lighting, then, should be one of the first things that a student writer pays attention to.

The way in which the camera moves or doesn't move and the movement before it of the subject matter is also extremely important in establishing the effect the image will have on the viewer. Movement is a fine subject for a paper, but it is one of the most difficult elements of the image to remember. Still, practice and attention to movement in film can increase one's ability to recall film movement.

Again, in a good film, movement is not random but purposeful. Movement of the camera toward the subject (either by **tracking** or by using a **zoom lens**) draws the viewer into a closer, more intense relationship with the subject, and movement of the camera away from the subject creates emotional as well as physical distance. The effect will also vary in relation to the speed with which movement in or out is accomplished, creating surprise, suspense, tension. Movement across the subject, and the speed with which it occurs, also creates mood and establishes the viewer's relationship to the subject. A slow, leisurely **pan** across a landscape will feel quite different from a **flash pan** which blurs the subject and tends to be dizzying. A camera mounted on a **boom** or a helicopter can produce liberating, swooping movements, or it can gaze at the subject coolly from a godlike distance. Moreover, the camera can move with a moving subject or lose it from the film frame, leaving behind an empty space. Indeed, subject movement in conjunction with camera movement creates complex spatial relationships which are constantly in flux. Sometimes, as in the opening sequence of Orson Welles's *Touch of Evil* (1958), these relationships are extremely important to the thematic and narrative content of the film.

What we see on the screen — the film image — is the complex combination of the various elements discussed. Images can seem straightforward, showing us characters executing the maneuvers of the plot and not calling attention to themselves, while other images can be obviously flamboyant and expressive. The simpler the image, the more straightforward in its presentation of the subject matter of the film, the more difficult it will be to discuss it in a paper. These simple images, of course, are significant, but those images which fascinate the viewer visually and also relate to the film's subject matter in their formal properties usually provide the most interesting paper topics. This student writer calls attention to details of composition in an examination of *Jeremiah Johnson* (Sydney Pollack, 1972):

```
The camera does not merely capture scenery through composition;
it sees nature with human response. With human vision, the lens
peers through soft hazy smoke in the campfire scenes and through
tall reeds that web the beauty of nature. The image of a deer
obscured by branches produces the effect of a human eye looking
through a rifle sight — which is just what Jeremiah is doing.
```

The writer who wishes to explore elements of the images in a film might ask himself the following questions before starting a paper. These questions should also stimulate a wealth of other — more narrowly focused — questions.

1. Was the film's imagery particularly expressive?
2. What elements of the cinematography (film stock properties, composition, lighting, camera angle, movement, etc.) stood out, either because of their artistry or because they seemed inappropriate?
3. Did an awareness of the technique clarify the content and theme of the film — or did it obscure them?
4. With all the various aesthetic possibilities open to him, why did the filmmaker choose to create his images the way he did? What function does his use of the stock, composition, angles, lighting, decor, and movement perform?

Editing
Editing is the linking together of separate images to form an entire and coherent film. This linking has some kind of narrative logic if it is a

fiction film, some kind of intellectual logic if it is a documentary, and some kind of aesthetic logic if it is an abstract film. Whether accomplished within the camera, in the editing room, or in the laboratory with an **optical printer,** editing provides the various kinds of transitions a filmmaker uses to get from one idea, time, place, or action to another. Editing — through its organization of time and space — creates the structure of every film.

The most common form of editing, **invisible editing,** attempts to smooth over the transitions from shot to shot so that they are not perceptible. Usually, the transitional sequence, cutting together a **long shot** to **medium shot** to close-up, goes unnoticed by the viewer who has long ago learned to accept the cinema's ability to move through time and space effortlessly. Another common form of invisible editing is that accomplished by camera movement, the camera performing a quiet but essential selection process as it moves in for a close-up and then backs off into a **two-shot** and finally moves upward on a boom to photograph an overhead shot at a great height. This kind of **mise-en-scène** editing is — in one sense — not editing at all in that there are no physical separations (joined together at a later time) in the film material. Nonetheless, in another sense editing is going on — transitions in time and space are occurring and variety is being achieved.

The first kind of invisible editing is difficult to write about because it is both common and hard to see when one is viewing the film. Usually it is in the service of a narrative and little can be said about its use in a specific film that cannot be generally applied to other films similarly edited. Thus the student may end up talking in generalities about this sort of invisible editing. Writing about mise-en-scène editing presents other problems. First, the student must recognize the presence of such an editorial style (usually by the relatively fewer **cuts** in the film), and then he must attempt to remember and uncover what relationships are established in the frame by the movements of the camera and the long shot/**long take** technique. The context established by mise-en-scène editing must be read for its clues to the relationships it creates among people, objects, and environment and then those clues must be interpreted for meaning.

What is generally referred to as **montage** editing is a great deal easier for the beginning student to see and to write about. The meanings inherent in any particular shot are kept relatively clear (often through the use of close-ups) and the shots will usually be edited together quite rapidly — or obviously — in order to create a specific meaning or mood through their juxtaposition. Often other highly visible transitional devices will be used in addition to the **straight cut.** The **dissolve,** the **su-**

perimposition, the **fade,** the jump cut are all relatively flamboyant and often call attention to themselves, thus providing the viewer with visual material he is able to recall more easily than invisible editing (Figure 9-7). It is much easier to recall Charlie Chaplin's commuters rushing for a train juxtaposed with a herd of sheep in *Modern Times* (1936) than to remember how, in Jean Renoir's *Grand Illusion* (1937), the camera movement created — in mise-en-scène style — the relationships between the men putting on the show in the prison camp.

Because most films combine montage and mise-en-scène or invisible editing styles, the student can contrast the use of both in a single film. A contemporary film like Michael Ritchie's *Smile* (1975), for instance, depicts a small-town beauty pageant, using both techniques for their respective effects. Mise-en-scène predominates, giving the film a realistic, semi-documentary atmosphere. Yet the film also uses montage sequences to make intellectual points and to create **satire;** short, rapidly cut shots of contestants responding with the same clichés to judges' questions are funny and thought-provoking. The student who chooses to write about the editing in a given film must be alert to the different editorial methods being employed and attempt to show how they work and what they mean. The dissolve, for example, is recognized in this excerpt from a student paper which discusses Buster Keaton's *Go West* (1925):

```
Keaton needs to show the time elapsing during a cross-country
train ride. To compress time, he uses a series of dissolves on
a sausage that show the meat slowly shrinking. The sausage is
the only food Keaton has with him on the freight train, and its
disappearance through the dissolves very tersely and effectively
represents the long train ride.
```

In addition to addressing particular editorial techniques and devices, a paper on editing might also focus on the manipulation of time and/or space in a film. Editing controls these two basic aspects of film form. Time can be compressed or expanded or reshuffled into nonchronological arrangement. Space can be extended or abridged, can be relatively continuous or highly fragmented. The rhythms and mood of a film can also be established through the patterns of editing and this may serve as a good focal point for a paper. Films often strike the viewer as exciting or boring, lyrical or staccato in tempo and this response is most often primarily influenced by the rhythm of the editing.

Editing always conveys some kind of information about the film's intent and focus. If the editing is natural and unobtrusive, it tells the viewer to watch the other filmic elements — the unfolding of the plot, the characters' interaction and dialogue, the lighting, composition, and

★ 9-7 The difference between mise-en-scène and montage images is visible in
these two shots. In the montage shot, from the shower murder sequence
in PSYCHO (Alfred Hitchcock, 1960), very little meaning can be gathered
from this one image selected from the seventy-eight that make up the sequence. The character is clearly in the shower, but the opaque shower curtain
cuts off any depth to the image, thus isolating the figure against a flat
background. The viewer needs to see the images which come before and
after to understand the relationship between the visible figure and the shadow
behind the curtain. On the other hand, the image from CITIZEN KANE
(Orson Welles, 1941), is extremely complete. The frame is full of information: in the foreground, the medicine bottle nearly empty suggests overdose;
in the middle plane, Susan's figure on the bed, her face in shadow, suggests
the deep sleep of death and recalls Kane's shadow as he towered over her
earlier; and Kane himself, coming through the door in the deep background,
reminds the viewer of his role in Susan's suicide attempt. Because information in all planes of the image is visible, the relationships between the
planes can be seen.

camera movement. If the editing is, on the other hand, conspicuous, it has — or should have — a particular significance; images juxtaposed in an obvious way have a special relationship to each other. Again, there are questions which the viewer might ask himself about the editing in a particular film, before actually beginning to write a paper about the subject, or more precisely, while jotting down the notes that will be the stuff of the first draft.

1. Was the editing noticeable?
2. If the editing was not noticeable, was it traditional invisible editing in service to the narrative? Or was it mise-en-scène, using camera movement and long takes to establish editorial relationships?
3. In those scenes in which the editing was noticeable, was it used as a signal, a signpost of something important?
4. Did the editing create meaning? How?
5. Did the editing contract or expand or distort chronological time? How?
6. What rhythm did the film have and how did the editing contribute?
7. What are some of the reasons the filmmaker might have had for editing the film the way he did?

Sound
Sound in a film falls into four categories: spoken dialogue and **narration, sound effects,** music, and silence. All of the aural elements in a film may be used simultaneously or individually to create aesthetic effects and convey information about the film's content. All are as subject to editing as is the visual image. Because most films a student is likely to see will be sound films, it is important to keep in mind the various ways in which sound can be used to amplify and articulate meaning. Sound can be **synchronous** with the onscreen image (source sound) or it can be **asynchronous.** It can have a temporal and spatial relationship which is coincident with the images on the screen, or it can evoke another time and space. It can be used to authenticate the images, lending credibility to what the viewer sees, creating an extension of the world seen in the frame into offscreen space, or it can make the images seem unreal, fantastic. It can change the entire tone of a scene, causing the viewer to regard the visual images on the screen ironically, comically, nostalgically, tragically, or romantically. Sound can subtly support what is in the frame, so that one is hardly aware of hearing it, or it can loudly contradict and act contrapuntally to what is seen, creating tension or humor or irony. The tension of a ski race in *Downhill Racer* (Michael Ritchie, 1969) is, in part, created by sound as this student paper demonstrates:

★ **9-8** In Ingmar Bergman's appropriately titled THE SILENCE (1963), both sound and silence combine to convey the film's theme aurally as well as visually. In one scene, the little boy Johann walks down the empty corridors of a decaying hotel and there is absolute silence. The camera, mounted on the ceiling, looks down on the boy as he pauses before walking away from the camera down another corridor, making the boy almost an abstract part of the rug's pattern.

```
The viewer is constantly reminded of the presence of the crowd
by effective dubbing of the spectators' cheers. Cutting from
cheers to silence to the sound of skis on snow and back to
cheers on the sound track heightens the suspense of the
race and helps to produce in the audience the drive and con-
centration that all competitors feel.
```

Certain films seem to lend themselves particularly to a discussion of sound not merely as technique but also as contributing to meaning. Indeed, a film like Francis Ford Coppola's *The Conversation* (1974) is about the creative and dangerous ways sound can be regarded. And in Ingmar Bergman's appropriately titled *The Silence* (1963), a film about the difficulty of human communication, both sound and silence combine to convey the film's theme aurally as well as visually. In one scene, for example, the little boy Johann walks down the empty corridors of the decaying hotel in which he is staying and there is absolute silence — no footfalls, no background noise of any kind (Figure 9-8). The effect produced creates a sense of isolation and (despite the space on the screen) claustrophobia, communicating the psychic states of the film's central characters.

Here are some questions the viewer might answer before deciding to write a paper about the sound in a film.

1. Was the sound noticeable? (Did the viewer pay more than usual attention to it?)
2. What kinds of sound were used in the film? What were their separate functions?
3. Did the sound support or complement the image? Was it synchronous or asynchronous? Did it authenticate the image or invalidate it?
4. Was sound at any time isolated, distorted, heightened or obscured? If so, to what purpose?
5. Did sound serve as a transitional device? What images and/or scenes did it link and how did it function?
6. Was silence used to any special effect?
7. Was the use of sound of more than average importance to the film?

★★★ ## What to Write About: Multiple Films and Extra-Filmic Issues

Thus far, this chapter has explored the various possibilities for paper topics involving one film, its content and form. This emphasis on the single work of art allows even the student with the most limited cinematic experience to write successfully about a film. This methodology rightly focuses attention on the work itself — not on other films, not on the film's place in film history or its place in a general historical and social context, not on its relation to other art forms.

Other critical positions, however, can be taken toward the film experience and the writing of a paper about film. Nearly all students have seen not just one film, but many. It is therefore natural and automatic that comparisons will be made between films, that films will be related to extra-filmic experience both personal and historical, and that films will be grouped together on the basis of their similarities of content and form. All of these relationships among films may provide interesting and suitable topics for papers about film.

Thinking about films in relation to each other and to personal and extra-filmic experience can give rise to fascinating questions, many of them answerable within the context of a written paper. The viewer may ask: Why do Alfred Hitchcock's films almost always sustain my interest? What is horror — and are horror films really horrifying? Why were there so many lavish musicals made during the Depression when people did not have jobs? What makes explicit violence and sex such a box office draw? Although it comes with different titles, stars, dialogue, and budgets, why do we go to see what seems to be the same movie again and again? All of these questions — central to cinematic concerns — are best discussed with reference to several films. All of them imply relationships between films, between film and history, film and society, film and the viewer's own personal cinematic history.

All the elements of content and form discussed in the section on writing about the individual film are also applicable to writing about more than one film. The image — or editing — or sound does not disappear because a student decides to write about the western rather than about one western, or about musicals and their economic relationship to the Depression. Usually, however, thorough discussion of these elements must be somewhat subordinated to the broader topic. Although the topic of a paper about more than one film is larger than an analysis of a single filmic element in a single film, the writer should be careful not to neglect the kind of specificity he would apply to a paper dealing with one movie.

COMPARISON AND CONTRAST

Although most students have seen many movies, some may have seen only a handful of extremely popular contemporary films and whatever films are shown in class. A student who has not seen a great many movies may feel uncomfortable in trying to relate films to history, to cultural trends, or to film genres. The easiest and usually the most successful approach for such a student is to compare and contrast two films he has seen. That way, he need not make any large generalizations which can't be supported from his own firsthand viewing experience.

If an instructor's assignment is very specific — a list of topics such as "Compare the editing patterns in Eisenstein's *Potemkin* with those in Pudovkin's *Mother*" or "Select any two westerns seen this term and discuss the nature of the hero" — there is no problem. But if the student is required to select his own two films for comparison, then he should be certain that there are enough common elements to make the comparison sensible rather than farfetched. There is no sense in comparing a Marx Brothers film with *Citizen Kane*. One could ostensibly write a paper comparing a banana with a football — but once one had finished pointing out they were both objects, both composed of organic material, and both with skins, what is there left to say? Similarly, the fact that all films are made on a sensitized plastic base and require light to capture the image does not form the basis of a meaningful comparison. Films do not have to be extremely similar or diametrically different to be suitable for a comparison, but they do have to have a reason for being compared. For example, since all films use light, it is fairly safe to discuss lighting in any two films. But the comparison may seem random unless it is further strengthened. A better and more selective focus would be to discuss the lighting in two horror films, because both films seek to elicit the same response in the viewer. Or one could discuss the lighting in two films directed by the same person or produced by the same studio. In each case, the range of discussion has narrowed, and the particular selection of the two films seems reasonable, the comparison for a purpose.

If the selection of films for comparison is appropriate and the focus is narrow enough, the variety of possible comparison-contrast papers is immense. One could compare the variations on a well-known plot using *The Poseidon Adventure* (Ronald Neame, 1972) and *The Towering Inferno* (John Guillerman, 1974). One could discuss the treatment of a common theme — the distinction between illusion and reality, for instance — in Ingmar Bergman's *Persona* (1967) and Luis Buñuel's *Belle du Jour* (1968). Any of the formal elements of film — editing, camera movement, composition, sound — are fair game for selective comparison. Social attitudes toward crime revealed in two gangster films of the 1930s might be interesting to compare — as would be the same attitudes revealed in two films from two eras. The variety of comparisons that might be made between films is nearly boundless. The student writer should take advantage, therefore, of the comparative form and the possibilities it opens up for exploring film issues within a fairly easy-to-learn paper structure.

One of the most intriguing and frequently assigned comparison-contrast topics treats a film adapted from some previous work of art, say a novel or a play or even an earlier film. Because the writer of a paper on **adaptation** is dealing with two works — the film and the source from which it was made — the most convenient form the paper can take is comparative, the identification of like and unlike things in the film and in its source. There are, however, special questions which the writer of an adaptation paper should address, questions which do not necessarily arise in other comparisons. Essentially, comparing a film adaptation to its source raises basic theoretical issues about the nature of the film medium and its unique qualities which allow it to function better than or less well than other media. Some of the issues the writer might wish to focus on (and, again, one or two at most should be selected for a short paper) are: How are interior states of being communicated in both media? How and where does action occur in each? What is omitted or added in the adaptation process? Do the themes of the works differ or are they the same? This thesis statement from a student paper shows one specific focus a paper on adaptation might take:

> In <u>Slaughterhouse Five</u>, Kurt Vonnegut said, "Life is just
> a collection of moments." He went on to demonstrate this state-
> ment in his novel through the time transitions made by the main
> character, Billy Pilgrim, from one moment to the next. In the
> book, these transitions were instantaneous and made with great
> ease. Translation of the book into a movie, however, caused
> unusual transitional problems that demanded the director and
> editor find new and effective means to convey the character's
> "time-tripping."

Generally, the least interesting papers on adaptation pit one work against the other as if they were enemies; the writer then proceeds to take sides and judges one work better than the other. A much more productive and interesting way to deal with adaptation is to see each work as valid in itself; the comparison is being made not to settle a contest, but to raise and clarify questions about the nature of the two media. Thus, Anthony Burgess's novel and Stanley Kubrick's adaptation of *A Clockwork Orange* (1972) can be seen not as competitors but as complementary and different works of art. Similarly, Ingmar Bergman's *The Magic Flute* (1975) is Mozart's opera and it is also something quite different.

Any comparison paper begins, of course, with at least two works. But one can add more titles and make comparisons within a larger group. What follows are suggested groupings of films into categories around which the student might shape a paper topic. Although the form of the paper will usually be less clearly structured than a comparison-contrast between two films, it will still depend upon choosing a topic that makes worthwhile the discussion of the films together.

GENRE GROUPINGS

Film genres are groups of films linked by similar subject matter, plotting, **conventions** of action and dialogue, and the use of particular objects, landscapes, and costumes which through their familiarity take on **iconic** significance. Genres are also most usually *popular* films seen by a lot of people representative of the culture at large. The genres most clearly defined in terms of form and content and the ones most written about as genres are the western, the horror film, the science fiction film, the gangster film, the musical, and the adventure film. Within such genres other smaller groupings of film arise: the caper film (a kind of gangster film), the disaster film (a kind of adventure film), the suspense film (a kind of horror film).

★ **9-9** Fritz Lang's METROPOLIS (1926) might suggest a variety of papers which could be written about film groupings. It might be a part of a study of German expressionism, a look at the science fiction genre, or part of an auteur study of Lang.

Film genres are the most obvious groupings for a paper concerning multiple films (Figure 9-9). The writer can focus on the identifying marks of an established genre (**formula** plots, conventions, icons) or attempt to do the same for a less well-known grouping. Or, one can focus on a specific element of a genre — the western hero, the use of landscape, the theme of West vs. East — and use several westerns to illustrate similarities, differences, and/or the evolution of these elements. An example of a good student paper on genre can be found at the end of this chapter.

AUTEUR GROUPINGS

The **auteur** of a film is the film artist or personality whose force of vision or charismatic qualities dominate and structure the finished work. Initially, it was thought that only a **director** could be an auteur, but now critics speak of auteurism in relation to performers, **screenwriters,** cinematographers, and editors.

An auteur grouping of films is a natural way to link films. There is no need to explain why the films are being discussed as a group if they are all films by Alfred Hitchcock, if they all star Bette Davis, if they are all written by Dudley Nichols, if they are all shot by James Wong Howe or edited by Dede Allen. Thus, instead of spending a great deal of time and space explaining why the films are being grouped, the bulk of an auteur paper will focus on describing similarities of form and content in the work of a single film artist. One could write, for example, about John Ford's use of landscape in his many westerns, or one could shift the emphasis slightly and discuss the way in which Ford's landscapes accentuate his basic theme of man against the wilderness. One might look at a number of Hitchcock films in order to isolate his thematic concerns with guilt and authority, or to point out his skillful use of objective and subjective point of view to create audience identification and anxiety.

Again, it is advisable to narrow the focus to a single area, deciding in advance whether to concentrate on an auteur's editing or imagery or whatever. Too broad a focus will result in a paper which is far too general to be illuminating.

NATIONAL CINEMA GROUPINGS

One can scarcely discuss all German films, or all French films, but a national grouping can be a first step in choosing a topic. A writer can seek evidence of a national "style," or evidence that the films are preoccupied with a particular theme. Much Japanese cinema, for instance, has a clear pictorial relationship to Japanese art, and can be discussed on the basis of its composition and formal camera movements. Italian films of the late 1960s and early 1970s seemed to be preoccupied with the relationship between sexuality and politics. The rhythms of Indian films are distinctly un-Western and can be discussed in terms of their editorial techniques.

FILM MOVEMENT GROUPINGS

A **film movement** is the result of the conscious effort of certain film artists who see themselves as a group committed to a particular aesthetic and/or sociopolitical purpose during a given period of historical time. Generally, the movement is quite self-conscious, its filmmakers not only producing films but also writing and interacting among themselves. Its period of existence is relatively well defined and often quite brief; it usually starts in reaction to an established tradition and then either exhausts its own devices or is co-opted and accepted within the establishment.

Film movements are most often closely associated with national cinemas. There have been, for example, **German expressionism, Soviet social realism, Italian neorealism,** the **French new wave,** and so on. However, a film movement cannot be considered equivalent to a national cinema; it is a much smaller group of films with a much narrower range of

★ **9-10** Film movements have both formal and contextual characteristics which link them together. *The Bicycle Thief* (Vittorio de Sica, 1949), like other Italian neorealist films, uses unprofessional actors, realistic settings, and documentary-like images to tell its story of postwar problems.

stylistic and thematic concerns. Other film movements are less clearly allied to a particular country; **surrealism,** for example, can be connected with France but is really much more international in practice and scope than such an alliance suggests.

An essay on film movements may focus on contextual issues regarding the circumstances which led to a movement's birth and decline, but it may also deal with stylistic and thematic consistencies within a movement. A paper might be written, for instance, on the use of chiaroscuro lighting in German expressionist film, or on the use of the ordinary individual as protagonist in Italian neorealist films (Figure 9-10).

THEORETICAL GROUPINGS

Film theory asks and attempts to answer the question "What is cinema?" It seeks to identify what is common to all films and yet unique to the medium. It attempts, also, to organize its findings in a systematic and coherent fashion.

Up to this point, the groups of films about which one might profitably write have been relatively narrow and circumscribed. Grouping films together by auteur precludes discussing any films not influenced by that person. Writing about the horror film means eliminating all other film genres from consideration (unless, of course, one refers to other genres by way of comparison). However, when one begins to ask theoretical questions about the basic properties of the cinematic medium, it is possible to consider all films. To the beginning film student, such a topic can be particularly intimidating, indeed overwhelming. A paper on film theory, however, should be as limited in scope as any other kind of paper previously discussed. The general question "What is the nature of the medium?" is far too broad to deal with successfully except, perhaps, in a book-length study. The student who wishes to discuss the theoretical basis of cinema must, therefore, narrow his focus to a manageable area of inquiry.

Instead of asking, "What is cinema?" the student writer can comfortably ask, "What is the function of the zoom?" or "What are the properties of the close-up?" (Figure 9-11). The question itself helps the writer select appropriate examples from a spectrum of films. It helps a great deal, obviously, if the writer has seen many films from which to choose illustrative examples. The most important thing to remember, however, is to *use* examples. Too often, students attempting to discuss theoretical points neglect to ground their abstract and generalized writing in concrete illustration. This is perhaps the commonest and most serious defect of such theoretical papers. Although familiarity with basic film theory is helpful, it is not essential to the writing of a theoretical paper. The very working out of a personal theory or aesthetic of film — grounded in concrete details — can be extremely productive in helping the student to define his own attitudes and observations about the cinema — and in allowing the instructor to see that student's mind at work. And it can be extremely exciting to deal with large ideas. That excitement, however, should be translated into logical and coherent prose, and abstract language should be supported by precise, detailed descriptions of actual moments in actual films.

CONTEXTUAL GROUPINGS

The context of a film or group of films can include such broad areas as social and political history and such narrow areas as the design of contemporary small theaters. Although it is possible (and sometimes even preferable) to discuss a single film in relation to contextual matters, most student writing about extrinsic issues relevant to film generally con-

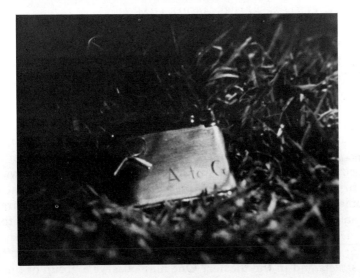

★ **9-11** One subject for a paper on film theory could be the discussion of one aspect of film form, for example, the close-up. The close-up allows film to give life to inanimate objects. In *Strangers on a Train* (Alfred Hitchcock, 1951), this monogrammed cigarette lighter travels from its rightful owner to the murderer, who later attempts to incriminate the hero with this bit of evidence.

cerns a number of films. It is easier and safer to make sociological and political observations about films when talking about a group of films that show a trend of some sort, or that reveal the particular concerns of a culture at a given time. One of the student papers at the end of this chapter does this quite well. A student might, of course, research and write about the production history of a single film and in that way deal with it in context. Or a student might discuss an individual film in relation to the other arts; indeed, one of the most common of all papers that deals with single films contextually is that which discusses the adaptation of a film from another medium. Generally, however, writing about film and its relation to the world around it seems most successful when it deals with several films.

Because a film depends on a mass audience, it can often tell us something about the society which produced it: the attitudes prevalent toward certain subject matter, standards of normality, and morality. Because large numbers of people attend movies, social commentators have wondered to what extent the screen image affects the viewer. They have asked the question: Do films of a particular time in a particular place reflect the society or does the society respond to the influence of the films it sees? Although the answer to this question is debatable, the question points out the close relationship which exists between film and everyday life. This relationship can be the starting point for a fascinating paper which focuses on a selected area of this relationship.

A sociological analysis of film is always concerned with history — time and its passage and the changes it brings about. One may group films together to indicate some theory or to raise questions: What does the new permissiveness in the depiction of sex and violence tell us about ourselves as a nation? Do films dealing with minorities in America exploit their subject matter to assuage liberal guilt or do they serve some other purpose? Do political films raise revolutionary consciousness, reflect something which already exists in the body politic, or are they really maintaining the status quo by substituting movie action for real action? Do pornographic films spur the latent sex criminal to overt action, or do they serve as a cathartic which keeps the potential offender off the streets and in the theater? One may observe a group of films and intelligently speculate on this relationship to the attitudes and emotional stresses of people at the time the films were made. Relating film to social and political history is a fascinating occupation, but one should recall that the generalizations offered, however plausible, cannot be proved. One cannot, for example, *prove* that people in the 1930s went to see James Cagney and Edward G. Robinson in gangster films because the very popular film genre perverted the Horatio Alger myth of American "get-up-and-go" and thus satisfied people's secret lack of faith in the American way of life. Certainly an analysis of gangster films and of the short and scrappy actors who played their protagonists could offer such a thesis and explore it with supportive detail from the films, relating it to the Depression and other social realities of the times. Such a thesis is subject to exploration, but it is also impervious to proof; one could pose any number of other reasons for the films' success, some of which might contradict the one already suggested. The best sociologically oriented papers explore an issue by looking at a variety of potential alternatives.

Before assuming too patly that a film reflects the culture of which it is a part, one can check the assumption by studying the evidence offered by documents such as newspapers. D. W. Griffith's *The Birth of a Nation* (1915), for instance, gives a one-sided portrayal of blacks during the Reconstruction period after the Civil War, but before we assume that Griffith's view was the common view of the period, we should study the accounts of the reception of the film in newspapers of the time. Such a study will reveal that many reviewers strongly objected to Griffith's picture of blacks.

Films which deal overtly with social problems can also tell us much about changes in social attitudes over a period of time. The cinema's changing treatment of racial or ethnic prejudice, poverty, war, crime, capital punishment, alcoholism, drug addiction, and psychological disorders not only can reveal the social and historical context in which a film was made, but also can reveal to the contemporary viewer the history of an attitude. By watching a number of films made over a period of years dealing with alcoholism, for example, the student can see what is initially considered a bestial, if not criminal, habit turn into a disease, something for which its victims cannot be held morally responsible. The same is true of mental illness. Some films, however, do not display an evolving and progressive attitude toward socially relevant subject matter. This does not mean such films would not provide good material for a paper focusing on their *lack* of responsiveness to social changes. Some films about war, for example, may stress the horror and futility of mass aggression, while others made at the same time may underscore the honor involved in combat, the glory connected with the patriotic sacrifice of one's life for one's country. One has to look at the historical context of the particular films in question to arrive at any kind of intelligent analysis of the attitudes expressed: Was there a war going on at the time the film was made? Was it made after a war — or before one? What actual war was contemporaneous with the film? Was it generally thought of as a "good" war like World War II or a "bad" war like the Vietnamese war?

Films, particularly popular films, are inextricably intertwined with history, society, and politics, with a culture's reality and its fantasy. The student who wishes to write a paper about some aspect relating film to culture must carefully narrow his focus as much as possible and must carefully select examples to support his speculations. Of all the approaches a student writer might take, the contextual approach just described is the hardest to keep organized and focused; it is also the easiest to inflate with hot air.

★★★ Research Papers

Although one may be required to do some research in connection with a short paper dealing with an individual film or group of films, generally the student will draw chiefly on his immediate experience of seeing the film and his memory of it. If, however, one chooses or is assigned to write about some aspect of the history of film, research is the essential first step.

Unfortunately, the films themselves are not often the student's primary resource material. Few students, for example, have seen enough early films to rely on their personal experience for the bulk of their source material. To write about the history and the development of film or about the history of a single film or film artist, one must use the library and its various source materials. The student must seek his information in books, in memoirs and letters written by actors, directors, production people, technicians, in biographies and autobiographies, in newspaper stories, movie reviews, magazine articles written at the time in which one is interested, histories of the cinema, and scholarly journals which might have already printed material on the subject matter the student is researching. In the body of the paper, the student will organize and present material selected from what he has read, combined with his own analysis of that material, appropriately citing his sources through footnotes and a bibliography. (A section on manuscript preparation follows, but the student should consult a handbook like *The MLA Style Sheet* for detailed information and examples.)

The research paper ultimately depends on the careful selection and use of source material. But the evaluation, organization, and interpretation of that material is the student's own contribution to the paper. Indeed, a research paper can be creative from its inception, offering an interesting thesis which the research illustrates and supports. A paper which argues that Metro-Goldwyn-Mayer's success was largely due to the artistic control wielded by production head Irving Thalberg will be much more interesting to read than one which merely recounts the facts and figures surrounding that studio's eminence. A paper which deals with the changing style of American movie palaces could be thought-provoking or tedious, depending upon the author's skill in presenting significant details. A research paper should not be considered a dry demonstration of the student's ability to use the library and the correct annotations. Instead, the research paper should offer an interesting hypothesis, support it with evidence, and draw reasonable conclusions.

★★★ ## Manuscript Preparation

The material in this section — modified to reflect the differing subject matter — is taken from Sylvan Barnet's *A Short Guide to Writing About Literature*, 4th edition.[2]

The following suggestions can be taken as a guide for the preparation of the film paper unless your instructor specifies something different.

FORMAT

1. Use 8½ x 11-inch paper of good weight. Turn in the original, not a copy.

2. Write on one side of the page only. If you typewrite, double-space. If you submit a handwritten copy, use lined paper and write, in ink, on every other line if the lines are closely spaced.
3. Put your name and course number at the top of the first page. It is a good idea to put your last name on each page in case a page gets mixed in with other papers.
4. Give your essay a title rather than a number such as "Assignment No. 1." Place the title about two inches from the top of the first page. Capitalize the first letter of the first and last words of your title and of all the other words except articles, conjunctions, and prepositions, thus:

    `The Light and the Dark in` <u>`Citizen Kane`</u>

    Notice that your title is neither underlined (indicating italics) nor enclosed in quotation marks, though material usually underlined or enclosed in quotation marks is so written, as is the film title in this example.
5. Begin the essay an inch or two below the title. If your instructor prefers a title page, begin the text on the next page.
6. Leave an adequate margin — an inch or an inch and a half — at top, bottom, and sides so that the instructor will have room for annotations.
7. Number the pages consecutively, using arabic numerals.
8. Fasten the pages in the upper left-hand corner with a paper clip or staple. Stiff binders are unnecessary; indeed, they are a nuisance to the instructor, adding bulk and making it awkward to write annotations.
9. Film titles like the titles of books are underlined (to indicate italics) or entirely capitalized. Do not use quotation marks.

FOOTNOTES

Avoiding Plagiarism

Though footnotes may sometimes be used to add material which would not smoothly fit the movement of the paper, their primary function is to acknowledge the writer's debt to other sources for ideas which are not common knowledge. When in doubt about whether to give credit or not, do. Not to acknowledge such borrowing is plagiarism — the theft of another person's ideas. This means you must give credit not only for direct quotations, but also for an attitude, insight, or interpretation created by someone else. Suppose, for example, you come across Gerald Mast's statement in *The Comic Mind* that Fatty Arbuckle was "so quick on his feet he could outrace a matador." You cannot use these words without giving credit to Mast. Nor can you retain the idea but alter the words, say, to "Arbuckle was so nimble he could run faster than a matador," presenting the idea as your own, for here you are simply lifting Mast's idea. If you want to use Mast's point, give him credit, using his exact words within quotation marks.

If you wish to use an idea which appears in a longer passage, do not quote the entire passage, but summarize the idea and give the author credit in a footnote or in the body of the paper itself. For instance, if you have read Stanley Cavell's book *The World Viewed* and want to use his idea that familiar stage character types are transformed into a whole new set of equally familiar film types, you might write in the body of your paper: "The Private Eye, the School Marm, the Swashbuckling Sea Captain, as Stanley Cavell points out, are only a few of the new types that film created from the old types found in popular theater.[20]" Note that the footnote number is placed after the final punctuation of the last sentence containing the material to be cited. Then the number is repeated at the bottom of the page, followed by the citation. (Some instructors will permit all the footnotes to go at the end of the paper, in which case they will be called "End Notes," or simply "Notes.")

Basic Footnote Forms

FIRST REFERENCE TO A BOOK

> [1] Gerald Mast, The Comic Mind (New York: Bobbs-Merrill, 1973), p. 263.

Notice that you give the author's name as it appears on the title page, first name first. The conventional abbreviation for page is "p." and for pages, "pp." If you give the author's name in the body of the page, do not repeat the name in the footnote. Merely begin with the title. If both title and author appear in the body, start with the parenthesis before the publication information, thus:

> [1] (New York: Bobbs-Merrill, 1973), p. 263.

For an edited or translated book:

> [2] John Grierson, Grierson on Documentary, ed. Forsyth Hardy (New York: Harcourt, 1947), p. 48.
>
> [3] Noel Burch, Theory of Film Practice, trans. Helen R. Lane (New York: Praeger, 1973), p. 68.

When you are quoting from an essay in an edited book, you begin with the essayist and the essay, then go on to give the title of the book and the name of the editor:

> 4 Raymond Durgnat, "Eyes Without a Face," in Focus on the Horror Film, ed. Roy Huss and T. J. Ross (Englewood Cliffs, N.J.: Prentice Hall, 1972), pp. 86-93.

FIRST REFERENCE TO A JOURNAL

Footnote 5 is for a journal (here, volume 25) paginated consecutively throughout the year; footnote 6 is for a journal that paginates each issue separately, for which the month, week, or day as well as the year must be given. Current practice favors omitting the volume number for popular weeklies (e.g., *Time*, *Newsweek*) and for newspapers, in which case the full date is given without parentheses.

> 5 Robert Brustein, "Film Chronicles: Reflections on Horror Movies," Partisan Review 25 (1958): 291.

> 6 Terence Fisher, "Horror Is My Business," Films and Filming 10 (July 1964): 7.

The author's name and the title of the article are given as they appear in the journal, the title of the article in quotation marks, and the title of the journal underlined. Current practices uses arabic numerals for both volume and page. When a volume number is given, as in notes 5 and 6, the page number is *not* preceded by "p." or "pp."

SUBSEQUENT REFERENCES

If you quote a second or third or fourth time from a work, use a short form in your footnote. The most versatile is simply the author's last name and the page number, thus:

> 7 Fisher, p. 8.

If you use the author's name in the sentence to which the footnote is keyed — "Fisher also says . . ." — the footnote need only be:

> 8 P. 8.

If you are referring to more than one work by the same author, however, you must indicate by a short title which work you mean, thus,

> 9 Brustein, "Film Chronicles," p. 290.

A subsequent reference to a book or journal should be kept as brief as clarity allows.

BIBLIOGRAPHY

A bibliography is a list of works cited in the piece of writing. Normally a bibliography is given only in a long manuscript such as a research paper or a book, but instructors may require it even for a short paper.

Because a bibliography is arranged alphabetically by author, the author's last name is given first. If a work is by more than one author, it is alphabetized under the first author's name; the last name is given first, but the other authors' names are given in normal order. In addition, a bibliographic entry differs from a footnote in putting a period after the author's name, a period after the title of a book, and in not enclosing the publication information in parentheses. And of course no page numbers are given for books, though the page numbers that an essay spans in a journal or a book are included. Begin the entry flush with the left-hand margin and indent subsequent lines if an entry is long. Single space each entry and double space between entries. Here are some samples:

Butler, Ivan. The Horror Film. Cranbury, N.J.: A. S. Barnes, 1967.

Dillard, R. H. W. "Even a Man Who Is Pure at Heart." In Man and the Movies. Ed. W. R. Robinson. Baton Rouge: Louisiana State University Press, 1967, pp. 129-74.

Gifford, Denis. Movie Monsters. New York: Dutton, 1969.

Kinder, Marsha, and Beverle Houston. "Rosemary's Baby." Sight and Sound, 28 (Winter 1968-1969): 17-19.

Sypher, Wylie. "The Meanings of Comedy." In Comedy. Ed. Sypher. Garden City, N.Y.: Doubleday Anchor, 1956, pp. 193-255.

★★★ # Helpful Hints for Writing Papers

SOME THINGS TO AVOID

1. *Don't* recount the entire plot of a film. Writing about what happens in film rather than what the film means or how its effects are achieved is *not* criticism. Summarize the plot in a sentence or two: "*Shane* is a western which concerns an ex-gunfighter who helps a family of sodbusters in a range war." Then, selectively use plot

incidents to clarify, illustrate, and solidify points within the body of the paper.

2. *Don't* write generally about an entire film. In a short paper you cannot cover the acting, directing, editing, lighting, sound, and so forth and say anything significant. Focus on a single element and explore it as thoroughly as you can. It is better to exhaust an idea than to flit from one idea to another.

3. *Avoid* words like "great," "good," "effective," "emotional," "well-done," and "interesting" as simple adjectives in phrases like: "The use of location was very effective," or "Light was used in a very interesting way." Statements like these strung out on a page fill up the white space but don't say anything. If these words are used at all, they must be immediately qualified by more specific information, and supported by concrete details. In what way was the location used? And why was it effective? How was light used? What did it have to do with the story or characters that made it interesting?

4. *Don't* use examples from the films just to let the instructor know you've seen the film or because you merely want to pepper the paper with examples. Make sure the examples are relevant to the point you're making. Once the example is located in context to the rest of the film (e.g., the scene when the gunfighter first comes to town), be as selective and specific as possible with that material which relates to your argument.

5. *Don't* leave gaps in your thought and in the logical development of your paper. Be sure that your argument moves coherently and with appropriate transitions from point A to point B to point C. Don't move about from point A to point K back to point B or omit the interim points. Don't expect the reader to think the way you think or to fill in the gaps for you.

SOME THINGS TO DO

1. *Do* focus on a particular and relatively narrow topic suitable to the length of your assigned paper. Have a thesis — a one-sentence summation of what your paper is about — clearly in mind before beginning to write. Make sure the paper has a function: argue with a critical position, make a statement and prove it.

2. *Do* use specific examples from the films to illustrate your points. Be precise and accurate in describing your example. General assertions such as "The acting was awful," "The cinematography was breathtaking," or "The editing was monotonous" have no validity without support by examples from the film(s) under discussion.

3. *Do* take the writing of the paper seriously. Consider that most instructors take time and effort to read and annotate your work. Regard your own mind and time as too valuable to waste in simply filling up pages with bland material.
4. *Do* try to be imaginative in relation to your material. This does not mean inventing material simply for originality's sake, but it does mean that your views, your intuition, your insights can be valuable.
5. *Do* check your paper carefully for typographical errors, errors in grammar, and the like before turning it in. Finish the paper in advance if possible and put it aside. Proofread it a day later, and you may well be able to spot any inconsistencies in logic or any other problems not apparent in the heat of composition. For some people, reading the paper aloud is a helpful way to detect errors.

★★★ Student Papers

Several sample student papers follow. One examines a specific cinematic element (music) and its artistic use in a single film. One is an example of contextual criticism, discussing political ideology in relation to several films. One isolates and identifies the characteristics of a subgenre, the caper film. Each paper has a specific point to make, is well organized, and backs up assertions with well-chosen and accurately described examples from the films. The papers were all written by students in introductory film classes. They are not completely free of problems and mistakes, but their success should be both relevant and encouraging to the student who is first beginning to write papers about film.

Focused title states topic and thesis.

Clear statement of thesis and elaboration indicate direction of essay.

THE USE OF MUSIC IN MICHAEL RITCHIE'S SMILE

In Michael Ritchie's SMILE (1975), music is used to expand the meaning and emotional content of the film. The choice of songs significantly contributes to the film's powerful satire of American values. Ritchie exposes the hypocrisies, superficialities, and contradictions of these values by creating an effective relationship between sight and sound. It is by examining, specifically, the relationship of music and image that one learns how Ritchie successfully produced a meaningful commentary on American life.

Illustrates thesis with first specific example. Example thoroughly developed.

The song "Smile" is an appropriate theme song. The lyrics, which are heard in the opening sequence of the film, immediately create an atmosphere of conflict and contradiction. "Smile though your heart is breaking" accompanies images of young girls posing and wearing artificial smiles. The song suggests that appearances may prove deceiving. A smile is usually a reflection of an internal feeling, but in Ritchie's film, smiles are worn as masks hiding feelings of fear, anger, and disappointment. The young beauty contestants are constantly told to smile so that they will look happy. As long as they "keep on smiling," real problems will not exist and therefore need not be faced. Characters such as Brenda and Big Bob wear the "Vaseline" smile which is symbolic of their superficial and artificial lives. They have developed attitudes based on the "American Miss" philosophy that "to look happy is to feel happy" and, as a result, they live in a narrow, unrealistic, and finally fragile world.

Further example builds argument by showing contradiction between image and music.

The American Miss Pageant theme song, which is sung by the contestants while they dance, expresses what is considered important and valuable by society. The girls sing, "We are proud to be all-American girls," while the camera focuses on various parts of their bodies. This scene suggests that the girls are commodities being used by the Santa Rosa Jaycees for profit and prestige. The girls are not individuals, but a club project through which the Jaycees may gain a good image.

Using whatever means available, the contestants try to meet the standards of the "All-American Girl." The American Miss theme song states they are proud Americans who have "faith and hope in a brighter day." The girls' words sound trite and meaningless as the camera scans their plastered smiles and their effervescent but uncoordinated gestures. This contradiction, presented through image and music, exposes the girls' real faith in externals and their hopes of winning the competition.

According to the judges, the All-American Girl should be physically attractive and full of "vim and vigor." Although she should possess talent, she doesn't have to have a great deal if she is well built. The American Miss should always appear happy, express the desire to help others, and respond to all controversial subjects with safe answers. The All-American Girl is a living tribute to the values of her country.

The old popular rock tunes which Ritchie uses also contribute ironic counterpoint to the images

Cumulative quotation of song titles and lyrics add specificity and strengthen argument. Writer interprets rather than merely describing relevant scenes.

and have some significant common characteristics. The songs, "Yes Sir, That's My Baby," "California Girl," "Sweet Sixteen," and "Come On Baby, Let the Good Times Roll," all have catchy, carefree melodies, trite and repetitive lyrics, and express a naive and unrealistic attitude toward life and love. In these songs, the American girl is described as "baby," "sweet sixteen" and "angel divine." Although these are not sensitive or perceptive descriptions, they do express an apparent need to define and maintain social roles. Ritchie makes many comments on the roles of men and women in American society and uses music to do so. In one scene, for example, he accompanies the ritual initiation ceremony of a club of over-35 males with the song, "Come On Baby, Let the Good Times Roll." The image of men clad in white sheets kissing a dead rooster counterpointed to the lyrics, "Come on baby, let me thrill your soul," illustrates a distorted sense of manhood.

Writer saves strongest point for last. Example pulls together previous points.

One of the most powerful comments made by the film is achieved through the music of "The Star-Spangled Banner" and images of various characters standing proudly with hands placed over their hearts. This gesture of pride and loyalty appears as superficial and hypocritical as all the other behind-the-scenes gestures we have seen. "The Star-Spangled Banner" presumably stands for honesty, truth, courage, and dedication, and, when played at the pageant, serves as a seal of approval on the values represented by the pageant. In this scene, the sound of "The Star-Spangled Banner" clashes with the pasted-on smiles and empty gestures which communicate hypocrisy, insincerity and phoniness. This scene is a fine example of Ritchie's ability to expand the meaning of his film through the use of music and imagery.

Concluding paragraph brings argument full circle and restates thesis.

At the very end of the film, the song "Smile" is played once again. The impact of this song is even more effective the second time, for it elicits a web of remembered images which intensifies the emotional impact of Ritchie's message. Music is successfully used by Ritchie to expand the meaning and emotional content of SMILE.

Title announces topic.

POLITICS IN MOVIES

Writer starts too generally; first sentence could be dropped.

Whenever a political movement is represented in the movies, we seem to be asking ourselves more about what motivates people to belong to it, than whether that movement is good or bad. Few of us question the fact that Nazism and Fascism were evil, but we do wonder how whole nations could become converted to them. We are a bit smug as we think, "I would never have been blindly loyal to Hitler," "Our nation could never succumb to Fascism." Then why did other people and nations succumb? Movies give us some interesting answers to that question, at the same time that they prod us out of our self-complacency. As we witness what happened to other people, it seems more possible to comprehend how the same thing could happen to us. What seemed remote before is now immediate — for a good movie has the peculiar quality of absorbing us into itself, of making us abandon our own lives for those of the characters on the screen, at least for a few hours.

Thus in Triumph of the Will, Nazism is no longer a terrible part of the past that we merely read about in our history books; it is real and alive before us. The film reinforces one striking characteristic that would motivate anyone to become a Nazi: an overpowering sense of organization. Nothing could be more organized than the thousands and thousands of marchers, every step synchronized, every uniform identical, every gun, shovel, or banner held at exactly the same angle as hundreds of other guns, shovels, and banners. The camera is constantly giving us high shots of the marchers, emphasizing and reemphasizing their organization. We get an enormous sense of power, a power that comes from everyone belonging, from everyone being in their places ready to carry out any of Hitler's orders. No wonder the young faces we see in the film are so intense and dedicated: they actually belong to this immense power, they are part of an almost inconceivably well-organized nation that proposes to conquer the earth. And so who wouldn't want to belong to those endless files of perfectly ordered, perfectly united soldiers? There is also a feeling of safety in belonging: how could anything so organized, so planned, ever be destroyed?

In Cabaret and Amarcord we do not see people fall under the spell of perfect, unified organization, yet we still sense in the characters a terrible desire to "belong," to be part of it all, this time on a different level: that of simple, basic emotion.

In Cabaret we hear a young Nazi, still only a boy, singing a song called "Tomorrow Belongs to

---

Thesis moves from implicit to explicit statement. Writer involves reader through use of "we."

Focuses on specific film to develop major point.

Shows how formal elements create viewer response.

Appropriate use of rhetorical questions relates thesis to reader.

Smooth transition to new issues and new films summarizes material to follow.

Examples carefully selected to further argument.

Me." Not only the melody, but every image in the song is beautiful: "the sun on the meadow . . . the stag in the forest runs free . . . but gather together to greet the sun, tomorrow belongs to me . . ." Halfway through, the crowd around him joins in, and we in the audience also want to burst out singing. It doesn't matter that we know from countless history lessons that Nazism was evil and destroyed millions of lives, we still want to sing. It is a wonderful and inspiring song in a quite inexplicable way, for we can never really explain our emotions. And so who wouldn't want to belong: something is happening, we don't quite know what, but it <u>does</u> seem glorious, and it is a basic human desire to be where "it's" happening, whatever that "it" may be, good or bad.

New example strengthens and extends point.

It is this same emotion we see in <u>Amarcord</u>, the story of an oceanside Italian village in the 1930s. The life of "S'Il Vous Plaît," one of the main characters, is symbolic of why people may have succumbed to Fascism. All during the movie, S'Il Vous Plaît, an "old maid," is searching for something beautiful, something wonderful; she is trying to find out where "it" is happening without knowing what "it" is. She does not need to say anything; we need merely to look at her excited, intense face, her eyes always darting about, always on the verge of discovering something. We have merely to watch her as she goes out to greet an ocean liner with an expedition of boats that includes the whole town. As the ship draws majestically near, she weeps and throws kisses, trying to give away some of that "sentiment" she is so full of, as she herself has explained. We do not know why she is excited about the ship, except that it is so beautiful, and everyone else is cheering and shouting, and something <u>is</u> happening, whatever it may be. In the same way she throws kisses to the soldiers marching through the streets, and finally marries a Fascist. At last S'Il Vous Plaît has found her "something," at last she belongs.

Further example and discussion develop variant while still supporting major point.

In <u>The Conformist</u> we see the need to belong arising from quite a different source. The protagonist has joined the Fascist movement in order to erase that which has heretofore set him apart from others: as a young boy he murdered a homosexual. By joining a movement where it is an acceptable, everyday occurrence to kill, he is becoming "normal," he is making his past acceptable so he can live with it. Only later after the fall of Mussolini does he meet up with Lino, the homosexual he thought he had murdered, and realizes how useless and unnecessary it was for him to become "normal." Ironically, then, he was actually "normal" before joining the Fascists, and only became "abnormal" — a killer — when he participated in the murders of Professor and Anna Quadri. His desire to belong has destroyed him when he thought that it would make him whole.

Thus the desire to belong is brought terribly close to us, for it is a universal human desire, it is <u>our</u> desire. All of the above motives could be our motives. No longer can we remain smugly aloof. Instead we must ask ourselves: What are <u>we</u> going to succumb to? What are <u>we</u> going to belong to? It is a frightening question but one that must be asked, and any movie that makes us ask it is certainly worth seeing.

Conclusion returns to opening strategy of involving reader and implicitly restates thesis. Final sentence emphasizes relevance of thesis

THE CAPER FILM

Title announces topic.

Thesis implicit. Definition of genre initiated through what "caper" is not. Useful references to other films help support generalizations.

One film genre is the crime film, and if the crime film is divided into sub-genres, one type could be called "caper" film. The caper film is not a typical gangster film involved with the rise and/or fall of a thug (<u>Little Caesar</u>, <u>Scarface</u>), or a pursuit film (<u>The Getaway</u>, <u>Sugarland Express</u>), or a whodunit film (<u>The Maltese Falcon</u>, <u>Chinatown</u>, <u>Murder on the Orient Express</u>), although it may contain elements found in some or all of these. The typical caper film seems to follow its own formula, with only the locale and the individual mechanics of the crime altered to fit the specific situation.

Paper organization based on hierarchy of genre ingredients. Topic sentence announces subject of paragraph.

All major operations need a leader, even a crime. The caper film is not about petty theft, or robbing the Cattlemen's Bank in Tonopah; it is about a bold scheme to do an impossible job. Planning such an undertaking requires extraordinary talent and leadership, and thus we have the first requirement of the caper: the mastermind, the brain, the frustrated executive, the bored computer specialist, the genius, the ex-commando looking for thrills, the quiet professor, or the cultured gentleman. Rarely, if ever, is the leader a <u>professional</u> criminal. He is often an upstanding member of the community (the professor in <u>Grand Slam</u>) organizing the caper as a thrill, a way to beat the system, or from idle curiosity: "Can I really do this?" or "Why not?"

Topic sentence parallels previous construction. Characteristics of genre further defined through multiple examples.

A leader needs someone to lead, a gang. These operations are expected to be professional, and so must the men. No amateur gunmen quick on the trigger will do when the job involves opening an impregnable vault guarded by every device known to mankind. There must be technicians: computer specialists (<u>The Italian Job</u>), electricians (<u>Ocean's 11</u>), mechanics, ex-commandos, demolition men, acrobats, race car drivers, etc. The military usually provides men with just such skills and it is not mere chance that many gangs consist of old buddies from the same Army unit. Where criminals are required to supply the necessary skills, they are not usually common convicts. They must be the best in the business, legends among those in the field who know of such things.

With a leader and a gang, an objective is needed. What could be more worthy of such a group than a vault ten feet thick guarded by the most sophisticated alarm system in the entire world (<u>Grand Slam</u>), or robbing not one but five casinos simultaneously in Las Vegas (<u>Ocean's 11</u>), or a mobile fortress monitored continuously by television, totally bulletproof, and following a random route impossible to locate (<u>They Came to Rob Las Vegas</u>). Whatever the objective, it must be impregnable, impossible and worth millions.

The objective is reached through a plan. Developed for months or years and conceived in boldness and daring, it is a brilliant masterpiece of flawless logic. Every detail is considered; alarms must be bypassed, cameras deceived, vaults of solid neutronium breached, and perhaps all this must occur undetected at Times Square during rush hour. The plan usually takes advantage of such things as holidays and public celebrations: the New Year's Eve celebration in Las Vegas (<u>Ocean's 11</u>), Mardi Gras in Rio de Janeiro (<u>Grand Slam</u>), the running of the bulls in Pamplona (<u>Caper of the Golden Bulls</u>).

Selective use of humor and exaggeration emphasize genre characteristics.

The execution proceeds like clockwork, smooth as silk, exactly by the timetable until . . . a newly installed alarm is discovered, a key man dies of an acute hickey (or heart attack as in <u>Ocean's 11</u>), for the first time in thirty years a guard feels restless and begins to prowl, the explosives man left the detonators in his other pair of pants, the polarity of the gee-gaw is right-handed and only a left-handed widget was brought to deactivate it! There is no time; it is all or nothing! With the entire audience breath-

*Organizational strategy
allows writer to
discuss climax of
genre at climax of
paper.*

less for the last forty minutes, enter the dilemma, the random flaw, the suspense multiplier.
The name of the game is tension, and there is usually plenty of it.

Finally, after the audience has aged ten years,
success is achieved. All the jewels in the world
are loaded into the false-bottomed tank truck,
the money bags are picked up with the garbage
(Ocean's 11), the high-speed cars head out of
town loaded with the gold bullion (The Italian
Job), the police personally escort the car with
the solid gold bumpers through the blockade.

And for what? For millions of dollars to be
cremated with a dead companion (Ocean's 11), for
a purse-snatcher to unwittingly steal all the
diamonds (Grand Slam), for an anxious accomplice
to blast millions heavenward (They Came to Rob
Las Vegas), for a bus loaded with the gold to get
stuck on the edge of a cliff (The Italian Job).
The point of the caper film seems to be not how
much you've won or whether you get to keep it, but
how you've played the game. The fact that the job
was done at all is usually the only reward.

*Last paragraph
skillfully summarizes
elements of
definition. Last
sentence illuminates
by ironic twist on
old cliché.*

Somewhere in film archives there probably exist
every variation and combination of the caper film
imaginable. But the basic elements seem to be
these: a brilliant leader, a gang of skilled professionals, a plan of great detail and daring,
a major portion of the film concerned with either
the preliminary training and preparation and/or
the actual execution of the job, and finally (but
not always) the momentary achievement of success
and riches, for an ironic ending seems to be the
norm. For even when successful, crime cannot pay.

NOTES

1 *Day for Night* (New York: Grove Press, 1975), p. xii.

2 *A Short Guide to Writing About Literature*, 4th ed. (Boston: Little, Brown, 1979),
pp. 59–70.

Selected Sources for Further Reading

The following selection of reading materials is intended to help students enlarge their general knowledge of film history, theory, and criticism, and to aid them in discovering further source materials which may be of help in writing critical and research papers. It is not meant to be a basic bibliography and includes only a few volumes which focus on auteur studies, individual genres, or other specialized subjects. Some of this kind of material is cited in appropriate sections of the text. For an introduction to specialized subject matter and to theoretical texts, consult some of the anthologies listed below in which excerpts from such original sources have been reprinted. Consult the Historical Overview before Chapter 9 for books most frequently cited as the seminal works of film criticism. The bibliography is divided into several sections for convenience: Theory and Criticism, Film History, Contextual Criticism, Guides to Film Information, Selected Interviews with Filmmakers, Bibliographical Guides, and Film Periodicals.

THEORY AND CRITICISM

Andrew, Dudley J. *The Major Film Theories: An Introduction.* New York: Oxford University Press, 1976.

Grant, Barry K., ed. *Film Genre: Theory and Criticism.* Metuchen, N.J.: Scarecrow Press, 1977.

Kaminsky, Stuart. *American Film Genres: Approaches to a Critical Theory of Popular Film.* Dayton, Ohio: Pflaum, 1974.

MacCann, Richard Dyer, ed. *Film: A Montage of Theories.* New York: Dutton, 1966.

Mast, Gerald, and Marshall Cohen, eds. *Film Theory and Criticism: Introductory Readings,* 2nd ed. New York: Oxford University Press, 1979.

Nichols, Bill, ed. *Movies and Methods.* Berkeley: University of California Press, 1977.

Perkins, V. F. *Film as Film.* Baltimore: Penguin Books, 1972.

Sitney, P. Adams, ed. *Film Culture Reader.* New York: Praeger, 1970.

———. *The Avant-Garde Film: A Reader of Theory and Criticism.* New York: New York University Press, 1978.

Wollen, Peter. *Signs and Meaning in the Cinema,* 2nd ed. New York: Viking, 1972.

FILM HISTORY

Balio, Tino, ed. *The American Film Industry.* Madison: University of Wisconsin Press, 1976.

Barnouw, Erik. *Documentary: A History of the Non-Fiction Film.* New York: Oxford University Press, 1974.

Brownlow, Kevin. *The Parade's Gone By.* New York: Ballantine Books, 1968.

Ellis, Jack. *A History of Film.* Englewood Cliffs, N.J.: Prentice-Hall, 1979.

Fell, John. *A History of Films.* New York: Holt, Rinehart and Winston, 1979.

Fielding, Raymond. *A Technological History of Motion Pictures and Television.* Berkeley: University of California Press, 1967.

Jacobs, Lewis, ed. *The Documentary Tradition: From Nanook to Woodstock.* New York: Hopkinson & Blake, 1971.

Jowett, Garth. *Film: The Democratic Art.* Boston: Little, Brown, 1976.

Knight, Arthur. *The Liveliest Art: A Panoramic History of the Movies,* rev. ed. New York: New American Library, 1979.

Mast, Gerald. *A Short History of the Movies,* 2nd ed. New York: Bobbs-Merrill, 1976.

Sklar, Robert. *Movie-Made America: A Social History of the American Movies.* New York: Random House, 1975.

CONTEXTUAL CRITICISM

Alloway, Lawrence. *Violent America: The Movies 1946–1964.* New York: Museum of Modern Art, 1971.

Bluestone, George. *Novels into Film.* Berkeley: University of California Press, 1957.

Gluckman, Andre, ed. *Violence on the Screen.* Translated by Susan Bennett. London: British Film Institute, Education Department, 1971.

Harrington, John. *Film and/as Literature.* Englewood Cliffs, N.J.: Prentice-Hall, 1977.

Jarvie, I. C. *Movies and Society.* New York: Basic Books, 1970.

MacBean, James Roy. *Film and Revolution.* Bloomington: Indiana University Press, 1975.

Wright, Will. *Sixguns and Society: A Structural Study of the Western.* Berkeley: University of California Press, 1975.

GUIDES TO FILM INFORMATION

Aaronson, Charles S. *International Motion Picture and Television Almanac.* New York: Quigley Publications, 1930 — . Annual.

Ash, Réné. *The Motion Picture Film Editor.* Metuchen, N.J.: Scarecrow Press, 1974.

Bawden, Liz-Anne, ed. *The Oxford Companion to Film.* New York: Oxford University Press, 1976.

Cawkwell, Tim, and John M. Smith. *The World Encyclopedia of Film.* New York: A & W Visual Library, 1972.

Corliss, Richard, ed. *The Hollywood Screenwriters.* New York: Avon, 1972.

————. *Talking Pictures: Screenwriters in the American Cinema.* New York: The Overlook Press, 1974.

Cowie, Peter, ed. *International Film Guide.* New York: A. S. Barnes, 1964 — . Annual.

Enser, A. G. S., ed. *Filmed Books and Plays: 1928–1974.* New York: Academic Press, 1974.

Film Daily Year Book of Motion Pictures. New York: Film Daily Publishers, 1918 — . Annual.

Gottesman, Ronald, and Harry M. Geduld. *Guidebook to Film: An Eleven-in-One Reference.* New York: Holt, Rinehart & Winston, 1972.

Halliwell, Leslie. *The Filmgoer's Companion,* 6th ed. New York: Hill and Wang, 1977.

————. *Halliwell's Film Guide: A Survey of 8,000 English-Language Movies.* London & New York: Granada Publishing, 1977.

Higham, Charles. *Hollywood Cameramen.* Bloomington: Indiana University Press, 1970.

Kozarski, Richard, ed. *Hollywood Directors, 1914–1940.* New York: Oxford University Press, 1976.

————. *Hollywood Directors, 1941–1976.* New York: Oxford University Press, 1977.

Krafsur, Richard, ed. *The American Film Institute Catalogue of Motion Pictures Produced in the United States: Feature Films 1961–1970.* New York: R. R. Bowker, 1976.

Manchel, Frank. *Film Study: A Resource Guide.* Rutherford, N.J.: Fairleigh Dickinson University Press, 1973.

Manvell, Roger, and Lewis Jacobs, eds. *International Encyclopedia of Film.* New York: Crown, 1972.

Monaco, James. *Film: How and Where to Find Out What You Want to Know.* New York: Zoetrope, 1976.

Munden, Kenneth W., ed. *The American Film Institute Catalogue of Motion Pictures Produced in the United States: Feature Films 1921–1930,* 2 vols. New York: R. R. Bowker, 1971.

The New York Times Directory of the Film. New York: Arno Press, 1974.

The New York Times Film Reviews 1913–1968, 6 vols. New York: Arno Press, 1970.

Roud, Richard, ed. *A Critical Dictionary of the Cinema.* New York: Viking Press, 1977.

Sadoul, Georges. *Dictionary of Film Makers.* Translated and edited by Peter Morris. Berkeley: University of California Press, 1972.

————. *Dictionary of Films.* Translated and edited by Peter Morris. Berkeley: University of California Press, 1972.

Sarris, Andrew. *The American Cinema: Directors and Directions, 1929–1968.* New York: Dutton, 1968.

Sitney, P. Adams. *The American Avant-Garde.* New York: Oxford University Press, 1974.

Thomson, David. *A Biographical Dictionary of Film.* New York: Morrow, 1976.

SELECTED INTERVIEWS WITH FILMMAKERS

Baker, Fred, with Ross Firestone, ed. *Movie People: At Work in the Business of Film.* New York: Douglas Book Corp., 1972.

Geduld, Harry M., ed. *Filmmakers on Filmmaking.* Bloomington: Indiana University Press, 1969.

Gelmis, Joseph. *The Film Director as Superstar.* Garden City, N.Y.: Doubleday & Co., 1970.

Higham, Charles, and Joel Greenberg. *The Celluloid Muse: Hollywood Directors Speak.* New York: New American Library, 1972.

Kantor, Bernard R., Blacker, Irwin R., and Kramer, Anne, eds. *Directors at Work: Interviews with American Film-Makers.* New York: Funk & Wagnalls, 1970.

Levin, G. Roy. *Documentary Explorations: 15 Interviews with Film-Makers.* Garden City, N.Y.: Doubleday & Co., 1971.

Samuels, Charles Thomas, ed. *Encountering Directors.* New York: Putnam, 1972.

Sarris, Andrew, ed. *Interviews with Film Directors.* New York: Bobbs-Merrill Co., 1967.

Sherman, Eric, and Martin Rubin. *The Director's Event: Interviews with Five American Film-Makers.* New York: New American Library, 1972.

BIBLIOGRAPHICAL GUIDES

Aceto, Vincent J., Jane Graves, and Fred Silva. *Film Literature Index.* Albany, N.Y.: Filmdex, Inc. Quarterly.

Batty, Linda. *Retrospective Index to Film Periodicals 1930–1971*. New York: R. R. Bowker, 1975.

Bowles, Stephen E., ed. *Index to Critical Film Reviews in British and American Film Periodicals, 1930–1972*. New York: Burt Franklin Co., 1975.

————. *Index to Critical Reviews of Books About Film, 1930–1972*. New York: Burt Franklin Co., 1975.

Bukalski, Peter J. *Film Research: A Critical Bibliography with Annotations and Essay*. Boston: G. K. Hall, 1972.

Gerlach, John C. and Gerlach, Lana. *The Critical Index*. New York: Teachers' College Press, 1974.

International Index to Film Periodicals (FIAF Index). New York: R. R. Bowker, 1972 — . Annual.

Kowalski, Rosemary Ribich. *Women and Film: A Bibliography*. Metuchen, N.J.: Scarecrow Press, 1976.

Leonard, Harold, ed. *The Film Index: A Bibliography. Vol. 1. The Film as Art*, reprint ed. New York: Arno Press, 1966.

MacCann, Richard Dyer and Edward S. Perry. *The New Film Index: A Bibliography of Magazine Articles in English, 1930–1970*. New York: E. P. Dutton, 1974.

Monaco, James, and Susan Schenker, eds. *Books About Film: A Bibliographical Checklist*, 3rd ed. New York: Zoetrope, 1976.

Rehrauer, George. *Cinema Booklist*. Metuchen, N.J.: Scarecrow Press, 1972. *Supplement One*, 1974. *Supplement Two*, 1976.

Schuster, Mel. *Motion Picture Directors: A Bibliography of Magazine and Periodical Articles, 1900–1969*. Metuchen, N.J.: Scarecrow Press, 1973.

FILM PERIODICALS

American Film. (Monthly). American Film Institute, Kennedy Center, Washington, D.C. 20006.

Cineaste. 333 Sixth Avenue, New York, New York 10014.

Cinema Journal. (Semiannual). Film Division, Northwestern University, Evanston, Illinois 60201.

Film Comment. (Bimonthly). Film Society of Lincoln Center, 1865 Broadway, New York, New York 10023.

Film Criticism. (Three issues a year). Box 825, Edinboro, Pennsylvania 16412.

Film Culture. G.P.O. Box 1449, New York, New York 10001.

Film Heritage. University of Dayton, Dayton, Ohio 45469.

Film Quarterly. University of California Press, Berkeley, California 94720.

Film Reader. (Annual). Northwestern University Film Division, Evanston, Illinois 60201.

The Journal of Popular Film and Television. (Quarterly). Popular Culture Center, Bowling Green State University, Bowling Green, Ohio 43403.

Jump Cut. (Bimonthly). 3138 West Schubert, Chicago, Illinois 60647.

Literature/Film Quarterly. Salisbury State College, Salisbury, Maryland 21801.

Quarterly Review of Film Studies. Redgrave Publishing Company, 430 Manville Road, Pleasantville, New York 10570.

Screen. (Quarterly). 29 Old Compton Street, London W1V 5PL, England.

Sight and Sound. (Quarterly). British Film Institute, 81 Dean Street, London W1V 6AA, England.

Take One. (Bimonthly). Unicorn Publishing, Box 1778, Station B, Montreal H3B, 3L3, Quebec, Canada.

Wide Angle. (Quarterly). Box 388, Athens, Ohio 45701.

The following concise definitions are meant as either quick introductions or brief reminders. For further information, consult the index, which will refer you to the pages that give a fuller discussion. Whenever possible, we have used the definitions (or parts of definitions) published by the University Film Association (Monograph No. 2) as *Glossary of Film Terms* (University Film Association, 1978). Compiled by John Mercer, this recent and thorough glossary draws upon a previous work published in 1955 by the University Film Producers Association. When our definitions are derived from the *Glossary of Film Terms,* they are followed by the letters *UFA;* when that *Glossary* uses the 1955 definitions, it appends the letters *UFPA.* Because the *Glossary* is much more extensive than ours and also more technical in some respects, occasionally we decided to simplify or to write new definitions more appropriate to this book. For more complete terminology, we urge the reader to write to the editor of the *Journal of the University Film Association* for information about obtaining a copy of the *Glossary of Film Terms.* As the editorship changes hands regularly, check a recent copy of the *Journal* for the name and address of the current editor.

abstract film   A film which shows only the essential elements of the original forms. Also, loosely, any nonrepresentational film. *UFA*

Academy aperture   The size of the frame mask in 35mm cameras and projectors as standardized by the Academy of Motion Picture Arts and Sciences. *UFA*

adaptation   The movement to the screen of a story, novel, play, or other work suitably treated so as to be realizable through the motion picture medium.

ambiguous time   Time on the screen that is either inadvertently or intentionally unclear. Dissolves, fades, and other transitional devices are not precise in their indication of the extent of the passage of time. Superimpositions also reveal time passing, but do not indicate how much. Often, ambiguous time is used in montage sequences whose purpose is to create mood and atmosphere, or to convey general rather than specific narrative information, e.g., the lovers have spent time together and their love has deepened.

analytic documentary   A form of nonfiction film which attempts to analyze its subject matter rather than simply to record it. That analysis involves the filmmaker's own interaction with the subject, within the film, or his purposeful juxtaposition of footage to make a point. Unlike the persuasive documentary, which is a sort of propaganda film, the analytic documentary tries to show many facets of the subject matter although it makes no claim to objectivity.

anamorphic lens   A lens which "squeezes" the material it perceives so that its wider than normal scope can be recorded on a normal size film frame. During projection the image will be widened and appear as normal in size on a wider-than-normal screen (2.5 or 2.85 to 1).

angle   See **camera angle.**

aperture   *1) Lens aperture:* The orifice, usually an adjustable iris, which limits the amount of light passing through a lens. *2) Camera aperture:* In 16mm motion picture cameras, the mask opening, 0.410 × 0.294 inches, which defines the area of each frame exposed. *3) Projector aperture:* In 16mm projectors, the mask opening, 0.380 × 0.284 inches, which defines the area of each frame projected. *4) Printer aperture:* The limiting orifice through which light passes to expose the film to be reproduced. *UFA (UFPA)*

art director   The person who assesses the staging requirements for a production and arranges for and supervises the work of set design and preparation. *UFA*

aspect ratio   The width-to-height ratio of a motion picture frame as photographed. Also, the ratio of the frame dimensions as projected on a screen.

associational editing, relational editing, associative editing   The juxtaposition of shots in order to present contrast, comparison, similarities, or ideas. *UFA*

asynchronous sound   Sound derived from a source not in the image on the screen at the time it is heard, i.e., sound not in synchronization with corresponding lip movement or object movement in the film.

auteur   (French, literally "author") The person primarily responsible for the entire style and treatment of the content of the film. Generally used in reference to a director with a recognizable style and thematic preoccupation, the term is also used for other production personnel (writers, performers, cinematographers, editors) who are seen as the major force behind a given film. More particularly, film auteurs function within the boundaries of studio production systems and are distinguishable from film artists, who have nearly total control over all aspects of production. Sometimes the two terms are used interchangeably.

avant-garde, avant-garde film   (French, literally "advance guard") *1)* A movement toward innovation in the arts in the twenties, encompassing such approaches as cubism, surrealism, and Dadaism, and including experimentation in filmmaking. *2)* Any current innovative movement in the arts. *UFA*

background music   Nonindigenous music which accompanies a film, usually on the sound track, but may be from a live performance of one or more instrumentalists, or from records or tapes. Most background music in nontheatrical films is not scored to fit the action; in theatrical films the music is usually written to reinforce and emphasize the action. *UFA*

backlighting   Light coming from behind objects or performers being photographed. *UFA*

blimp   A camera housing which, because it is soundproof, prevents the noise of the camera's operation from being recorded on the sound track. Once immobile or awkward and bulky, blimps are now light and portable.

boom, camera boom   A sturdy vehicular support providing vertical, horizontal, pivotal, and translational movement for camera and operator, enabling them to assume, rapidly and conveniently, almost any desired angle in relation to the scene to be photographed. *UFA (UFPA)*

British Free Cinema   See **Free Cinema.**

camera angle, angle   The physical relationship between camera and subject. If the camera is low, tilted up toward the subject, the result is a low-angle shot. If the camera is high, tilted down toward the subject, the result is a high-angle shot. If the camera is tilted neither up nor down, the result is a normal-angle shot. If the camera is not tilted but is placed at the eye-level of a person standing or seated, the angle is called an eye-level shot. If the camera is tilted off its horizontal and vertical axes, the result is a tilt angle or dutch-tilt angle. If the camera and subject are so positioned that approximately 75 per cent of one side, surface, or plane of the subject and 25 per cent of a second side, surface, or plane are facing the camera, the camera angle is a three-quarter angle. *UFA*

camera movement   Any motion of a camera during a shot, such as panning, tilting, dollying, craning, rolling, or wobbling. *UFA*

camera speed   The rate at which film is run through a camera in frames per second (fps) or feet or meters per minute. The normal speed for sound film today is 24 fps, for silent 18 fps.

cel   A transparent sheet of cellulose acetate or similar plastic serving as a support for drawings, lettering, etc., in animation and title work. Usually, it is punched, outside the limits of the camera field, with holes which fit pegs similarly arranged to facilitate registration of successive cels during preparation and photography. *UFA*

characters, characterizations   The fictional people within a narrative film, not to be confused with the actors who play them.

Cinema Novo   A film movement which arose in Brazil in the 1960s and kindled contemporary filmmaking (often for political purpose) in Latin America.

CinemaScope, Scope   Trade name (Metro-Goldwyn-Mayer) for wide screen films made and projected by the use of anamorphic lenses on camera and projector. *UFA*

cinema verité   (French, literally "film truth") A style of filmmaking begun in Europe in the fifties involving the use of portable sound cameras and recorders, and the cinematography of interviews and events on location. Commentary, sometimes obtained from interviews and hidden recorders, was used as well as lip-synchronous sound. Cinema verité films usually sought strong, sometimes radical, opinion. Often one of the filmmakers asked questions. *UFA*

Cinerama A wide screen process which originally used three cameras, three corresponding projectors, and stereophonic sound. *UFA*

city symphony A type of nonfiction film which uses images of cities both lyrically and socially. Often structured around a dawn-to-dusk movement and edited rhythmically.

close-up shot, close-up, CU, close-shot, CS A shot in which the image of the subject or its most important part fills most of the frame. A close-up shot of a person usually includes the head and part of the shoulders. *UFA*

code The rules or forms which can be observed to allow a message to be understood, to signify. "Codes" are the rules operating on the means of expression (and thus are distinct from the means of expression). *UFA*

collage film A type of experimental or avant-garde film that uses single-frame cinematography to control the speed with which images of various objects, cutouts, and drawings are overlaid, animated, and presented to the viewer.

color film Color film carries one or more emulsions in which, after processing, brightness values of a scene are reproduced in terms of color scales. *UFA*

color saturation The measure applied to how vividly a color appears on the film, i.e., whether it seems washed out or dense.

comedy Generally, a work of literature, drama, or film which has a non-tragic ending and which creates a climate considered humorous by a majority of viewers. There are many different types of comedy (slapstick, parody, screwball comedy), and comedy may be created around any subject matter.

compilation film A film made by editing large amounts of footage shot usually without a script for record or news purposes. *UFA*

composition The distribution, balance, and general relationship of masses and degrees of light and shade, line, and color within a picture area. *UFA* *(UFPA)*

constructivism An art movement of the 1920s, especially popular in Soviet Russia. It emphasized geometric and abstract forms, often based on mechanical principles and machinery.

contextual criticism A form of criticism which sees film in relation to the context in which it was created and in which it is shown. Considerations of specific films and groups of films touch on history, politics, sociology, psychology, and other disciplines.

continuity The cinematic portrayal of a flow of events. *UFA*

contrapuntal sound, counterpoint Sound, especially music, which contrasts or conflicts with the action in a motion picture. *UFA*

convention   A recurrent unit of activity, dialogue, or cinematic technique which is used in films and is familiar to audiences, e.g., the shoot out in a western, the line "There are some things man was not meant to know" in a horror film, the editing of a chase scene.

counterpoint   See **contrapuntal sound.**

crane, camera crane   A movable vehicle which has a long boom on which a camera can be mounted and moved up much higher than on a small dolly. *UFA*

credits, credit titles   Titles of acknowledgment for story, sets, direction, etc. *UFA (UFPA)*

cross-cut   A cut from one line of action to another. Also applies as an adjective to sequences which use such cuts. *UFA*

cubism   An art movement, beginning about 1910, in which people and objects were broken down into their geometric components.

cue sheets   Sheet music available to accompanists of silent films. Cue sheets indicated moods or dramatic sequences like the chase and then provided appropriately paced music which might be played for any movie.

cut   1) The instantaneous change from one shot to another. 2) A command used to stop operation of the camera, action, and sound recording equipment. 3) To sever or splice film in the editing process. *(UFPA)* Also, to eliminate a shot, sequence, or some sound from a film. Loosely, to edit a film. *UFA*

cut-away shot, cut-away, CA   A shot of action occurring at the same time as the main action, but which is not part of the main action. A cut-away shot may be preceded by a definite look or glance out of frame by an actor or actors. Conversely, it may show something of which actors in the preceding shot are unaware. Example: during a chase, a shot of what is going on back at the ranch. *UFA*

dada   An art movement of the 1920s which predated surrealism. Like surrealism, it promoted incongruity, illogic, and shock. Its aims were anarchic and nihilistic.

decor   The furnishings and decorations used in a motion picture action field, especially set furnishing and decorations. *UFA*

deep-focus cinematography, deep-field cinematography   Cinematography which renders objects in focus at both near and far distances through the use of small f-stops, short focal length lenses, or both. *UFA.*

depth-of-field, D/F   The distance in front of a camera and its lens in which objects are in apparent sharp focus. *UFA*

dialogue   Lip-synchronous speech in a film with the speaker usually, but not always, visible. *UFA*

direct cinema, uncontrolled documentary   A type of location, nonfiction, "close observation" cinema in which lightweight cameras and sound recorders are used to record action as it actually happens with indigenous sound only. The origin of the term, used to distinguish this kind of filmmaking from cinema verité, is attributed to Albert Maysles. *UFA*

direct cut   See **straight cut.**

director   The individual who interprets the script in terms of performances and cinematic technique, and who supervises all phases of the work involved in achieving a coherent, unified film presentation. *UFA (UFPA)*

director's script   See **shooting script.**

discontinuity   A mismatch of action, properties, furnishings, objects, or lighting as one shot ends and another starts. A jump cut. *UFA*

disorientation cut   Two pieces of film edited together for their disorienting or dislocating effect on the viewer. The cut is made to confuse the viewer as to content, space or time.

dissolve, lap dissolve   A shot-linking effect which results when one shot fades out at the same time that a second shot fades in. *UFA (UFPA)*

documentary   A nonfiction film. It uses actuality as its raw material and may be of many different types with many different purposes.

Dolby system   Trade name for a noise-reduction system designed to reduce the noise level of a tape or optical recording and thus achieve better fidelity. *UFA*

dolly   *1)* A small, sturdy wheeled platform built to carry camera and cameraman to facilitate movement of the camera during shooting. *2)* To move the camera by means of a dolly while shooting. *UFA (UFPA)*

double exposure, multiple exposure   The photographic recording of two (or more) images on a single strip of film. The images may be either superimposed or side-by-side in any relationship, sometimes individually vignetted. *UFA (UFPA)*

double-system sound recording   The recording of sound on a recorder which is separate from the camera. The recorder is usually a magnetic tape recorder with sync-pulse capability or a magnetic film recorder. *UFA*

dramatization   The acting out and the realization of that acting out in images on the screen of a fictional or factual event. Narration tells us what happened, dramatization shows it to us as it happens.

dub   To transfer sound from one medium to another, from units which are for playback only. Also, to put dialogue, sometimes foreign, into a film after it has been shot. *UFA*

edge numbers, edge numbering   Numbers placed on the edge film to facilitate matching (conforming) of original film and sound to edited workprints. *UFA*

editing, cutting   The process of assembling, arranging, and trimming film, both picture and sound, to the best advantage for the purpose at hand. *UFA (UFPA)*

effects, FX   Depending on context, either sound effects, optical effects, or special effects. *UFA*

elevator shot   A shot in which the camera moves straight up and down, not in an arc as on a crane. *UFA*

emulsion   The coating, consisting of gelatin and silver salts (unprocessed film) or gelatin and metallic silver (processed film) or iron oxide (for magnetic sound) bonded to and supported by a film base. *UFA*

epic   A film which stresses spectacle and large casts, often with a historical or biblical plot. The emphasis is on scope, and so, appropriately, many epics have been filmed in various wide-screen processes.

epic documentary   A recent form of documentary which is distinguished by its great length, its combination of interviews and stock footage, and its attempts to be accurate and fair through its complexity and scope.

establishing shot   Usually, a long shot which shows the location of the ensuing action, but may be a close-up or even a medium shot which has some sign or other clue which identifies the location. Sometimes called a cover shot. *UFA*

ethnographic film   An anthropological film which combines visual raw data and analysis through commentary and editing. *UFA*

experimental film   An independent, noncommercial film which is the product of the personal vision of the filmmaker. *UFA*

exposé   An investigative documentary which presents factual material ignored or unknown, with an eye to effecting viewer action. Sometimes it approaches yellow journalism and is more exploitative than socially oriented.

expressionism, expressionist, expressionistic   Fantasy and distortion in sets, lighting, and costumes used as a means of expressing the inner feelings of both filmmaker and characters. *UFA*

extended image   Composition within the film frame which draws the viewer's eye and consciousness beyond the frame itself and suggests the completion of the image outside the camera field, e.g., an image of half a man's face in the frame will provoke the viewer to complete the image mentally, and so to extend the face beyond what is shown in the actual image.

extreme close-up, ECU, extreme close shot, ECS   A very close shot of some detail, such as an actor's eyes or a small object. *UFA*

extreme long shot, ELS, XLS   A shot which shows considerable distance. Usually used only in reference to outdoor shots. *UFA*

fade   An optical or sound effect in which the screen or sound track gradually changes from black to an image or silence to sound (fade-in) or the reverse (fade-out).

fast film   A film which has relatively high sensitivity to light, usually an exposure index of 100 or higher. *UFA*

fast motion Action which has been photographed at a filming rate less than normal, then projected at normal speed. Sometimes called accelerated motion. *UFA*

feature film, feature Usually, a fictional narrative film lasting more than an hour, made for showing in commercial theaters. *UFA*

film *1)* A strip of flexible, transparent base material, usually cellulose triacetate, having various coatings such as photographic emulsions and iron oxide, and usually perforated. *2)* To photograph a motion picture. *3)* The cinema in general. *UFA*

film actors Performers who play fictional roles on the screen. Generally, less well-known personalities than film stars and more likely to submerge their personal characteristics in the characters they portray.

film archive A depository of films and associated print materials, used for study and research. *UFA*

film artist Generally, a filmmaker who has as much control over the idea, production, realization, and final form of a released film as is possible, given the collaborative nature of the commercial medium. Unlike the film auteur, who faces many studio-determined obstacles in realizing his personal vision on the screen, the film artist often works independently and with hand-chosen collaborators. (Often loosely used as a synonym for film auteur.)

film auteur See **auteur.**

film craftsman A filmmaker who realizes a given film on the screen competently and aesthetically, in accordance with production dictates of a studio, or other commercial considerations. Generally not the originator of the story and not preoccupied thematically, the film craftsman does not develop a personal style, but matches his style to the needs of a particular production.

film criticism The analysis and evaluation of films, usually in relation to theoretical principles including both aesthetics and philosophy. *UFA*

film movement The films and filmmakers who constitute a cinema (usually national) at a given period of historical time. Most often, social and political factors cause a film movement, bringing together artists who have common aesthetic and political goals and who recognize themselves as a group.

film noir (French, literally "black film") The term refers to a group of films which share a common cinematic style and related themes dealing with corruption, generally in urban settings. Most often used in reference to a group of films made in Hollywood during the 1940s and 1950s.

film review, review A summary of the content of a film, usually accompanied by information about the cast and the production, and often by the reviewer's judgment as to the worth of the film, published in print media or delivered orally on radio or television. *UFA*

film speed *1)* The general term used to indicate a film emulsion's sensitivity to light; the higher (or faster) the film speed, the better it is able to record an image with low illumination. 2) The rate of speed at which the film progresses through the camera and the projector, measured in frames per second or feet or meters per minute.

film stock   Unprocessed film and the various sizes of rolls in which it is available. *UFA*

film theory   General principles which explain the nature and capabilities of film as an independent art. *UFA*

filmic time and space   The expansion, condensation, or elimination of time and space, as well as shifts from a film's present to past time, through flashbacks, and to future time, through flash-forwards, as characteristically done through the use of editing and significant cues in picture and sound track. *UFA*

filter   A device used both in sound recording and mixing and in cinematography to block out unwanted sounds, light, or color, or to change the natural quality of sound, light, or color.

final cut   The editing of the film as it will be released in theaters. The filmmaker who has the right to final cut will guarantee that his version of the film is not tampered with prior to its release.

fisheye lens   An extreme wide-angle lens that distorts the image so that straight lines appear bowed at the edges of the frame.

flash pan, swish pan   An extremely rapid pan in which the subject becomes blurred.

flashback   A shot or sequence (sometimes quite long) showing action which occurred before the film's present time. *UFA*

flash-forward   A shot or sequence which shows future action or action which will be seen later in the film. *UFA*

flatbed editor, flatbed editing machine, horizontal editor   A table on which there are upright spindles for film and sound tracks, sprocket drives, heads for picture projection and sound reading, provision for interlock and advancing or retarding sound, and other features, used in various ways in the editing of films. *UFA*

floodlight, flood   Any of various types of luminaires which cast wide beams of light. *UFA*

focal length   The distance from the optical printer of a lens to the film plane when the lens is focused at infinity. *UFA*

focus   1) The sharpness or definition of the image. 2) To adjust the sharpness and clarity of the image by adjusting the lens or light source so as to create sharp or soft focus or to change focus.

foreground music   Often synchronous, music which finds its source within the actual narrative of the film. It can be heard realistically over the radio or from a television set, or performed on screen by the narrative characters (both major and minor) or by performers in the background.

formal criticism   Criticism which approaches film primarily as an art form and which discusses specific films as independent works which can be illuminated through an exploration of their cinematic technique and narrative content and structure.

formalism, formalist   A cinematic or critical approach to film which stresses form over content in the belief that meaning occurs in the way that content is presented.

formula   A pattern of dramatic actions or plot (for example, the reluctant hero of a western forced to take up his guns once more for the final shootout) which becomes familiar as it is repeated with minor variations from film to film.

frame, framing   *1)* One individual picture, as defined by the limits of the camera aperture, on a piece of motion picture film. *2)* To compose a shot. *UFA (UFPA)*

Free Cinema, British Free Cinema   A film movement which arose in Britain in the 1950s, initially emerging from the work of experimental documentarists and then influencing feature narrative films. The emphasis was on a realistic treatment of working-class Britons.

freeze frame, stop frame, hold frame   A frame which is printed repetitively so that although the projector is still operating, the image in the print can be seen without movement for a desired length of time. *UFA*

French New Wave   See **New Wave.**

futurism   An art movement around the time of World War I, emphasizing speed and dynamism in its forms as a response to modern life in the machine age.

gate   A hinged support for projector or camera pressure plate. Also, loosely, the camera or projector film aperture. *UFA (UFPA)*

genre   A film type, such as a western or science fiction film, which usually has conventional plot structure and characters; loosely, a "formula" film. *UFA*

German Expressionism   A film movement in Germany from 1919 through the 1920s, peaking about 1925. Following earlier expressionist movements in fine art and literature, filmmakers used decor, lighting, and cinematic technique to express interior states of being and feeling rather than to record an objective reality.

glass shot   A shot taken through a sheet of glass bearing titles or other art work in order to superimpose titles or art work on the moving background. *UFA (UFPA)*

grainy, graininess, grain   An image is grainy if it appears to be made up of distinguishable particles or grains. Actually, this is due to the grouping together, or "clumping," of the individual silver grains, which are by themselves far too small to be perceived under normal viewing conditions. *UFA (UFPA)*

hand-held Shot with a camera by a cameraman. Also, the somewhat wobbly image on the screen which results from such shooting. *UFA*

high-angle shot, high shot See **camera angle.**

high contrast The appearance of an image in which tones grade quickly from white to black with few intermediate values. *UFA*

high grain See **grainy.**

high-key A quality of any picture in which the emphasis is distinctly on the lighter tones. Also, in lighting, a relatively high level of illumination of subject, with relatively short-scale tonal rendition. *UFA (UFPA)*

high-speed film *1)* Film which has extra perforations for use in high-speed camera. *2)* Film which is very sensitive to light. *3)* A film made using mostly high-speed cinematography. *UFA*

holography Photography using laser light instead of sunlight or conventional artificial light, producing three dimensional images.

icon, iconography An object, landscape, or performer who accrues symbolic as well as particular meaning and conveys that meaning through recurrent presence in a group or genre of films. Not to be confused with a motif, which accrues such meaning in a single film only.

image (photographic) Any photographically obtained likeness in a processed photo-sensitive material. *UFA*

impact cut The editing together of two pieces of film for startling effect or impact. It may shock in its juxtaposition of content or temporarily confuse or unsettle the viewer.

independent filmmaking Film production initiated by a person or persons not under contract to a commercial studio. Some independents may produce without making use of union personnel or commercial facilities, other than a laboratory. Others may subcontract the production to union personnel and commercial facilities. *UFA*

insert shot, insert A shot of some detail of the main action or parallel action which can be made at any time during production, then inserted into the action during the editing process. *UFA*

intellectual montage An assembly of shots through editing which results in conveying an abstract or intellectual concept. A group of people being menaced and beaten by mounted police next to a shot of cattle being slaughtered in a slaughterhouse provokes the idea that the people in the first shot are being victimized and are helpless, considered no better than dumb animals by their oppressors. This idea is not pictured; it is suggested by the relationship of the two shots.

intercutting Insertion into a series of related shots of other shots for contrast or other effect. *UFA*

invisible editing, invisible cut A cut made during the movement of a performer, achieved either by overlapping the action, or by using two cameras and then matching the action during editing. Such cuts make shifts of camera position less noticeable. *UFA*

iris A circular masking device, so called because of its resemblance to the iris of the human eye.

Italian Neorealism See **Neorealism.**

jump cut An instantaneous advance in the action within a shot or between two shots due to the removal of a portion of film, to poor pictorial continuity, or to intent. *UFA*

key light The luminaire which creates the main, brightest light falling on a subject. *UFA*

lens aperture See **aperture.**

light, lighting *1)* Radiant energy. *2)* Illumination used in connection with filming. *3)* To arrange illumination for shooting. *UFA*

live action The action of living things, as distinguished from action created by animation. *UFA*

location shooting Shooting which is done away from a studio. *UFA*

long shot, LS A shot which shows all or most of a fairly large subject (for example, a person) and usually much of the surroundings.

long take A single shot (or take, or run of the camera) which lasts for a relatively lengthy period of time before it is juxtaposed with another shot. It reveals information within an unbroken context of space and time, and through camera and subject movement rather than through editing.

low-angle shot, low shot See **camera angle.**

low contrast Of a photographic image, having a long gradation of tones from white to black. *UFA*

low-key *1)* Pictures in which the majority of tones lie toward the darker end of the scale. *2)* In lighting, a generally low level of illumination of subject, with relatively short-scale tonal rendition. *UFA (UFPA)*

magnetic tape, magnetic sound Thin tape bearing an iron oxide coating on which sound may be recorded and from which sound may be reproduced. *UFA*

mask A device used to block or limit the passage of light from one area while admitting whole or reduced illumination to another area. *UFA (UFPA)*

master shot, master scene   A long shot or moving shot which includes all of the action in a particular sequence, with the camera fairly distant. After it is made, if only one camera is being used, medium shots and close ups are made of the repeated action and are inserted into the master shot during editing. *UFA*

matte shot   A shot in which a portion of the action field is masked off with action put in later either in the original camera, in a bipack camera, or in an optical printer.

medium shot, MS   A shot which shows part of a person or object. A medium shot of a person is usually considered to be one which includes head, shoulders, chest, and enough additional space for hand gestures to be seen. *UFA*

melodrama   A work of literature or film which treats serious subject matter (often life and death situations), but which is distinct from tragedy because the ending is always happily resolved with the protagonist overcoming all obstacles to achieve his or her desired goal. In those cases where the protagonist does not fully have the audience's sympathy (i.e., the socially unacceptable ambitious female of the 1940s or the gangster hero of the 1930s), the happy ending may be somewhat ambiguous.

microcinematography   Cinematography accomplished through the use of a microscope. Mostly used in scientific filmmaking, but also used in documentary and fiction films.

minimal film, minimal cinema   A type of experimental film which attempts to reduce film to its basic properties (its recording of actuality in continuous space and time) with minimal intervention by the filmmaker.

mise-en-scène   *1)* A term generally used to describe those elements of the film image which are placed before the camera and in relation to it, rather than to the process of editing which occurs after the interaction between camera and subject. *2)* Also, the images in which context and relationships are revealed in units which preserve continuous space and time.

mix, sound mix   To combine sound from two or more sources into a single recording, usually with adjustment of tonal quality and/or relative volume level. *(UFPA)* Also, the completed recording itself. *UFA*

montage   The assembly of shots, hence, editing, and especially the portrayal of action and creation of ideas through the use of many short shots. In the 1920s, the Russians formulated several kinds of montage styles. Later, in the U.S.A., montage came to mean a series of shots, often with superimpositions and optical effects, showing a condensed series of events, e.g., a crime wave in a city. *UFA*

motif   An object or sound which becomes linked to a film's narrative in a meaningful way so that it becomes symbolically identified with a character or action. The glass paperweight in *Citizen Kane* and the "attack" music in

Jaws are motifs. Not to be confused with icons, which function from film to film, motifs convey specific meaning in a single film only.

multiple exposure   The addition of images to a strip of film after the initial exposure, done by rewinding and re-exposing the film in the camera more than twice, or by combining images in printing. *UFA*

multiple-image   Having several images, not superimposed, within the frame.

multiple track, multiple channel   More than one recording source for motion picture sound. For easier control in sound mixing, dialogue, music, and effects are recorded on separate tracks which are then mixed into one track, or several tracks for stereophonic sound. As many as eight tracks can be used for the final optical sound track.

narration   Commentary spoken by an off-screen voice. In informational films, the voice is usually that of an "anonymous expert." In dramatic films, it may be the voice of one of the characters. *UFA*

negative image   An image in which the light and dark areas in the original subject are rendered correspondingly as dark and light areas. In the case of a negative color image, the subject color values are represented in the film as colors complementary to the colors producing them, in addition to the usual inversion of the black and white tonal scale. *UFA*

Neorealism, Italian Neorealism   A style of filming and kind of film content which became prominent in Italy after World War II, characterized by concern with man's struggles against inhumane social forces, filmed mostly on location with untrained actors, and using unsoftened realism throughout. *UFA*

New German Cinema, Das Neue Kino   A film movement begun in Germany in the late 1960s, fostered by support from German television. The films and filmmakers are linked through their political concerns and questioning of traditional narrative forms.

newsreel   About ten minutes of newsfilm, edited with titles, music, speed, and commentary, formerly seen regularly in theaters, but now no longer produced in the United States. *UFA*

New Wave, French New Wave, nouvelle vague   The films of a group of young French directors, most of whom started making feature films in 1959 and 1960, who emphasized conscious filmic manipulation and psychological reality over plot and characters. *UFA*

noise   Unwanted sound in an audio pickup. *UFA*

nonfiction film   Any film which records action for analysis, demonstrates a skill, presents information, or which attempts persuasion through the use of documentary or propaganda techniques. *UFA*

nuevo cine, el   A Latin American film movement which followed and was influenced by Cinema Novo of Brazil. The movement is politically radical and sees film as an educational as well as aesthetic force for social change. It combines documentary and fictional technique and subject matter, and attempts to break with what it considers the cultural imperialism of Hollywood narrative.

objective camera angle, objective camera Camera coverage which places the audience in the position of an observer of the action. *UFA*

objective time Time as it is recorded and revealed through camera movement and editing, unallied with any specific character in the narrative, or with a narrator. The camera functions as an omniscient third person narrator and the viewer is to perceive the time it perceives as undistorted by emotion or personality. Objective time often coincides with screen time.

off-screen space That space which is out of the camera field, but which is implied by the film through the movement of the camera and subject movement into and out of the field of vision.

optical cut, optical effect, optical Any systematic progressive alteration of a motion picture scene, or transition from one scene to another, commonly introduced in duplication. Includes the fade, the dissolve, and the wipe, as well as a host of more spectacular effects. *UFA (UFPA)*

optical printer A printer consisting essentially of a projector and a camera. Light passing through the film to be printed subsequently passes through a lens system before striking the print stock. The lens system and associated devices permit reduction and enlargement and the making of various kinds of effects. *UFA*

optical sound Sound recorded on or reproduced from photographic sound tracks, as distinguished from sound recorded on or reproduced from disks, tapes, and magnetic film. *UFA*

out-take In general, any shot which is removed from a film. More specifically, shots which are not workprinted. *UFA*

overhead shot A shot made from a position directly above the action. *UFA*

pan, pan shot A movement of the camera from left to right or right to left along a horizontal plane. Unlike the tracking shot in which the camera moves with the subject, the pan is shot from a stationary point.

parallel editing, parallel action, cross-cutting The intercutting of shots of two or more simultaneously occurring lines of action. *UFA*

persistence of vision A time-lag effect between visual stimulation of the eye and cessation of response to that stimulation. *UFA (UFPA)*

persuasive documentary A form of documentary which is aimed at convincing the viewer of a given thesis. Raw footage is assembled so as to make that point, and narration is not uncommon. At its most extreme, persuasion is attempted through dramatization presented on screen as actuality, or distortion of actual fact through editing or commentary; this form of persuasion is called propaganda.

pin spot   A spotlight or luminaire in which light is directed through lens and reflectors into an extremely narrow beam. Often used to add illumination to a performer's eyes.

pixilation, pixilation animation   Animation of people, achieved by having performers move slightly between exposures, then hold position while one or two frames are exposed. *UFA*

point-of-view shot, p.o.v. shot, POV   A shot made from a camera position close to the line of sight of a performer who is to be watching the action shown in the point-of-view shot. *UFA*

post-synchronized sound, dubbed sound   Lip-synchronous sound which is recorded after film has been shot, either in the language used by the performers or in foreign language, which fits the lip movements of the performers. *UFA*

process shot   A shot made of action in front of a rear projection screen having on it still or moving images for the background. *UFA*

producer   The entrepreneur who initiates and/or manages film production activities. *(UFPA)* Also, the administrator who is assigned to manage the production of a contract film. *UFA*

production personnel   Persons working on a film in any capacity. A list of job titles might include the following: writer, art director, assistant director, head gaffer, best boy, cameraman, casting director, choreographer, continuity girl, editor, director, director of photography, gaffer, grip, juicer, make-up artist, mixer, operating cameraman, producer, production supervisor, script girl, second-unit director, special effects supervisor, stunt supervisor, technical advisor, and unit manager. *UFA*

propaganda film   A type of film used for persuasive purposes (often political) which tends to manipulate and distort actuality and to appeal to emotion rather than to rational thought.

psychological time   The time the film seems to take to the viewer, generally felt as a sense of rhythm and pacing, i.e., the film felt long and boring or excitingly fast. Not to be confused with subjective time which belongs to a screen character rather than to the film viewer.

puppet animation   Animation of puppet figures which often have numerous heads and body parts with slightly different expressions and positions. *UFA*

rack focus, pull focus, shift focus   To change the focus of a lens during a shot. *UFA*

raw footage   Exposed film which has recorded desired subject matter but which has not yet been assembled into any kind of narrative or informative order, or selected on considerations of its satisfactory or unsatisfactory technical qualities.

reaction shot   Any shot, usually a cut-away, in which an actor reacts to action which has just occurred. *UFA*

realism, realistic film   The use of scripts, staging, costuming, and camera coverage which renders action as being real, not fantasy. *UFA*

reflector   A surface used to direct reflected sunlight (or artificial light) onto the subject matter to be photographed. It is used to either soften and diffuse harsh light or to enhance available light.

reverse motion, reverse action   Action which goes backward on the screen, achieved by shooting with the camera upside down, then turning the processed film end-over-end, or by shooting with camera rightside up and action reversed, or by reverse printing in an optical printer. *UFA*

running time   The time of the film's duration on the screen, its "length," e.g., two and a half hours.

satire   A work of literature or film which ridicules or exposes the vices, follies, foibles, and shortcomings of its subject, most often society and its institutions.

scene   A dramatic unit composed of a single or several shots. A scene usually takes place in a continuous time period, in the same setting, and involves the same characters.

screen time   The time covered by the film's story, or narrative time, i.e., a lifetime, a week, two days.

screenplay   See **script.**

screenwriter, script writer   One who prepares stories, treatments, and scripts for motion pictures. *UFA*

screwball comedy   A kind of American feature film which got its start in the 1930s, characterized by satire, sexual candor, romance, comically impossible and incongruous situations involving likeable people from different social classes, and fast-moving events. *UFA*

script   A set of written specifications for the production of a motion picture. (*UFPA*) There are several different kinds of scripts and they contain specifications for settings, action, camera coverage, dialogue, narration, music, and sound effects, in varying degrees of explicitness. *UFA*

selective focus   Rendering only part of the action field in sharp focus through the use of shallow depth of field. *UFA*

selective sound   A track in which some sounds are removed while others are retained. It can sound realistic, but it can also be so selective that its lack of ambient sound makes it seem artificial or expressionistic.

semiotics, semiology   *1)* The study of signification via codes or systems in texts. *2)* The general science of signs, of systems of signification. *UFA*

sequence   A dramatic unit composed of several scenes, all linked together by their emotional and narrative momentum. A sequence can span time and space so long as its dramatic elements and structure are unified.

setting   The location for a film or parts of a film. *UFA*

set-up   One camera position and its associated lighting. Also, loosely, any arrangement of settings, lights, and cameras. *UFA*

shooting ratio   The amount of film shot compared to the length of the edited film, with the edited film having a value of one. *UFA*

shooting script   A final script which is followed by performers and the director during filming. *UFA*

shooting time   The time it takes to set up, perform, and record photographically the images and sound of a motion picture.

shot   1) A single run of the camera. 2) The piece of film resulting from such a run. Systematically joined together in the process of editing, shots are synthesized into sequences, and the sequences in turn are joined to form the film as a whole. *UFA (UFPA)*

shot analysis   A careful and thorough recording of the separate shots which constitute an entire film or specific sequences. The analysis describes the visual images, camera movement, duration, sound, and transitions from shot to shot. Sometimes such an analysis is drawn as if it were a storyboard.

shutter   In a motion picture camera, the mechanical device which shields the film from light at the aperture during the film movement portion of the intermittent cycle. Also, a similar device in projectors for cutting the projection light during the time the film is moving at the aperture. *UFA (UFPA)*

silent speed   Originally, about sixteen frames per second, although cameramen varied their speed and projectionists were often instructed to crank more slowly for love scenes and faster for chases. Now, eighteen frames per second. *UFA*

simultaneous time   Created by the parallel editing or cross-cutting of events which are narratively understood to be occurring at the same moment, e.g., the heroine being tied to the railroad tracks, cut back and forth with the hero riding to her rescue. Can also be created through multiple image and split-screen technique, in which different events actually do occur in simultaneous running and screen time.

single-frame cinematography, single-frame shooting, single-framing   Releasing the starting switch or release for each frame of film exposed. Often used to greatly speed up the normal motion of persons and objects, to give apparent motion to lifeless objects, and to speed up the growth and development of plants and animals (time-lapse cinematography), when the film is projected at normal speeds. *UFA*

slapstick comedy, slapstick   Violent, acrobatic comic acting, generally depicting aggressive and destructive behavior.

slow motion   Action which takes place on the screen at a rate less rapid than the rate of the real action which took place before the camera. This occurs when the camera is operated at a frame repetition rate greater than standard, but the projection frame repetition rate is maintained at standard or below. *UFA (UFPA)*

slow-speed film   A film whose emulsion needs a greater or slower exposure to light to register an image satisfactorily. Compared to high-speed film (fast film), slow film produces a finer-grained, slicker looking image.

soft focus   An effect in which sharpness of image is reduced by the use of an optical device, usually a soft-focus lens, diffusion disc, or open-weave cloth over the lens. Usually confined to closeups. *(UFPA)* Also used to indicate an image or parts of an image which are slightly out of focus. *UFA*

solarization, color solarization   A process (either chemical or electronic) which reverses or shifts color values in color film. The image appears somewhat like a color negative.

sound bridge   A segment of sound track (dialogue, music, effects) which continues from one shot into another quite different shot, i.e., time, space, or characters change radically enough for the two shots to be part of two separate scenes. The sound track thus acts as a unifier, a bridge, between the two and the transition is less abrupt.

sound effects, SFX   Any sound from any source other than synchronized dialogue, narration, or music.

sound-on-disc, sound-on-record   The first commercially used sound process, which was then superseded by the more efficient and economical sound-on-film (or optical sound) process. Sound on phonograph records was synchronized to the projector, and thus image and sound synchronization on the screen was achieved.

sound-on-film   See **optical sound.**

sound perspective, aural perspective   The impression of distance in sound. *UFA*

sound track, track   The portion of the length of film reserved for the sound record, of any recording so located. Also, any length of film bearing sound only. *UFA (UFPA)*

Soviet Social Realism   A film movement in postrevolutionary Russia which joined ideology and aesthetics to celebrate the new Soviet Union cinematically. The emphasis was on documentary realism illuminated by artistic and purposeful editing and camera technique. The movement lost all its imagination and energy after Stalin came to power and saw its earlier practitioners as too elite and formalist.

special effects   Shots unobtainable by straightforward motion picture shooting techniques. In this category fall shots requiring contour matting, multiple image montages, split screens, vignetting, models, and the like. *(UFPA)* Term also applies to explosions, ballistics effects, and mechanical effects. *UFA*

Spieler, der (German and Yiddish, literally "the player")   A term applied to the person who told the story and read the title cards during the exhibition of silent movies so that non–English speaking immigrants and illiterates could follow the plot.

splice   The act of joining two pieces of film by any of several methods — by cementing, butt-welding, taping, or, for processing, by staples or grommets. Also, the resulting lapped or joined portions of film. *UFA (UFPA)*

split screen effect, split screen, split screen shot   The division of the film frame into two or more separate nonoverlapping images, done either in the camera or in an optical printer. *UFA*

spotlight, spot   A luminaire in which light from a contained source is directed by means of a reflector and lens into a relatively narrow beam. *UFA (UFPA)*

sprockets, sprocket roller, sprocket wheel   A roller having teeth which engage the perforations of a film in order to pull the film along. *UFA*

star system   The system of developing audience appeal through publicity stressing a leading performer rather than other elements of a film. Begun in the second decade of this century with such stars as Mary Pickford and Charlie Chaplin, the system allows star actors to command extremely high salaries. *UFA*

Steadicam   Trade name for a camera support which is attached to the operator's body. A movement-dampening mechanism holds the camera steady, and the outfit uses a small television monitor as a viewfinder. *UFA*

stereophonic sound   Sound which was recorded through two or more microphones each of which has its own track, and which is played back in two or more corresponding loud speakers in order to achieve a three-dimensional effect. *UFA*

stock shots, stock footage, SS   Film footage of scenery and action which is catalogued and stored for possible future use. *UFA*

story board   A pictorial outline of a film presentation, with sketches or photographs representing shots, and usually having in writing the speech, music, and sound effects which are to go with each shot. *UFA*

straight cut   Descriptive of two shots butted together with no optical effects. *UFA*

structural film, perceptual film   Films using slow camera movements, repeated loops, extended zooms, flickers, or images photographed from the screen on which they are projected, but usually not more than one of these techniques at a time. *UFA*

structuralism   The study of how institutions and art forms are structured on basic notions of conflict and opposition (e.g., light and dark, good and evil) and how those structures are repetitive and archetypal.

subjective camera, subjective viewpoint   A situation in which the audience involvement with a scene is intensified through identification with the camera point-of-view. In some dramatic films, the camera has taken the place of an actor, with other actors looking directly at the lens. *UFA (UFPA)*

subjective time   The time experienced or felt by a characer in a film, as revealed through camera movement and editing, e.g., a fearful character climbs a flight of stairs to find out what is making a noise and the climb is prolonged to match his terror, or a character dreams and time has no meaning.

subtitle, subtitling   A title superimposed over action, usually at the bottom of the frame, used to translate foreign language, or to identify the scene. *UFA (UFPA)*

sun screens   Screens made out of mesh or gauze used to diffuse sunlight during exterior shooting.

superimpose, superimposition, super   To place a smaller image over another image by double exposure, double printing, or other technique. *UFA*

surrealism   An art movement of the 1920s which attempted to tap the world of dreams and the unconscious for its sources. Incongruity, shock, and a rejection of causality were its major characteristics. Because of its ability to move instantaneously in time and space, film greatly interested surrealist artists.

synchronization   Achieving a precise match between picture and sound. *UFA*

synchronous sound   Sound whose source is apparent in the picture, and which matches the action. *UFA*

take   A shot. Also, a term used to indicate the number of times a given shot has been made. Takes are usually numbered sequentially and identified in picture by slate and in track by voice. *UFA (UFPA)*

telephoto lens, telephoto shot   An extremely long lens which is able to bring far distant objects into close view, acting as a magnifier. It has a very narrow angle of view and therefore tends to foreshorten and flatten its distant subject matter. It also makes motion toward the camera appear extremely slow, creating a treadmill effect.

theme   The story subject matter from which the general value or idea forming the intellectual background for a film is evolved. *UFA (UFPA)*

360-degree pan   A pan shot which makes a complete circle. *UFA*

three-shot   A shot of three performers. *UFA*

title, title card   The name or designation of a film. Also, any inscription contained in a film for the purpose of conveying information about the film, its message, or its story to the viewer. *UFA (UFPA)*

tone   The mood or atmosphere of a film (e.g., ironic, comic, nostalgic, romantic) which is created as the sum of the film's cinematic techniques.

tracking shot, traveling shot, trucking shot   A shot made while the camera and its entire support are moving. *UFA*

tragedy A work of literature or drama which focuses on the downfall of an admirable character whose defeat (physical or moral) usually is brought about through a flaw in an otherwise noble nature.

travelogue A short, nondramatic film showing events in distant places or foreign countries. *UFA*

treatment, treatment outline A short summary of a proposed film, giving information about the kind of production and describing the main sequences to be developed. *UFA (UFPA)*

trucking shot See **tracking shot.**

two-shot A shot of two people. *UFA*

typecasting, typage The selecting or casting of actors because of their looks or type rather than for their acting experience. *UFA*

uncontrolled documentary See **direct cinema.**

underground cinema A term often used synonymously with independent film, avant-garde film and experimental film. It also, however, connotes films which deal with shocking subject matter, or which are purposefully antitraditional.

universal time Time created through imagery (often edited in a montage sequence) which abstracts its subject matter from a specific temporal or spatial context. The actions perceived could occur, therefore, anywhere and at any time, and the experiences on the screen are universalized.

viewer's script, cutting continuity script Often published after the critical and commercial success of a film, this script is a recording in dialogue or frames of the film as it appears on the screen in its final release. It may differ quite a bit from the actual shooting script.

viewpoint The apparent distance and angle from which the camera views and records the subject. Not to be confused with point-of-view shots or subjective camera shots.

voice-over, VO 1) A sound and picture relationship in which a narrator's voice accompanies picture action. 2) Any off-screen voice. 3) A narration job. *UFA*

wide-angle lens, wide-angle shot. A short lens able to capture a broad field of action. It appears to create depth and, in its extreme forms (such as the fisheye), distorts linear perspective so that the edges of the image may appear bowed.

wild Descriptive of any device or process not susceptible to precise control. Variable-speed motors are termed "wild" since control of their speed is not sufficiently accurate for synchronous picture and sound recording work. In a similar sense, either picture or sound, shot without synchronous relationship to the other. *UFA (UFPA)*

wipe An optical effect used to join one shot to another. In its commonest form, scene *A* appears to be "wiped" off the screen by the progressive revelation of scene *B* as a vertical dividing line separating the two advances across the screen from left to right. Many modifications of this basic form have been used, such as vertical, diagonal, iris, spiral, and even "atomic bomb" wipes. *UFA (UFPA)*

workprint Any positive duplicate picture, sound track print, or magnetic duplicate intended for use in the editing process to establish through a series of trial cuttings the finished version of a film. The purpose is to preserve the original intact and undamaged until the cutting points have been established. *UFA (UFPA)*

writer's script The screenplay for a motion picture conceived by the writer and recorded to best represent the story and characters to potential commercial backers. Such a script will have a minimum of camera direction, lighting information, or technical specificity, but will attempt instead to convey mood, tone, plot, and characterization.

zoom lens, varifocal lens, variable-focal-length lens A lens with effective focal length continuously variable within a limited range. Changing the focal length of such a lens as a shot progresses simulates the effect of movement of the camera toward or away from the subject. *UFA (UFPA)*

★★★ Index